MW00996595

LAST DAYS MADNESS

Obsession of the Modern Church

Gary DeMar

Copyright © 1999 by American Vision, Atlanta, Georgia. All rights reserved.
Fourth revised edition, 1999
Printed in the United States of America.
04 03 02 01 00 99   10 9 8 7 6 5 4 3 2 1

No part of this publication may be reproduced, stored in a retrieval system, or transmitted in any form by any means, electronic, mechanical, photocopy, recording, or otherwise, without the prior written permission of the publisher, except for brief quotations in critical reviews or articles. Such quotations must be in context.

Unless otherwise noted, all Scripture quotations are from the *New American Standard Bible*, © 1960, 1963, 1971, 1972, 1973, 1975, 1977, by the Lockman Foundation and are used by permission.

Last Days Madness: Obsession of the Modern Church is produced by American Vision, a Christian educational and communications organization. American Vision publishes a monthly magazine, *Biblical Worldview*. For more information about American Vision and how to obtain a subscription to *Biblical Worldview* and receive a catalog of materials, write:

American Vision
P.O. Box 220
Powder Springs, Georgia 30127
or call 1–800–628–9460.

E-mail: avision1@aol.com
World-Wide Web: americanvision.org
For prophecy-related books: prophecybooks.com

ISBN: 0–915815–35–4

Elder: Larry E. Brown

LAST DAYS MADNESS

Contents

Preface

The response to *Last Days Madness* has been overwhelming. With little advertising, *Last Days Madness* has had a profound effect on thousands of Christians around the world. It is gratifying to get letters from readers who have been blessed by its content. Many write and tell me that they have gained a renewed appreciation of God's Word since they no longer have to ignore passages that seemed to be mistaken about the timing of Jesus' return. They can now read the Bible with confidence.

The interpretive methodology outlined in *Last Days Madness* is not innovative. For the past 150 years Christians have been sidetracked by a novel interpretive methodology known as dispensational premillennialism. While *Last Days Madness* is not primarily directed at dispensationalism, much of what is addressed herein is critical of this very popular interpretive belief system.

Like the second (1994) and third (1997) editions, this fourth edition is not a revision in the usual sense. After doing numerous radio interviews and debates, I learned where certain arguments could be better stated and supported by Scripture and history. These additions made up the bulk of the new material in the third edition of *Last Days Madness*. In this edition, I have continued my policy of interacting with the latest Bible prophecy books to keep *Last Days Madness* current. Most of the new books on prophecy simply restate the tired and still unproven assumptions of the old books.

The additional study that went into this edition of *Last Days Madness* has continued to solidify my conviction that the time texts are key indicators of when certain prophetic events will take place. Most books on prophecy do not interpret time texts literally. In fact, some books ignore the time texts altogether. For example, Robert Van Kampen quotes a portion of Revelation 1:1, leaving out this very important phrase: "the things which must *shortly* take place." He follows the same method when he does not quote all of Revelation 1:3, leaving out "for the time is *near*."[1] he claims to interpret the Bible literally, but he refuses to handle these texts in a literal way.[2] In his latest book, Van Kampen once again suspiciously fails to deal with the time texts. There is no discussion of Revelation 1:1 ("shortly") and 1:3 ("near"). Matthew 16:27–28, a crucial time text, is not dealt with. On the dedication page, he concludes with "Come quickly, Lord Jesus," and yet he does not expound on Revelation 22:20 where Jesus said nearly 2000 years ago, "Yes, I am coming quickly." In his analysis of those of us who believe the time texts are supremely important, he writes:

> Both the allegorical and spiritualized views must deny a literal understanding of the prophecies found in the Book of Daniel, the Olivet Discourse, and the greater part of the Book of Revelation. Preterists view these passages as past, historical events (even though nothing historically has ever happened that bears any resemblance to these specific passages), with minimal end-time relevance.[3]

A preterist is someone who believes that certain prophecies have been fulfilled, that is, their fulfillment is in the *past*. For example, Floyd Hamilton, writes that there "are in the Old Testament 332 distinct predictions which are literally fulfilled in Christ."[4] All Christians are preterists regarding these prophecies since they believe they have been fulfilled in Jesus Christ. Jews who are still waiting for the promised Messiah are anti-preterists since they believe these prophetic passages have not been fulfilled. They are futurists. Van Kampen believes that the preterist interpretation of prophecy regarding the judgment coming of Christ in the first century is indefensible because *"nothing* historically has ever happened that bears *any* resemblance to these specific passages," that is, the Olivet Discourse of Matthew 24.

Notice that Van Kampen writes that there is "nothing" in history that shows that the events of the Olivet Discourse happened in the first century.

Nothing? Jesus predicted that there would be earthquakes before that first-century generation passed away. There were earthquakes (Matt. 27:54; 28:2; Acts 16:26) and famines (Acts 11:28; cf. Rom. 8:35), just like Jesus predicted (Matt. 24:7). Paul tells us that the "gospel" had been preached "to all the nations" in his day (Rom. 16:25–26), just like Jesus predicted (Matt. 24:14). This says nothing of the promise by Jesus that the temple would be destroyed within a generation (Matt. 24:34). All of history attests to the fact that the temple was destroyed within a generation of Jesus' Olivet Discourse. Therefore, Van Kampen's assertion that "*nothing* historically has ever happened that bears *any* resemblance to these specific passages" is absurd. Van Kampen dismisses the preterist perspective hoping his readers will not check out the evidence for themselves. That's why *Last Days Madness* was written—to examine the evidence, all the evidence.

Dispensationalists and other futurists realize that an honest analysis of biblical texts related to the timing of prophetic events jeopardizes their prophetic views. In fact, the entire thesis of futurism rests on a non-literal reading of the time texts. This arbitrary manner of dealing with Scripture has proven to be a foundation of sand for the entire prophetic system called dispensationalism and the newly promoted pre-wrath rapture position.[5] Dispensational scholars and former rank and file dispensationalists recognize the problem and are doing everything to prop up the faltering system. Some like Marvin Rosenthal and Robert Van Kampen advocate "A *new* understanding of the Rapture, the Tribulation, and the Second Coming."[6]

Dispensational author Robert L. Saucy, professor of systematic theology at Talbot School of Theology, tells us, "Over the past several decades the system of theological interpretation commonly known as dispensationalism has undergone considerable development and refinement."[7] The change has been radical enough to warrant the label "the new dispensationalism" or "progressive [dispensationalism] ... to distinguish the newer interpretations from the older version of dispensationalism."[8]

In *Dispensationalism, Israel and the Church: The Search for Definition*, the contributors describe how dispensationalism has changed and will continue to change. One writer states that "dispensationalism has been in the process of change since its earliest origins within the Plymouth Bretheren [*sic*] movement of the nineteenth century."[9] In the same series, Craig Blaising admits of and welcomes "modifications currently taking place in dispensational thought."[10] Similar to Saucy, the contributors to *Dispensationalism, Israel and the Church* have no discussion of those texts which describe the "soon" return of Jesus in judgment. Even those contributors from amillennial and historical premillennial positions who respond to the ten lengthy chapters make no mention of the time texts. They, too, are trapped in eschatological systems filled with contradictions.

A Christian should never fear having his "system" scrutinized by the plain teaching of the Bible. The rallying cry of the Reformation was *ecclesia reformata quia semper reformanda est,* "the church reformed because it must always be reforming." This should be every Christian's rallying cry. *Last Days Madness* is an appeal to the church to take another look at the topic of eschatology, the study of last things. The topic has not been settled in spite of a great deal of misplaced dogmatism. If you decide to read on, be prepared to be challenged. Moreover, be prepared to gain a greater respect for the integrity of the Bible.

Last Days Madness is unique because it argues its case rather than just states it. Most popular prophecy writers simply declare their position with little analysis or interaction with competing systems, assuming that their position is the only viable interpretive model. This is especially true in books like John Hagee's *Beginning of the End: The Assassination of Yitzhak Rabin and the Coming Antichrist*[11] and Ed Dobson's *50 Remarkable Events Pointing to the End: Why Jesus Could Return by* A.D. *2000.*[12] These authors dismiss, without sustained analysis, any view that does not agree with their opinion. In fact, for them no other views on prophecy even exist. Readers are left with the impression that the Church has *always* believed what these men claim is true. *Last Days Madness* takes a different approach. It acknowledges the existence of opposing views, lists their supporting evidences, considers their line of argumentation, and offers a counter opinion with detailed exegetical and historical testimony. Unlike most books on Bible prophecy, *Last Days Madness* is not "an ill-digested rehash of someone else's views"[13] but a careful and detailed analysis of Bible prophecy.

Notes

1. Robert D. Van Kampen, *The Rapture Question Answered: Plain and Simple* (Grand Rapids, MI: Revell, 1997), 135.

2. Van Kampen even admits that he does not interpret the Bible literally when it comes to the wound suffered by the Beast (Rev. 13:14), which he believes is either Nero or Hitler: "Antichrist must have died by a 'wound of the sword' (Rev. 13:14). Neither Nero nor Hitler died literally by the sword, but both died by weapons used in warfare, and Hitler in particular took his life during battle rather than surrender." (Robert Van Kampen, *The Sign of Christ's Coming and the End of the Age* [Wheaton, IL: Crossway Books, 1999], 14.).

3. Van Kampen, *The Sign of Christ's Coming and the End of the Age*, 14.

4. Floyd E. Hamilton, *The Basis of Christian Faith: A Modern Defense of the Christian Religion*, rev. ed. (New York: Harper & Row, 1964), 160.

5. Marvin Rosenthal, *The Pre-Wrath Rapture of the Church* (Nashville, TN: Thomas Nelson, 1990).

6. Cover-copy to Rosenthal, *The Pre-Wrath Rapture of the Church*.

7. Robert L. Saucy, *The Case for Progressive Dispensationalism: The Interface Between Dispensationalism and Non-Dispensational Theology* (Grand Rapids, MI: Zondervan, 1993), 8.

8. Saucy, *Case for Progressive Dispensationalism*, 9.

9. Stanley N. Gundry, "Foreword," *Dispensationalism, Israel and the Church: The Search for Definition* (Grand Rapids, MI: Zondervan, 1992), 11.

10. Craig A. Blaising, "Dispensationalism: A Search for Definition," *Dispensationalism, Israel and the Church*, 15.

11. Nashville, TN: Thomas Nelson, 1996.

12. Grand Rapids, MI: Zondervan 1997.

13. William Graham Scroggie, *The Unfolding Drama of Redemption*, 3 vols. (Grand Rapids, MI: Kregel, [1953–71] 1994), 3:357.

Introduction

Prediction is very difficult, especially about the future.[1]

—*Neils Bohr*

Prophecy is easier to explain after it has been fulfilled than before.[2]

—*Henry M. Morris*

In 1973, after a series of extraordinary acts of providence, I found myself sitting at a table in a dimly lighted pub in Ann Arbor, Michigan, listening to a high school friend explain the intricacies of Bible prophecy through the interpretative grid of someone named Hal Lindsey. This seemingly chance encounter was my first introduction to *The Late Great Planet Earth*. I was fascinated. Certainly the topic of Bible prophecy interested me, but I was more captivated by the Bible itself. I had been raised Roman Catholic. The only knowledge of the Bible that I had came from a Gideon New Testament that my father had brought back from his tour of duty in the Pacific during World War II. While I had read from it on a number of occasions, the Bible had remained a closed book until the day my friend convinced me that there was contemporary relevance in its pages. For him, that contemporary relevance was prophecy.

An in–depth study of prophecy was not what I needed at the time, but the curiosity factor that the prophecy issue raised did motivate me to read the Bible in a systematic way. Through another friend's direction, I read C.S. Lewis's *Mere Christianity*, and through it became interested in the defense of the Christian faith. In time I realized that I was a sinner in need of salvation. In the solitude of my room, in a rented house shared by six other students, one vagrant, two dogs, and three cats at 715 Village Street,

Kalamazoo, Michigan, I turned to Jesus Christ as my Savior and Lord. Those dark days in that dilapidated house prior to Christ will never be forgotten.

Soon after graduation from college in 1973 I began to delve into the complexities of Bible prophecy once again. By this time I was no longer the biblically ignorant convert. Bible study had become a daily affair. While I was certainly far from being an expert, I noticed that a number of verses did not fit with the prevailing system of Bible prophecy offered by Hal Lindsey and others who shared his views. A number of questions were raised when I tried to put together all the pieces of Lindsey's prophetic jigsaw puzzle. Too many pieces were missing. That is, a number of verses were either not discussed or were so twisted as to have no real meaning. At the time it seemed as if a prophetic *system* was trying to govern what the Bible says.

In 1974 I entered Reformed Theological Seminary (RTS) in Jackson, Mississippi. Two new worlds were opened up to me at RTS: the theological library and campus bookstore. Most bookstores typically carry only those books that sell well. This means that the average Christian is introduced to a small number of new books each year. Many great books are never read or even seen. There is no such limitation at a seminary library or a bookstore like the one at RTS. I scrutinized Bible commentaries and history books. My dissatisfaction with the Lindsey system forced me to go digging for answers to solve the hermeneutical puzzle.

I believed the Bible. There is no way that it could err. This was my starting presupposition. Scripture had to be taken at face value. Pet interpretations had to go, no matter how dearly held or how popular they were. This is why it was disheartening for me to read Bible passages that could not be reconciled with what I had been reading about the last days in prophetic best sellers like *The Late Great Planet Earth*. Either Lindsey was wrong or the Bible was wrong. Hal Lindsey was egregiously wrong. But Lindsey wasn't the only one who was dodging the plain meaning of the Bible. I soon learned that there were others who did not share Lindsey's end-time scenario but who still fudged on some of the most crucial prophetic texts.

The first area of dissatisfaction came with how commentators handled Matthew 24:34: "Truly I say to you, this generation will not pass away until all these things take place." At first reading one gets the distinct impression that Jesus is saying that the people with whom He was speaking would live to see and experience the events described in Matthew 24. This seemed impossible! And yet, there it was. I looked up every other occurrence of the phrase "this generation," and each time I came up with the same answer: Jesus was referring to *His* generation, the generation of people alive when He uttered the words. Every Bible commentator danced around the text. "It means the generation alive when the events described in the previous verses begin to manifest themselves," one respected commentator wrote. If that's true, I thought, then this is the only place where "this generation" means a future generation. That's not sound Bible interpretation. Another commentator, skirting the obvious, claimed that the Jewish race was in view. "The Jewish race," he wrote, "would not pass away until all these things took place." This interpretation has even more interpretive problems. My discontent grew. I was stuck with the obvious, straightforward, literal, plain interpretation: The generation to whom Jesus was speaking would not pass away until all those things listed in Matthew 24:1–34 came to pass.

If this is the correct interpretation, as I believe it is and hope to prove in the course of this book, then today's speculative madness related to repeated failed attempts at predicting the end must be attributed to a gross misunderstanding of Bible prophecy. As I soon learned, I was not alone in coming to this conclusion. For centuries great Bible expositors had taught that many New Testament prophecies had already been fulfilled. They taught that many texts that are often futurized actually describe events in the first century. This literature made sense of the passages that millions of Christians struggle to understand. Moreover, I soon learned that today's prophetic scenario, so popular with radio and television evangelists and multi-million-copy best sellers, has a short history. The system of prophetic interpretation that is familiar to most Christians had its beginning in 1830.

But what about world conditions? Aren't we seeing prophecy being fulfilled right before our eyes? This protest is offered when people are hit with an interpretation that no longer fits their doctrinal views. They shift from the clear teaching of Scripture to current events. The Bible is then read through the lens of today's newsprint, a form of "newspaper exegesis." When current events change, somehow the clear teaching of the Bible on these subjects also changes. Few people ever take the time to check what prophecy "experts" wrote ten years earlier.

Our nation, and every nation, could go through the most tumultuous upheaval that history has ever experienced, and this still would not mean that Jesus was returning "in our generation." For date setters, history is ignored and the Bible is twisted to fit a preconceived view of prophecy; the result is that the church experiences wild gyrations in the field of biblical prophecy. W. Ward Gasque writes:

> The problem with the evangelicals who turn the Bible into a kind of crystal ball is that they show very little historical awareness. They speak assuredly about the signs that are being fulfilled "right before your very eyes" and point to the impending end. Lindsey confidently refers to our own as "the terminal generation." However, these writers do not seem to be aware that there have been many believers in *every* generation—from the Montanists of the second century through Joachin of Fiore (*c.* 1135–1202) and Martin Luther to those Russian Mennonites who undertook a "Great Trek" to Siberia in 1880–84 and the nineteenth-century proponents of dispensationalism—who have believed that *they* were living in the days immediately preceding the second coming of Christ. So far they have all been mistaken. How many people have lost confidence in clear doctrines of Scripture affecting eternal life because misguided prophetic teaching is, unfortunately, not likely to be investigated?[3]

Gasque's admonition is borne out by considering the religious and cultural conditions prior to the Reformation of the sixteenth century. Medieval life was dominated by a corrupt church which positioned itself to be the ruler of all life, from personal thought and behavior to political power. The theology of the majority in the church could be described as heretical. It's no wonder that the Reformers saw the Papacy as the Antichrist. The Westminster Confession of Faith of the seventeenth century, for example, named the Roman Pontiff as the Antichrist in the chapter on "Of the Church."

> There is no other head of the Church but the Lord Jesus Christ: nor can the Pope of Rome in any sense be the head thereof; but is the Antichrist, that man of sin and son of perdition that exalteth himself in the Church against Christ, and all that is called God.

In addition to apostasy, the outbreak of bubonic plague nearly decimated Medieval Europe. The Black Death or "The Great Dying" had started its trek through the great trade routes from the East in the fourteenth century. All ages and classes were affected, and death, when it came, struck quickly and with a vengeance. While estimates vary on the number of deaths—from one-third to one-half of Europe's population—no epidemic since has matched its black scourge.

The plague reached Constantinople in 1347 and spread through Europe to England by late 1348. As one could imagine, all of society was affected. The burial of the dead was a major task since the living were often outnumbered by victims who had succumbed to the epidemic. Courts were closed. Food prices dropped because people were afraid to buy meat. Crops lay in the field for want of workmen. Those laborers who would work demanded exorbitant wages.

The time was ripe for prophecy advocates to predict the near-demise of the times. The English Reformer John Wycliffe (1329—1384) "describes the 'covetousness, sensuality, and fraud' of the clergy as infecting all of humanity, thus causing the chastisement under which Europe mourned."[4] In addition to plague, heresy, social unrest, monumental economic changes, and class conflict there were "exaggerated forms of religious mysticism," and "the lack of educated clergy reduced the church's intellectual vigor."[5] While Wycliffe was right about the theological and moral climate of his era, it was not the last days.

Then there was the Hundred Years' War (1337—1453), which could be described as years of war interrupted by peace, a series of invasions and treaties, challenged succession to the French throne, disputes over trade and ports, territorial claims and counter claims. But this was not the end, although there were certainly enough people around making their predictions, using the same Bible verses and the same methodologies that are being used today.

Last Days Madness was written to take a fresh look at the Bible. There is little that is new in the following pages. As you will read, the views expressed herein have been around for centuries. Unfortunately, they have been buried under millions of copies of paperback books that have assured us year after year that the end is near. If you are afraid to have your views challenged, then I suggest that you stop reading now.

Notes

1. Quoted in Chris Morgan and David Langford, *Facts and Fallacies: A Book of Definitive Mistakes and Misguided Predictions* (Toronto, Canada: John Wiley & Sons Canada Limited, 1981), 57.
2. Henry M. Morris, *Creation and the Second Coming* (El Cajon, CA: Master Books, 1991), 36.
3. W. Ward Gasque, "Future Fact? Future Fiction?" *Christianity Today* (15 April 1977), 40.
4. "Wycliffe's England: A Time of Turmoil," *Christian History*, Issue 3 (1983), 8.
5. "Wycliffe's England," 8.

Chapter One

THE DATING GAME

D ip into any period of history and you will find prophets of all types, from any number of theological traditions, who claimed they knew when the next endtime event would occur. Some have pointed to the rise in apostasy, lawlessness, natural disasters, signs in the heavens, and an increase in rival religions in their day as unmistakable evidence that the end was near for them. Finding hidden meanings in biblical numbers was another favorite pastime that assured the faithful that the end had to be at hand.

In the second century, Tertullian, in *Ad Nationes*, wrote, "What terrible wars, both foreign and domestic! What pestilences, famines ... and quakings of the earth has history recorded!"[1] Evaluating current events and concluding that they offer "compelling evidence" that Jesus would return soon has been a common practice among prophecy writers. In the sixth century, Pope Gregory assured the world that the return of Christ could not be far off since he claimed that so many prophecies were being fulfilled in his day.

> Of all the signs described by our Lord as presaging the end of the world some we see already accomplished.... For we now see that nation arises against nation and that they press and weigh upon the land in our own times as never before in the annals of the past. Earthquakes overwhelm countless cities, as we often hear from other parts of the world.

Pestilence we endure without interruption. It is true that we do not behold signs in the sun and moon and stars but that these are not far off we may infer from the changes of the atmosphere.[2]

Peculiar sectarian cults arose during periods of hype and hysteria, when endtime prophetic speculation was fueled by expected promises of imminent catastrophe and the hope of a future millennium. "At first sight, one could hardly imagine two more dissimilar ideas. The first suggests death and desolation; the second, salvation and fulfillment. Yet the two intertwine again and again. Those who regard the Millennium as imminent expect disasters to pave the way. The present order, evil and entrenched, can hardly be expected to give way of itself or dissolve overnight."[3] Some took advantage of perilous times by heightening eschatological expectations to agitate the faithful, knowing that "men cleave to hopes of imminent worldly salvation only when the hammerblows of disaster destroy the world they have known and render them susceptible to ideas which they would earlier have cast aside."[4]

Others stirred the revolutionary fires in those preoccupied with a coming apocalypse. The zealous were duped into joining a "vision of a new moral order, a world purified and freed from conflict and hatred,"[5] a world based on socialistic and communistic ideals that proved tragic for those caught up in the frenzy.[6]

The End is Near—Again!

The small and the great, the sane and the insane, the sacred and the profane have been quick to predict when the end might come. For example, Billy Graham and Barbra Streisand—two people on different ends of the spiritual spectrum—have at least one thing in common: They both believe that we cannot hold out much longer. Barbra Streisand believes "the world is coming to an end." She just feels "that science, technology, and the mind have surpassed the soul—the heart. There is no balance in terms of feeling and love for fellow man."[7] Billy Graham, feeling equally pessimistic, writes: "If you look in any direction, whether it is technological or physiological, the world as we know it is coming to an end. Scientists predict it, sociologists talk about it. Whether you go to the Soviet Union or anywhere in the world, they are talking about it. The world is living in a state of shock."[8]

Billy Graham does not "want to linger here on the who, what, why, how, or when of Armageddon." He simply states that "it is near."[9] What does Graham mean by "near"? The Book of Revelation states that the time was "near" for those who first read the prophecy (Rev. 1:1, 3). Since Revelation was written during Nero's reign, prior to the destruction of Jerusalem in A.D. 70, the prophetic events of Revelation were fulfilled during the lifetime of those who first read the prophecy.[10]

Prophetic Déjà Vu

As early as the second century, prophets were suggesting dates for the bodily return of Christ. The "prophet" Montanus was one of the first to propose such a date. He proclaimed the imminent appearance of the New Jerusalem, the signal for which was to be a new outpouring of the Holy Spirit. Montanus as a new convert to Christianity believed himself to be the appointed prophet of God. Two prophetesses, Prisca and Maximilla, soon joined him. They claimed to be mouthpieces of the Paraclete, the Greek title used in John's Gospel for the Holy Spirit. The Montanists' predictions failed. Their failures, however, did not deter other date setters:

> In the third century, a prophet called Novatian gathered a huge following by crying, "Come, Lord Jesus!" Donatus, a fourth-century prophet, commanded attention when he stressed that only 144,000 people would be chosen by God. He found this magic figure in Revelation 14:1 (a verse which the Jehovah's Witnesses use to proclaim their own version of this heresy). Both Novatian and Donatus were branded as heretics by the Church.[11]

The sack of Rome by the Vandals (A.D. 410) was supposed to bring on the end; the birth of the Inquisition (1209–44) prompted many well-meaning saints to conclude that it was the beginning of the end; the Black Death that killed millions was viewed as the prelude to the demise of the world (1347–50). The plague disrupted society at all levels. Giovanni Boccaccio wrote a vivid description of how some people responded. For some,

> debauchery was the road to salvation, or, if there was to be no salvation [from the plague], to happiness in the few days that remained. These

profligates abandoned all work and drifted from house to house, drinking, stealing, fornicating. "People behaved as though their days were numbered," Boccaccio wrote, "and treated their belongings and their own persons with equal abandon. Hence most houses had become common property, and any passing stranger could make himself at home.... In the face of so much affliction and misery, all respect for the laws of God and man had virtually broken down.... Those ministers and executors of the laws who were not either dead or ill were left with so few subordinates that they were unable to discharge any of their duties. Hence everyone was free to behave as he pleased."[12]

Martin Luther "frequently expressed the opinion that the End was very near, though he felt it was unwise to predict an exact date. Christians, he said, no more know the exact time of Christ's return than 'little babies in their mothers' bodies know about their arrival.'" This, however, did not stop him from concluding that the end was not a distant event. In January 1532, he wrote, "The last day is at hand. My calendar has run out. I know nothing more in my Scriptures."[13] As it turned out, there was a lot more time to follow. Many other disasters, natural and political, gave rise to the same speculation, century after century.

Contemporary events like the Lisbon earthquake of 1755 were interpreted as evidence of the fulfillment of biblical prophecies. Above all, the French Revolution excited a spate of interpretations on both sides of the Atlantic designed to show that the world was entering upon the last days. Millennialism was widely espoused by leading scholars and divines. In America the names of Timothy Dwight (President of Yale), John H. Livingston (President of Rutgers), and Joseph Priestly come to mind: in Britain, George Stanley Faber, Edward King, and Edward Irving. A spate of pamphlets and sermons by Church of England clergy and orthodox American ministers poured forth from the 1790s; and there was a constant reference back to the prophetical studies of Sir Isaac Newton, Joseph Mede, and William Whiston. The usual method of interpretation was some variant of the year–day theory, by which days mentioned in the prophecies were counted as years, weeks as seven–year periods, and months as thirty years. There was general agreement in the late eighteenth century that the 1,260 days mentioned in Revelation 12:6 were to be interpreted as 1,260 years, and that this period was now ended. An alternative theory, which became increasingly popular after 1800, emphasized the importance of the 2,300year period of Daniel 8:14 and the 'cleansing of the sanctuary' which would fall due some time in the 1840s. The fulfillment of the time prophecies meant that mankind was living in the last days, that the 'midnight cry' might soon be heard, and that the coming of the messiah might be expected shortly. Such beliefs had an influence far beyond the members of explicitly adventist sects. They were part and parcel of everyday evangelical religion.[14]

The lessons of history are recorded for all to heed. For many, however, the past is a distant memory. All that counts is the present. Sure, *they* were wrong, the prophecy "experts" warn us, but it will be different with *us*.

The First Millennium

As the last day of 999 approached, "the old basilica of St. Peter's at Rome was thronged with a mass of weeping and trembling worshipers awaiting the end of the world," believing that they were on the eve of the Millennium.[15] Land, homes, and household goods were given to the poor as a final act of contrition to absolve the hopeless from sins of a lifetime. Some Europeans sold their goods before traveling to Palestine to await the Second Coming. This mistaken application of biblical prophecy happened again in 1100, 1200, and 1245. Prophetic speculation continued. "In 1531, Melchior Hofmann announced that the second coming would take place in the year 1533.... Nicholas Cusa held that the world would not last past 1734."[16]

As the second Millennium approaches, we can expect increased activity among the prophetic speculators as we are assured that the time of the end is imminent. Lester Sumrall wrote in his book *I Predict 2000* A.D.: "I predict the absolute fullness of man's operation on planet Earth by the year 2000 A.D. Then Jesus Christ shall reign from Jerusalem for 1000 years."[17] In *Armageddon Now!*, Dwight Wilson observed that there had been no significant increase regarding "hazardous speculation" because "the quarter century that remains makes the year 2000 too far removed to induce a sense of crisis or terror; but as it approaches, the cry of impending doom may be expected to swell. To the extent that this cry is reinforced by continuing crises in the Middle East there will grow an ever more deafening roar of 'Armageddon

Now!'"[18] Remember, this was written in 1977, a full fourteen years before Saddam Hussein invaded Kuwait.

Was Wilson right? Mikkel Dahl predicated in *The Midnight Cry* that the present era would end by 1980. Reginald Edward Duncan predicted in *The Coming Russian Invasion of America* that the Millennium would begin in 1979. Emil Gaverluk of the Southwest Radio Church predicted that the rapture would occur by 1981. The year 1988 saw an abundance of books predicting the rapture of the church since this was thought to be the final year of the "terminal generation" because of the resettlement of the nation Israel in 1948. The most notorious was Edgar C. Whisenant's *88 Reasons Why the Rapture Is in 1988.*[19] Upon the release of his calculations, Whisenant remarked, "Only if the Bible is in error am I wrong, and I say that unequivocally. There is no way Biblically that I can be wrong; and I say that to every preacher in town."[20] When the author's intricate system of predicting the end failed, he went on undaunted with a new book called *The Final Shout: Rapture Report 1989*. It seems that he had made a critical error because he was following the wrong calendar:

> My mistake was that my mathematical calculations were off by one year.... Since all centuries should begin with a zero year (for instance, the year 19*00* started this century), the first century A.D. was a year short, consisting of only 99 years. This was the one–year error in my calculations last year [1988]. The Gregorian calendar (the calendar used today) is always one year in advance of the true year. Numbered correctly from the beginning, *i.e.,* 1 A.D., 1989 Gregorian would be only one thousand nine hundred eighty eight years of 365.2422 days each.[21]

Whisenant was not alone in making 1988 the termination point of the last days. Many others succumbed to last days madness. Clifford Hill writes that "two young men from Denmark announced that they were the two witnesses of Revelation 11:3 sent by God to prepare the way for Messiah. Two years earlier I had met two young Americans camping on the Mount of Olives also claiming to be the two witnesses."[22]

On the heels of Whisenant came Grant R. Jeffrey's *Armageddon: Appointment with Destiny*. Jeffrey writes that through his own research into biblical prophecies he has discovered a number of indications "which suggest that the year A.D. 2000 is a probable termination date for the 'last days.'"[23] His argument is little different from that of Edgar Whisenant's *88 Reasons* thesis. Instead of Whisenant's 365.2422 days, Jeffrey concludes that a biblical year is made up of only 360 days. Here is an example of his reasoning:

> The year when [Jesus' reading from Luke 4:18–21] occurred, *the fall of* A.D. *28, was, in fact, not only a Jubilee Year, but also the thirtieth Jubilee* since the Sabbatical-Jubilee system of years began when Israel crossed the Jordan River in 1451 B.C. Thus, Jesus Christ precisely fulfilled **"the acceptable year of the Lord"** on the exact year of Jubilee—the year of liberty and release.
>
> Please note that He stopped reading at **"the acceptable year of the Lord"** because He knew that the next phrase of the prophet's sentence, **"and the day of vengeance of our God,"** which refers to Armageddon, would be postponed exactly 2000 biblical years (2000 biblical years times 360 days equals 720,000 days divided by 365.25 equals 1971.25 calendar years).
>
> If we add 2000 biblical years (1971.25 calendar years) to the beginning of Christ's ministry on a Jubilee Year when He read the prophecy about **"the acceptable year of the Lord"** in the fall of A.D. 28; we arrive at the year A.D. 2000, forty Jubilee Cycles later.
>
> The next Jubilee Year will occur in A.D. 2000, completing the Sabbatical—Jubilee system of years—the seventieth Great Jubilee.[24]

Part of Jeffrey's interpretive method is based on where Jesus stopped reading in Isaiah. Supposedly the "day of vengeance" (Isa. 61:2; cf. 63:4) has been postponed for nearly two thousand years because Jesus did not continue reading Isaiah 61:2. Nothing in the New Testament supports this interpretation. In fact, Luke's Gospel later indicates that the "days of vengeance" (Luke 21:22) would be poured out before that first-century generation passed away. This means that the "days of vengeance" are past for us since these "days" refer to the destruction of Jerusalem in A.D. 70. The "days of vengeance" were future for those who first heard Jesus' reading.

Jesus began His public ministry by reading from an Old Testament Scripture that identified Him as the promised Messiah. He would spend three years preaching and teaching to learn how He would be received by His countrymen. They despised and rejected Him, turning Him over to the Roman authorities to be crucified as a common criminal. Peter, an eyewitness to these events, said of his countrymen: "But you disowned the Holy and Righteous One, and asked for a murderer to be granted to you, but put to death the Prince of life, the one whom God raised from the dead..." (Acts 3:14–15). Their cry, when Jesus was presented to them as their king, was, "We have no king but Caesar!" (John 19:15). In the Olivet Discourse as recorded by Luke, Jesus quotes from Isaiah 61:2, warning His disciples of the coming "days of vengeance" that would befall their city and temple. In fact, Jesus told them that this would befall their generation, not some future *postponed* generation (Matt. 24:34; Mark 13:30; Luke 21:32).

There is no need for mathematical schemes to determine hidden timetables that are not self-evident for all to see and understand. When God wants to set a timetable, He sets a timetable: 7 years (Gen. 45:6), 40 years (Num. 14:34), 70 years (Jer. 25:10), 430 years (Gen. 15:13).

There was a lull on the prophetic scene after the dismal failure of Edgar Whisenant's *88 Reasons*. Then Iraq invaded Kuwait, and the prophecy books once again came rolling off the presses. Hal Lindsey's *Late Great Planet Earth* found new life. John F. Walvoord reissued a revised edition of *Armageddon, Oil and the Middle East Crisis* to fit new developments in the Mideast. Walvoord claimed that Saddam Hussein's "move into Kuwait was motivated by a desire to 'set up a power base from which to attack Israel.'"[25] Charles Dyer, a professor at Dallas Theological Seminary, claimed that modern Babylon was a fulfillment of end-time prophecy. Using events leading up to and including the events of the Gulf War with Saddam Hussein, Dyer sought to "prove" that prophecy was being fulfilled right before our eyes. His book *The Rise of Babylon* now sells for pennies on the dollar.[26] Sensationalism, not sound biblical study, sells.

A Korean group placed newspaper advertisements predicting that the rapture would take place on October 28, 1992. As we all know, the rapture did not take place. When asked about the non-event, Kim Tae-jin replied, "We got the message from God wrong. Jesus will be back in several years."[27] The only message from God we have is found in the Bible, and that message clearly states that Jesus' coming was near for the first-century church.

Charles R. Taylor wrote in *Bible Prophecy News* in the summer of 1992 that Jesus' return would occur in the fall of the same year: "What you are starting to read *probably* is my final issue of *Bible Prophecy News*, for Bible prophecy fulfillments indicate that Jesus Christ our Lord will most likely return for us at the rapture of the Church before the Fall 1992 issue can be printed." Not to be outdone, Harold Camping wrote *1994?* Camping's approach is similar to Edgar Whisenant's. Through a series of intricate calculations based on a number of unproven assumptions, Camping concluded that Jesus would return sometime in the fall of 1994. He based his calculations on the belief that Adam was created in 11,013 B.C. and that the numbers 13, 130, 1,300, and 13,000 are significant biblical numbers. For Camping, judgment day was to be 13,006 years after Adam's creation.[28]

"Ranch Apocalypse"

David Koresh and his Branch Davidian sect believed that the end was near. Koresh based his prophetic premonitions on a contemporary application of the "seven seals" found in the Book of Revelation (5:1, 5; 6:1; 8:1), a method not unlike the theories of modern-day fundamentalists and evangelicals who believe we are living in the last days.

> If America could learn these seals, they would respect me…. I'm the anointed one. I teach the seven seals…. It's the fulfillment of prophecy. This is it. This is the end…. They don't want to be bound by the truth. There's one truth that ties men into God, and that's the seven seals. And the anointed one is the only one that can present it. And that's me.[29]

While we will never know Koresh's true understanding of the application of the seven seals, there is little doubt that the Branch Davidian's fiery end fit well with his understanding of the seventh seal: "And the angel took the censor; and he filled it with the fire of the altar and threw it to the earth; and there followed peals of thunder and sounds and flashes of lightning and an earthquake" (8:5). In the last two weeks of the standoff with federal agents, three scrawled communiqués were retrieved from outside the compound. Although apparently written by Koresh, they were signed "God." They threatened that catastrophe would befall God's enemies, an allusion to the judgment theme in the Book of Revelation (14:7). "Open your eyes and not your mouth," read one. "Fear the hour of judgment, for it has come."[30] FBI agent Bob Ricks stated that Koresh was following his "apocalyptic theory of resolution. He says that the final days are being fulfilled by what is occurring. I think he has put forth a self-fulfilling prophecy, and we're hoping that something will happen to interrupt that prophecy."[31] The events in Waco serve as a tragic lesson for those who maintain that the judgment themes depicted in Matthew 24, Mark 13, Luke 21, and the Book of Revelation are still in our future. How many more such tragedies will it take before Christians realize that these prophetic events have been fulfilled?

Because of the mix of eschatology and violence among some fringe groups, the FBI has been keeping a close eye on apocalyptic cults. *USA Today* reports that FBI Director Louis Freeh is preparing for possible violence from rightwing extremists, religious cults, and apocalyptic groups.[32] The FBI was unprepared for the end-time logic of Vicki and Randy Weaver in the Ruby Ridge disaster. The Weavers were treated like fringe political extremists who were tied to white supremacist, anti-semitic, and Aryan Nation groups rather than believers in an imminent apocalypse that they (the Weavers) concluded would be led by governmental powers ("the Beast").

> The Weaver family's flight to Ruby Ridge was greatly influenced by *The Late Great Planet Earth*. Though Vicki Weaver, the family's spiritual leader, was also influenced by H.G. Wells and Ayn Rand, it was Lindsey's prophetic work, coupled with her home-spun visions, that convinced her to pack up her family and move to Ruby Ridge. She believed that the enemies of God predicted by Lindsey were prepared to strike at any moment.[33]

The Weavers mixed conspiracy theories, apocalypticism, and paranoia to conclude that the end was near.[34] You can imagine what the Weavers thought as they saw armed soldiers attacking their homestead. Was this happening everywhere? Was this the prelude to the end that they read so much about in popular prophecy books and expected in their lifetime? The Book of Revelation was being acted out right before their eyes, so they thought.

The history of date setting is long and tortuous. Francis Gummerlock catalogs more than a thousand false predictions over the past two millennia, everything from the identity of the antichrist to the date of Christ's coming. Two common streams run through all of them: they were sure of their prediction and they were wrong.[35]

Crying Wolf

Historian Mark Noll serves us a warning: "At the very least, it would be well for those in our age who predict details and dates for the End to remember how many before them have misread the signs of the times."[36]

As children we learned Aesop's fable of the "Shepherd Boy and the Wolf." In the end we learn that the sheep are the ones that are harmed by the shouts of "Wolf!" by the Shepherd Boy. In the same way the people of God—the sheep—are harmed by continual shouts of "the end is near!" God is looking for shepherds after His own heart, "who will feed" the flock "on knowledge and understanding" (Jer. 3:15), not on the latest newspaper headlines.

> Day after day, a Shepherd Boy tended a flock of sheep in the hills above his village. One day, just to cause some excitement, the Shepherd Boy ran down from the hills shouting "Wolf! Wolf!"
>
> The townsfolk came running with sticks to chase the Wolf away. All they found was the Shepherd Boy, who laughed at them for their pains.
>
> Seeing how well his trick worked, the Shepherd Boy tried it again the next day. Again he ran down from the hills shouting, "Wolf!" Again the townsfolk ran to his aid in vain.
>
> But the day after, it happened that a Wolf really came. The Shepherd Boy, now truly alarmed, shouted, "Help! Come and help me! The Wolf is killing the sheep!"
>
> But this time the townsfolk said, "He won't fool us again with *that* trick!" They paid no attention to his cries, and the Wolf destroyed the entire flock.
>
> When the people saw what happened to their sheep, they were very angry. *"There is no believing a liar,"* they said, *"even when he speaks the truth!"*[37]

Of course, if you cry "last days" long enough, you just might be the one to get it right, but by then there might not be anyone listening. Preaching about the soon coming of Christ has long been used by Christian prophecy teachers as a way of pleading with the lost to commit themselves to Jesus Christ. Such a motivating device can backfire on even the most well–intentioned evangelist. What happens if a listener shouts out, "Preachers like you have been telling us for centuries that Jesus is coming soon. Why should we believe you now?" By crying wolf and being wrong each time, the church is

perceived as unreliable. Skeptics of the Christian faith are likely to conclude
that since these self-proclaimed prophets were wrong on the timing of Jesus'
return when they seemed so certain (particularly of the nearness of the
rapture, the rise of Antichrist, the Great Tribulation, and Armageddon), then
maybe they are wrong on other issues which they teach with equal certainty. Maybe the entire Christian message is a sham.

The New Testament does use the *near* and *soon* coming of Jesus *in judgment* as a way of spurring the church on to greater works. The near judgment spoken of in Scripture refers to the destruction of Jerusalem in A.D. 70,
not a distant future coming of Christ. Peter wrote, "The end of all things *is
at hand*; therefore, be of sound judgment and sober spirit for the purpose of
prayer" (1 Peter 4:7). At hand for whom? If words mean anything, then
Peter must have had his contemporary readers in mind. What end was he
describing? In Luke's Gospel we read Jesus saying, "But keep on the alert at
all times, praying in order that *you* may have strength to escape all these
things that *are about to take place*, and to stand before the Son of Man" (Luke
21:36). John says in his first epistle, "Children, it is the *last hour*; and just as
you heard that antichrist is coming, *even now many antichrists have arisen; from
this we know it is the last hour*" (1 John 2:18).

The Bible is not a book that can be taken lightly. The integrity of the
Bible is at stake if we dismiss these clearly worded statements of time. As
students of the Bible, we are obligated to take God at His word, even when
it contradicts what we've been taught by popular prophecy writers.

Notes

1. Quoted in Carl Olof Jonsson and Wolfgang Herbst, *The "Sign" of the Last Days—When?* (Atlanta, GA: Commentary Press, 1987), ix.

2. Quoted in T. Francis Glasson, *His Appearing and His Kingdom* (London: Epworth, 1953), 45.

3. Michael Barkun, *Disaster and the Millennium* (New Haven, CT: Yale University Press, 1974), 1.

4. Barkun, *Disaster and the Millennium*, 1.

5. Clarke Garrett, *Respectable Folly: Millenarians and the French Revolution in France and England* (Baltimore, MD: Johns Hopkins University Press, 1975), 2.

6. Igor Shafarevich, *The Socialist Phenomenon,* trans. William Tjalsma (New York: Harper and Row, [1975] 1980). Also see Norman Cohn's *The Pursuit of the Millennium* (New York: Oxford University Press, [1957] 1970).

7. Quoted in Mike Evans, *The Return* (Nashville, TN: Thomas Nelson, 1986), 222.

8. Quoted in Evans, *The Return*, 22.

9. Billy Graham, *Storm Warning* (Dallas, TX: Word, 1992), 294. This is a revised version of *Approaching Hoofbeats: The Four Horsemen of the Apocalypse* (Waco, TX: Word, 1983). Graham had to revise the 1983 edition because historical circumstances changed.

10. For a defense of this position, see Kenneth L. Gentry, Jr., *Before Jerusalem Fell: Dating the Book of Revelation*, 2nd ed. (Atlanta, GA: American Vision, 1999). "Indeed, it is becoming an increasingly persuasive argument that all the New Testament books were written before 70 A.D.—within a single generation of the death of Christ." John Ankerberg and John Weldon, *Ready With An Answer: For the Tough Questions About God* (Eugene, OR: Harvest House Publishers, 1997), 364–65.

11. John C. Souter, "The Sky is Falling," *Future* (Wheaton, IL: Tyndale, 1984), 6.

12. Otto Friedrich, *The End of the World: A History* (New York: Coward, McCann and Geoghegan, 1982), 116.

13. Mark Noll, "Misreading the Signs of the Times," *Christianity Today* (6 February 1987), 10–11. Also see Mark U. Edwards, Jr., "Apocalyptic Expectations: The Scourge of God," *Luther's Last Battles: Politics and Polemics, 1531–46* (Ithaca, NY: Cornell University Press, 1983), 97–114.

14. J.E.C. Harrison, *The Second Coming: Popular Millenarianism, 1780–1850* (New Brunswick, NJ: Rutgers University Press, 1979), 5.

15. Richard Erdoes, *AD 1000: Living on the Brink of Apocalypse* (San Francisco, CA: Harper and Row, 1988), 1. Other scholars dispute the claim that the year 1000 was a key prophetic date. See Dick Teresi and Judith Hooper, "The Last Laugh?," *Omni* (January 1990), 84.

16. Souter, "The Sky is Falling," 6.

17. Quoted in Ron Rhodes, "Millennial Madness," *Christian Research Journal* (Fall 1990), 39.

18. Dwight L. Wilson, *Armageddon Now!: The Premillenarian Response to Russia and Israel Since 1917* (Tyler, TX: Institute for Christian Economics, [1977] 1991), 13.

19. Edgar C. Whisenant, *88 Reasons Why the Rapture Is In 1988* (Nashville, TN: World Bible Society, 1988).

20. Quoted in Ralph Lyman, *A Critique on the 1988 Rapture Theory* (Oklahoma City, OK: Southwest Radio Church, 1988), 2.

21. Edgar Whisenant and Greg Brewer, *The Final Shout: Rapture Report 1989* (Nashville, TN: World Bible Society, 1989), 1.

22. Clifford Hill, *Prophecy Past and Present: An Explanation of the Prophetic Ministry in the Bible and the Church Today* (Ann Arbor, MI: Servant, 1989), 5.

23. Grant R. Jeffrey, *Armageddon: Appointment with Destiny* (Toronto: Frontier Research, 1988), 193. In Jeffrey's *The Millennium Meltdown: The Year 2000 Computer Crisis* (1998), copy on the back cover reads: "Grant Jeffrey's new prophecy blockbuster explores the potential of the disastrous Year 2000 computer meltdown that will set the stage for the rise of the world government of the Antichrist." This is a prediction!

24. Jeffrey, *Armageddon: Appointment with Destiny*, 192.

25. Stephen L. Lutz, "Evangelical Publishers Cash in on Iraq War," *World* (26 January 1991), 16.

26. Charles H. Dyer, *The Rise of Babylon: Sign of the End Times* (Wheaton, IL: Tyndale), 1991. Fellow dispensationalist Ed Hindson disagrees with Dyer on the identity of Babylon: "Babylon is still in ruins in fulfillment of Old Testament prophecies. Saddam Hussein's attempt to 'rebuild' it as a tourist trap hardly qualifies it as the great city of the last days. Besides, his attempts have failed. Babylon has no sacred significance to the religion of Islam. Muslims are interested in protecting only their holy sites. They have no interest in rebuilding ancient pagan sites, including Babylon." (*Approaching Armageddon: The World Prepares for War with God* [Eugene, OR: Harvest House, 1997], 245).

27. B.J. Lee, "'Sorry, Let's Go Home': Miracle of the Rapture a No-Show in South Korea," *Atlanta Constitution* (29 October 1992), A4.

28. Harold Camping, *1994?* (New York: Vantage Press, 1992), 444.

29. Cited in Mark Potok, "Sect leader charismatic, 'dangerous,'" *USA Today* (2 March 1993), 2A. Koresh had granted interviews to CNN, KRLD radio, and others during the siege at his cult's compound near Waco, Texas. In these interviews, Koresh mentioned the "seven seals," a reference to biblical prophecies he believed foreshadowed the imminent return of Jesus.

30. Sam Howe Verhovek, "F.B.I. Saw the Ego in Koresh But Missed Willingness to Die," *New York Times* (22 April 1993), A1.

31. "Is Koresh hoping his followers get killed?," *Atlanta Journal/Constitution* (28 March 1993), B3. None of this is to exonerate the FBI, the Bureau of Alcohol, Tobacco and Firearms (BATF), and the Justice Department in the way they handled the situation. See "Waco: The Rules of Engagement," a video documentary that is critical of the way the FBI and BATF handled the Davidian group.

32. "FBI: Violence possible as 2000 approaches," *USA Today* (February 5, 1998), 13A.

33. Paul T. Coughlin, *Secrets, Plots & Hidden Agendas: What You Don't Know About Conspiracy Theories* (Downers Grove, IL: InterVarsity, 1999), 145–46.

34. Jess Walter, *Every Knee Shall Bow: The Truth and Tragedy of Ruby Ridge and the Randy Weaver Family* (New York: Regan Books/Harper Collins, 1995).

35. Francis X. Gummerlock, *The Day and the Hour: Christianity's Perennial Fascination with Predicting the End of the World* (Atlanta, GA: American Vision, 1999).

36. Noll, "Misreading the Signs of the Times," 10–11.

37. "The Shepherd Boy and the Wolf," *Aesop's Fables* as retold by Ann McGovern (New York: Scholastic Book Services, 1963), 33.

Chapter Two

WHEN WILL THESE THINGS BE?

W ith rockets soaring over the land of the apocalyptic prophets, many people have turned to end-times experts for insights."[1] It seems that any time a war breaks out or an earthquake is recorded on the Richter scale or famine sweeps through a third-world country, books predicting that the end is near are hurriedly readied for publication. Such books have little regard for the historical context of Bible prophecy and the failed predictions of past writers who were equally certain. As we've seen, there is nothing new in any of this. Floods in the Midwest in the summer of 1993 led one Baptist minister to conclude: "The Bible says that in the latter days, there will be earthquakes, and all of that refers to natural disasters.... We live in a time like that."[2] Such comments are not unusual. Books long ago discarded by anxious Christians contain similar assessments of world conditions and their supposed relationship to end-time events.

Based on current events in the late 1970s and early '80s, Hal Lindsey wrote, "We are the generation that will see the end times ... and the return of Christ."[3] When Saddam Hussein invaded Kuwait and coalition forces led by the United States sent troops to force him out, John F. Walvoord revised his *Armageddon, Oil and the Middle East*, first published in 1974, to address how the Bible applies to "the future of the Middle East *and the end of Western Civilization.*"[4] Based on current events coupled with Bible passages which he believes throw light on the state of affairs just prior to a so-called Rapture, Jerry Falwell boasts, "We will not be here for Armageddon."[5] On a December 27, 1992, television broadcast, Falwell stated, "I do not believe there will be another millennium … or another century." Like Falwell, Walvoord, who is in his eighties, "expects the Rapture to occur in his own lifetime. So many people will be suddenly missing, he muses, 'I wish I could be around to see how the media explains [*sic*] it.'"[6] According to William T. James in *Storming Toward Armageddon*, "We live in days such as delineated in 2 Timothy 3:1–5. The evidence is astoundingly abundant to anyone not wishing to be a foolish, deceived, brute beast but rather desiring to seek to be wise unto salvation."[7] A careful reading of 2 Timothy 3 will show that Paul was describing conditions in Timothy's day, what the writer of Hebrews characterizes as the "last days" of the Old Covenant (Heb. 1:1–2; cf. 1 Cor. 10:11). Notice Paul's optimism when he states that those who perform such deeds "will not make further progress; for their folly will be obvious to all" (2 Tim. 3:9). Second Timothy 3 is *not* a description of what the world will be like before the so-called rapture.

"Your Timing Is Off"

Why is there so much speculation and error about when the end might be, whether the "end" has reference to the rapture, the return of Christ to set up His millennial kingdom, or the return of Christ to inaugurate the "new heavens and new earth" (2 Peter 3:13; Rev. 21:1)? While there are a number of reasons why prophetic speculation continues unabated, as we will see in subsequent chapters, one reason stands above them all: *Fulfilled* prophecy is being interpreted as if it were *unfulfilled* prophecy. This error was also made by the first-century Jews. When Jesus "came to His own … those who were His own did not receive Him" (John 1:11). These unbelieving Jews did not believe Jesus was the fulfillment of centuries of prophetic pronouncements that are found in "the Law of Moses and the Prophets and the Psalms" (Luke 24:44).

Let's look at a similar contemporary example. Many Jews today are still awaiting the Messiah. Like their first-century counterparts, they do not believe that the messianic prophecies were fulfilled in the person and work of Jesus in the first century. The messianic prophecies have been taken from their first-century fulfillment context and have been projected into the distant future as unfulfilled prophecy. In effect, present-day Jews are still awaiting the first coming of the Messiah. In a similar way, many Christians take prophecies that have been fulfilled—either in Old Testament events or in events following the ascension of Jesus—and view them as still unfulfilled. They then manipulate these fulfilled prophecies and apply them to contemporary events. Their speculations are wrong because they are applying fulfilled prophecies to current events. As we will see, they ignore the time texts that speak of a *near* coming of Jesus in judgment upon an apostate Judaism that rejected its Messiah in the first century.

The Last Days

One of the first things a Christian must learn in interpreting the Bible is to pay attention to the time texts. Failing to recognize the proximity of a prophetic event will distort its intended meaning. The New Testament clearly states that the "end of all things" was at hand for those who first read 1 Peter 4:7; that is, the Old Covenant with its types and shadows was about to pass away. The Book of Hebrews opens with two verses that put the timing of certain eschatological events into perspective: "God, after He spoke long ago to the fathers in the prophets in many portions and in many ways, *in these last days has spoken* to us in His Son, whom He appointed heir of all things, through whom also He made the world" (Heb. 1:1–2). Prior to the coming of Jesus, God spoke via dreams, prophets, written revelation, and types. Through the New Covenant God "has made the first obsolete. But whatever is becoming obsolete and growing old is ready [lit., *near*] to disappear" (8:13).

The New Covenant is better than the Old Covenant because the blood of Jesus is better than the blood of animals (Heb. 7:22; 8:6). In addition, the way God communicates with His people has changed. For example, under the Old Covenant no man could look upon the face of God and live (Ex. 33:20). At the dawning of the New Covenant, however, God was no longer hidden. He had taken on human flesh in the person of Jesus Christ:

• "The Word became flesh and dwelt among us, and *we beheld His glory*, glory as of the only begotten from the Father, full of grace and truth" (John 1:14).

- "What was from the beginning, what we have heard, *what we have seen with our eyes,* what we beheld and our hands handled, concerning the Word of Life" (1 John 1:1).

God spoke in this new way "in *these* last days." The last days were in operation in the *first century* when God was manifested in the flesh in the person of Jesus Christ! Those Hebrew Christians who read the letter addressed to them were being told that an important covenantal era was about to end, the era of "the fathers in the prophets." The proof that the last days had come was that God "*has* spoken in His Son." The last days are not way off in the distant future. The end came to an obsolete covenant in the first century.

In A.D. 70 the "last days" ended with the dissolution of the temple and the sacrificial system. A similar pronouncement is made in 1 Peter 1:20: "For He was foreknown before the foundation of the world, but has appeared *in these last times* for the sake of you." Gordon Clark comments on what Peter means by "these last times": "'The last days,' which so many people think refers to what is still future at the end of this age, clearly means the time of Peter himself. I John 2:18 says it is, in his day, *the last hour.* Acts 2:17 quotes Joel as predicting the last days as the life time of Peter."[8]

Certain destructive events confronted the early Church, events that were "near" for those who first read the New Testament prophecies (Matt. 24:32–33; Rev. 1:3; 22:10). The Apostle Paul mentions "the *present* distress" (1 Cor. 7:26). There is no getting around this language, that most of the verses that many believe are yet to be fulfilled already have been fulfilled. Forcing the following verses to describe a time nearly two thousand years in the future is the epitome of "Scripture twisting":

- "And you will be hated by all on account of My name, but it is the one who has endured to the end who will be saved. But whenever they persecute you in this city, flee to the next; *for truly I say to you, you shall not finish going through the cities of Israel, until the Son of Man comes*" (Matt. 10:22–23).
- "For the Son of Man is going to come in the glory of His Father with His angels; and WILL THEN RECOMPENSE EVERY MAN ACCORDING TO HIS DEEDS. Truly I say to you, *there are some of those standing here who shall not taste death until they see the Son of Man coming in His kingdom*" (Matt. 16:27–28).

- "Jesus said to [the high priest], 'You have said it yourself [that I am the Christ, the Son of God]; nevertheless I tell you, hereafter *you shall see the Son of Man sitting at the right hand of power, and coming on the clouds of heaven*'" (Matt. 26:64).
- "Peter therefore seeing him [John] said to Jesus, 'Lord, and what about this man?' Jesus said to him, '*If I want him* [John] *to remain until I come*, what is that to you? You follow Me!'" (John 21:21–22).
- "And this do, knowing the time, that it is already the hour for you to awaken from sleep; for *now salvation is nearer to us than when we believed*" (Rom. 13:11).
- "*The night is almost gone and the day is at hand.* Let us therefore lay aside the deeds of darkness and put on the armor of light" (Rom. 13:12).
- "And the God of peace will *soon* crush Satan under your feet" (Rom. 16:20).
- "But this I say, brethren, *the time has been shortened*, so that from now on both those who have wives should be as though they had none" (1 Cor. 7:29).
- "For the form of this world *is passing away*" (1 Cor. 7:31).
- "Now these things happened to [Israel] as an example, and they were written for our instruction, *upon whom the ends of the ages have come*" (1 Cor. 10:11).
- "And *you know what restrains him now*, so that in his time he may be revealed" (2 Thess. 2:6).
- "For the mystery of lawlessness *is already at work*" (2 Thess. 2:7).
- "Let your forbearing spirit be known to all men. *The Lord is near*" (Phil. 4:5).
- "*But now once at the consummation of the ages He has been manifested* to put away sin by the sacrifice of Himself" (Heb. 9:26).
- "Not forsaking our own assembling together, as it is the habit of some, but encouraging one another; and all the more, *as you see the day drawing near*" (Heb. 10:25).
- "FOR YET IN *A VERY LITTLE WHILE*,[9] HE WHO IS COMING WILL COME, AND WILL NOT DELAY" (Heb. 10:37).
- "Be patient, therefore, brethren, *until the coming of the Lord*. Behold, the farmer waits for the precious produce of the soil, being patient about it, until it gets the early and late rains" (James 5:7).
- "You too be patient; strengthen your hearts, *for the coming of the Lord is at hand*" (James 5:8).

- "Do not complain, brethren, against one another, that you your-selves may not be judged; behold, *the Judge is standing right at the door*" (James 5:9).
- "For He was foreknown before the foundation of the world, *but has appeared in these last times* for the sake of *you*" (1 Peter 1:20).
- "*The end of all things is at hand*; therefore, be of sound judgment and sober spirit for the purpose of prayer" (1 Peter 4:7).
- "And when the Chief Shepherd *appears, you will receive*[10] the unfading crown of glory" (1 Peter 5:4).
- "Children, *it is the last hour*, and just as you heard that antichrist is com-ing, even now many antichrists *have arisen*; from this *we know that it is the last hour*" (1 John 2:18).
- "The Revelation of Jesus Christ, which God gave Him to show to His bond-servants, *the things which must shortly take place...*" (Rev. 1:1).
- "Blessed is he who reads and those who hear the words of the prophecy, and heed the things which are written in it; *for the time is near*" (Rev. 1:3).
- "'Because you have kept the word of My perseverance, I also will keep you from the hour of testing, that hour which *is about to come* upon the whole world,[11] to test those who dwell upon the earth [land]'" (Rev. 3:10).
- "*I am coming quickly*; hold fast what you have, in order that no one take your crown" (Rev. 3:11).
- "The second woe is past; behold, the third woe is coming *quickly*" (Rev. 11:14).
- "The beast that you saw was and is not, and *is about to come up* out of the abyss" (Rev. 17:8).
- "And he said to me, 'These words are faithful and true'; and the Lord, the God of the spirits of the prophets, sent His angel to show to his bond-servants *the things which must shortly take place*" (Rev. 22:6).
- "And behold, *I am coming quickly*. Blessed is he who heeds the words of the prophecy of this book" (Rev. 22:7).
- "And he said to me, 'Do not seal up the words of the prophecy of this book, *for the time is near*'" (Rev. 22:10)
- "Behold, *I am coming quickly*, and My reward is with Me, to render to every man according to what he has done" (Rev. 22:12; cf. Matt. 16:27).
- "He who testifies to these things says, 'Yes, *I am coming quickly*.' Amen. Come, Lord Jesus" (Rev. 22:20).

These passages and others like them tell us that a significant eschatological event was to happen in the lifetime of those who heard and read the prophecies. Dispensationalists reject this literal approach to interpreting the time texts by fabricating a doctrine called *imminency*. The following definition is typical:

> The primary thought expressed by the word "imminency" is that something important is likely to happen, and could happen soon. While the event may not be immediate, or necessarily very soon, it is next on the program and may take place at any time.[12]

There is nothing in the above texts that would support this definition. Words such as "likely," "could happen," and "may take place" are nowhere indicated. The biblical writers are straightforward in their claim that the events described were to happen "soon" for those who first read the prophecies. No other interpretation is possible if the words are taken in their "plain, primary, ordinary, usual, or normal" sense. If the biblical authors had wanted to be tentative in the way they described future events, they would have used words expressing probability.

The time texts are the most important element in Bible prophecy. If they are ignored or manipulated in any way, then God's Word can be made to mean anything. A Bible that can mean anything is a Bible without meaning.

Notes

1. Joe Maxwell, *Christianity Today* (11 March 1991), 60.

2. Quoted in Alan Bash, "Some see signs of doom in storms' clouds," *USA Today* (13 July 1993), 3D.

3. Back-cover copy of Hal Lindsey, *The 1980s: Countdown to Armageddon* (King of Prussia, PA: Westgate Press, 1980).

4. Cover copy of John F. Walvoord, *Armageddon, Oil and the Middle East*, rev. ed. (Grand Rapids, MI: Zondervan, [1974, 1976] 1990).

5. Cited in Kenneth L. Woodward, "The Final Days are Here Again," *Newsweek* (18 March 1991), 55.

6. Cited in Woodward, "The Final Days are Here Again," 55.

7. William T. James, "What the Future Holds," *Storming Toward Armageddon: Essays in Apocalypse* (Green Forest, AR: New Leaf Press, 1992), 45.

8. Gordon H. Clark, *II Peter: A Short Commentary* (Nutley, NJ: Presbyterian and Reformed, 1975), 64.

9. "Little while" is used to describe events that take place in the lifetime of the audience: Mark 14:17; John 7:33; 12:35; 13:33; 14:19; 16:16; Heb. 2:7, 9; James 4:14; 1 Peter 1:6; 5:10; Revelation 6:11; 17:10.

10. If Peter had a distant generation in mind, he would have written, "*they* will receive."

11. The Greek word translated "world" is not *kosmos* but *oikoumenes*, "the inhabited earth," most often interpreted as "the Roman Empire" (see Luke 2:1 and Matt. 24:14).

12. Gerald B. Stanton, "The Doctrine of Imminency: Is It Biblical?," in Thomas Ice and Timothy Demy, eds., *When the Trumpet Sounds* (Eugene, OR: Harvest House, 1995), 222.

Chapter Three

WHEN DID JESUS "COME IN GLORY"?

Almost any interpretation can be put on a verse or series of verses if the grammatical and historical contexts are not first determined. The *time* when Jesus said certain events would take place is all-important. To miss the identification of the time when an event is said to occur will mean that the discourse can be made to fit any generation. This, of course, would lead to tremendous confusion. There is no doubt that this error is the chief problem for those who maintain that the events of Matthew 24–25 and other prophetic passages are yet to be fulfilled, either in our generation or in some future generation. A few examples will put this concept in proper perspective.

In Matthew 16:27–28, Jesus proclaims, "For the Son of Man is going to come in the glory of His Father with His angels; and will then recompense every man according to His deeds. Truly I say to you, *there are some of those who are standing here who shall not taste death* until they see the Son of Man coming in His kingdom." If we maintain that the event Jesus is describing is still in our future, then how should we interpret His statement that some of those with whom He was speaking would still be alive when He did in fact "come in the glory of His Father with His angels"? Some claim that the "coming" Jesus had in mind was the transfiguration. But the transfiguration cannot be its fulfillment since Jesus indicated that *some* who were standing with Him would still be alive when He came but *most* would be dead. If we adopt the view that the transfiguration is the fulfillment, we must conclude that most of the people with whom Jesus spoke were dead within a week of Jesus' prediction (Matt. 17:1)! Dispensationalist Stanley D. Toussaint disagrees: "The Lord is simply asserting the fact that it would not be a long time before some of them saw Christ coming in His kingdom, which occurred in the Transfiguration."[1] If this is what Jesus wanted to communicate, then why did He say that some of those who were standing before Him would not *taste death* before they saw Him coming in His kingdom? Toussaint comments that preterists, those who believe that these verses were fulfilled nearly forty years later, read "more into the text than is being said." In reality, Toussaint dismisses what is plainly said. Moreover, if he believes that Matthew 16:27–28 has been fulfilled in the transfiguration, then he is a preterist! He has refuted his own anti-preterist argument since he believes that the fulfillment is in the past.

Others see Pentecost, with the coming of the Holy Spirit, as the fulfillment. But the same problem arises—nearly all the disciples would have had to die within a period of a few months after the events described by Jesus in Matthew 16:27–28. Such a scenario does not fit with the language of the text and what we know took place. Anyway, finding a fulfillment in these two proximate events does not solve the problem for futurists who maintain that "the Son of Man coming in His kingdom" is language that refers exclusively to the second-coming.

The Bible Interprets Itself

A helpful biblical commentary on Matthew 16:27–28 is found in John 21:18–23. After Jesus describes for Peter how he will die (21:18), Peter asks of John's fate, "Lord, and what about this man?" (21:21). Jesus says to Peter, "If I want him to remain until I come, what is that to you? You follow Me!" (21:22). History tells us that Peter died before Jerusalem was destroyed, and John lived beyond Jerusalem's destruction, a perfect and expected fulfillment of Matthew 16:27–28. If we are still waiting for the fulfillment of Jesus' prediction of His coming "in the glory of His Father with His angels," then *some* of those who were with Jesus are still alive! An impossibility, to be sure. So, then, we must look for an event that was far enough in the future where *most* of Jesus' hearers would be dead, but not so far in the future where they *all* would be dead. Is there such an event? Yes! The destruction of Jerusalem in A.D. 70 by the Romans. Henry Hammond (1605–1660) offers a helpful harmony of Matthew 16:27–28, John 21:18–23, and Matthew 24 and their relationship to Jesus' judgment on Jerusalem:

> The nearness of this to the story of *Christ's* Transfiguration, makes it probable to many, that this *coming of Christ* is that Transfiguration of his, but that cannot be, because the 27th *verse* of the *son of man's coming in his glory with his Angels to reward,* &c. (to which this verse clearly connects) cannot be applied to that. And there is another place, *John* 21:23. (which may help to the understanding of this) which speaks of a real coming, and one principal person (agreeable to what is here said of *some standing here*) that should *tarry,* or *not die,* till *that coming* of his. And that surely was fulfilled in *John's* seeing the …*famous destruction* of the Jews, which was to fall in that generation, *Matthew* 24, that is, in the lifetime of some there present, and is called the *Kingdom of God,* and the *Coming of Christ,* and by consequence here most probably the *son of man's coming in his kingdom,* … that is, his coming in the exercise of his Kingly office, to work vengeance on his enemies, and discriminate the faithful believers from them.[2]

Hammond's view is not unusual. In fact, most evangelical commentators applied these passages to the destruction of Jerusalem in A.D. 70. Henry Alford states that this passage refers *"to the destruction of Jerusalem,* and the full manifestation of the Kingdom of Christ by the annihilation of the Jewish polity…."[3] The Dutch commentator S. Greijdanus offers a helpful summary of Matthew 16:27–28 in his comments on the parallel passage in Luke 9:27:

> Then this coming of God's dominion cannot refer to our Lord's resurrection, nor to the gift of the Holy Spirit which were to be realized within the year…. Nor can it refer to our Lord's coming in judgment which is yet even now in abeyance…. Nor can the powerful spread of the gospel be meant, for this already came about within comparatively few years…. We shall have to think of the destruction of Jerusalem…. In it God revealed his kingly dominion in his judgment, a precursor of his judgment on the last day.[4]

Charles H. Spurgeon's comments get to the heart of the matter when he writes, "If a child were to read this passage I know what he would think it meant: he would suppose Jesus Christ was to come, and there were some standing there who should not taste death until really and literally he did come. This, I believe, is the plain meaning." Though plain, Spurgeon still could not accept it.[5]

Mark's gospel adds more to the context. "For whoever is ashamed of Me and My words in *this adulterous and sinful generation*," Jesus dclares, "the Son of Man will also be ashamed of him when He comes in the glory of His Father with the holy angels" (Mark 8:38). A distant generation is not in view; it's Jesus' contemporaries who will experience His wrath. And how does Jesus define the time context of "this adulterous and sinful generation"? "And He was saying to *them*, 'Truly I say to *you*, there are *some of those who are standing here* who shall not taste death until *they see* the kingdom of God after it has come with power'" (Mark 9:1).

Questioning Jesus and the Bible

Why is a discussion of these texts so important? First, we want to be accurate in our understanding of Scripture since it is God's only Word to us, the expression of His will. To misinterpret Scripture is to misinterpret God's will. Second, the integrity of the Bible is at stake. Critics of the Bible have studied Jesus' words in these passages and have concluded that He was wrong! Jesus predicted that He would return within a generation, as Matthew 24:34 clearly states, and He did not. The conclusion? The Bible cannot be trusted as a reliable book. It is filled with errors. The well-known atheist Bertrand Russell seized on what he perceived to be a mistake and concluded that the Bible was not trustworthy. He wrote the following in *Why I Am Not a Christian*:

I am concerned with Christ as he appears in the Gospel narrative as it stands, and there one does find some things that do not seem to be very wise. For one thing, He certainly thought that His second coming would occur in clouds of glory before the death of all the people who were living at that time. There are a great many texts that prove that and there are a lot of places where it is quite clear that He believed that His coming would happen during the lifetime of many then living.

That was the belief of His earlier followers, and it was the basis of a good deal of His moral teaching.[6]

If Jesus was wrong on the timing of His coming, Russell concludes, then His moral worldview should be questioned as well. Jesus' moral teaching is based on His character. If His characater is flawed, so is His morality.

A similar line of argument is attempted by the skeptic Tim Callahan in *Bible Prophecy: Failure or Fulfillment?* Callahan's arguments are identical to those used by futurists who claim that Jesus coming in His kingdom (Matt. 16:27–28) and the events of the Olivet Discourse prophecy (Matt. 24–25) could not have been fulfilled prior to the destruction of the temple in A.D. 70. "Obviously," Callahan writes, "the gospel had not been preached to the entire world by 70. C.E., even if we interpret the whole world as being nothing more than the Roman Empire."[7] This is the same argument used by dispensationalists to get around what Jesus said so clearly, that He would come in judgment before that generation passed away.

Writing for the *Skeptical Inquirer*, Gerald A. Larue takes a position similar to that of Russell and Callahan and concludes that the Bible is riddled with errors because Jesus' was wrong about the timing of His coming:

> Although apocalyptic mythology is found throughout the New Testament and is portrayed in its most organized form in Revelation, the gospel writers gave authority for the idea to John the Baptizer, who introduced the theme in the gospels, and to Jesus, who explained signs of the end of the age and promised his disciples that the new kingdom of God would be ushered in during their lifetime (Matt. 16:28). Jesus was wrong. Indeed, during the second century CE, some Christians asked, "Where is the promise of His coming? For ever since the fathers fell asleep, all things have continued as they were from the beginning of creation." (2 Peter 3:4). All we can say is that from that time on, every prophetic pronouncement of the ending of time has been wrong.[8]

If Jesus was wrong, then critics like Russell, Callahan, and Larue can rightly conclude that we cannot trust anything He said. In addition, if *Jesus*, being the Son of God, was wrong, then how can we trust the writers of the New Testament, who claimed to be nothing more than finite and fallible sinners?

Evangelicals have done a poor job in reconciling these time texts with other parts of the Bible and with history. Their argument goes something like this: "It *seems* that Jesus was predicting that He would return before the last disciple died, but He didn't *really* mean to leave that impression." Even C.S. Lewis understood the dilemma present in Jesus' statement in Matthew 24:34, that He would return before that first-century generation passed away. After dealing with critics who maintain that Jesus was just another Palestinian seer, Lewis confronts the more serious objection:

> "But there is worse to come. 'Say what you like,' we shall be told, 'the apocalyptic beliefs of the first Christians have been proved to be false. It is clear from the New Testament that they all expected the Second Coming in their own lifetime. And, worse still, they had a reason, and one which you will find very embarassing. Their Master had told them so. He shared, and indeed created, their delusion. He said in so many words, "this generation shall not pass till all these things be done." And He was wrong. He clearly knew no more about the end of the world than anyone else.'"[9]

Lewis considers Matthew 24:34 "the most embarrassing verse in the Bible." His attempts to reconcile this and other time texts with the reality that Jesus' coming did not take place in the first century are ineffective. He's not alone.

Gleason Archer believes that there "are three possible fulfillments of [Matthew 16:28]": the transfiguration, Pentecost, and the destruction of Jerusalem in A.D. 70. He dismisses the transfiguration and the destruction of Jerusalem and opts for Pentecost as the fulfillment.[10] Nowhere does he explain how verse 28 fits: "there are some of those who are standing here who shall not taste death until they see the Son of Man coming in His kingdom" (16:28). J. Carl Laney believes that the transfiguration is the fulfillment. How does he explain verse 28? "Jesus was not mistaken in thinking that some of the disciples would witness the inauguration of His kingdom. He simply encouraged them with the promise that some would experience a foretaste of His kingdom glory!" Laney avoids dealing with what the text actually says and puts words in Jesus' mouth.[11] Larry Richards ignores the time element in the passage by failing to explain how verse 28 could be fulfilled in either the transfiguration or Pentecost.[12] R. A. Torrey follows a similar line of argument.[13] A note in *The Believer's Study Bible* (1991) suggests that Matthew 16:28 might refer to Jesus' "triumphal entry into Jerusalem a few days hence" (1366) without ever discussing the time issue.

But What Does It Mean?

But how can we maintain that Jesus came "in the glory of His Father with His angels" in A.D. 70? As we've seen, the time indicator in the passage precludes either an immediate fulfillment (transfiguration, resurrection, Pentecost) or a distant fulfillment (the second coming of Christ). The language of Matthew 16:27–28 is similar to the way Jehovah came to "the sons of Israel" under the Old Covenant:

> "The LORD came from Sinai, and dawned on them from Seir; He shown forth from Mount Paran, and He came from the midst of ten thousand holy ones. At His right hand there was flashing lightning for them" (Deut. 33:1–2).

Jude presents a similar picture in the New Testament. But his is a description of God's coming in judgment: "Behold, the Lord came with many thousands of His holy ones, to execute judgment upon all, and to convict all of the ungodly of all their ungodly deeds which they have done in an ungodly way, and of all the harsh things which ungodly sinners have spoken against Him" (Jude 14–15). The language is almost identical with that of Matthew 16:27. In addition, "Jesus alludes to Daniel 7:13–14 and thus applies Old Testament language for God as judge to Himself (Ps 62:12; Prov 24:12; Jer 17:10; 32:19; Ezek 18:30). The reference to angels is probably from Zechariah 14:5, though it also fits the context of the image in Daniel 7:13–14."[14] Jesus assumes the Old Testament apocalyptic language referring to Jehovah's coming and applies it to Himself. A similar pattern is found in Revelation 2:5: "Remember therefore from where you have fallen, and repent and do the deeds you did at first; or else I am coming to you, and will remove your lampstand out of its place—unless you repent." Similar "coming" language is used in Revelation 2:16, neither of which refer to Christ's second coming.

Notes

1. In a paper presented at the Fourth Annual Pre-Trib Study Group in Dallas, Texas (December 11–13, 1995), 20.

2. Henry Hammond, *A Paraphrase, and Notations Upon all the Books of the New Testament*, 7th ed. (London: John Nicholson, [1653] 1702), 74–75. For similar comments on John 21:18–21, see John Lightfoot, *A Commentary on the New Testament from the Talmud and Hebraica: Matthew—1 Corinthians*, 4 vols. (Peabody, MA: Hendrickson Publishers, [1859] 1989), 3:451–54 and John Gill, *Exposition of the Old and New Testaments*, 9 vols. (London: Mathews and Leigh, 1809), 8:135.

3. Henry Alford, *The New Testament for English Readers* (Chicago, IL: Moody Press, [1886] n.d.), 122.

4. S. Greijdanus, *Het heilig Evangelie naar de beschrijving van Lukas* (1940), 1:424, 425. Quoted in Herman Ridderbos, *The Coming of the Kingdom*, trans. H. de Jongste (Philadelphia, PA: Presbyterian and Reformed, 1975), 504.

5. Charles H. Spurgeon, "An Awful Premonition," in *12 Sermons on the Second Coming of Christ* (Grand Rapids, MI: Baker Book House, 1976), 3–6.

6. Bertrand Russell, *Why I Am Not a Christian* (New York: Simon and Schuster, 1957), 16.

7. Tim Callahan, *Bible Prophecy: Failure or Fulfillment?* (Altadena, CA: Millennium Press, 1997), 185–89.

8. Gerald A. Larue, "The Bible and the Prophets of Doom," *Skeptical Inquirer* (January/February 1999), 29.

9. C. S. Lewis, *The World's Last Night and Other Essays* (New York: Harcourt, Brace and Company, 1960), 97–98.

10. Gleason L. Archer, *Encyclopedia of Bible Difficulties* (Grand Rapids, MI: Zondervan/Regency Reference Library, 1982), 326–27.

11. J. Carl Laney, *Answers to Tough Questions: A Survey of Problem Passages and Issues from Every Book of the Bible* (Grand Rapids, MI: Kregel, 1997), 198–99.

12. Larry Richards, *735 Baffling Bible Questions Answered* (Grand Rapids, MI: Revell, [1993] 1997), 249.

13. R. A. Torrey, *Difficulties and Alleged Errors and Contradictions in the Bible* (New York: Fleming H. Revell, 1907), 116–118.

14. Craig S. Keener, *The IVP Bible Background Commentary: New Testament* (Downers Grove, IL: InterVarsity Press, 1993), 91.

Chapter Four

TIMING IS
EVERYTHING

O nce the timing of prophetic events is established, the next step is to survey the events that are to take place during the time intervals. Two large prophetic passages are outlined for us in the Bible where both time indicators and sign indicatiors are used: the Olivet Discourse (Matt. 24–25; Mark 13; Luke 21) and the Book of Revelation. Revelation, with its visions, apocalyptic imagery, and symbols is a difficult book to interpret for those who are not intimately familiar with the Bible as a whole. The best place to start to understand Jesus' prophetic plan is the Olivet Discourse. We are given a time text (Matt. 24:34) and specific events that are said to unfold prior to that first-generation's passing. Therefore, we can test the events that Jesus said would take place before that first-century generation passed away with the Bible and history.

To understand Matthew 24, we must begin with a brief background study of Matthew 23. The disciples had just heard Jesus pronounce His "woes" on the Pharisees. Jesus ended His denunciation of Israel's religious leaders with this bombshell: "Behold, your house is being left to you desolate!" (23:38). What "house" did Jesus have in mind? Matthew 24 begins: "And Jesus came out from the *temple* and was going away when His disciples came up to point out the temple buildings to Him" (24:1). So then, the "house" that is being left to them "desolate" in Matthew 23:38 is the "temple" that will soon be judged and torn down, stone by stone (24:1).

The disciples were obviously curious since the temple was the most holy site in all Israel. Earlier in His ministry, Jesus pronounced to the religious leaders that His own body was the true temple. The temple of stone was a temporary edifice that pointed to a greater, permanent temple (John 2:19–22). Only after Jesus' resurrection did the disciples begin to understand that the true and everlasting temple is "the temple of His body" (2:21). The physical temple was designed to be temporary. To make the temple of stone a permanent structure in the light of Jesus' atoning work would be a denial of the Messiah and His redemptive mission.

The disciples were surprised when Jesus told them that the temple was going to be destroyed, with not one stone left on top of another (Matt. 24:2). In response, they asked this multifaceted question: "Tell us, when will these things be, and what will be the sign of Your coming, and of the end of the age" (24:3)? It is crucial that we pay close attention to *when Jesus* said these events would take place.

Jesus told the scribes and Pharisees, "Truly I say to you, *all these things* shall come upon *this generation*," that is, the destruction of their temple and city will be realized before the then-existing generation passes into history (23:36). It was the generation of those who rejected Jesus who would experience His wrath. The "this generation" of Matthew 23:36 is the generation upon whom Jesus pronounced judgment.

But what of those who say that the Olivet Discourse is a prophecy about a still-future temple that must be rebuilt in Jerusalem and destroyed like the temple that was destroyed by the Roman military leader Titus in A.D. 70? This supposed future temple would have to be rebuilt with the same stones that made up the temple that was destroyed. Not just any stones will do. Jesus said that "not one stone *here* shall be left upon another, which will not be torn down" (Matt. 24:2).

The temple that Jesus said would be destroyed is the same temple with the same stones that were pointed out by Jesus to His disciples. No future temple is in view. Jesus gives no indication that He has a future *rebuilt* temple in mind. Certainly Jesus' disciples would not be thinking of a rebuilt temple when they were looking at an existing temple that Jesus said would be destroyed! But what if the Jews are able to rebuild the temple? Such a temple will have nothing to do with the fulfillment of any part of this prophecy.

The Severity of Judgment

Why did Jesus treat this first-century generation of Jews so harshly? Why was their generation destined for destruction? *They made up the generation that had to make a choice either to accept or reject the promised Messiah* who "became flesh and dwelt among" them (John 1:14). Certainly every generation must make a decision about Jesus. But no other generation will ever have the chance to turn Him over to the Romans to be crucified. Jesus "came to His own, and those who were His own did not receive Him" (John 1:11). No other generation will be given such an opportunity. The Lord of glory was in their midst, and they crucified Him, choosing a murderer in place of God's only begotten Son (Matt. 27:20–26; Acts 3:14–15). The following verses are biblical descriptions of "this generation," that is, the generation that Jesus addressed:

- They were "sons of those who murdered the prophets" (Matt. 23:31).
- The measure of their fathers' guilt was filled up with their generation (23:32).
- They were "serpents" and a "brood of vipers" who would not "escape the sentence of hell" (23:33).
- They will "scourge," "persecute," "crucify," and "kill" some of the "prophets and wise men and scribes" that Jesus will send (23:34).

Of course, these indictments had been heard before. During the ministry of John the Baptist these same men were described as a "brood of vipers" who had heard of a "wrath to come," a wrath they thought they could escape in the baptismal waters of the Jordan River (3:7).

"But to what shall I compare *this* generation? It is like children sitting in the market places, who call out to other children, and say, 'We played the flute for you, and you did not dance; we sang a dirge, and you did not mourn.' For John came neither eating nor drinking, and they say, 'He has a demon!' The Son of Man came eating and drinking, and they say, 'Behold, a gluttonous man and a drunkard, a friend of tax-gatherers and sinners!' Yet wisdom is vindicated by her deeds."

Then He began to reproach the cities in which most of His miracles were done, because they did not repent. "Woe to you, Chorazin! Woe to you, Bethsaida! For if the miracles had occurred in Tyre and Sidon which occurred in *you*, they would have repented long ago in sackcloth and ashes" (11:16–21).

Not long after this pronouncement of judgment the religious leaders accused Jesus of being in league with Satan because He cast out demons (12:24). Jesus once again called them a "brood of vipers" (12:34). They were "condemned" by their words (12:37). The scribes and Pharisees asked for a sign (12:38), and Jesus informed them that "an evil and adulterous generation craves for a sign" (12:39). Jesus warned the unregenerate of His day that "the men of Nineveh shall stand up with *this generation* at the judgment, and shall condemn it because they repented at the preaching of Jonah" (12:41). Judgment was certain to come upon "this generation" because "something greater than Jonah is here" (12:41). Jesus compared "this generation" to that of "unclean spirits" who occupy a man's house, exacerbating the man's spiritual condition. "That is the way it will also be with *this evil generation*," Jesus said (12:45). This all took place in one of their synagogues (12:9). Is this the "house" that will be occupied by "unclean spirits," which the Book of Revelation describes as a "synagogue of Satan" (Rev. 2:9)?

Jesus told them on another occasion, "The kingdom of God will be taken away from you, and be given to a nation producing the fruit of it. And he who falls on this stone will be broken to pieces; but on whomever it falls, it will scatter him like dust" (Matt. 21:43–44). There is no mistaking the context, the audience, and the time of judgment; the generation with whom Jesus spoke would be destroyed within forty years, along with the temple and the city. "And when the chief priests and the Pharisees heard His parables, *they understood that He was speaking about them*," not a generation two thousand years in the future (21:45).

This is why Dave Hunt's strained interpretation of "this generation" is so off-base. He ends up, unwittingly, of course, indicting all Jews throughout history with his novel interpretation of the phrase "this generation." In fact, he turns a passage that is addressed specifically to Jews of the first century and applies it to Jews in general. Hunt states, "Certainly anyone living at any time who exhibited the same evil tendencies would also be part of that 'generation of vipers.'"[1] This explanation makes "this generation" meaningless. Jesus isn't describing any time or any generation; He has the generation of His own day in mind: "All these things shall come upon *this* generation.... *This* generation will not pass away until all these things take place" (Matt. 23:36; 24:34). How could Jesus have said it more clearly? How could Jesus have better designated the generation to whom He was speaking?

The "woes" of Matthew 23 and the destruction of the temple and the city of Jerusalem were a result of all that John the Baptist and Jesus had been warning the scribes, Pharisees, and chief priests regarding the judgment that would come upon them if they did not repent. "All these things," Jesus cautioned, "shall come upon *this* generation" (23:36). It is after hearing about the desolation of "their house" (temple)[2] that the disciples ask about the "temple buildings" (24:1). Jesus answered the disciples' questions relating to the time and signs of Jerusalem's destruction, always with the background of Matthew 23 in view, since His comments in that chapter had raised the questions (24:3). The Old Covenant order would end with the destruction of Jerusalem. This would be the "sign" of the "end of the age," the end of the Old Covenant, and the consummation of the New Covenant.

The Time Text: "This Generation"

Since the events described in Matthew 23 precipitated the questions of Matthew 24, we should expect to see some connection between the two chapters. If Matthew 24 is an elucidation and expansion of Matthew 23, then we should expect the events of both chapters to describe the same period of time. We only assume this to be true because we have biblical cause to make the connection. The two chapters contain two verses that speak of time. The time texts are found in Matthew 23:36 and 24:34.

- "Truly I say to you, all these things shall come upon *this generation*" (23:36).
- "Truly I say to you, *this generation* will not pass away until all these things take place" (24:34).

These verses form eschatological bookends for determining when the predicted events that occur between these two time markers are to be fulfilled. Sandwiched between the time texts are the "sign" texts. The futurist interpreters of Matthew 24 assert that "this generation" does not mean the generation to whom Jesus was speaking. Rather, they maintain that it refers to a distant generation alive at the time when these events will take place. There are a number of difficulties with this position.

First, "this generation" always means the generation to whom Jesus was speaking. How do we know this? Scripture is our interpreting guide. We do not have to speculate about the meaning of "this generation." Those who deny that "this generation" refers to the generation to whom Jesus was speaking in the Matthew 24 context must maintain that "this generation" means something different from the way it is used in every other place in Matthew and the rest of the New Testament. Matthew 23:36 clearly refers to the Pharisees and their associates. Why should we interpret "this generation" in Matthew 24:34 in a way different from 23:36, since Jesus is answering His disciples' questions regarding His statement in Matthew 23:36 to the Pharisees about their house—the temple— being left to them desolate? The usual rejoinder is, "All of Matthew 24 could not have been fulfilled during the life of the apostles. There must be a future fulfillment even though 'this generation' seems to refer to those who lived between A.D. 30 and 70."

But this is not the way we should interpret Scripture. If Jesus said that all the events prior to Matthew 24:34 would occur before the contemporary generation (within forty years) passed away, then we must take Him at His word. Dispensationalists insist on literalism. Why not in this instance? "If 'this generation' is taken literally, all of the predictions were to take place within the life-span of those living at that time."[3] An honest assessment of Scripture can lead to no other conclusion. The integrity of the Bible is at stake in the discussion of the biblical meaning of "this generation."

Second, the use of "this generation" throughout the Gospels makes it clear that it means the generation to whom Jesus was speaking. The following is a list of every occurrence of "this generation" in the New Testament:

- "But to what shall I compare *this generation*?" (Matt. 11:16).
- "The men of Nineveh shall stand up with *this generation* at the judgment, and shall condemn it because they repented at the preaching of Jonah; and behold, something greater than Jonah is here" (Matt. 12:41).
- "The Queen of the South shall rise up with *this generation* at the judgment and shall condemn it, because she came from the ends of the earth to hear the wisdom of Solomon; and behold, something greater than Solomon is here" (Matt. 12:42).

- "Truly I say to you, all these things shall come upon *this generation*" (Matt. 23:36).
- "Truly I say to you, *this generation* will not pass away until all these things take place" (Matt. 24:34).
- "Why does *this generation* seek for a sign? Truly I say to you, no sign shall be given to this generation" (Mark 8:12).
- "Truly I say to you, *this generation* will not pass away until all these things take place" (Mark 13:30).
- "To what then shall I compare the men of *this generation*, and what are they like?" (Luke 7:31).
- "*This generation* is a wicked generation; it seeks for a sign, and yet no sign shall be given to it but the sign of Jonah" (Luke 11:29).
- "For just as Jonah became a sign to the Ninevites, so shall the Son of Man be to *this generation*" (Luke 11:30).
- "The Queen of the South shall rise up with the men of *this generation* at the judgment and condemn them, because she came from the ends of the earth to hear the wisdom of Solomon; and behold, something greater than Solomon is here" (Luke 11:31).
- "The men of Nineveh shall stand up with *this generation* at the judgment and condemn it, because they repented at the preaching of Jonah; and behold something greater than Jonah is here" (Luke 11:32).
- "For this reason also the wisdom of God said, 'I will send to them prophets and apostels, and some of them they will kill and some they will persecute, in order that the blood of all the prophets, shed since the foundation of the world, may be charged against *this generation*, from the blood of Abel to the blood of Zechariah, who perished between the altar and the house of God; yes, I tell you, it shall be charged against *this generation*'" (Luke 11:49–51).
- "But first He must suffer many things and be rejected by *this generation*" (Luke 17:25).
- "Truly I say to you, *this generation* will not pass away until all things take place" (Luke 21:32).

Without exception, these verses describe events within the lifetime of the then-present generation. All the evidence points to the generation of Jews who heard Jesus' words and would suffer the same judgment as the scribes, Pharisees, and the chief priests if they did not heed Jesus' warning and escape before the Roman armies surrounded the city and destroyed it (Matt. 24:15–22; Luke 21:20–24). David Chilton summarizes the argument:

> *Not one* of these references is speaking of the entire Jewish race over thousands of years; *all* use the word in its normal sense of *the sum total of those living at the same time.* It always refers to *contemporaries.* (In fact, those who say it means "race" tend to acknowledge this fact, but explain that the word suddenly *changes* its meaning when Jesus uses it in Matthew 24! We can smile at such a transparent error, but we should also remember that this is very serious. We are dealing with the Word of the living God.)[4]

Third, the adjective *this* points to the contemporary nature of the generation Jesus was referencing (cf. Matt. 11:23; 27:8; 28:15). If some future generation had been in view, Jesus could have chosen the adjective *that* (cf. 7:22; 10:19; 24:10, 36; 26:29). The passage would then read this way: "*That* generation will not pass away until all these things take place."   A study of the way Matthew uses the adjective "this" will show that Jesus had the generation to whom He was speaking in mind when He described its soon destruction:

- "Give us *this day* our daily bread" (6:11).
- "And *this news* went out into all the land" (9:26).
- "But whenever they persecute you in *this city,* flee to the next" (10:23).
- "*This is the one* about whom it was written" (11:10).
- "*This man* casts out demons only be Beelzebul the ruler of the demons" (12:24).
- "And whoever shall speak a word against the Son of Man, it shall be forgiven him; but whoever shall speak against the Holy Spirit, it shall not be forgiven him, either in *this age,* or in the age to come" (12:32).

Fourth, notice how many times Jesus uses the plural *you* in Matthew 24 and in the parallel passages in Mark 13 and Luke 21: "They will lay their hands on *you* and will persecute *you,* delivering *you* to the synagogues and prisons, bringing *you* before kings and governors for My name's sake" (Luke 21:12; see verses 13–20, 28, 30). Now, if *you* heard Jesus say that all these things would happen to "this generation" while you were standing there listening to Him, and in every other instance of its use "this generation" meant the present generation, and *you* also heard Him say that when "you" would see these things, what would you conclude? The most natural (literal) interpretation is that it would happen to *your generation*, and maybe even to you personally (Matt. 16:27–28). Again, if it were a future generation, we would expect Jesus to have said, "when *they* see ... they will bring *them* ... they will persecute *them*."

This overwhelming evidence does not phase futurists. Stanley D. Toussaint writes that "the second person plural may be employed of those who are not contemporaries." (Notice that he says "may be.") He turns to Matthew 23:35 for support. In this passage, Toussaint argues, "the Lord Jesus referred to the death of Zechariah and says, 'whom you murdered.' Obviously Zechariah was killed centuries before Christ."[5] Note that Jesus makes it clear that He is referring to the contemporary generation of Jews who heard His message of judgment. The "you" refers to *them* as Toussaint admits, regardless who murdered Zechariah. It was their generation that "filled up the measure of the guilt" begun by their fathers (23:32). Jesus tells us that "you" refers to them. The "you" does not refer to a past generation of murderers. Nowhere are we told that "you" refers to anyone but them. The burden of proof is on Toussaint to prove otherwise. And since there is a great deal of speculation as to the identity of this Zechariah, it is possible that they had indeed killed him.

Fifth, a survey of Bible commentators will show that for centuries, prior to the advent of dispensational premillennialism, "this generation" was interpreted as the generation of Jesus' day and not a distant generation. In addition, these same commentators understood that all the events prior to Matthew 24:34 referred to events leading up to and including the destruction of Jerusalem in A.D. 70. Here are some examples:

- "Hence it appears plain enough, that the foregoing verses are not to be understood of the last judgment, but, as we said, of the destruction of Jerusalem. There were some among the disciples (particularly John), who lived to see these things come to pass. With Matt. xvi. 28, compare John xxi. 22. And there were some Rabbins alive at the time when Christ spoke these things, that lived until the city was destroyed."[6]
- "It is to me a wonder how any man can refer part of the foregoing discourse to the destruction of Jerusalem, and part to the end of the world, or any other distant event, when it is said so positively here in the conclusion, *All these things shall be fulfilled in this generation*."[7]

- "[T]he obvious meaning of the words 'this generation' is the people contemporary with Jesus. Nothing can be gained by trying to take the word in any sense other than its normal one: in Mark (elsewhere in 8:12, 9:19) the word always has this meaning."[8]
- "This is a full and clear proof, that not any thing that is said before [v. 34], relates to the second coming of Christ, the day of judgment, and the end of the world; but that all belongs to the coming of the son of man in the destruction of Jerusalem, and to the end of the Jewish state."[9]
- "[This generation] can only with the greatest difficulty be made to mean anything other than the generation living when Jesus spoke."[10]
- "The significance of the temporal reference has been debated, but in Mark 'this generation' clearly designates the contemporaries of Jesus (see on Chs. 8:12, 38; 9:19) and there is no consideration from the context which lends support to any other proposal. Jesus solemnly affirms that the generation contemporary with his disciples will witness the fulfillment of his prophetic word, culminating in the destruction of Jerusalem and the dismantling of the Temple."[11]

In the past, there has been almost unanimous agreement among Bible-believing commentators that "this generation" means the generation of Jews who lived between A.D. 30 and 70.

On One Condition

"For I say to you, from now on you shall not see Me until you say, 'BLESSED IS HE WHO COMES IN THE NAME OF THE LORD!'" (Matt. 23:39)

Stanley Toussaint believes that Matthew 23:39 speaks against a first-century fulfillment of the Olivet Discourse because it holds out hope for a future conversion of the Jews as a nation. He agrees that "your house" (23:38) refers to the destruction of the temple in A.D. 70 but that "verse 39 describes Israel's future repentance when as Zechariah 12:10[12] says they shall mourn for their great sin."[13] This interpretation is impossible.

The word *"For"* with which the verse begins unambiguously links it with God's abandonment of his house in v. 38."[14] Part of the problem in understanding the relationship between verses 38 and 39 in Matthew 23 is in the way "until" is used. R.T. France contends that "the words *until you say* are expressed in Greek as an indefinite possibility rather than as a firm prediction; this is the condition on which they will see him again; but there is no promise that the condition will be fulfilled."[15] The following verses demonstrate the conditional use of "until":

- "Truly I say to you, you shall not come out of there, *until* you have paid up the last cent" (Matt. 5:26).
- "He was unwilling however, but went and threw him in prison *until* he should pay back what was owed" (Matt. 18:30).
- "And his lord, moved with anger, handed him over to the torturers *until* he should repay all that was owed him" (Matt. 18:34).
- "And when it was day, the Jews formed a conspiracy and bound themselves under and oath, saying that they would neither eat nor drink *until* they had killed Paul" (Acts 23:12).

Throughout the period between the crucifixion and the destruction of Jerusalem, Jews cried out, "Blessed is He who comes in the name of the Lord" and were saved from judgment. Until these religious leaders do the same, Jesus warns them, they will die in their sin and face Him as their judge (Acts 3:11–26). Many Jews did embrace Jesus as the promised Messiah. They came to Christ by the thousands in Jerusalem alone just days after Jesus' ascension (2:41; 4:4). The restoration had begun in Jerusalem and would extend throughout the Roman Empire prior to the destruction of the temple and city in A.D. 70.

> There is nothing in Jesus' teaching in this Gospel which suggests that *after* this period of judgement there will be a restoration; the 'seven evil spirits enter and live there' ([Matt.] 12:45), the 'vineyard is leased to others' (21:41), the city is 'burnt' (22:7), the Temple is 'abandoned' (23:38); the Apocalyptic Discourse (ch. 24) moves away from Jerusalem to focus on the coming of the Son of Man.[16]

Toussaint is willing to dismiss repeated references to an impending judgment by straining to find a single passage to bolster his argument that a pretribulational rapture, a rebuilt temple, and the reinstitution of Old Covenant Judaism during an earthly millennium remain to be fulfilled. A careful study of the New Testament will dispel such notions. Once again, the time texts are the key.

Does this mean that there was no hope for these Jews after Jesus declared that their house was being left to them desolate? Not at all. As James DeYoung writes, "Although the temple shall be destroyed, a new religious order will be instituted in which the Jews are still invited to come to Christ and greet him as the Messiah within the new temple, the spiritual house that God will build, the Church. But there is in this passage no expression of the thought that this judgment on the temple, and hence on Jerusalem as the religious center of God's people, will ever be reversed; that God will ever return to his temple in Jerusalem and once again make it the place where he exercises his redemptive revelational relation with his people."[17]

Notes

1. Dave Hunt, *How Close Are We?: Compelling Evidence for the Soon Return of Christ* (Eugene, OR: Harvest House, 1993), 288.

2. Prior to the Olivet Discourse Jesus had described the temple as "My house" (Matt. 21:13) and "My Father's house" (John 2:16). Now that the temple is coming under judgment, it is now "your house."

3. William Sanford LaSor, *The Truth About Armageddon: What the Bible Says About the End Times* (Grand Rapids, MI: Baker Book House, 1987), 122.

4. David Chilton, *The Great Tribulation* (Ft. Worth, TX: Dominion Press, 1987), 3. Emphasis in original.

5. Stanley D. Toussaint, "A Critique of the Preterist View of the Olivet Discourse" (presented at the Fourth Annual Pre-Trib Study Group, held in Dallas, Texas, December 11–13, 1995), 19.

6. John Lightfoot, *A Commentary on the New Testament from the Talmud and Hebraica: Matthew–1 Corinthians*, 4 vols. (Peabody, MA: Hendrickson Publishers, [1859] 1989), 2:320.

7. Thomas Newton, *Dissertations on the Prophecies, Which Have Remarkably Been Fulfilled, and at This Time are Fulfilling in the Whole World* (London: J.F. Dove, 1754), 377.

8. Robert G. Bratcher and Eugene A. Nida, *A Translator's Handbook of the Gospel of Mark* (New York: United Bible Socieites, 1961), 419.

9. John Gill, *Exposition of the Old and New Testaments*, 9 vols. (London: Mathews and Leigh, 1809), 3:296.

10. D.A. Carson, "Matthew" in *The Expositor's Bible Commentary*, gen. ed. Frank E. Gaebelein, 12 vols. (Grand Rapids, MI: Zondervan, 1985), 8:507.

11. William L. Lane, *Commentary on the Gospel of Mark* (Grand Rapids, MI: Eerdmans, 1974), 480.

12. John 19:37 quotes Zechariah 12:10 as something that "came to pass, that the Scripture might be fulfilled" at the time of the crucifixion (19:36).

13. Toussaint, "A Critique of the Preterist View of the Olivet Discourse," 4.

14. R. T. France, *The Gospel According to Matthew: An Introduction and Commentary* (Grand Rapids, MI: Eerdmans, 1990), 333.

15. France, *The Gospel According to Matthew,* 332.

16. P.W.L. Walker, *Jesus and the Holy City: New Testament Perspectives on Jerusalem* (Grand Rapids, MI: Eerdmans, 1996), 42. Also see John Forster, *The Gospel-Narrative* (London: John W. Parker, 1847), 227.

17. James Calvin De Young, *Jerusalem in the New Testament: The Significance of the City in the History of Redemption and in Eschatology* (Amsterdam: J.H. Kok/N.V. Kampen, 1960), 89.

Chapter Five

SEE THAT NO ONE MISLEADS YOU

Journalist Hap Cawood says he shares "the fascination with the Bible and its mysteries" with those he calls "Armageddon-here guys." But he has a problem. When he was around ten years old, he found a huge old book that offered an interpretation of what the author said were biblical prophecies. "I got more and more engrossed as I read on about how world events would unfold," Cawood wrote. "Finally, the author said when the world would END—in 1934, or thereabouts. What a relief that it all had happened before I was born!"[1] What impact did that failed 1934 prophecy have on Mr. Cawood's perceptions of the Christian faith? Do you think today's speculative prophetic dogmatism about "robots that can reproduce themselves" and "an artificial brain created by Japanese scientists" are having similar effects?[2]

In our day, prophetic speculators are misleading millions of people with their supposed certainties about the next series of events they believe are signs that Jesus is about to return to "rapture" His church. For example, in 1988 John F. Walvoord wrote that "in these present closing years of the twentieth century, evidence is pointing to the fulfillment of end-time events leading up to the second coming of Christ."[3] In his book on the continual crisis in the Middle East, Walvoord writes, "[T]he events of history clearly indicate that the world is poised and ready for the Rapture of the church and the beginning of the countdown to Armageddon."[4] He tells us that "the world is like a stage being set for a great drama. The major actors are already in the wings waiting for their moment in history. The main stage props are already in place. The prophetic play is about to begin.... All the necessary historical developments have already taken place."[5]

But we have heard all of this before. In fact, also in 1988, we were assured that the rapture would occur sometime in a three-day period in September of that year. "But by sunset Tuesday [September 13, 1988], the end of the 48–hour period pinpointed by former NASA rocket engineer and author Edgar G. Whisenant as the time of the Rapture, it was apparent that The End was not quite at hand."[6] Whisenant remained confident. He later "revised his prediction, saying the Rapture could possibly occur by 10:55 A.M. Wednesday [September 14]."[7] A final modification was made, predicting that 1989 would be the year.[8] As one might suspect, such predictions can have a negative effect on Christians and non-Christians. "Too much wild-eyed speculation could eventually discredit the essential message we are called to proclaim. Remember, [Jack] Van Impe himself was certain the Soviet flag would fly over Independence Hall in Philadelphia by 1976."[9] Van Impe, after uttering one failed prediction after another, goes on undaunted, revising his prophetic pronouncements as current events change: "I just can't believe that I've preached this all my life and that I've lived to see these things happening."[10] Self-proclaimed Bible prophecy "experts" like Van Impe are as eager to predict the future as they are eager to forget their failed past predictions. They count on the people forgetting as well. These failed prophecy "experts" are the "Christian" equivalent of the "Psychic Network." We'll never know how much damage they've done to the credibility of the Bible and the Christian faith.

The airwaves are filled with prophecy pundits who continually assure us the end is threatening. *Praise the Lord*, the official newsletter of the Trinity Broadcasting Network (TBN), which boasts being "on the air worldwide," states emphatically that "the end of the world is coming soon." In the same issue of *Praise the Lord*, Hal Lindsey and Chuck Smith, described by TBN as "two of the most respected Bible prophecy teachers," believe that "the signs in our world today clearly point to the imminent return of our Lord."[11]

Confusion over Fulfilled Prophecy

One of the most wonderful benefits of fulfilled prophecy, over against the speculations of self-appointed prophetic speculators, is that fulfilled prophecy can be used to support the Bible's own claim that it is indeed the very Word of God. For example, the crucifixion of Jesus was outlined in remarkable detail centuries before Roman soldiers pierced Jesus' hands and feet and divided His garments among them (Psalm 22:11–18) on that horrible day at Golgotha. Isaiah 53 reads like an eyewitness account of the Crucifixion. But Isaiah was not an eyewitness. He wrote centuries before Jesus lived and died.

The faith of Christians is strengthened when they read what was predicted in the Old Testament and fulfilled in the New Testament pertaining to the coming Messiah. "Canon Liddon is authority for the statement that there are in the Old Testament 332 distinct predictions which were literally fulfilled in Christ,"[12] all demonstrating the veracity of the Bible's assertion that "all Scripture is God-breathed" (2 Tim. 3:16, NIV).

The New Testament continues with its own prophetic pronouncements. We should expect prophecies found in the New Testament to be fulfilled with equal precision. While there are many who believe that much from the New Testament is yet to be fulfilled, many fine scholars have taught that much *has been fulfilled.*

No Stone upon Another

Before embarking on a verse by verse exposition of the Olivet Discourse, setting the context for the prophetic material outlined by Jesus in Matthew 24–25 must be considered. It begins with Jesus' full-scale indictment of the Pharisees in Matthew 23 and the questions the promised desolation of the temple raises for the disciples. Jesus warned the Pharisees that their "house"— the temple— would be left to them "desolate" (23:38). When Jesus finished His verbal indictment, He "came out from the temple and was going away when His disciples came to point out the temple buildings to Him" (24:1). It was at this point that Jesus makes a remarkable prediction.

> *"And He answered and said to them, 'Do you not see all these things? Truly I say to you, not one stone here shall be left upon another, which will not be torn down'" (Matt. 24:2).*

Notice that Jesus says, "not one stone *here* shall be left upon another." Jesus is not describing what will happen to some future rebuilt temple. No mention is ever made in the New Testament about a rebuilt temple. Those who claim that the temple must be rebuilt during a future period of "great tribulation" cannot point to one verse in the New Testament that describes such a rebuilding program. Even those who teach that the temple will be rebuilt admit, "There are no Bible verses that say, 'There is going to be a third temple.'"[13] The temple under discussion throughout the Olivet Discourse is the one that was standing during the time of Jesus' ministry, the same temple that was destroyed by the Romans in A.D. 70. Probably stunned at this point, the disciples ask the following multi-faceted question.

"Tell us, when will these things be, and what will be the sign of Your coming, and of the end of the age?" (Matt. 24:3)

The disciples' question involves three interrelated, contemporary events: (1) the *time* of the temple's destruction; (2) the *sign* that will signal Jesus' coming related to the destruction of the temple; and (3) the *sign* they should look for telling them that "the end of the age" has come. These questions are related to the destruction of the temple and the end of the Old Covenant redemptive system and nothing else. Alfred Plummer offers a helpful summary of the significance of the end of the age terminology: "'The end' of course means the end of the age, and in interpreting that we must remember the subject of this discourse and the persons to whom it is addressed. Our Lord is speaking of the overthrow of Jerusalem and of the Temple to men who would inevitably think of such an overthrow as the end of the age. . . . What was important for them to know was that the Temple was doomed and its end near."[14]

Jesus never indicates that He has a distant coming in mind. There is nothing in the Olivet Discourse that would give the reader the impression that a distant event is in view. Remember, Jesus told his disciples that He was "going to come in the glory of His Father with His angels" before the last apostle died (Matt. 16:27–28). While they did not understand the full implications of this coming in judgment, they did know that it would happen within the span of their generation. Jesus confirms the timing of His coming as He outlines the events leading up to the temple's destruction. We know the temple was destroyed just as Jesus prophesied. This happened within a generation.

For when the Romans had taken Jerusalem, Titus ordered his soldiers to dig up the foundations both of all the city and the temple.... As we read in the Jewish Talmud and in Maimonides, Turnus Rufus, or rather Terentius Rufus, who was left to command the army at Jerusalem, did with a ploughshare tear up the foundation of the temple; and thereby signally fulfilled those words of Micah, (iii. 12,) "Therefore shall Zion for your sake be ploughed as a field." Eusebius too affirms, that it was ploughed up by the Romans, and he saw it lying in ruins.[15]

Flavius Josephus (A.D. 37–101), the Palestinian Jewish historian of priestly decent who compiled a history of the Jewish people for the Romans, was an eyewitness to these events. His *Wars of the Jews* was written about A.D. 75, five years after the fall of Jerusalem. He wrote of the temple's destruction that "there was left nothing to make those who had come thither believe it had ever been inhabited."[16]

The End of the Age

Notice that the disciples did not ask about the end of the "world" (*kosmos*), as some Bible versions translate the Greek word *aion*. In context, with the temple and city as their primary focus, they asked about the end of the "age." They were asking when time would run out for the temple, the city of Jerusalem, and the covenant promises that were related to the Mosaic system of animal sacrifices, ceremonial washings, and the priesthood.

Time was divided by the Jews into two great periods, the age of the law and the age of the Messiah. The conclusion of the one was the beginning of the other, the opening of that kingdom which the Jews believed the Messiah was to establish, which was to put an end to their sufferings, and to render them the greatest people upon the earth. The apostles, full of this hope, said to our Lord, immediately before his ascension, "Lord, wilt thou at this time restore the kingdom to Israel?" [Acts 1:6]. Our Lord used the phrase of his coming to denote his taking vengeance upon the Jews by destroying their city and sanctuary.[17]

The "end of the age" refers to the end of the Old Covenant redemptive system with its attendant sacrifices and rituals. These were designed to be temporary symbols of the coming atoning work of Christ. The "end of the age" refers to the termination of the exclusive Jewish entitlement to the covenant promises and the inclusion of the Gentiles into the blessings of the covenant and the privileges of the gospel and kingdom (Matt. 21:41, 43; 22:10). "End of the age" is a covenantal phrase. With the temple destroyed, there would be no way and no need to carry out the rigorous demands of the sacrificial system, a system that was predestined to pass away with the incarnation, death, resurrection, ascension, and enthronement of Jesus. Jesus replaces the sacrificial system as the "lamb of God" (John 1:29), God's dwelling place as the "temple of God" (2:13–22), God's sanctuary as the "true tabernacle" (Heb. 8:2; John 1:14), and God's earthly sinful high priest as the "perfect High Priest" (Heb. 2:17, 3:1, 5:1–10, 7:26–28).[18]

The End of the Old Covenant

The temple was a constant reminder that a wall separated Jew from Gentile. In Christ, the wall was removed (Eph. 2:11–22). There is no longer any need for the blood of "bulls and goats" (Heb. 10:4; 9:1–28), and thus, no need for a temple of stone or a future, rebuilt, millennial temple as dispensationalism requires.[19] In opposition to this view, Don Stewart and Chuck Missler use more than 230 pages to convince readers that a temple will be rebuilt *according to Bible prophecy*. What *biblical* evidence do they offer?[20] Not a single verse states that another temple will be or needs to be rebuilt to fulfill Bible prophecy. The passages from the New Testament that they do cite (Matt. 24:15, 2 Thess. 2:4, and Rev. 11:1–2) were written *before* the temple was destroyed in A.D. 70. Anyone who read these texts when they were first written would have immediately assumed that they referred to the temple still standing in Jerusalem.

With these facts in mind, the destruction of the temple inaugurates a new era in which "the blood of Christ" cleanses our "conscience from dead works to serve the living God" (Heb. 9:14). Therefore, the expression "end of the age" refers "to the end of the 'Jewish age,' *i.e.,* the time of transference from a national [Israel only] to an international people of God [the world]," [21] what the Apostle Paul describes as the "ends of the ages," a period of time that had come upon the first-century church (1 Cor. 10:11). The phrase the "ends of the ages" is used in the same way by the author of Hebrews: "But now once at the *consummation of the ages* He has been manifested to put away sin by the sacrifice of Himself" (Heb. 9:26). Jesus was manifested, not at the beginning, but "at the consummation of the ages." Notice that the text says, "He *was* manifested," an event already past. The period between A.D. 30 and 70 is, as the apostle Peter describes it, "these last times" (1 Peter 1:20). As time drew near for Jerusalem's destruction, Peter could say that "the end of all things was at hand" (4:7). Milton Terry defines "end of the age" in covenantal terms:

> It is, according to Matthew's phraseology, the end or "consummation of the age."... It is the solemn termination and crisis of the dispensation which had run its course when the temple fell, and there was not left one stone upon another which was not thrown down. That catastrophe, which in Heb. xii, 26, is conceived as a shaking of the earth and the heaven, is *the end* contemplated in this discourse; not "the end of the world," but the termination and consummation of the pre-Messianic age.[22]

Again, the Bible establishes the time parameter for when the "end" was to take place. We are told that it was "at hand," that is "near" for those reading Peter's letter.

The Coming of Christ

But how can we maintain that Jesus "came" in A.D. 70? Keep in mind that Jesus stated that the generation to whom He was speaking would not pass away "until *all* these things take place," that is, all those things He specified in verses 2 through 34 of Matthew 24. Jesus was very dogmatic about the timing of these events.

Jesus' "coming" in judgment upon Jerusalem (Matt. 24:27) and His coming "*up* to the Ancient of Days" (Dan. 7:13) were two events that occurred within the time span of the first generation of Christians. There is no future fulfillment of these events. Since Jesus left no doubt that He would "come" before that first-century generation passed away, we must conclude that the idea of "coming" in this context is different from the way many contemporary Christians understand the concept. Jesus' coming in judgment upon Jerusalem in A.D. 70 was an event that would occur within a specified time frame—the generation between A.D. 30 and 70 would not pass away until all the events predicted in the Olivet Discourse took place.

Since Scripture is the best interpreter of Scripture, we must allow the Bible to direct us to the best interpretation of what "coming" means based on the context and an evaluation of parallel passages. The "Son of Man coming on the clouds of the sky with power and great glory" appears later in the Olivet Discourse (24:30). We will discuss its meaning there. At this point, however, it is enough to say that Jesus' coming in Matthew 24 is little different from the way God came many times in the Old Covenant (e.g., Gen. 11:5; Ex. 3:8; 19:9; 34:5; Psalm 18:6–17; 72:6; 104:3; Isa. 19:1–4; 31:4; Micah 1:3–5) and the way Jesus promised to come in the New Testament (e.g., Matt. 10:23; 16:27–28; 18:30; 26:64; Mark 14:61–62; Luke 10:1; John 14:21, 23, 30).

Jesus warned the Church at Ephesus that He would come and remove their lampstand "unless you repent" (Rev. 2:5). He issued a similar warning to the church at Pergamum: "Repent therefore; or else *I am coming to you quickly*, and I will make war against them [i.e., the Nicolaitans] with the sword of My mouth (2:16; see 19:15). Sardis is forewarned using similar judgment language: "If therefore you will not wake up, I will come like a thief, and you will not know at what hour I will come to you" (3:3; see 1 Thess. 5:2, 4; 2 Peter 3:10; Rev. 16:15). These are judgment comings that were threatened on a particular church at a particular time similar to Jesus' promised coming in judgment against apostate Judaism in the first century. The passages that describe the coming of Christ to first-century churches are not descriptive of the "second coming" (consummating coming) of Christ, contrary to Robert L. Thomas' strained efforts to make them so.[23]

Jesus clearly states that He would come in some way before the last apostle died: "For the Son of Man is going to come in the glory of His Father with His angels; and WILL THEN RECOMPENSE EVERY MAN ACCORDING TO HIS DEEDS. Truly I say to you, *there are some of those who are standing here who shall not taste death until they see the Son of Man coming in His kingdom*" (Matt. 16:27–28). Henry Alford states that this passage refers "*to the destruction of Jerusalem, and the full manifestation of the Kingdom of Christ by the annihilation of the Jewish polity....*"[24] The question about the "end of the age" was asked against the backdrop of this text. Peter certainly understood that Jesus' coming was near. He specifically asked whether John would be alive when Jesus came (John 21:21–22). Of course, as we saw earlier, Peter states in his first epistle that he was writing in the "last times" (1 Peter 1:20) and that the "end of all things was at hand" (4:7).

"And Jesus answered and said to them, 'See to it that no one misleads you. For many will come in My name, saying, "I am the Christ," and will mislead many'" (Matt. 24:4–5).

By comparing the New Testament with secular histories of the period, we can see that all of what Jesus said in the Olivet Discourse about signs was fulfilled prior to the Roman invasion of Jerusalem and in events leading up to the destruction of the temple in A.D. 70. Notice that the warning was addressed to Jesus' disciples: "See that no one misleads *you*." *They* would be hearing of "wars and rumors of wars." Jesus said, "See that *you* are not frightened." The *disciples* would be delivered up to tribulation: "They will kill *you*," and *"you* will be hated." The conclusion is obvious: Jesus' warning was to the generation of disciples who asked the question about the temple and those who heard His response.

"False Messiahs"

False messiahs made regular appearances in Israel. The book of Acts lists a number of them. Gamaliel mentions "Theudas" who claimed "to be somebody" (Acts 5:36). He describes another false messiah, Judas of Galilee, who "rose up in the days of the census, and drew away some people after him" (5:37). Simon is probably the best known: "Now there was a certain man named Simon, who formerly was practicing magic in the city, and astonishing the people of Samaria, claiming to be someone great; and they all, from smallest to greatest, were giving attention to him, saying, 'This man is what is called the Great Power of God. And they were giving him attention because he had for a long time astonished them with his magic arts'" (Acts 8:9–11).

Secular historians record these and other examples of false messiahs and prophets who rose up soon after the death, resurrection, and ascension of Jesus. "Jerome quotes Simon Magus as saying, 'I am the Word of God, I am the Comforter, I am Almighty, I am all there is of God.' ... And Irenaeus tells us how Simon claimed to be the Son of God and the creator of angels."[25] Eusebius records the words of one Justin and his description of Simon in a communique to Antonine in one of the earliest defenses of Christianity. This is an early testimony of the truthfulness of Jesus' words:

> And after the ascension of our Lord into heaven, certain men were suborned by demons as their agents, who said they were gods. These were not only suffered [permitted] to pass without persecution, but were even deemed worthy of honours by you. Simon, a certain Samaritan of the village called Githon, was one of the number, who, in the reign of

Claudius Caesar, performed many magic rites by the operation of demons, was considered a god, in your imperial city of Rome, and was
honoured by you with a statue as a god, in the river Tiber—(on an is-
land)—between the two bridges, having the superscription in Latin, *Simoni
Deo Sancto*, which is, To Simon the Holy God; and nearly all the Samaritans, a few also of other nations, worship him, confessing him as the
Supreme God.[26]

Josephus tells of "a certain impostor named Theudas [who] persuaded a
great number to follow him to the river Jordan which he claimed would divide for their passage."[27] Cuspius Fadus, procurator of Judea, "sent a troop of
horse[s] against them, who falling unexpectedly upon them, killed many, and
made many prisoners; and having taken Theudas himself alive, they cut off
his head, and brought it to Jerusalem."[28] Dositheus, a Samaritan, "pretended
that he was the lawgiver prophesied of by Moses."[29] There were so many of
these impostors preying on the gullibility of the people that under the
procuratorship of Felix, "many of them were apprehended and killed every
day. They seduced great numbers of the people still expecting the Messiah;
and well therefore might our Saviour caution his disciples against them."[30]

While this particular prophecy relates to events leading up to the destruction of Jerusalem in A.D. 70, this does not mean that false messsiahs no
longer appear on the scene. Their appearance in our day, however, has nothing to do with the fulfillment of the events outlined in the Olivet Discourse.

Notes

1. Hap Cawood, "If Buying Armageddon Theories, Insist on Money-back Guarantee," *Atlanta Constitution* (9 February 1991), A19.
2. An advertisement for a video tape produced by Jack and Rexella Van Impe, *Last Days: Hype or Hope?* (October 1996).
3. John F. Walvoord, *The Nations in Prophecy* (Grand Rapids, MI: Zondervan/ Academie, 1988), xiv.
4. John F. Walvoord, *Armageddon, Oil and the Middle East: What the Bible Says About the Future of the Middle East and the End of Western Civilization*, rev. ed. (Grand Rapids, MI: Zondervan, [1974, 1976] 1990), 219.
5. Walvoord, *Armageddon, Oil and the Middle East*, 227.
6. Joe Drape, "Ready or Not, The Rapture Didn't Come," *Atlanta Journal/Constitution* (14 September 1988), 1A.
7. Drape, "Ready or Not, The Rapture Didn't Come," 14A.
8. Edgar Whisenant and Greg Brewer, *The Final Shout: Rapture Report 1989* (Nashville, TN: World Bible Society, 1989).
9. Ed Hindson, "The End Is Near ... Or Is It?," *World* (24 November 1990), 12.
10. Quoted in Kenneth L. Woodward, "The Final Days Are Here Again," *Newsweek* (18 March 1991), 55.
11. Paul Crouch, "Argentina on the Air," *Praise the Lord* (February 1993).
12. Floyd E. Hamilton, *The Basis of Christian Faith: A Modern Defense of the Christian Religion* (New York: Harper & Row, 1964), 160.
13. Thomas Ice and Timothy Demy, *The Truth About the Last Days' Temple* (Eugene, OR: Harvest House, 1996), 13.
14. Alfred Plummer, *An Exegetical Commentary on the Gospel According to Matthew* (Minneapolis, MN: James Family Christian Publishers, [1915] n.d.), 331–32.
15. Thomas Newton, *Dissertations on the Prophecies, Which Have Remarkably Been Fulfilled, and at this Time are Fulfilling in the World* (London: J.F. Dove, 1754), 329.
16. Quoted in J. Marcellus Kik, *An Eschatology of Victory* (Phillipsburg, NJ: Presbyterian and Reformed, 1975), 83.
17. George Hill, "Predictions Delivered by Jesus," *Lectures in Divinity* (New York: Robert Carter, 1847), 103–104.
18. Jesus is said to be "the end [*telos*] of the law" (Rom. 10:4). Jesus, through His life, death, resurrection, and ascension, brought to an end one age and inaugurated a new age based on His finished redemptive work. "Therefore the

Law has become our tutor *to lead us to Christ*.... But now that faith has come, we are no longer under a tutor" (Gal. 3:15–26, especially verses 24–25).

19. John F. Walvoord, *The Prophecy Knowledge Handbook* (Wheaton, IL: Victor Books, 1990), 198–206. For fanciful interpretations of Bible prophecy relating to rebuilding the temple, see Thomas Ice and Randall Price, *Ready to Rebuild: The Imminent Plan to Rebuild the Last Days Temple* (Eugene, OR: Harvest House, 1992) and Peter and Patti Lalonde, *The Edge of Time: The Final Countdown Has Begun* (Eugene, OR: Harvest House, 1997), 41–52.

20. Don Stewart and Chuck Missler, *The Coming Temple: Center Stage for the Final Countdown* (Orange, CA: Dart Press, 1991).

21. R. T. France, *The Gospel According to Matthew: An Introduction and Commentary* (Grand Rapids, MI: Eerdmans, 1985), 337.

22. Milton S. Terry, *Biblical Apocalyptics: A Study of the Most Notable Revelations of God and of Christ* (Grand Rapids, MI: Baker Book House, [1898] 1988), 225.

23. Robert L. Thomas, "The 'Comings' of Christ in Revelation 2–3," unpublished paper, n.d.).

24. Henry Alford, *The New Testament for English Readers* (Chicago, IL: Moody Press, [1886] n.d.), 122.

25. Kik, *An Eschatology of Victory,* 92.

26. Eusebius Pamphilus, *The Ecclesiastical History of Eusebius Pamphilus* (Grand Rapids, MI: Baker Book House, 1988), 2:13, 62.

27. Ralph Woodrow, *The Great Prophecies of the Bible* (Riverside, CA: Ralph Woodrow Evangelistic Association, 1971), 54. See Flavius Josephus, *The Antiquities of the Jews* in *The Works of Josephus*, trans. William Whiston (Peabody, MA: Hendrickson Publishers, 1987), 20:5:1, 531.

28. Newton, *On the Prophecies,* 332–33.

29. Alexander Keith, *The Evidence of the Truth of the Christian Religion Derived from the Literal Fulfillment of Prophecy Particularly as Illustrated by the History of the Jews* (Philadelphia, PA: Presbyterian Board of Publication, n.d.), 59.

30. Newton, *On the Prophecies,* 333.

Chapter Six

SIGNS FOR ALL TO SEE

In each new prophecy book that hits the bookstores we are told that Bible prophecy is being fulfilled before our eyes. The authors point to various signs that they say are compelling evidence that Jesus' return is near. In no other time in history, we are led to believe, have eschatological events converged to prove that we must be living in the last days. William T. James writes that "No previous generation has experienced the number, frequency and intensity of signals so similar to things prophesied to be witnessed by the generation alive at the consummation of human history."[1] The history of the world is the history of war and bloodshed. Plagues and famines have been common place. Jesus clearly set a time frame for the signs that He said would occur before He came in judgment against apostate Judaism: "This generation will not pass away until *all these things take place*" (Matt. 24:34). He could not have said it more definitely or more clearly. Even so, modern-day prophecy writers dismiss His clear testimony and the facts of history and propose that our generation being described. And yet, as we will see, all the signs that Jesus said would take place before that first-century generation passed away came to pass between A.D. 30 and 70. Such testimony is purposely ignored by today's prophecy writers. "Jesus' words about the signs of the times just before His return at the time of Armageddon are becoming reality before our eyes as we move through our daily lives. False christs, false prophets, wars and rumors of wars and all the other signals our Lord said will be happening concurrently in birth-pang fashion convulse our world with continuing regularity."[2]

Withought a doubt, the signs Jesus outlines in the Olivet Discourse were familiar to and experienced by His first-century audience.

And you will be hearing of wars and rumors of wars; see that you are not frightened, for those things must take place, but that is not yet the end. For nation will rise against nation, and kingdom against kingdom, and in various places there will be famines and earthquakes. But all these things are merely the beginning of birth pangs. Then they will deliver you to tribulation, and will kill you, and you will be hated by all nations on account of My name. And at that time many will fall away and will deliver up one another and hate one another. And many false prophets will arise, and will mislead many. And because lawlessness is increased, most people's love will grow cold"' (Matt. 24:6–12).

"Wars and Rumors of Wars"

There were to be "wars and rumors of wars" before the generation to whom Jesus spoke would pass away. But how could there be wars and rumors of wars during the era of the *Pax Romana* (Roman Peace), which began with the reign of Augustus and his establishment of the "Age of Peace" in 17 B.C.? "Wars and rumors of wars" can only be a sign during times of supposed peace! As we will see, the Roman Peace was fragile, to say the least.

> The Jews resisted the erection of the statue of Caligula in the temple; and such was the dread of Roman resentment, that the fields remained uncultivated. At Caesarea, the Jews and Syrians contended for the mastery of the city. Twenty thousand of the former were put to death, and the rest were expelled. Every city in Syria was then divided into two armies, and multitudes were slaughtered. Alexandria and Damascus presented a similar scene of bloodshed. About fifty thousand of the Jews fell in the former, and ten thousand in the latter. The Jewish nation rebelled against the Romans; Italy was convulsed with contentions for the empire; and, as a proof of the troublous and warlike character of the period, within the brief space of two years, four emperors, Nero, Galba, Otho, and Vitellius, suffered death.[3]

The *Annals of Tacitus*, covering the period from A.D. 14 to the death of Nero in A.D. 68, describes the tumult of the period with phrases such as "disturbances in Germany," "commotions in Africa," "commotions in Thrace," "insurrections in Gaul," "intrigues among the Parthians," "the war in Britain," and "the war in Armenia." Wars were fought from one end of the empire to the other. With this description we can see further fulfillment: "For nation will rise against nation, and kingdom against kingdom" (Matt. 24:7). Josephus writes that Roman civil wars were so common in the empire that there was no need to write about them in any great detail: "I have omitted to give an exact account of them, because they are well known by all, and they are described by a great number of Greek and Roman authors; yet for the sake of the connection of matters, and that my history may not be incoherent, I have just touched upon everything briefly."[4] The Jews were often the target of these wars. At Seleucia "more than 50,000 Jews were killed."[5]

"Famines"

Beginning with the book of Acts, we see that famines were prevalent in the period prior to Jerusalem's destruction in A.D. 70: "Now at this time some prophets came down from Jerusalem to Antioch. And one of them named Agabus stood up and began to indicate by the Spirit that there would certainly be *a great famine all over the world* [*oikoumene*]. *And this took place in the reign of Claudius.* And in the proportion that any of the disciples had means, each of them determined to send a contribution for the relief of the brethren living in Judea" (Acts 11:27–29). The famine was dramatic evidence that Jesus' prophecy was coming to pass in their generation just like He said it would. The famine was so great that the church as far away as Corinth participated in relief efforts (1 Cor. 16:1–5; Rom. 15:25–28). The entire Roman Empire was affected. Futurist William T. James writes that "God's Word has much to say about famine,"[6] and yet he does not mention Acts 11:27–29. Why? Is he afraid that his readers will ask why this passage is not a fulfillment of what Jesus said would happen?

Contemporary secular historians such as Tacitus, Suetonius, and Josephus mention other famines during the period prior to A.D. 70. In Tacitus we read a description of famine conditions in A.D. 51 in Rome: "This year witnessed many prodigies [signs or omens] ... [including] repeated earthquakes.... Further portents were seen in a shortage of corn, resulting in famine.... It was established that there was no more than fifteen days' supply of food in the city [of Rome]. Only heaven's special favour and a mild winter prevented catastrophe."[7] Tacitus remembers the days when Italy "once exported food for the army in distant provinces!"[8]

War is the number-one contributor to famine and its disastrous effects. It is no accident that Jesus lists "famines" after "wars." Josephus reports on the miserable famine conditions brought on by the siege of Jerusalem by Titus. The siege stopped the people from leaving the city and provisions from entering. "Then did the famine widen its progress, and devoured the people by whole houses and families; the upper rooms were full of women and children that were dying by famine; and the lanes of the city were full of the dead bodies of the aged; the children also and the young men wandered about the marketplaces like shadows, all swelled with the famine, and fell down dead wheresoever their misery seized them."[9]

Upon hearing the reports of these famines, could the disciples have dismissed them as having nothing to do with the words spoken by Jesus on the Mount of Olives?

"Earthquakes"

Today's prophecy writers contend that it is the *increase* and *magnitude* of modern earthquakes that make them significant for determining that we are living in the last days. "The Lord obviously meant earthquakes of unprecedented seismological dimension."[10] Jesus simply says that "in various places there will be famines and earthquakes" (24:7). He says nothing about an increase in their number. Luke writes that "there will be great earthquakes" (Luke 2:11). The historical record of earthquakes that occurred before Jerusalem was destroyed in the first century fulfills Jesus' prophecy to the letter. Two earthquakes are mentioned in Matthew: When Jesus was crucified (27:54) and when the angel came down to roll the stone away from the tomb where Jesus was buried (28:2). This second earthquake is said to have been "severe." The Book of Acts records "a great earthquake" that shook "the foundations of the prison house" (Acts 16:26). Three earthquakes are mentioned prior to the destruction of Jerusalem in A.D. 70. One is described as "severe," and one is said to be "great." Were Jesus' words fulfilled? Yes.

Secular historians support the biblical record. "And as to earthquakes, many are mentioned by writers during a period just previous to 70 A.D. There were earthquakes in Crete, Smyrna, Miletus, Chios, Samos, Laodicea,

Hierapolis, Colosse, Campania, Rome, and Judea. It is interesting to note that the city of Pompeii was much damaged by an earthquake occurring on February 5, 63 A.D."[11] The number of earthquakes during this era is staggering. Josephus describes an earthquake in Judea of such magnitude "that the constitution of the universe was confounded for the destruction of men."[12] He goes on to write that this earthquake was "no common" calamity, indicating that God Himself had brought it about for a special purpose.[13] One commentator writes: "Perhaps no period in the world's history has ever been so marked by these convulsions as that which intervenes between the Crucifixion and the destruction of Jerusalem."[14] Since the generation between A.D. 30 and 70 is past, there is no reason to attach prophetic significance to earthquakes in our day as a fulfillment of Matthew 24:7. They are not signs of the imminency of Jesus' return in our generation. But they were a prelude to the coming of Jesus in judgment upon Jerusalem in the generation of the apostles.

"Signs in the Heavens"

Matthew's recording of the Olivet Discourse does not mention "terrors and great signs from heaven." This phrase is found in Luke's gospel on the same subject (Luke 21:11). It appears with Luke's discussion of earthquakes, plagues, and famines; therefore, it is parallel to Matthew's account.

The appearance of comets in the sky was often taken as a warning of some approaching calamity or a sign of change in existing political structures: "It is a disorder of the heavens 'importing change of times and states,' as William Shakespeare put it, and is bad news, especially for eminent persons."[15] For example, a comet appeared in the sky in 44 B.C., the year of Julius Caesar's assassination. Another comet appeared in 11 B.C. This time it was thought to have had something to do with the death of Marcus Agrippa, a Roman statesman who died the year before. We know that the "star in the east" was a sign of joy for the magi, but it was a bad omen for Herod who feared political competition (Matt. 2:1–12).

Were there any "signs from heaven" prior to A.D. 70 that would be a fulfillment of Luke 21:11? A comet appeared around A.D. 60 during the reign of Nero. The public speculated that some change in the political scene was imminent: "The historian Tacitus wrote: 'As if Nero were already dethroned, men began to ask who might be his successor.'"[16] Nero took the comet's "threat" seriously. This is the man who murdered his mother, his two wives, and most of his family, burned Rome, and used Christians as flaming torches. He knew the intricacies of political intrigue. The appearance of a comet might just give somebody an idea. "Nero took no chances as another historian, Suetonius, related: 'All children of the condemned man, were banished from Rome, and then starved to death or poisoned.' The policy worked like a charm. Nero survived that comet by several years."[17]

Nero may have thought that he was finished with warnings from heaven. Halley's Comet appeared in A.D. 66. Not long after this Nero committed suicide. Historians have linked the appearance of Halley's Comet not only with the death of Nero, but with the destruction of Jerusalem four years later. A seventeenth-century print graphically depicts the phenomenon as it passes over Jerusalem.[18] The following caption accompanies the print: "Halley's Comet of A.D. 66 shown over Jerusalem. . . . The Comet was regarded as an omen predicting the fall of the city to the Romans which actually occurred four years later."

In addition to Halley's Comet, Josephus recounts that "there was a star resembling a sword, which stood over the city, and a comet, that continued a whole year."[19] Josephus goes on to describe other unusual phenomena. Here is clear testimony that Jesus' words were fulfilled within a generation. None of this historical data satifies the sensationalists. Chuck Missler concocts an elaborate UFO-alien-demonic scenario that he says must take place in order for Luke 21:11 to be fulfilled. Again, Jesus' words are stretched beyond their intended meaning to avoid the obvious first-century fulfillment.[20]

"Tribulation"

No one can doubt that persecution followed the church soon after Pentecost. Jesus warned His disciples that those who hated Him would hate them as well (John 15:18; Matt. 23:34). From its inception the church underwent relentless tribulation. The Book of Acts records many instances of persecution. Peter and John were arrested and put in jail (Acts 4:3). They were warned not to speak to any man in the name of Jesus (4:17). After another arrest, they were again instructed not to teach in the name of Jesus. But this time, upon their release, they were "flogged" (5:40) as a warning. The tribulation worsened with the death of Stephen (7:54–60).

After this first wave of mistreatment, "a great persecution arose against the church in Jerusalem; and they were all scattered throughout the regions of Judea and Samaria, except the apostles" (8:1). Persecutions continued as Saul was "breathing threats and murder against the disciples of the Lord" (9:1). In addition to the religious terrorism of Saul, "Herod the king laid hands on some who belonged to the church, in order to mistreat them. And he had James the brother of John put to death with a sword" (12:1–2). Herod, seeing that this pleased the Jews, "proceeded to arrest Peter also" (12:3).

In time the crowds even turned on the disciples in frenzied persecution: "Jews came from...Iconium, and having won over the multitudes, they stoned Paul and dragged him out of the city, supposing him to be dead" (14:19). Thomas Newton comments: "Some are 'brought before rulers and kings,' as Paul before Gallio, (xviii. 12) Felix, (xxiv) Festus and Agrippa, (xxv).... Some are *beaten*, as Paul and Silas: (xvi. 23).... But if we would look farther, we have a more melancholy proof of the truth of this prediction, in the persecutions under Nero, in which (besides numberless other Christians) fell those two great champions of our faith, St. Peter and St. Paul."[21] Paul writes: "Five times I received from the Jews thirty-nine lashes. Three times I was beaten with rods, once I was stoned.... I have been on frequent journeys, in dangers from rivers, dangers from robbers, dangers from my countrymen, dangers from the Gentiles" (2 Cor. 11:24–26). "Tacitus says that Nero, for the conflagration of Rome, persecuted the Christians, '*a race of men detested for their crimes*.' also see 1 Pet. ii.12; iii.16; iv.14–16."[22] As Tertullian wrote, "There was war against the very name" of Christ.[23] As the testimony of the Bible confirms, the disciples were delivered up to tribulation, and some were killed (Matt. 24:9). The apostle John writes that he is a "fellow-partaker in the tribulation" (Rev. 1:9).

None of this means that the church is presently exempt from tribulation: "In the world you have tribulation, but take courage; I have overcome the world" (John 16:33; see Rom. 5:3; 8:35; 12:12; 1 Thess. 1:6). But between A.D. 30 and 70, the tribulation the church experienced was a fulfillment of the specific prophecy outlined in Matthew 24:9.

Falling Away and Betrayal

While many today are looking for a future "falling away," there is no doubt that the first-century church had to contend with betrayal and apostasy. Those who once proclaimed the name of Christ went on to do harm to the church they formerly claimed as their own. Paul stated: "All who are in Asia turned away from me, among whom are Phygelus and Hermogenes" (2 Tim. 1:15). Demas, who was said to have "loved this present world," deserted Paul (4:10). This does not seem to be an isolated event: "At my first defense no one supported me, but all deserted me; may it not be counted against them" (4:16). Bishop Newton writes: "But they shall not only apostatize from the faith, but also 'shall betray one another, and shall hate one another.' To illustrate this point we need only cite a sentence out of Tacitus, speaking of the persecution under Nero. At first, says he, several were seized who confessed, and then by their discovery a great multitude of others were convicted and barbarously executed."[24]

Then there were the Judaizers who were consistently distorting the gospel, actually preaching a "gospel" that was contrary to "the gospel of Christ" (Gal. 1:6–10). They claimed that to be a Christian, a person had to be circumcised: "And some men came down from Judea and began teaching the brethren, 'Unless you are circumcised according to the custom of Moses, you cannot be saved'" (Acts 15:1).

"False Prophets"

The Apostle Peter writes that "false prophets also arose among the people, just as there will also be false teachers among you, who will secretly introduce destructive heresies, even denying the Master who bought them, bringing swift destruction upon themselves" (2 Peter 2:1). These false prophets will malign the truth, "and in their greed they will exploit *you* with false words" (2:2–3). Paul describes the Judaizing teachers as "false apostles, deceitful workers, disguising themselves as apostles of Christ" (2 Cor. 11:13). On his first missionary journey, Paul encountered "a Jewish false prophet whose name was Bar-Jesus" (Acts 13:6). The pronouncements of false prophets like Hymenaeus and Philetus "will lead to further ungodliness, and their talk will spread like gangrene" (2 Tim. 2:16–17).

Paul says that these two "have gone astray from the truth saying that the resurrection has already taken place, and thus they upset the faith of some" (2:18). The Ephesian elders are warned about "savage wolves [who] will come in among you, not sparing the flock; and from among your own selves men will arise, speaking perverse things, to draw away the disciples after them" (Acts 20:29–30). In "later times," that is, in the near future, according to Paul, "the Spirit explicitly says that …some will fall away from the faith, paying attention to deceitful spirits and doctrines of demons" (1 Timothy 4:1). In Timothy's day "evil men and impostors will proceed from bad to worse, deceiving and being deceived" (2 Tim. 3:13).

John tells us that "many false prophets have gone out into the world" (1 John 4:1), *in John's day*. In another context John tells the church that "many deceivers have gone out into the world, those who do not acknowledge Jesus Christ as coming in the flesh. This is the deceiver and the antichrist" (2 John 7). John offers evidence that it was "the last hour" (1 John 2:18): "They went out from us, but they were not really of us; for if they had been of us, they would have remained with us; but they went out, in order that it might be shown that they all are not of us" (2:19).

Increased Lawlessness

The New Testament writers were constantly battling sensual living that had the effect of destroying relationships so that the love of many would grow cold (Matt. 24:12). Paul was shocked at the behavior of the members of the Corinthian church: "It is actually reported that there is immorality among you, and immorality of such a kind as does not exist even among the Gentiles, that someone has his father's wife. And you have become arrogant, and have not mourned instead, in order that the one who had done this deed might be removed from your midst" (1 Cor. 5:1–2).

> By reason of these trials and persecutions from without, and these apostasies and false prophets from within, the love of many to Christ and his doctrine, and also their love to one another shall wax cold. Some shall openly desert the faith, (as ver. 10;) others shall corrupt it, (as ver. 11;) and others again, (as here) shall grow indifferent to it. And (not to mention other instances) who can hear St. Paul complaining at Rome, (2 Tim. iv. 16,) that "at his first answer no man stood with him, but all men forsook him"; who can hear the divine author of the Epistle to the Hebrews, exhorting them, (x. 25,) "not to forsake the assembling of themselves together, as the manner of some is"; and not conclude the event to have sufficiently justified our Saviour's prediction?[25]

The increase of lawlessness was not confined to the church. A history of the Roman era, especially the history of the Roman emperors, is proof positive that lawlessness was on the rise. The names Caligula and Nero are synonymous with "lawlessness."

Through it all the church was not defeated. The church continues to this day while all of its first-century enemies lie in the dust. In our day new enemies are equally intent on destroying the church. Their end is equally sure. Seeing how God fulfilled this extraordinary prophecy should bolster our faith that He will do the same for His church in our day. If non-Christian "folly [was made] obvious to all" in the first century (2 Timothy 3:9), can we expect any less in our day?

"The one who endures to the end, he shall be saved" (Matt. 24:13).

The end of what? Jesus is answering questions about the destruction of the temple and the "end of the age," the end of the Jewish dispensation, the Old Covenant order. Remember, the disciples had just heard Jesus predict that the temple was going to be left "desolate" (Matt. 23:38), and that these things would happen to "this generation," that is, to the generation of Jews then living in Israel (23:36). This is the end Jesus had in mind. Great social, religious, and political upheavals would come upon the Roman Empire that would engulf the first-century state of Israel. Those who endured to the end of this conflagration would be saved; that is, they would not die in Rome's war with the Jewish rebels. "The *primary* meaning of this seems to be, that whosoever remained faithful till the destruction of Jerusalem, should be preserved from it. No Christian, that we know of, perished in the siege or after it."[26]

Even for those who interpret the "end" in Matthew 24:13 to be some future "end," that future "end" is not *the* "end." A number of events supposedly follow the "end": the Great Tribulation, the Millennium, and the New Heaven and New Earth. Each time "end" is used, the context specifies what end is in view. In the case of the Olivet Discourse, the "end" is related to the question regarding the destruction of the temple which took place within the lifetime of the first-century church.

[A]s far as the disciples, good first-century Jews as they were, were concerned, there was no reason whatever for them to be thinking about the end of the space-time universe. There was no reason, either in their background or in a single thing that Jesus had said to them up to that point, for it even to occur to them that the true story of the world, or of Israel, or of Jesus himself, might include either the end of the space-time universe, or Jesus or anyone else floating down to earth on a cloud.[27]

The Apostle Paul tells us that the "ends of the ages" were not in the distant future: "Now these things happened to them [the Israelites in the wilderness] as an example, and they were written for our instruction, *upon whom the ends of the ages have come*" (1 Cor. 10:11). The "ends of the ages"— the end of the Old Covenant—had come upon the first-century church. In another place, Paul describes the end of the Old Covenant era this way: "Having therefore such a hope, we use great boldness in our speech, and are not as Moses, who used to put a veil over his face that the sons of Israel might not look intently *at the end of what was fading away*" (2 Cor. 3:12–13). The writer of Hebrews told his readers that "now once at the consummation of the ages He was been manifested to put away sin by the sacrifice of Himself" (Heb. 9:26). "Now" is equal to "the consummation of the ages." "Now" does not mean later or the distant future.

The New Testament describes the nearness of the Lord's coming and the "end of all things," that is, the end of the distinctly Jewish era with the shadows of the Old Covenant. These events were "near" for those Christians who read the Book of Revelation (Rev. 1:3). There is no other explanation except that time was running out for the shadows of the Old Covenant. Forcing this verse and others like it to describe a period nearly two thousand years in the future makes the interpreter conclude that biblical time texts are meaningless. Jesus made it clear to the religious leaders of His day that the kingdom of God would be taken away from them to be "given to a nation producing the fruit of it" (Matt. 21:43). When would this happen? "And when the chief priests and the Pharisees heard His parables, *they understood that He was speaking about them*" (21:45). Their generation would experience the kingdom transfer. For them it was the "end."

"This gospel of the kingdom shall be preached in the whole world for a witness to all the nations, and then the end shall come" (Matt. 24:14).

Robert Van Kampen, a prophecy author who believes the events outlined by Jesus in Matthew 24 are yet to be fulfilled, writes, "Christ tells His disciples that only after the gospel is preached to all nations, 'then the end shall come.'"[28] Since the Bible clearly states that that the gospel "was proclaimed in *all* creation under heaven" (Col. 1:23), then the end spoken of by Jesus is a past event for us. Earlier in his letter to the Colossians, Paul describes how the gospel was "constantly bearing fruit and increasing in *all* the world [*kosmos*]" (1:6). The faith of the Romans was "being proclaimed throughout the whole world [*kosmos*]" (Rom. 1:8), "to all the nations" (16:26). These statements by Paul reveal a fulfillment of what Jesus told His disciples would be a prelude to the destruction of Jerusalem. "The Gospel had been preached through the whole *Roman world*, and every nation had received its testimony, before the destruction of Jerusalem: see Col. i. 6, 23; 2 Tim. iv. 17. This was necessary not only as regarded the Gentiles, but to give God's people the Jews, who were scattered among the nations, *the opportunity of receiving or rejecting the preaching of Christ.*"[29]

In addition, we learn that Paul was making plans to go "to Spain" (Rom. 15:24, 28). It is possible that a church already existed there. This would mean that the gospel had nearly reached the western border of the Roman Empire in Paul's day. This may explain why Paul quoted from Psalm 19:4: "But I say, surely they have never heard, have they? Indeed they have: 'THEIR VOICE HAS GONE OUT INTO ALL THE EARTH, AND THEIR WORDS TO THE ENDS OF THE WORLD [*oikoumene*]'" (Rom. 10:18; cf. 2 Tim. 4:17). Luke records that "*all who lived in Asia* heard the word of the Lord, both Jews and Greeks" (Acts 19:10).

The Greek word translated "world" in Matthew 24:14 is *oikoumene*, "the inhabited earth." The same Greek word is used in Luke 2:1: "Now it came about in those days that a decree went out from Caesar Augustus, that a census be taken of all *the inhabited earth.*" In the New American Standard Version, the marginal note in Luke 2:1 reads "the Roman empire" (also see Acts 11:28, 24:5). The marginal reading of Luke 21:26—a verse parallel to Matthew 24:14—is also translated as "inhabited earth." The translators of the NASV have no such notation for Matthew 24:14, even though the same Greek word (*oikoumene*) is used. Matthew 24:14 clearly shows that the gospel would be preached throughout the Roman Empire before Jesus returned in judgment upon Jerusalem. Thomas Ice writes of those who advocate a first-century application of Matthew 24:14: Are they "saying that the gospel was preached before A.D. 70 in the Western hemisphere?"[30] The same question could be asked of Luke 2:1 and the geographical extent of the Roman census: "Is Luke saying that Caesar Augustus sent out a decree 'that a census be taken of the Western hemisphere,' since *oikoumene* is used in both places?"

But even if *kosmos* had been used in Matthew 24:14, we have seen from Romans 1:8 and Colossians 1:6 that the "gospel of the kingdom" being "preached in the whole world" was a pre-A.D. 70 fulfillment. Is there any historical evidence outside the biblical testimony that the gospel did reach the extreme parts of the Roman Empire, which Scripture describes as the "inhabited earth"? Philip Doddridge made the following remarks in *The Family Expositor*:

> It appears, from the most credible records, that the *gospel* was preached in Idumea, Syria, and Mesopotamia, by Jude; in Egypt, Marmorica, Mauritania, and other parts of Africa, by Mark, Simon, and Jude; in Ethiopia, by Candace's Eunuch and Matthias; in Pontus, Galatia, and the neighbouring parts of Asia, by Peter; in territories of the seven Asiatic churches, by John; in Parthia, by Matthew; in Scythia, by Philip and Andrew; in the northern and western parts of Asia, by Bartholomew; in Persia, by Simon and Jude; in Media, Carmania, and several eastern parts, by Thomas; through the vast tract from Jerusalem round about unto Illyricum, by Paul, as also in Italy, and probably in Spain, Gaul, and Britain; in most of which places Christian churches were planted, in less than thirty years after the death of Christ, which was before *the destruction of Jerusalem.*[31]

Prior to A.D. 70 the inhabited earth had heard the gospel ("all creation under heaven") as Paul wrote in Colossians 1:23. This section of Matthew 24 was fulfilled within a generation, as Doddridge writes, "in less than thirty years after the death of Christ," in direct fulfillment of Jesus' prophecy.[32]

Some commenators claim that the phrase "all the nations" governs the extent of the gospel's expansion. Since all the nations had not been reached prior to the destruction of the temple in A.D. 70, so the argument goes, Matthew 24:14 has not been fulfilled. The Apostle Paul writes otherwise in Romans 16:25–27:

> Now to Him who is able to establish you according to my gospel and the preaching of Jesus Christ, according to the revelation of the mystery which has been kept secret for long ages past, but now is manifested, and by the Scriptures of the prophets, according to the commandment of the eternal God, *has been made known to all the nations*, leading to obedience of faith; to the only wise God, through Jesus Christ, be the glory forever. Amen.

According to Paul, the gospel had "been made known to *all the nations*" in his day. If the expression "all the nations" governs the extent of fulfillment in Matthew 24:14, then according to Paul, Matthew 24:14 has been fulfilled.

Notes

1. William T. James, "Daniel's Last-Days Flood," *Foreshadows of Wrath and Redemption*, William T. James, gen. ed. (Eugene, OR: Harvest House, 1999), 7.

2. James, "Daniel's Last-Days Flood," 8.

3. Alexander Keith, *The Evidence of the Truth of the Christian Religion Derived from the Literal Fulfillment of Prophecy Particularly as Illustrated by the History of the Jews* (Philadelphia, PA: Presbyterian Board of Publication, n.d.), 59-60.

4. Flavius Josephus, *The Wars of the Jews*, in *The Works of Josephus*, trans. William Whiston (Peabody, MA: Hendrickson Publishers, 1987), 4:9:2, 688.

5. Henry Alford, *The New Testament for English Readers* (Chicago, IL: Moody Press, [1886] n.d.), 162.

6. James, "Famines Pestilences, Earthquakes," *Foreshadows of Wrath and Redemption*, 90.

7. Tacitus, *The Annals of Imperial Rome*, trans. Michael Grant (London: Penguin Books, 1989), 271.

8. Tacitus, *The Annals of Imperial Rome*, 271

9. Josephus, *The Wars of the Jews*, 5:12:3, 723.

10. James, "Famines, Pestilences, Earthquakes," 94. For an up-to-date analysis of the claim that earthquakes are increasing in number and magnitude, see Steven A. Austin and Mark L. Strauss, "Are Earthquakes Signs of the End Times? A Geological and Biblical Response to an Urban Legend," *Christian Research Journal*, 21:4 (1999), 30–39.

11. J. Marcellus Kik, *An Eschatology of Victory* (Phillipsburg, NJ: Presbyterian and Reformed, 1975), 93. See Alford, *The New Testament for English Readers*, 163.

12. Quoted in Thomas Scott, *The Holy Bible Containing the Old and New Testaments, According to the Authorized Version; with Explanatory Notes, Practical Observations, and Copious Marginal References*, 3 vols. (New York: Collins and Hannay, 1832), 3:108.

13. Quoted in Keith, *Evidence*, 60.

14. Edward Hayes Plumptre, "The Gospel According to St. Matthew," *Ellicott's Commentary on the Whole Bible*, ed. Charles John Ellicott, 8 vols. (London: Cassell and Company, 1897), 6:146.

15. Nigel Calder, *The Comet is Coming!: The Feverish Legacy of Mr. Halley* (London: British Broadcasting Corporation, 1980), 12.

16. Calder, *The Comet is Coming!*, 12.

17. Calder, *The Comet is Coming!*, 13.

18. The print is reproduced in *Asimov's Guide to Halley's Comet: The Awesome Story of Comets* (New York: Walker and Company, 1985), 6.

19. Josephus, *The Wars of the Jews*, 6:5:3, 742.

20. Chuck Missler, "Signs in the Sun, Moon and Stars," *Foreshadows of Wrath and Redemption*, 99–113.

21. Thomas Newton, *Dissertations on the Prophecies, Which Have Remarkably Been Fulfilled, and at this Time are Fulfilling in the World* (London: J.F. Dove, 1754), 339.

22. Alford, *The New Testament for English Readers*, 163. Emphasis in the original.

23. Tertullian, "The Apology," *The Ante-Nicene Fathers*, eds. Alexander Roberts and John Donaldson, vol. 3 (Grand Rapids, MI: Eerdmans, [1885] 1986), ch. 2, 18–20.

24. Newton, *On the Prophecies*, 339.

25. Newton, *On the Prophecies*, 340–41.

26. Alford, *The New Testament for English Readers*, 164.

27. N. T. Wright, *Jesus and the Victory of God* (Minneapolis, MN: Fortress Press, 1996), 345.

28. Robert Van Kampen, *The Rapture Question Answered: Plain and Simple* (Grand Rapids, MI: Fleming H. Revell, 1997), 74.

29. Alford, *The New Testament for English Readers*, 164. Emphasis in original.

30. H. Wayne House and Thomas D. Ice, *Dominion Theology: Blessing or Curse?* (Portland, OR: Multnomah Press, 1989), 298.

31. Philip Doddridge, *The Family Expositor*, 6 vols. (Charlestown, MA: S. Etheridge, 1807), 2:365, note *n*.

32. Most futurist commentators, especially dispensationalists, do not discuss the relationship between Matthew 24:14 and Colossians 1:23 and the use of *oikoumene* instead of *kosmos*. See, for example, Stanley D. Toussaint, *Behold the King: A Study of Matthew* (Portland, OR: Multnomah Press, 1981); William Hendriksen, *New Testament Commentary: Exposition of the Gospel According to Matthew* (Grand Rapids, MI: Baker Book House, 1973); John F. Walvoord, *Matthew: Thy Kingdom Come* (Chicago, IL: Moody Press, 1974); Arno C. Gaebelein, *The Gospel According to Matthew: An Exposition* (Neptune, NJ: Loizeaux Brothers, [1910] 1961).

Chapter Seven

THE TEMPLE OF DOOM

" The temple of Israel will be rebuilt. Of that we have no doubt whatso-
ever."[1] Orthodox Jews are planning for the day when they will once
again have their temple with a re-established priesthood. "Spurred by both
religious belief and nationalistic fervor and backed by the government, a
group of Israelis and Jews abroad are quietly planning the construction of
the third Jewish temple."[2] Many of the temple utensils have been manufactured and await the day when all will be as it was before the Romans destroyed the temple in A.D. 70. Stories about rocks being supplied from quar-
ries in Indiana and underground temple construction make their way through
the Christian rumor mill. There is even talk about a prefabricated temple
ready to be constructed when the time is right.

But does any of this have anything to do with Bible prophecy? Rabbi
Leon Ashkenazi, a Jerusalem-based scholar, pointed to the war between
Iraq and the allies as the fulfillment of "many texts that speak of a conflict
between Babylonia and Rome and Greece."[3] In his view, the "preparation
for the Messiah began with the Balfour Declaration in 1917, followed by
the 'unification' of Israel in 1967; it will be completed in 1992 with the
rebuilding of the temple."[4] Nineteen-ninety-two has passed and the temple
remains a future hope. The Jews who look for a rebuilt temple are not
searching the Torah for their instructions but rather the Babylonian Tal-

mud. Jews are even divided over the subject of a rebuilt temple. "Rabbinical advocates of researching the new temple remain cautious. They consistently remind their followers that their work is to prepare for the coming of the Messiah, not to replace him."[5]

Does the Bible, especially the New Testament, predict that the temple will be rebuilt? It does not. Why are Jews wanting to rebuild the temple? For the same reason that the temple was maintained prior to its destruction in A.D. 70—apostate Jews do not believe that Jesus is the promised Messiah. If the Jews once again build a temple and begin to offer sacrifices, this will only confirm their rejection of the atoning blood of Jesus. It was this rejection that led to the destruction of the temple that was standing in Jesus' day.

Because of the consistent futurizing of the events of Matthew 24, contemporary prophetic speculators who teach the imminency of the rapture envision the *need* for a rebuilt temple. Supposedly in this rebuilt temple the Antichrist will set up a statue to be worshipped, the "abomination of desolation" that Jesus said would be "standing in the holy place" (Matt. 24:15). As this chapter will demonstrate, this is a past event. The temple was still standing in the "holy city" called Jerusalem (4:5; 27:53) when Jesus spoke of the "abomination of desolation." The temple had been pointed out by the disciples, the very temple that Jesus said would be left desolate and the same temple that Jesus walked away from (23:38). Jesus' disciples would have immediately thought of the temple that they had pointed out to Him, not a temple that had to be rebuilt. To propose that Jesus was describing a *rebuilt* temple must be proven from Scripture. The New Testament mentions *nothing* about a rebuilt temple. There is nothing in Matthew 24 that even hints at the rebuilding of the temple. Why would Jesus confuse His listeners and those of us who read His recorded prophecy by leaving out a crucial detail like a rebuilt temple? It does not make sense.

What's Future Is Past

The key to the futurizing interpretation of Matthew 24 is the belief that the seventieth week of Daniel 9:24–27 has been disconnected from the sixty-ninth week. The seventieth week, according to dispensationalists, is still future. It is during this "week," actually seven years, that the Antichrist supposedly will make and break a covenant with the Jews (in the middle of the week, that is, after three and a half years) and desecrate a newly rebuilt temple by proclaiming himself to be God and setting up a statue of himself for the world to worship (2 Thess. 2).

Again, this prophetic scenario is dependent on splitting the seventieth "week" (seven years) from the previous sixty-nine "weeks" (483 years) and inserting a "gap" of nearly two thousand years after the sixty-ninth "week" and before the seventieth "week" of Daniel 9:24–27. There is nothing in Daniel 9:24–27 that even hints that there will be a rebuilt temple. The temple being discussed in Daniel 9:24–27, Matthew 24:15, 2 Thessalonians 2:4, and Revelation 11:1–2 is the temple that Jesus cleansed on at least two occasions (John 2:13–22; Matt. 21:12–17) and left for a future judgment that history attests occurred in A.D. 70 (Matt. 23:38).

There is one major problem with the futurizing scenario that views the seventieth week as not being fulfilled in the first century: There is no *biblical* warrant for stopping Daniel's prophecy of the seventy weeks after the sixty-ninth week. *The idea of separation and the placement of an indeterminable gap between the two sets of weeks is one of the most unnatural and nonliteral interpretations of Scripture found in any eschatological system.* This interpretation is taught by those who insist on a literal hermeneutic. If dispensationalists were consistent in their literalism, they would never manipulate Scripture to fit an already established prophetic system. The weeks form a unit without separation or a gap. Interpreters who place a gap between the sixty-ninth and seventieth weeks of Daniel 9:24–27 should be challenged to produce a single Bible verse that even implies such a division. Why is there no mention of this "great parenthesis" either in the Bible or in nearly nineteen hundred years of church history?

Futurism mandates that a temple must be rebuilt so the events of Matthew 24 can be fulfilled again! History records that the temple was destroyed in A.D. 70, with the events of Matthew 24 preceding its demise. *Not one verse in the New Testament mentions the need for a rebuilt temple*, a fact admitted by those who believe a future temple is necessary for prophecy to be fulfilled. Thomas Ice and Timothy Demy write: "There are no Bible verses that say, 'There is going to be a third temple.'"[6] Of course, there's a good reason for this. The real temple of God in the New Testament is obviously the church of Christ with Jesus as the "cornerstone" (1 Peter 2:7). The Old Testament prophecies predicting a rebuilt temple were fulfilled in the post-exile period and in the first coming of Christ.[7] Some point to the temple of Ezekiel 40–48 as an example of a prophecy that is yet to be fulfilled. But this passage is simply a visionary expression of the faithful remnant that returned after the exile and the glorious future they would have.

> With the exception of the Messianic section in ch. xlvii. 1–12 [of Ezekiel], the fulfillment of all the rest of the prophecy belongs to the times immediately after the return from the Chaldean exile. So must every one of its first hearers and readers have understood it ... Jeremiah the prophet, whom Ezekiel follows throughout, ... had prophesied that the city and temple should be restored seventy years after the date of the Chaldean servitude, falling in the fourth year of Jehoiakim. Of these seventy years, thirty-two had already elapsed at the time when our prophecy was delivered. Ezekiel himself had announced, in ch. xxix. 13, that forty years after the desolation of Egypt, the nations visited by the Chaldeans would return to their former state. And what is more obvious, according to ch. xi. 16, the restoration is to follow in a brief space after the destruction of the temple. Accordingly the first hearers and readers could not but expect that, with respect to the restoration of the temple and city, the word holds good which Habakkuk uttered (ch. i. 5) with regard to the destruction, "I do a deed in your days;" and we enter upon the interpretation with the presupposition that here also the word of the Lord applies, "Verily I say unto you, This generation shall not pass till all these things be fulfilled [Matthew 24:34]."[8]

By extension, Ezekiel's temple is a picture of the New Covenant under which the church, made up of believing Jews and Gentiles, is the new temple. Peter, in describing the church of his day, wrote: "You also, as living stones, are being built up as a spiritual house for a holy priesthood, to offer up spiritual sacrifices acceptable to God through Jesus Christ" (1 Peter 2:5). What could be more clear? Christians—converted Jews and Gentiles from every tribe, tongue, and nation—are "living stones" being joined together in a living temple (Eph. 2:19–21; 1 Cor. 3:16; 6:19; 2 Cor. 6:16). This new edifice is called "a holy temple in the Lord" (Eph. 2:21). In the previous chapter we saw how Jesus abandoned the earthly temple of stone by walking away from it and turning His back to it (Matt. 23:38). The physical temple, taken over by the corrupt Pharisees and priests, would be left to them "desolate." It is in this new temple made from "living stones" (1 Peter 2:5) that God's Spirit dwells (Eph. 2:22). Scripture could not be more clear.

The call for another temple simply energizes the spreading of last days madness and denies the truth of the Bible.

Four Temples?

Those who believe that the Bible requires a rebuilt temple in fulfillment of Bible prophecy actually teach the need for *two* rebuilt temples: "The Jewish people themselves speak of the possibility of two future temples. Christian scholars who study both the Old and New Testaments see a third temple, built upon Mt. Moriah, which will be desecrated by the man of great evil (Antichrist). A concept of the Antichrist is also found in traditional writings of Jewish scholars. He is called anti-messiah or the 'golem.' The third temple will be of short duration. The final temple [the fourth], which will be built in the Millennium under the auspices of the Messiah Himself, is described in chapters 40 to 48 of Ezekiel."[9]

This supposed millennial temple is of special interest since it depicts animal sacrifices "to make atonement" (Ezek. 45:15, 17, 20). The word "atonement" is used in the Pentateuch to describe Old Testament propitiatory sacrifices, the very thing Jesus came to abolish through His own shed blood (Lev. 6:30; 8:15; 16:6, 11, 24, 30–34; Num. 5:8; 15:28; 29:5; Rom. 3:25; 1 John 2:2; 4:10). The Book of Hebrews was written to show beyond a shadow of a doubt that the entire Old Covenant system—with its priests, sacrifices, ceremonies, and temple—has been done away with in Christ. No mention is made in the Book of Hebrews that the temple that would be destroyed in A.D. 70 must be rebuilt during a so-called future Great Tribulation, or that a millennial temple must be built by Jesus. Such a millennial temple would require Jesus to officiate over the very animal sacrifices that He shed His blood to replace.

How does the futurist (dispensationalist) get around this obvious theological problem? The *New Scofield Reference Bible* understands the dilemma. The editors of the 1909 version give two possible interpretations: "(1) Such sacrifices, if actually offered, will be memorial in character.... (2) the reference to sacrifices is not to be taken literally." In the first case, nothing in the text gives any indication that the sacrifices are "memorial in character." In the second case, dispensationalism demands strict literalism. It is a pillar of the system.[10] But when a rebuilt temple with blood flowing during the supposed millennial reign of Jesus on the earth obviously contradicts the clear teaching of the New Testament, dispensationalism rejects literalism. This is convenient, but it is hardly convincing. The prophecy of Ezekiel's temple is a picture of the restored covenant community that returned to the land after the exile. This vision should not be projected nearly twenty-five hundred years into the future into some earthly millennial kingdom where sacrifices will be offered *for atonement* in the presence of the crucified Christ!

Planned Obsolescence

The earthly temple was designed as a temporary edifice that would no longer be needed when the true temple of God, Jesus Christ, was manifested on earth. Just like heaven is God's true throne and dwelling place and earth is His footstool (Isa. 66:1), Jesus is the true temple with the earthly temple being a mere copy of heaven (2 Sam. 22:7). God asks: "Where then is a house you could build for Me?" (Isa. 66:1b). "The rebellious Jews believed that they might construct the Temple as a place of rest for Yahweh. In that Temple, however, He would have no place of rest nor would it be His sanctuary. Those who would build a house influenced by such conceptions were seeking to render the infinite finite, the eternal temporal, and the Creator a mere creature."[11]

The New Testament situation is no different. Jesus is the true and abiding temple. The earthly temple was designed with obsolescence in mind, while the temple of His body was designed for permanency (John 2:13–22). Even the city of Jerusalem is no longer considered to be a focal point of worship (John 4:21–26; Gal. 4:21–31). Therefore, those religious leaders who continued to offer animal sacrifices after Jesus offered Himself as "the Lamb of God who takes away the sin of the world" (John 1:29) were offering the equivalent of "swine's blood" in the temple that would cease to exist in A.D. 70 (Isa. 66:3c). "He who burns incense is like the one who blesses an idol. As they have chosen their own ways, and their soul delights in their abominations" (66:3e). Here we see that those priests who offered the biblically prescribed Old Covenant sacrifices are said to "delight in their abominations." Why did these sacrifices constitute an abomination?

> If there is any historical reference, it is to those who, having returned from exile, desired to serve God by means of their own appointment. The reference may be in part to some who built the second Temple, but more

fully it is to those who built Herod's temple and continued offering the sacrifices even after the one true sacrifice had been offered. John 12:38 expressly applies Isaiah 53:1 to the unbelief of the Pharisees.[12]

In anticipation of the promised Redeemer, a warning was issued by God through Isaiah to those who fail to recognize God's plan of salvation: "I will choose their punishments, and I will bring on them what they dread" (66:4a). The temple, earthly priesthood, and animal sacrifices were designed to pass into oblivion when the promised High Priest, Jesus, offered Himself as the perfect and final sacrifice. All other sacrifices, no matter how well intentioned, would be an abomination in the light of the cross of Christ.

Notes

1. David Allen Lewis, *Prophecy 2000: Rushing to Armageddon* (Green Forest, AR: New Leaf, 1990), 131.
2. Steve Rodan, "Move to Build 3rd Jewish Temple in Jerusalem Stirs Resistance," *Washington Post* (25 November 1989), D11.
3. Kenneth L. Woodward, "The Final Days are Here Again," *Newsweek* (18 March 1991), 55.
4. Woodward, "The Final Days are Here Again," 55.
5. Rodan, "Move to Build," D11.
6. Thomas Ice and Timothy Demy, *The Truth about the Last Days' Temple* (Eugene, OR: Harvest House, 1996), 13.
7. William Hendriksen, *Israel in Prophecy* (Grand Rapids, MI: Baker Book House, 1968).
8. Ernst Wilhelm Hengstenberg (1802–69), *The Prophecies of the Prophet Ezekiel Elucidated*, trans. A.C. Murphy and J.G. Murphy (Edinburgh: T. & T. Clark, 1869), 348–49.
9. Lewis, *Prophecy 2000*, 175.
10. Charles Ryrie, certainly a respected representative of dispensationalism, states, "Dispensationalists claim that their principle of hermeneutics is that of literal interpretation. This means interpretation which gives to every word the same meaning it would have in normal usage, whether employed in writing, speaking or thinking" (*Dispensationalism Today* [Chicago, IL: Moody Press, 1965], 86). Therefore, atonement must mean atonement. Blood sacrifices must mean blood sacrifices. You cannot, using dispensationalism's view of literalism, turn blood atonement into a memorial.
11. Edward J. Young, *The Book of Isaiah*, 3 vols. (Grand Rapids, MI: Eerdmans, 1972), 3:518–19.
12. Young, *The Book of Isaiah*, 3:520.

Chapter Eight

THE ABOMINATION OF DESOLATION

F uturists need a rebuilt temple in order to project the fulfillment of prophecies related to the abomination of desolation to another time. Is this
what Jesus had in view in Matthew 24:15? A careful reading of Scripture
will show that the abomination of desolation mentioned by Jesus was an
event that would be fulfilled during the lifetime of His disciples. Jesus said,
"This generation"—the generation He addressed—"will not pass away until
all these things take place" (24:34). One of the "things" was the "abomination
of desolation ... standing in the holy place" (24:15).

The abomination of desolation is mentioned in one Old Testament book
(Dan. 9:27; 11:31; 12:11). The Book of Maccabees, a non-inspired book
written during the intertestamental period, mentions the abomination of
desolation and its relationship to Antiochus Epiphanes (168 B.C.) (1 Macc.
1:10–64; 4:36–59; 6:7; 2 Macc. 10:1–8). First-century Jews would have
been familiar with the theology and history surrounding the abomination
of desolation. There was no doubt in the minds of those who read and
understood Jesus' words in Matthew 24:15 that the abomination of desolation prophecy was fulfilled in events leading up to the temple's destruction
in A.D. 70. The Apostle Paul would later address the concerns of the

Thessalonians about the "day of the Lord" with a discussion of the man of lawlessness" (2 Thess. 2). The man of lawlessness was a contemporary figure who was identified with the "abomination of desolation."

The prophecy of Daniel concerning the appalling sacrilege had been called to mind in the year A.D. 40 when Caligula laid plans to have an image of himself set up in the Jerusalem Temple (see Philo, *Legatio ad Gaium*; Josephus, *Antiquities* XVIII. viii. 2–9; Tacitus, *History* V.9). After that catastrophe was averted, Josephus found the fulfillment of Daniel in the events of A.D. 66–70 (*Antiquities* X. xi. 7: "in the same manner Daniel also wrote about the empire of the Romans and that Jerusalem would be taken and the Temple laid waste"). He refers to an ancient prophecy concerning the desecration of the Temple *by Jewish hands* and found its fulfillment in a whole series of villainous acts committed by the Zealots in the Temple precincts from the period November 67 to the spring of 68.[1]

Further study on this important topic should leave no doubt that Matthew 24:15 was fulfilled in its entirety before the passing away of the generation that heard Jesus' prophecy on the Mount of Olives. Again, the time text of verse 34 compels us to look for a candidate within the time frame of the generation that heard the prophecy.

"Therefore when you see the ABOMINATION OF DESOLATION which was spoken of through Daniel the prophet, standing in the holy place (let the reader understand)..." (Matt. 24:15).

There is an unbroken transition from verse 14 to verse 15 in Matthew 24. By comparing Luke 21:20–21 and Matthew 24:15–18, we can pinpoint the time when the abomination of desolation was to appear. Luke tells us, "When you see *Jerusalem surrounded by armies,* then recognize that her desolation *is at hand.* Then let those who are in Judea flee to the mountains, and let those who are in the midst of the city depart, and let not those who are in the country enter the city" (Luke 21:20–21). Was Jerusalem ever surrounded by armies prior to A.D. 70? Yes! Did Jesus' disciples flee the city? Yes!

When Roman legions besieged Jerusalem, the Jewish Zealots were inflamed by predictions of apocalyptic rescue and maintained their resistance in the false expectation that God would supernaturally deliver the city as He had done in the time of King Hezekiah (701 B.C.).... When [the Christian Jews] saw the desolating abomination in the holy place, they were to understand this as the signal to flee immediately from the city and Judea. They should not expect God to deliver Jerusalem as the prophets Joel (chapter 3), Daniel (12:1), and Zechariah (chapters 12 and 14) had envisioned. The reason should be clear: these apocalyptic prophecies presuppose a faithful remnant of Israel on Mount Zion. But this time the faithful remnant was the messianic flock that was called out of the doomed city.[2]

While futurists (typically dispensationalists) generally acknowledge that Luke is describing events prior to A.D. 70, they assert that Matthew is recounting a different series of events that are still future.[3] For these futurists, Matthew's abomination of desolation will appear in a rebuilt temple during the so-called "seven-year tribulation period" after the pre-tribulational rapture of the church. Only a preconceived theological system could ever twist these verses in this way. It is obvious that all three gospel writers are describing the same series of events and period of time.

Some commentators maintain that only some of Matthew's description of the abomination of desolation was fulfilled in the Roman defilement of the temple. "Yes, the Roman armies did defile the holy place with their acts of emperor worship," they say. "But this did not happen in the 'holy of holies.'" For these commentators, a future fulfillment remains when the *antichrist* will proclaim himself to be God while standing in a rebuilt temple. There is no mention of the Antichrist in Matthew 24. The biblical doctrine of Antichrist is very different from today's fanciful teaching on the subject.

An Abomination of Bloodletting

An abomination in the Old Testament was "related to the desecrating of worship, either by outright false worship (Deut. 7:25; 27:15) or by a profanation of true worship (Lev. 7:18; Deut. 17:1)."[4] This definition fits the situation leading up to the temple's desolation in A.D. 70 in a number of ways. While there is little agreement on what the abomination was that brought on the desolation, nearly all the older commentators are agreed that the desolation occurred in the temple's destruction in A.D. 70. We do know, however, that the abomination that brings on the desolation happens sometime between Jerusalem being "surrounded by armies" (Luke 21:20) and the destruction of the temple. Four events are put forth as possible "abominations."

The Zealots

Because of Israel's oppression under the Romans, the Zealots appeared as advocates of political and religious freedom from the yoke of Roman oppression. We learn of the existence of the Zealots from the New Testament. Jesus chose Simon the Zealot as one of His twelve apostles (Matt. 10:4; Mark 3:18; Luke 6:15; Acts 1:13). Simon may have been a follower of this sect that some say had its origin in A.D. 6 following the death of Herod the Great. "The Zealots were nationalists, strong upholders of Jewish traditions and religion; [who] ... became a principal cause of the Jewish War in which Rome sacked Jerusalem."[5]

As hostilities grew between Rome and Judea, Zealot nationalism sharpened into what one could call a "holy war." Depending on one's perspective (Josephus called them brigands and robbers), the Zealots were either assassins or patriotic freedom fighters. The Zealots saw their chance for nationalistic and religious revival by storming the temple. Their tactics, however, were less than honorable.

> The zealots had got possession of the Temple at an early stage in the siege, and profaned it by these and other like outrages; they made the Holy Place (in the very words of the historian) "a garrison and stronghold" of their tyrannous and lawless rule; while the better priests looked on from afar and wept tears of horror. The mysterious prediction of 2 Thess. ii.4 may point, in the first instance, to some kindred "abomination."[6]

At the outbreak of the Jewish War, the Zealots moved in and occupied the temple area. They allowed persons who had committed crimes to roam about freely in the Holy of Holies, and they perpetrated murder within the temple itself. These acts of sacrilege climaxed in the winter of 67–68 with the farcical investiture of the clown Phanni as high priest.[7]

> It was in response to this specific action that the retired priest Ananus, with tears, lamented: "It would have been far better for me to have died

before I had seen the house of God laden with such abominations and its unapproachable and hallowed places crowded with the feet of murderers" (*Wars*, 4:3:10).[8]

The Zealots "went over all the buildings, and the temple itself, and fell upon the priests, and those that were about the sacred offices."[9] The Zealots believed that "God would intervene directly" to vindicate their cause. "The Zealots hoped to be able to overcome the power of Rome by the armed force of eschatological Israel under the people's messianic leader, in a situation in which God would send them his supernatural help as he had done when they had been led by Moses and Joshua."[10] As history attests, this did not happen. God's purpose was judgment upon the "city and sanctuary" (Dan. 9:26) for the nation's rejection of the promised Messiah (John 1:11). Eventually the surviving Zealots retreated to the mountain stronghold called Masada. The Romans pursued them but were hindered in leading troops up the mountain side. This obstacle was eventually overcome. By the time the soldiers entered Masada the 960 rebels, many of whom were women and children, had been killed by their own hand. Ten men had been selected for the execution of the remaining men. First to be granted death were the fathers and husbands who had just taken leave of their families. In rapid order the executions were carried out until the last ten remained. This was in May of A.D. 73.

The Idumeans

The Idumeans, who occupied the territory south of Judea, which had been the ancient kingdom of Edom, came to Jerusalem at the behest of Zealot leaders to participate in their revolutionary cause against the Romans. "With an army of some twenty thousand men and four generals, the Idumeans marched to Jerusalem only to find the gates tightly locked and guards on the walls."[11] Not able to enter the city, the Idumeans made camp outside the city walls. During an intense storm and the cover of night, the Zealots "went to the gate nearest the Idumeans and began to saw the bars" to open a passageway for the Idumeans to enter.[12] Once inside, the Idumeans, along with the Zealots, vented their fury on the city's occupants. Josephus reports that the outer court of the Temple was deluged with blood with the death of over eight thousand. The real target was the chief priest Ananus. Ananus had on an earlier occasion tried to persuade the people to rise up against the Zealots. Ananus and many other priests were killed, and their dead bodies were mocked by those who stood upon them. Their corpses were cast into the streets. Josephus believed that it was this act that brought on the judgment of God.

> I should not mistake if I said that the death of Ananus was the beginning of the destruction of the city, and that from this very day may be dated the overthrow of her wall, and the ruin of her affairs, whereon they saw their high priest, and the procurer of their preservation, slain in the midst of the people.[13]

If Josephus believed that the destruction of the city was due to the execution of Ananus the high priest, is it not probable that God would take His "vengeance" (Luke 21:22) on the city because of the death of His Son—the Greater High Priest—Jesus (Hebrews 5:6, 10; 6:20; 7:11, 17)? Jerusalem was destroyed because there were many in Israel, provoked and led by the religious leaders, who had years before "disowned the Holy and Righteous One, and asked for a murderer" (Acts 3:14; cf. 2:23). They "put to death the Prince of life" (3:15). In return God destroyed their city.

The Idumeans, having had enough of the atrocities, withdrew from the city. This, however, did not stop the savagery of the Zealots. "Some feel that it may have been at this point in time that the Christians left the city and fled to Pella [Matthew 24:16]."[14]

The Romans

Eventually the temple was taken by the Romans and burned,[15] an action which Titus opposed but could not stop. While the sanctuary was still burning, "the soldiers brought their legionary standards into the sacred precincts, set them up opposite the eastern gate, and offered sacrifices to them, there, acclaiming Titus *imperator* (victorious commander) as they did so. The Roman custom of offering sacrifices to their standards had already been commented on by a Jewish writer [the Qumran commentator on Hab. 1:16] as a symptom of their pagan arrogance, but the offering of such sacrifice in the Temple court was the supreme insult to the God of Israel."[16] This action by the Romans must have been understood by the Jews as the fulfillment of Daniel's vision when the burnt offering would cease and the abomination of desolation would be set up (Dan. 9:27). What Caligula could not do in A.D. 40, the Roman armies accomplished in A.D. 70.

The representations of Caesar, and of the eagle, on the Roman standards were worshipped by the soldiers of that nation, and thus were, in Hebrew phraseology, "an abomination."—With equal propriety is their army described by the word "desolation." They plundered and devastated without mercy, and, to use the indignant expression of a hostile chieftain, "Where they have made a desert, they call peace" (Speech of Galgacus, Tacitus; Life of Agricola 30).—They planted their standards before Jerusalem, several furlongs of land around which were accounted holy. The Temple was more particularly called "the holy place" (Acts vi. 13); and on the capture of the city, this prediction was fulfilled to the letter; for the Romans brought "the Eagles" into the Temple and sacrificed to them there. Out of respect to Jewish scruples, they had always before been left at Cesarea by the Roman Governors.[17]

This Roman abomination was reminiscent of what Antiochus Epiphanes did to profane the temple and altar more than two centuries before. On December 15, 168 B.C., Antiochus built a pagan altar on the site of the great altar where sacrifices were made (2 Maccabees 6:1–13). Ten days later a heathen sacrifice was offered on it. In 167 B.C. he set up a pagan statue in the temple. Antiochus went even farther in forcing Jews to participate in his abominations. Those who did not cooperate were killed: "Now Antiochus was not satisfied either with his unexpected taking of the city, or with its pillage, or with the great slaughter he had made there; but being overcome with his violent passions, and remembering what he had suffered during the siege, he compelled the Jews to dissolve the laws of their country, and to keep their infants uncircumcised, and to sacrifice swine's blood on the altar."[18]

The Roman abomination hypothesis is the most popular since it parallels the actions of Antiochus Epiphanes. Luke's description of "Jerusalem surrounded by armies"—Roman armies—(Luke 21:20) appears to point to a Roman "abomination."

The Jews

It is likely, however, that Jesus had more in mind than the abominable acts that took place in the temple by the Romans, Idumeans, or the "desecration of the temple by the Zealots in the winter of A.D. 67/8, shortly before the Roman siege began."[19] Antiochus, the Zealots, the Idumeans, and the Roman legions were not the ones who could defile the temple under the terms of the New Covenant. Only someone posing as an official religious representative of God could actually defile the temple. Israel's priesthood was corrupt, and the sacrifices were an abomination since the priests denied the atoning work of Christ. Earlier in Israel's history God threatened desolation "because the Jews had defiled the temple with detestable things and abominations."[20] "'So as I live,' declares the LORD GOD, 'surely, because you have defiled My sanctuary with all your detestable idols and with all your abominations, therefore I will also withdraw, and My eye shall have no pity and I will not spare'" (Ezek. 5:11).

The Jews of Jesus' day had turned the temple into a "house of merchandise" (John 2:16) and a "robbers' den" (Matt. 21:13). When a priest inspected a house and found it leprous, the house was to be torn down (Lev. 14:33–47). Jesus, as the High Priest, after the order of Melchizedek (Heb. 5:6), inspected the temple twice, found it leprous, and issued His priestly evaluation: "And Jesus came out from the temple" (Matt. 24:1), as the priest "shall come out from the house" (Lev. 14:38), and declared it "desolate" (Matt. 23:38), as the priest declared a leprous house to be "unclean" (Lev. 14:44). A leprous house could be cleansed in only one way: "He shall therefore *tear down the house, its stones,* and its timbers, and all the plaster of the house, and he shall take them outside the city to an unclean place" (Lev. 14:45). When Jesus' disciples pointed to the temple buildings after hearing of its desolation, Jesus answered: "Do *you* not see all these things? Truly I say to *you, not one stone here shall be left upon another, which will not be torn down"* (Matt. 24:2).

It was the priests, along with the scribes, elders, and Pharisees, who rejected Jesus as the Messiah (Matt. 26:57–68). Instead of choosing Jesus, they "persuaded the multitudes to ask for Barabbas, and to put Jesus to death" (27:20). With the true Lamb slain, the earthly temple could no longer operate as a place of sacrifice. The action of the high priest, "standing in the holy place" (24:15), continuing to offer sacrifices in the temple, was an abomination, a rejection of the work of Christ. James B. Jordan comments:

> False worship is idolatrous worship. When the Jews rejected Jesus and kept offering sacrifices, they were engaged in idolatry…. This was the "wing of abominations" [Dan. 9:27] that took place in the Temple. It is why the Temple was destroyed.
>
> A full picture of this is provided in Ezekiel 8-11…. There you will see that when the apostate Jews of Ezekiel's day performed the sacrifices,

God viewed it as an abomination. He called the holy shrine an "idol of jealousy, that provokes to jealousy" (8:3). The Jews had treated the Temple and the ark as idols, and so God would destroy them, as he did the golden calf. Ezekiel sees God pack up and move out of the Temple, leaving it empty or desolate. Once God had left, the armies of Nebuchadnezzar swept in and destroyed the empty Temple. (When we recognize that Ezekiel and Daniel prophesied at the same time, the correlation becomes even more credible.)[21]

Jesus' actions in Matthew 23:38 in proclaiming the temple "desolate" and walking away from the structure are what God had warned about when He saw abominations present: "Then the glory of the LORD departed from the threshold of the temple and stood over the cherubim" (Ezek. 10:18). John Calvin put forth a similar interpretation: God "deserted his Temple, because it was only founded for a time, and was but a shadow, until the Jews so completely violated the whole covenant that no sanctity remained in either the Temple, the nation, or the land itself."[22] As J. Marcellus Kik states, "The real cause for the desolation was found in the spiritual fornication of the Jews, especially their rejection of the Messiah."[23]

While disagreement remains as to what form the abomination took, Scripture makes it clear that it occurred soon after Jerusalem was surrounded by armies. As history attests, Jerusalem was surrounded just prior to the temple's destruction in the fall of A.D. 70. The abomination brought desolation.

Not the Real Thing

Those who look for a rebuilt temple to be destroyed during the "Great Tribulation" or a millennial temple where Jesus will sit have a problem with much of the Bible. The Book of Hebrews describes the temple, the daily sacrificial system, religious feasts, the altar, the holy of holies, and the priesthood as "a copy and shadow of the heavenly things" (Heb. 8:5). Copies and shadows are not the real thing. With the death of Jesus, no barriers separated the people from the holy of holies (Matt. 27:51). There was no longer a need for an earthly priesthood to offer up animal blood in atonement for sins. J.C. Ryle understood the meaning of the coming of Christ when he wrote:

Jerusalem and the temple were the heart of the Old Jewish dispensation. When they were destroyed the Old Testament system came to an end. The daily sacrifice, the yearly feasts, the altar, the holy of holies, and the priesthood were all essential parts of revealed religion till Christ came— but no longer. When He died upon the cross, their work was done: they were dead, and it only remained that they should be buried. But it was not fitting that this thing should be done quietly. The ending of a dispensation given with so much solemnity at Mount Sinai might well be expected to be marked with particular solemnity; the destruction of the holy temple, where so many old saints had seen "shadows of good things to come," might well be expected to form a subject of prophecy: and so it was. The Lord Jesus specially predicts the desolation of the "holy place" (verse 15). The Great High Priest describes the end of the dispensation which had been put in charge to lead people to Himself.[24]

Jesus had accomplished His mission with His cry of "It is finished" (John 19:30). The people, especially the priesthood, were warned by God when He tore "the veil of the temple … in two from top to bottom" (Matt. 27:51) that atonement would no longer be made in the temple. Jesus had told the Samaritan woman that "an hour is coming when neither in this mountain, nor in Jerusalem, shall you worship the Father.… But an hour is coming, and now is, when the true worshipers shall worship the Father in spirit and truth; for such people the Father seeks to be His worshipers" (John 4:21, 23).

"Then let those who are in Judea flee to the mountains; let him who is on the housetop not go down to get the things out that are in his house; and let him who is in the field not turn back to get his cloak. But woe to those who are with child and to those who nurse babes in those days! But pray that your flight may not be in the winter, or on the Sabbath" (Matt. 24:16–20).

These verses allude to Lot and his family escaping the judgment of Sodom. The acts of the people of Sodom were a type of abomination that brought desolation to the city and those who chose to reside there despite the warning God them through His messengers: "Behold, this was the guilt of your *sister* Sodom[25]: she and her daughters had arrogance, abundant food, and careless ease, but she did not help the poor and needy [see Mark 7:10–13; Matt. 23:23]. Thus they were haughty and committed *abominations* before

Me. Therefore I removed them when I saw it" (Ezek. 16:49–50). When the temple's approaching desolation was evident to the Christians still living in Jerusalem, it was time to head for the hills. They had been expecting the temple's destruction. The New Testament is filled with time texts that make it clear that the "end of all things was at hand" (1 Peter 4:7), literally, "has come near."

Matthew 24:16–20 clearly presents first-century-Israel living conditions. Most roofs in Israel were flat with an outside staircase (Mark 2:4; Acts 10:9). They were commonly occupied (Deut. 22:8) and used for storage (Joshua 2:6) and rest in the evening (2 Sam. 11:2). Once Jerusalem was surrounded by armies, not much time was left for a getaway. There was not even enough time to go inside the house to carry away prized possessions.

> [I]n the Oriental houses there are stairs on the outside of the house landing in the court, from which one could escape into the street through the porch. Occasionally, though not often, we are told of stairs which come directly from the roof on the street side of the house into the street below.[26]

In these verses, Jesus refers to the strict Sabbath laws that were operating in first-century Israel (Matt. 12:2, 10; Mark 2:24; 16:1; Luke 23:56; John 5:9, 16, 18; 9:16). Acceptable distances for travel on the Sabbath were measured in terms of a "Sabbath day's journey," approximately three-quarters of a mile as determined by Pharisaical law (Acts 1:12).[27] The Christians would have been prohibited from traveling on the Sabbath by the religious leaders due to the distorted travel restrictions imposed upon the populace. During the Jewish and Idumean revolts against Rome (A.D. 66–70), Pella, a rock fortress hidden in the hill country approximately sixty miles northeast of Jerusalem, became a refuge for many fleeing Christians.

Luke tells us that the warning sign of the approaching desolation would be *"Jerusalem surrounded by armies"* (Luke 21:20–21). How could armies surrounding a city give an opportunity for the people of the city to escape? Escape was made possible because Cestius and his armies suddenly and without warning withdrew from the temple area. As an eyewitness to the events, Josephus writes, "Without any just occasion in the world."[28] The Jews saw the withdrawal as a sign of weakness and pursued the retreating army, which gave the Jewish Christians the opportunity to escape unhindered. The translator of Josephus' *Wars of the Jews* supplies the following comment on this odd series of events. Notice that he identifies this event as the time of the "Great Tribulation":

> There may another very important, and very providential, reason be here assigned for this strange and foolish retreat of Cestius; which, if Josephus had been now a Christian, he might probably have taken notice of also; and that is, the affording the Jewish Christians in the city an opportunity to calling to mind the prediction and caution given them by Christ about thirty-three years and half before, that "when they should see the abomination of desolation" [the idolatrous Roman armies, with the images of their idols in their ensigns, ready to lay Jerusalem desolate] "stand where it ought not"; or, "in the holy place"; or, "when they should see Jerusalem encompassed with armies," they should then "flee to the mountains." By complying with which those Jewish Christians fled to the mountains of Perea, and escaped this destruction.... Nor was there, perhaps, any one instance of a more unpolitic, but more providential conduct than this retreat of Cestius, visible during this whole siege of Jerusalem; which yet was providentially such a "Great Tribulation, as had not been from the beginning of the world to that time; no, nor ever should be."[29]

Christian Jews heeded Jesus' warning long before the armies of Titus had captured the city. Jews who were expecting messianic deliverance remained in the city. Titus had been ordered by his father Vespasian to subdue Judea. "Those within the city were not only prevented from escape by the enemy but also by the Zealots within the city."[30] The Jews who remained were slaughtered. Estimates put the number killed at over one million! Thousands more were taken into captivity as slaves (Luke 21:24). Forty years earlier Jesus had given the warning to flee to the mountains when the holy city was seen encompassed by armies. Those who believed the prophecy and acted upon it escaped with their lives. Those who remained suffered untold misery. Josephus recounts one incident that describes the horrible tribulation of the period:

> There was one Mary, the daughter of Eleazar, illustrious for her family and riches. She having been stripped and plundered of all her substance and provisions by the soldiers, out of necessity and fury killed her own

sucking child, and having boiled him, devoured half of him, and covering up the rest preserved it for another time. The soldiers soon came, allured by the smell of victuals, and threatened to kill her immediately, if she would not produce what she had dressed. But she replied that she had reserved a good part for them, and uncovered the relics of her son. Dread and astonishment seized them, and they stood stupefied at the sight.[31]

Centuries before God had warned Israel what would happen if they ever renounced the covenant: "You shall eat the offspring of your own body, the flesh of your sons and of your daughters whom the LORD your God has given you, during the siege and the distress by which your enemy shall oppress you" (Deut. 28:53; cf. verse 55; Jer. 19:9). This prophecy came to pass during the Babylonian invasion. The siege from these foreign invaders was so oppressive that "The hands of the compassionate women boiled their own children; they became food for them... (Lam. 4:10; see 2:20; 2 Kings 6:24–31)."

Many people preferred death to undergoing the hardships brought on by the Roman siege in A.D. 70. "For the days shall come upon you," Jesus warned the Jews of His day, "when *your* enemies will throw up a bank before *you*, and surround *you*, and hem *you* in on every side, and will level *you* to the ground and *your* children within you, and they will not leave in *you* one stone upon another, because *you* did not recognize the time of *your* visitation" (Luke 19:43–44). These verses and the description in Matthew 24 make it clear that Jesus was describing "a local event, one that was limited to Palestine, and not descriptive of the second coming when the elect will be taken up with Christ. At that time there will be no necessity for believers to flee to the mountains."[32]

Notes

1. William L. Lane, *Commentary on the Gospel of Mark* (Grand Rapids, MI: Eerdmans, 1974), 468–69.

2. Hans K. LaRondelle, *The Israel of God in Prophecy: Principles of Prophetic Interpretation* (Berrien Springs, MI: Andrews University Press, 1983), 197–98.

3. This is the view of Arno C. Gaebelein: "The record of this prediction of the fall of Jerusalem under Titus is not at all given in Matthew twenty-four, but we find that the Spirit of God has put that in the Gospel of Luke" (*The Gospel of Matthew: An Exposition* [Neptune, NJ: Loizeaux Brothers (1910) 1961], 467).

4. Kenneth L. Gentry, Jr., "The Abomination of Desolation," *Dispensationalism in Transition*, 4:10 (October 1991), 1.

5. D.A. Carson, "Matthew," *The Expositor's Bible Commentary*, gen. ed. Frank E. Gaebelein, 12 vols. (Grand Rapids, MI: Zondervan, 1984), 8:239.

6. Edward Hayes Plumptre, "The Gospel According to St. Matthew," *A New Testament Commentary for English Readers*, ed. Charles John Ellicott, 3 vols. (London: Cassell and Company, 1897), 1:147.

7. Flavius Josephus, *The Wars of the Jews* in *The Works of Josephus*, trans. William Whiston (Peabody, MA: Hendrickson Publishers, 1987), 4:3:6–10 and 4:5:4, 671–672, 680.

8. Lane, *Commentary on the Gospel of Mark*, 469.

9. Josephus, *The Wars of the Jews*, 5:1:3, 697.

10. Martin Hengel, *The Zealots: Investigations into the Jewish Freedom Movement in the Period from Herod I until 70 A.D.*, trans. David Smith (Edinburgh: T. & T. Clark, [1976] 1989), 305.

11. Cleon L. Rogers, Jr., *The Topical Josephus: Historical Accounts that Shed Light on the Bible* (Grand Rapids, MI: Zondervan, 1992), 160.

12. Rogers, *The Topical Josephus*, 161.

13. Josephus, *Wars of the Jews*, 4:5:2, 679.

14. Rogers, *The Topical Josephus*, 162.

15. The Old Testament demanded that "the daughter of the priest" who "profanes herself by harlotry" shall be "burned with fire" (Lev. 21:9). Jerusalem had committed acts of harlotry with the nations, especially Rome (see John 19:15: "We have no king but Caesar!"). Israel had played the harlot many times before: "You trusted in your beauty and played the harlot because of your fame, and you poured out your harlotries on every passerby who might be willing. And you took some of your clothes, made for yourself high places

of various colors, and played the harlot on them, which should never come about nor happen" (Eze. 16:15–16). When God came for Israel's redemption, He was rejected and crucified. Instead of embracing the God of Israel, Israel embraced Caesar as god. Israel was a harlot (Rev. 17–18).

16. F.F. Bruce, *Israel and the Nations: From the Exodus to the Fall of the Second Temple* (Grand Rapids, MI: Eerdmans, 1963), 224. As Bruce comments in a footnote on the same page, "Josephus evidently recognizes the fulfillment of these prophecies in the events of A.D. 70 (*War*, vi. 94, pp. 311, 316)."

17. John Forster, *The Gospel-Narrative* (London: John W. Parker, 1847), 304, note 12. Josephus writes: "And now the Romans upon the flight of the seditious into the city, and upon the burning of the holy house itself, and all of the buildings lying round about it, brought their ensigns to the temple, and set them over against its eastern gate; and there did they offer sacrifices to them, and there did they make Titus imperator, with the greatest acclamations of joy" (*Wars of the Jews*, 6:6:1, 743).

18. Josephus, *Wars of the Jews*, 1:1:2, 546.

19. R.T. France, *The Gospel According to Matthew: An Introduction and Commentary* (Grand Rapids, MI: Eerdmans, 1985), 340.

20. J. Marcellus Kik, "Abomination of Desolation," *The Encyclopedia of Christianity*, ed. Edwin H. Palmer, 4 vols. (Wilmington, DE: The National Association for Christian Education, 1964), 1:19.

21. James B. Jordan, "The Abomination of Desolation: An Alternative Hypothesis," in Gary DeMar, *The Debate over Christian Reconstruction* (Ft. Worth, TX: Dominion Press, 1988), 240.

22. John Calvin, *Commentaries on the Book of the Prophet Daniel*, trans. Thomas Myers, 2 vols. (Grand Rapids, MI: Eerdmans, 1948), 2:390.

23. Kik, "Abomination of Desolation," 19.

24. J.C. Ryle, *Matthew* (Wheaton, IL: Crossway Books [1856], 1993), 228–29.

25. Jerusalem is called "Sodom" in the Book of Revelation: "And their dead bodies will lie in the street of the great city which mystically is called Sodom and Egypt, where also their Lord was crucified" (Rev. 11:8).

26. James M. Freeman, *Manners and Customs of the Bible* (Plainfield, NJ: Logos International, 1972), 375.

27. A Sabbath day's journey "was a distance of 2,000 cubits or around one kilometer, ingeniously reckoned by interpreting Ex. 16:29 ('let no one go out of his place on the seventh day') in the light of Num. 35:5 (where the Levites' pasturelands are defined by a radius of 2,000 cubits from any one of the six

'cities of refuge')" (F.F. Bruce, *The Book of the Acts*, rev. ed. [Grand Rapids, MI: Eerdmans, 1988], 39).

28. Josephus, *Wars of the Jews*, 2:19:1–9, 630–33. Others understand the "army" to be that of the Zealots and Idumeans.

29. William Whiston, note b in Josephus, *Wars of the Jews*, 2:19:6, 631–32.

30. J. Marcellus Kik, *An Eschatology of Victory* (Nutley, NJ: Presbyterian and Reformed, 1971), 113.

31. Thomas Newton, *Dissertations on the Prophecies, Which Have Remarkably Been Fulfilled, and at this Time are Fulfilling in the World* (London: J.F. Dove, 1754), 345–46.

32. Kik, *An Eschatology of Victory*, 115.

Chapter Nine

THE PAST GREAT TRIBULATION

"Messiah 1975? The Tribulation 1976?" This was the title of an article that appeared in *The Jack Van Impe Crusade Newsletter* in April of 1975. While Van Impe stated, "We do not believe in setting dates concerning the return of Christ," he does believe that we can ascertain the nearness of Jesus' return based on certain "signs." All we can know is that He "is near."[1]

Van Impe and many like him base their assumptions on a misreading and misdating of Jesus' Olivet Discourse. He wrote: "Jesus did say, 'When you shall see all these things, know that it [or He] is near, even at the doors.' His reference in that twenty-fourth chapter of Matthew is to false Christs, wars, famines, pestilences, earthquakes and numerous other happenings."[2]

Salem Kirban has struck a similar prophetic chord. When he wrote *Countdown to Rapture* in 1977, he was sure that the rapture was near. For Kirban, the stage was "being set for this final world catastrophe which will culminate in the Battle of Armageddon ... a battle where 200 million will die!"[3] In 1977, when the Shah of Iran was still in power, this Islamic nation was the prophetic bogeyman. Supposedly, with the infusion of aid from the United States and the former Soviet Union, Iran was "to be a principal force in the Middle

East."[4] The increased militancy of mid-eastern dictatorships and seemingly overnight revival of Islamic fundamentalism would "launch the Battle of Armageddon. And the stage is being set ... right now!"[5] After listing how the world has changed morally in past decades, Kirban concludes: "Those of us familiar with Scripture can easily see the handwriting on the wall as the way is prepared for the coming Antichrist.... Evidences that surround us show us that this old world is on the verge of a nervous breakdown ... and no amount of Valium can resolve the problem. Based on these observations, it is my considered opinion, that the time clock is now at *11:59.*"[6]

As has been shown in previous chapters, the "signs" that contemporary date-setters use to justify their belief that the rapture is the next prophetic event, followed by a great tribulation, the rise of antichrist, and Armageddon, are found in Matthew 24, Mark 13, and Luke 21. John F. Walvoord, a leading spokesman for the theory that the events described in Matthew 24 are yet to be fulfilled, believes that the time is near for the rapture. In an interview with *USA Today*, when asked if the prophetic clock is ticking, Walvoord answered "Yes."[7] Walvoord wrote in another context:

> In the predictions that Christ made almost 2,000 years ago, He accurately portrayed the progress in the present age. In [Matt. 24:]4–14 He predicted at least nine distinctive features of the period: (1) false christs (vv. 4–5); (2) wars and rumors of wars (vv. 6–7); (3) famines (v. 7); (4) pestilence (v. 7, KJV); (5) earthquakes (v. 7); (6) many martyrs (vv. 8–10); (7) false prophets (v. 11); (8) increase in wickedness with love growing cold (v. 12); (9) worldwide preaching of the Gospel of the kingdom (vv. 13–14). Luke 21:8–24 records similar prophecies.[8]

Of course, these predictions describe conditions prior to the destruction of Jerusalem in A.D. 70. That generation would not pass away until all these things took place (Matthew 24:34). It is inappropriate therefore to interpret them so that they are removed from their first-century context and their obvious application to the then-existing temple and Jewish nation and project them into the distant future.

In 1980 Hal Lindsey told his readers that "*The decade of the 1980s could very well be the last decade of history as we know it.*"[9] Lindsey has been so sure that the end is near that in 1970 he wrote in *The Late Great Planet Earth* that he believes the Antichrist "is alive today—alive and waiting to come forth."[10]

The Middle East war against Iraq in early 1991, Lindsey told us, was "'setting the stage' for that last, climactic war."[11]

Charles Ryrie, best known for the *Ryrie Study Bible,* expresses similar sentiments based on his understanding of Matthew 24. He writes that "Jesus said that these coming days will be uniquely terrible. Nothing in all the previous history of the world can compare with what lies in store for mankind. 'For then there will be great distress, unequaled from the beginning of the world ... and never to be equaled again'" (Matt. 24:21, NIV).[12]

Tim LaHaye believes in a future great tribulation based on passages of Scripture that found their fulfillment in the destruction of Jerusalem in A.D. 70. Because of his pre-tribulational rapture doctrine, he also believes that "the church will be raptured before the Tribulation begins...."[13] The determination on how near the rapture might be is based upon a faulty reading of the signs outlined by Jesus in Matthew 24. While LaHaye does not set a date for the rapture or for the great tribulation, he does tell us that "Jesus is coming. Soon! Maybe today. Maybe tonight. Maybe before I draw my next breath."[14] Jack Van Impe is equally emphatic when he writes, based on world conditions, "The Rapture is near, my friend ... the signs are all around us."[15]

Billy Graham writes that "the words of Christ in Matthew 24, in which He spoke of the signs of the end of the age," along with other prophetic passages, "remain powerful and evocative images of what may lie just ahead."[16] It is in this chapter of Matthew's gospel that Graham believes "Christ tells precisely how the last days of planet Earth will unfold."[17] It is Graham's misinterpretation and misplacement of the time when the "signs" in Matthew 24 appear that leads him to this erroneous conclusion. Jesus was describing events that would come upon that first-century generation.

A Past Great Tribulation

Can any of these modern-day predictions be justified by an appeal to Matthew 24, especially verse 21? I do not believe they can. Authors who promote such a scenario as being based on "Bible prophecy" ought to be held accountable for their repeatedly mistaken predictions: "Anyone who buys a prediction of a scriptural end-of-the-show schedule ought to ask for a double-your-money-back guarantee if the interpretation turns out to be a lot of hooey. Lindsey, John Walvoord and a whole string of evangelists would need a federal bailout."[18]

Is the great tribulation of Matthew 24 a description of a future seven-year period where the Antichrist makes a covenant with Israel and then turns on the Jews, bringing about worldwide destruction?

"There will be a great tribulation, such as has not occurred since the beginning of the world until now, nor ever shall" (Matt. 24:21).

One reason offered for the belief that the great tribulation is still a future event is the seemingly unqualified statement in Matthew 24:21 concerning a "great tribulation, *such as has not occurred since the beginning of the world until now, nor ever shall.*" This language is nearly identical to Ezekiel 5:9: "And because of all your abominations, I will do among you *what I have not done, and the like of which I will never do again.*" Ezekiel 5:9 refers to the destruction of Jerusalem in the sixth century B.C. by the Babylonians, and yet Bible commentators who hold out for a yet future great tribulation state that "never again would God execute a judgment like this."[19] But God did execute a greater judgment in the destruction of Jerusalem in A.D. 70, and dispensationalists claim that there will be yet an even greater tribulation sometime in the near future. The language of Ezekiel 5:9 and Matthew 24:21 is obviously proverbial and hyberbolic.[20]

While the fall of Jerusalem in A.D. 70 was certainly a calamity for the Jews, futurists argue, it was not the great tribulation that will take place on a *worldwide scale*. The tribulation described by Jesus in Matthew 24 was local, confined to Judea. Jesus condemns the scribes and Pharisees (chapter 23) and tells them that these judgments will come upon "this," that is, their generation (23:36). He mourns over the city of "Jerusalem" (23:37), not the world, and pronounces judgment upon the temple, leaving it, not a future temple, "desolate" (23:38; 24:2).

The people live in houses with flat roofs (24:17). The Sabbath is still in force with its rigid travel restrictions (24:20). In Mark's account of the Olivet Discourse we learn that the disciples will be delivered "up to the courts," "flogged in the synagogues," and made to "stand before governors and kings" (13:9). Jesus uses similar words in Matthew 10:17–18 when He sends the twelve out as witnesses to Israel: "But beware of men, for they will deliver *you* up to the courts, and scourge *you* in their synagogues; and *you* shall even be brought before kings for My sake, as a testimony to them and to the Gentiles." The Book of Acts records the fulfillment of Jesus' prediction of religious and political tribulation (4:1–22; 5:17–40; 8:1–3; 12:1–9; 14:19–20; 16:22–23; 22:30–23:11) in the period *before* the destruction of Jerusalem.[21] The existence of these religious and political tribunals is indicative of what life was like in first-century Judea. The tribulation had reference to the Jews, the people of Judea (Matt. 24:16; Luke 21:20–24); it was not a worldwide tribulation.[22]

Those who remained in Jerusalem up until the time of the temple's destruction had to be able to "see the abomination of desolation" (24:15). People around the globe will have no such advantage if what Jesus is describing here refers to a worldwide tribulation period. The only ones who can benefit are those who can see the temple. The tribulation period cannot be global because all one has to do to escape is flee to the mountains. Notice that Jesus says "let those who are in *Judea* flee to the mountains" (24:16). Judea is not the world; it's not even the nation of Israel!

"And unless those days had been cut short, no life would have been saved; but for the sake of the elect those days shall be cut short" (Matt. 24:22).

"Those days" refers to the tribulation period leading up to Jerusalem's destruction. The sign of "Jerusalem surrounded by armies" (Luke 21:20) was a warning to "the elect"—the Jewish Christians living in Jerusalem and its environs—to leave the city so they would not be caught in the impending conflagration. "No life would have been saved" refers to no life in Judea since Judea is the geographical context. James Stuart Russell comments:

> During the three years and a half which represent with sufficient accuracy the duration of the Jewish war, Jerusalem was actually in the hands and under the feet of a horde of ruffians, whom their own countryman [Josephus] describes as 'slaves, and the very dregs of society, the spurious and polluted spawn of the nation.' The last fatal struggle may be said to have begun when Vespasian was sent by Nero, at the head of sixty thousand men, to put down the rebellion. This was early in the year A.D. 70, and in August A.D. 70 the city and the temple were a heap of smoking ashes.[23]

One of the first things we should recognize about Jesus' words is an implied shortening of the tribulation that was coming. If God had allowed these "very dregs of society" to continue in their rebellion, not a single soul would have been left alive in Jerusalem. But for the sake of the elect the tribulation period was cut short. God also restrained the Romans from venting their anger completely.

Luke identifies the tribulation period as being confined to the land of Israel and the people living there in the first century: "Woe to those who are with child and to those who nurse babes in those days; for there will be great distress upon the *land*, and wrath to *this* people" (Luke 21:23). The land of Israel is in view, and "this people" refers to the Jews living in Israel at the time when Jerusalem is "surrounded by armies" (21:20), an event that occurred just prior to Jerusalem's destruction in A.D. 70. "*The land* should be taken in the restricted sense which we give the word, *the country*. —St Paul seems to allude to the expression, *wrath upon this people*, in Rom. ii.5–8 and 1 Thess. ii.16."[24] This means that the intention of "no life would have been saved" (24:22) refers to those living in Judea (24:16) at that time. If Jesus is referring to the entire world, then how would fleeing to the mountains help? Since Jesus offers a simple way to escape the coming judgment, the judgment must be local.

"Then if any one says to you, 'Behold, here is the Christ,' or 'There He is,' do not believe him. For false Christs and false prophets will arise and will show great signs and wonders, so as to mislead, if possible, even the elect. Behold, I have told you in advance. If therefore they say to you, 'Behold, He is in the wilderness,' do not go forth, or, 'Behold, he is in the inner rooms,' do not believe them" (Matt. 24:23–26).

It's possible that the description of events in Matthew 24:23 is different from the signs described by Jesus earlier when He said that many would come in His name saying "I am the Christ" (24:5) and that "false prophets" would arise to "mislead many" (24:11). In all likelihood, Jesus is describing events separated by an interval of time. Jesus gives the impression that His coming in judgment would be near the end of that present generation. False Christs and false prophets would appear soon after His ascension, "but that is not yet the end" (24:6). As Roman oppression increased, the unbelieving Jews embraced an increasing number of messianic figures hoping to be delivered. One of the earliest was Simon, a man who "astonished them with his magic arts." He was thought to be "what is called the Great Power of God" (Acts 8:10).

The Apostle Paul describes those in his day who acted like "Jannes and Jambres," the two sorcerer high priests who "opposed Moses" (2 Tim. 3:8).

They were said to "oppose the truth, men of depraved mind, rejected as regards the faith" (3:8). Jannes and Jambres used "great signs" in an attempt to mislead the people in Moses' day by using deception to duplicate the true miracle of Aaron's rod turning into a serpent (Ex. 7:10–12).

The men Paul had in mind in his day were the same people Jesus warned about in His Olivet Discourse. In fact, Paul himself was thought to be "the Egyptian who some time ago stirred up a revolt and led four thousand men of the Assassins out into the *wilderness*" (Acts 21:38). This incident is reminiscent of Jesus' words about those who will give support for a false prophet claiming that "He is in the *wilderness*" (Matt. 24:26). Those who had rejected their Messiah at the "time of [their] visitation" (Luke 19:44), the same people who wanted "to make Jesus king" to overthrow the tyrants of Rome (John 6:15), were still looking for a political savior right up until the time of Jerusalem's destruction. Josephus writes:

> A false prophet was the occasion of these people's destruction, who had made a public proclamation in the city that very day, that God commanded them to get upon the temple, and that there they should receive miraculous signs of their deliverance. Now, there was then a great number of false prophets suborned by the tyrants to impose upon the people, who denounced this to them, that they should wait for deliverance from God....[25]

Josephus describes how a star resembling a sword stood over the city. He also chronicles the sighting of a comet showing its brightness for a full year. Other inexplicable events are recounted, most of which were probably false but had the effect of persuading the people that their deliverance was at hand: "A heifer, as she was led by the high priest to be sacrificed, brought forth a lamb in the midst of the temple."[26] No doubt false prophets and false messiahs fabricated these stories to bolster their credibility with the terrorized population.

"For just as the lightning comes from the east, and flashes even to the west, so shall the coming of the Son of Man be" (Matt. 24:27).

Jesus would come "just as the lightning comes from the east," that is, quickly and without warning. In the Bible, lightning often signifies the presence of the Lord and His coming in judgment (Ex. 19:16; 20:18; Job 36:30; Ezek. 21:15, 28; Zech. 9:14). God was not physically present during any of these Old Testament comings, but His presence was obvious, as the reaction of the people will testify: "And when the people saw it, they trembled and stood at a distance" (Ex. 20:18). The lightning and thunder did not terrify the people. They had seen such things before. What frightened them was the reality that the Lord had come. What the people saw was the manifestation of the Lord's coming even though they did not actually see Him. In a similar way, lightning is associated with the coming of the Lord in Deuteronomy 33:2: "The LORD *came* from Sinai, and dawned on them from Seir; He *shone forth* from Mount Paran, and He *came* from the midst of ten thousand holy ones; at His right hand there was flashing lightning for them." Was God physically present? He was not. Did He come? Most certainly! Jesus warned the churches of Ephesus (Rev. 2:5), Pergamum (2:16), and Sardis (3:3) that He would come in judgment if they did not repent. Were any of these comings the second coming?

All of the signs listed in Matthew 24 have reference to the destruction of Jerusalem in A.D. 70. While there is no doubt that many today look at current world conditions and surmise that the rapture must be near, this view is impossible based on what we've learned thus far. Jesus established the time frame for Jerusalem's destruction—it would occur within a generation. Before forty years passed, Jerusalem would be "trampled underfoot by the Gentiles until the times of the Gentiles be fulfilled" (Luke 21:24). The "times of the Gentiles" refers to the four kingdom nations depicted in Daniel 2. Rome is obviously the fourth and final kingdom to oppress the Jews. With the destruction of the temple and the city of Jerusalem, the "time of the Gentiles" is completed (see Rev. 11:2).

Claiming that the great tribulation is a past event is not meant to minimize the realities of persecution that take place around the world in our day. We will always have tribulation, tribulation that is overcome in Jesus (John 16:33). Entry into the kingdom comes through "much tribulation" (Acts 14:22). What we will not have is a rapture that will remove us where tribulation is a reality.

The Wrath of the Lamb

Matthew 24:27 reveals that Jesus is somehow participating in Jerusalem's destruction. This is exactly the point. When the temple was ransacked by

Nebuchadnezzar, we read that "*the Lord gave Jehoiakim king of Judah into his hand,*
along with some of the vessels of the house of God" (Dan. 1:2).
Nebuchadnezzar "besieged" Jerusalem, but God orchestrated the entire affair.

> Who gave Jacob up for spoil, and Israel to plunderers?
> Was it not the LORD, against whom we have sinned,
> And in whose ways they were not willing to walk,
> And whose law they did not obey?
> So He poured out on him the heat of His anger
> And the fierceness of battle;
> And it set him aflame all around,
> Yet he did not recognize it;
> And it burned him, but he paid no attention.
>   (Isa. 42:24–25)

Jesus came "like lightning" to set Jerusalem "aflame all around." If you
recall, it was Titus, as God's representative agent, who set the temple on fire
and leveled the edifice. God calls Assyria the "rod of My anger, and the staff
in whose hands is My indignation" (Isa. 10:5). Assyria was sent by God
"against a godless nation ... to capture booty and to seize plunder, And to
trample them down like mud in the streets" (10:6).

In A.D. 70 Rome was sent by God to fulfill a similar task. "Our Lord
forewarns His disciples that His coming to that judgment-scene would be
conspicuous and sudden as the lightning-flash which reveals itself and seems
to be everywhere at the same moment."[27]

On His way to the cross, Jesus had prophesied what would happen to the
generation of Jews who rejected Him: "Daughters of Jerusalem, stop weeping for Me, *but weep for yourselves and for your children.* For behold, the days
are coming when they will say, 'Blessed are the barren, and the wombs that
never bore, and the breasts that never nursed.' Then they will begin TO SAY
TO THE MOUNTAINS, 'FALL ON US, ' AND TO THE HILLS 'COVER US'" (Luke
23:28–30). Who brought this judgment? As Jerusalem's destruction drew
near for that generation, "they said to the mountains and to the rocks, 'Fall
on us and hide us from the presence of *Him who sits on the throne, and from the
wrath of the Lamb*; for the great day of their wrath has come; and who is able
to stand?" (Rev. 6:16–17). It was the "wrath of the Lamb [Jesus]" that brought
judgment to Israel. Luke 23:28–30 was fulfilled before that generation passed

into oblivion. Remember, Jesus told the "Daughters of Jerusalem" to "weep for *yourselves and your children.*" No future generation was in view here. This is more evidence that the Book of Revelation was written *before* Jerusalem was destroyed.[28]

"Wherever the corpse is, there the vultures will gather" (Matt. 24:28).

The Greek word translated "eagle" in many Bible versions is best translated "vulture" in this context. Did Jesus' disciples understand what He had in mind when He uttered this seemingly cryptic saying? Being familiar with the Hebrew Scriptures, they would have immediately recognized the words of Jeremiah judging those who pervert God's covenant (Jer. 7:33).

Jesus was acting out in word and deed the prophecies given to Jeremiah centuries before. Notice the similarities between what Jeremiah and Jesus did. Jeremiah was to "stand in the gate of the LORD's house" and proclaim God's Word to the people (Jer. 7:2; compare with Matt. 23:36; 24:1). The people were not to "trust in deceptive words, saying, 'This is the temple of the LORD, the temple of the LORD, the temple of the LORD'" (Jer. 7:4; compare with Matt. 24:2). The temple was meaningless without obedience: "Thus says the LORD of hosts, the God of Israel, 'Amend your ways and your deeds, and I will let you dwell in this place'" (Jer. 7:3; compare with Matt. 24:5–11). The temple, the house "which is called by My name," God says, has "become a den of robbers" (Jer. 7:11; compare with Matt. 21:13; 24:15).

These deeds had led God to reject and forsake "the generation of His wrath" (Jer. 7:29b; compare with Matt. 23:36; 24:34). How would this rejection take place? Days would come when "*the dead bodies of this people will be food for the birds of the sky,* and for the beasts of the earth; and no one will frighten them away. Then I will make to cease from the cities of Judah and from the streets of Jerusalem the voice of joy and the voice of gladness, the voice of the bridegroom and the voice of the bride; for the land will become a ruin" (Jer. 7:33–34). Later in Jeremiah, God revives His complaint against His disobedient covenant people: "And I shall make void the counsel of Judah and Jerusalem in this place, and I shall cause them to fall by the sword before their enemies and by the hand of those who seek their life; *and I shall give over their carcasses as food for the birds of the sky and the beasts of the earth*" (Jer. 19:7; compare with Matt. 24:28).

The Jerusalem of Jesus' day, because of its dead rituals, was a carcass, food for the scavenging birds, the Roman armies. This is an appropriate description of Jerusalem's acts of abomination. In addition, we know that tens of thousands (Josephus says over a million) were killed during the Roman siege. Even the temple area was not spared. The Idumean and Zealot revolt left thousands slaughtered in and around the temple. A single carcass would render the city and temple area "unclean." According to Numbers 19:11–22, anyone touching the corpse of a human being is unclean: "Anyone who touches a corpse, the body of a man who has died, and does not purify himself, *defiles the tabernacle of the* LORD; and that person shall be cut off from Israel" (19:13). There was no life in Jerusalem since the Lord had departed. As our High Priest, Jesus could no longer remain in the city because of its defilement. It had to be burned with fire for purification.

Just as there is little life left once the vultures have gathered, so with the destruction of the temple and the desolation of the city, the shadow of heavenly things is no more. While the disciples pointed out the then-standing temple, it is up to Jesus' present disciples to point out the "temple of His body" (John 2:21; cf. 1 Cor. 6:19) to those who would seek salvation, not by the blood of bulls and goats, but by the lamb of God who takes away the sins of the world.

Notes

1. Jack Van Impe, "Messiah 1975? The Tribulation 1976?" *The Jack Van Impe Crusade Newsletter* (April 1975), 1.
2. Van Impe, "Messiah 1975?," 1.
3. Salem Kirban, *Countdown to Rapture* (Irvine, CA: Harvest House, 1977), 12.
4. Kirban, *Countdown to Rapture*, 176.
5. Kirban, *Countdown to Rapture*, 177.
6. Kirban, *Countdown to Rapture*, 181, 188.
7. Barbara Reynolds interviews John Walvoord, "Prophecy Clock is Ticking in Mideast," *USA Today* (19 January 1991), 13A. According to dispensationalism, the prophecy clock does not start ticking again until *after* the rapture.
8. John F. Walvoord, *The Prophecy Knowledge Handbook* (Wheaton, IL: Victor Books, 1990), 383.
9. Hal Lindsey, *The 1980's: Countdown to Armageddon* (King of Prussia, PA: Westgate Press, 1980), 8. Emphasis in original.
10. *The Late Great Planet Earth* (Grand Rapids, MI: Zondervan [1970] 1973), 15.
11. "Artswatch," *World* (2 March 1991), 15.
12. Charles Caldwell Ryrie, *The Living End: Enlightening and Astonishing Disclosures about the Coming Last Days of Earth* (Old Tappan, NJ: Fleming H. Revell, 1976), 21.
13. Tim LaHaye, *No Fear of the Storm: Why Christians Will Escape All the Tribulation* (Sisters, OR: Multnomah, 1992), 60. This book has been republished as *Rapture Under Attack: Will Christians Escape the Tribulation?* (1998).
14. LaHaye, *No Fear of the Storm*, 14.
15. Jack Van Impe, *The Great Escape: Preparing for the Rapture, the Next Event on God's Prophetic Clock* (Nashville, TN: Word, 1998), 146.
16. Billy Graham, *Storm Warning* (Dallas, TX: Word, 1992), 25.
17. Graham, *Storm Warning*, 25.
18. Hap Cawood, "If Buying Armageddon Theories, Insist on Money-back Guarantee," *Atlanta Constitution* (9 February 1991), A19.
19. Ralph A. Alexander, "Ezekiel," *The Expositor's Bible Commentary*, Frank E. Gaebelein, gen. ed. (Grand Rapids, MI: Zondervan, 1986), 6:773.
20. Also see William Greenhill, *An Exposition of Ezekiel* (Carlisle, PA: Banner of Truth Trust, [1647–1667], 1994), 145–46.

21. David J. Palm, "The Signs of His Coming: An Examination of the Olivet Discourse from a Preterist Perspective" (Deerfield, IL: Trinity Evangelical Divinity School, 1993), 12–13.

22. Any tribulation the Jews experience in other countries is not in view here. The death of six million Jews at the hands of the Nazis did not take place in the land of Israel. The great tribulation is a description of what happened to Jews living in Israel in the first century. Over one million Jews died at the hands of the Romans. Nothing will ever compare to it because of Israel's special covenantal status. Here sin was great, therefore her judgment was great: "For the iniquity of the daughter of my people is greater than the sin of Sodom, which was overthrown as in a moment, and no hands were turned toward her" (Lam. 4:2).

23. James Stuart Russell, *The Parousia: A Study of the New Testament Doctrine of Our Lord's Second Coming* (Grand Rapids, MI: Baker Book House, [1887] 1999), 429. For a helpful discussion of the meaning of "no life," literally, "all flesh" (Matt. 24:22), see Kenneth L. Gentry, Jr., "The Great Tribulation is Future: Rebuttal," in Thomas Ice and Kenneth L. Gentry, Jr., *The Great Tribulation: Past or Future?—Two Evangelicals Debate the Question* (Grand Rapids, MI: Kregel, 1999), 190–91.

24. Frederick Louis Godet, *Commentary on the Gospel of Luke*, 2 vols. (Grand Rapids, MI: Zondervan [1887] n.d.), 2:267.

25. Josephus, *Wars of the Jews*, 6.5.2, 742–43.

26. Josephus, *Wars of the Jews*, 6.5.3, 742.

27. Russell, *The Parousia*, 76.

28. For the most comprehensive defense of a pre-A.D. 70 date for Revelation, see Kenneth L. Gentry, Jr., *Before Jerusalem Fell: Dating the Book of Revelation*, 2nd ed. (Atlanta, GA: American Vision, 1999).

Chapter Ten

SIGNS IN THE HEAVENS

"Can you imagine 50-pound chunks of ice falling out of the sky? The hailstones would rip through the roof of your house as though it were paper. They would flatten your automobile. Where would you hide? How could you be safe?"[1] From 50-pound chunks of ice to piercing lead projectiles, today's prophetic speculators continue to stretch the imagination and the texts of Scripture to fit their contrived end-time scenarios. "The children of David Koresh's doomsday cult were so prepared for the final battle between good and evil that when bullets rained down on their commune seven weeks ago [February 28, 1993], they believed it was a prophecy fulfilled."[2]

Pat Robertson saw prophetic significance in the Hale-Bopp comet that could be seen with the naked eye in 1997, "one of the few times in recorded history that a comet's appearance coincided with a lunar eclipse." He also claims there might be something to the fact that "three recent eclipses of the moon have coincided with Jewish feasts." Following research done by Greg Killian, Robertson reports that "a Bible passage from Revelation may be playing out in the heavens." Killian maintains "that in Jewish tradition, the new moon represents the Messiah. Since last fall, the moon's path has intersected the constellation Virgo (which depicts a woman) in a way similar to what is described in Revelation 12:1–2." Following Killian, Robertson conjectures that "this scenario will culminate in 1999, when the moon moves across Virgo in a position that depicts a baby moving through the birth canal. Could this convergence be a prophetic fulfillment of that passage, pointing to the Messiah's soon return." After speculating about what the heavens reveal, Robertson closes with the obligatory "We must remember that no man knows the day or the hour...." Still peering over the prophetic edge, he then reminds us that Jesus instructed "us to look to the skies for 'signs' (Luke 21:25)."[3]

Because of heightened interest in things prophetic, the eyes of many biblical soothsayers are looking to the heavens for signs that the end is near. Today's talk about a stray planet or a wayward asteroid hitting Earth brings to mind the sci-fi classic *When Worlds Collide* and the more current *Sudden Impact* and *Armageddon*.[4] Just as a spaceship was built to rescue a few dozen earthlings in a high-tech version of Noah's ark in *When Worlds Collide*, prophecy teachers tell us that the church will escape the devastation of these projectiles by means of the rapture. Hal Lindsey writes: "Without benefit of science, space suits, or interplanetary rockets, there will be those who will be transported into a glorious place more beautiful, more awesome, than we can possibly comprehend.... It will be the living end. The ultimate trip."[5]

During World War II biblical references to falling heavenly bodies were thought to be bombs dropping on the cities of Europe. Supposedly there was even a Russian postage stamp to support the interpretation. The stamp showed apocalyptic symbols—lightning and a hail of bombs falling on the cities of Europe: "It is clear that this last judgment [Rev. 16:17–21] would be manifested through aerial warfare, the hailstones weighing about a talent (or 125 pounds, according to Thompson's Chain-Reference Bible), and the cities falling in heaps, being an exact picture of what the nations are today experiencing as a result of air raids."[6]

Here we have prophecy pundits, separated by a half century, who look at the same Scripture text and make a contemporary application. We know that the reference to World War II was misapplied and *wrong*. But how do we know that contemporary interpreters are any more correct? Why should we believe that "50-pound chunks of ice falling out of the sky" are in *our* future?

For centuries theologians have tried to attach prophetic significance to the appearance of comets and other happenings in the heavens. Increase Mather managed "to find records showing that some 415 comets had appeared 'since the world began.'"[7] In addition to the inventory of comets, he catalogued "the dates on which each comet had appeared, the intervals being filled in with lists of wars, deaths of leaders, famines, floods and plagues."[8] For example, he records that in A.D. 984 "A Blazing Star was seen. An Earth-Quake, Wars, Plague, Famine followed. The Emperor and the Pope died."[9] In retrospect, these heavenly signs were no evidence that the return of Christ was near. Like Mather, his correspondent John Richards saw their importance as God's warning to a sinful world: "God is again threatening a sinful world by tokens of His displeasure, a blazing star appearing again in the heavens…. Great is the patience and long-suffering of God, that is so often warning before He brings desolating judgments."[10]

The Jupiter Non-Effect

In 1982 there was to be an unusual alignment of the planets called the Jupiter Effect. The planets would be in a straight line formation perpendicular to the sun. This alignment—an event that occurs every 179 years according to Gribbin and Plagemann in their book *The Jupiter Effect*—supposedly exerts an uncommon gravitational pull on the planets. Hal Lindsey saw eschatological significance in the Jupiter Effect. He wrote in 1980, "This alignment causes great storms on the sun's surface, which in turn affect each of the planets. The sun storms will not only affect our atmosphere, as was previously mentioned, but they will slow down the Earth's axis slightly."[11] This slowdown, according to Lindsey and his "author-experts," would mean putting "a tremendous strain on the Earth's faults, touching off earthquakes."[12] This new wave of earthquakes was to bring about great floods because dams have been built over fault lines. In addition, we were to see "nuclear power plant meltdowns at facilities built on or near the Earth's faults."[13] What happened? Nothing.

UFO Nonsense

Lindsey included a section on UFOs in his *The 1980s: Countdown to Armageddon* and speculated that increased interest in UFOs fulfilled Jesus' prediction that there will be "terrors and great signs from heaven" just before His return (Luke 21:11).[14] Such terrors and great signs from heaven, Lindsey believes, are unidentified flying objects of the alien variety!

Authorities now admit that there have been confirmed sightings of unidentified flying objects. There are even some baffling cases where people
under hypnosis say they were taken aboard UFOs by beings from space.

Reports held in U.S. Air Force files reveal that whatever these flying
objects are, they move and turn at speeds unmatched by human technology.

It's my opinion that UFOs are real and that there will be a proven "close
encounter of the third kind" soon. And I believe that the source of this
phenomenon is some type of alien being of great intelligence and power.

According to the Bible, a demon is a spiritual personality in a state of
war with God. Prophecy tells us that demons will be allowed to use their
powers of deception in a grand way during the last days of history (2
Thessalonians 2:8–12). I believe these demons will stage a spacecraft
landing on Earth. They will claim to be from an advanced culture in
another galaxy.

They may even claim to have "planted" human life on this planet and
tell us they have returned to check on our progress.[15]

Did you notice Lindsey's progression of thought? First, he quotes a passage from the Bible concerning sun, moon, and stars and how "the powers
of the heavens will be shaken." Nowhere does he try to learn how this
language is used elsewhere in Scripture. Second, he moves to an unsubstan-
tiated belief in UFOs. Third, without ever proving his case, he assumes that
the Bible is actually describing spacecrafts occupied by demons passing
themselves off as aliens from other planets. Fourth, he easily moves to a
prediction that "demons will stage a spacecraft landing on Earth." Fifth, we
are supposed to believe this scenario and the claims of geophysical disrup-
tions based on the "Jupiter Effect" because it's "all in the Bible."

Is it any wonder that Christians are confused over prophecy? How can
the average Christian pick up a Bible and come to these fantastic conclusions? Does the Bible have UFOs and alien spaceships in mind when it
describes signs in the heavens? For example, Charles Ryrie, a noted dispensational writer and author of the notes in the best selling *Ryrie Study Bible*,
asks this question of the imagery in the Book of Revelation: "How do we
make sense out of all those beasts and thrones and horsemen and huge
numbers like 200 million? Answer: Take it at face value. If God intended to
disclose something to us in a book, then we can be confident He wrote it in
such a way as to communicate to us, rather than confuse us."[16]

But later Ryrie gives an example of the usefulness of his "face value" hermeneutic in seeking the correct interpretation of Revelation 9:1–12 (the locusts from the abyss): "John's description sounds very much like some kind of war machine or UFO. Demons have the ability to take different shapes, so it is quite possible that John is picturing a coming invasion of warlike UFOs. Until someone comes up with a satisfactory answer to the UFO question, this possibility should not be ruled out."[17] The first readers of this prophecy would have been utterly confused if this is what God was communicating. In fact, nearly two-thousand years of Christendom would have been confused.

Is this how we are to read the Book of Revelation? Is this interpreting Scripture at "face value"? Belief in UFOs is a rather recent curiosity based on evolutionary "science." Christians from time immemorial knew nothing of such happenings. (Of course, if Erich Von Däniken is to be believed, the Earth was visited by extraterrestrials centuries ago.)[18] If UFOs are the interpretative key to this section of Scripture, then God's Word would have remained a mystery for millions of Christians for centuries.

Cobra Helicopters?

Not to be outdone, Hal Lindsey makes the locusts in Revelation 9 "Cobra helicopters" in the following line of Vietnam-era logic:

> I have a Christian friend who was a Green Beret in Viet Nam. When he first read this chapter he said, "I know what those are. I've seen hundreds of them in Viet Nam. They're Cobra helicopters!"
>
> That may just be conjecture, but it does give you something to think about! A Cobra helicopter does fit the composite description very well. They also make the sound of "many chariots." My friend believes that the means of torment will be a kind of nerve gas sprayed from its tail.[19]

In his more recent works, Lindsey contends that he has been able to decipher the Apocalypse in a way that "many scholars of all Christian denominations have either marveled over ... scoffed at ... or allegorized its prophetic content into absurd historical allegories about the early Christian era."[20] Lindsey attempts to interpret the Book of Revelation as if its message was hidden from those who first read the detailed prophecy. When Lindsey interprets the first three verses of the first chapter, he conveniently passes over two key phrases: the events must "soon take place" (1:1) and the "time is near" (1:3). He concentrates on the "hidden things"—the apocalyptic elements—while dismissing what is explicit—the timing of the events.[21] Has he really cleared things up for us? Has he been able to decipher the "encrypted Biblical symbols"? You be the judge. After quoting Revelation 9:1–10 about "locusts that looked like horses prepared for battle," Lindsey offers the following commentary:

> Note that John keeps saying, "**looked like, something like, resembled, was like,** etc." By these qualifying terms, John sought to emphasize that he was aware of describing vehicles and phenomena far beyond his first century comprehension. So he used symbols drawn from 1st century phenomena that "looked like" these marvels of science. Using a mixed composite of things from the 1st century, he strove to represent what he saw.
>
> With that in mind, let's see if we can find the passage's meaning. The vehicle's overall shape looked to John like a **"locust."** The general outer shape of a helicopter is similar to that of a locust.
>
> The phrase **"horses prepared for battle"** probably means "the attack helicopters" were heavily armored. John had seen Romans drape armor over their horses to protect them from arrows, lances and swords.
>
> At this point John seems to switch to what he saw inside the machine. The phrase **"something like crowns of gold"** most likely describes the elaborate helmets worn by helicopter pilots. And **"their faces resembled human faces. . ."**—as John looked at the front of the helicopter, the face of the pilot appeared through the front windscreen.[22] The appearance of something that looked like **woman's hair** could describe the whirling propeller that looked like filmy hair. Remember, John had never seen a large instrument spinning so fast that it couldn't be seen clearly. The term **teeth** probably describes the weaponry projecting from the "chopper"— there is a monster six-barrel cannon suspended from the nose of most attack helicopters today.[23]

And he accuses preterists of allegorizing Revelation's "prophetic content into absurd historical allegories about the early Christian era." Many Christians will be taken in by this so-called literal interpretation of the Bible. The same passage, following Lindsey's methodology, could apply to the Middle Ages or any era where horses were used in fighting wars. Interpreting "woman's hair" as a "whirling propeller" is as far as one can get from a literal interpretation of the Bible. Did you notice that there was not mention of Vietnam? Lindsey's arguments change with the times. He hopes no one will notice.

Will we get a similar reading when we allow the Bible to interpret itself? In comparing Scripture with Scripture, there is no possible way to come to the conclusions of Ryrie and Lindsey. While it's certainly exciting to read about UFOs, aliens, spaceships, earthquakes, nuclear power plant meltdowns, and any number of fantastic end-time scenarios, we should always ask ourselves this basic question: What does the Bible mean when it describes falling heavenly bodies? In addition, Jesus gave us the time frame for the fulfillment of the events listed in the Olivet Discourse: All of these things, even the darkening of the sun and moon and the falling of the stars from the sky, were fulfilled within a generation. Is this possible? Let the Bible be your guide.

Notes

1. Chuck Smith, "The Second Coming: Any Day Now," *Charisma and Christian Life* (February 1989), 46.
2. Deborah Tedford and Kathy Fair, "Children Awaiting Doomsday Died," *Atlanta Constitution* (20 April 1993), A8.
3. Pat Robertson, "Signs in the Skies," *Pat Robertson's Notepad* (July/August 1997), 1–2.
4. Numerous magazines and newspapers covered the story of Swift-Tuttle, a comet that some say could strike the Earth in the year 2126, even though the odds of such a strike are about 1 in 10,000. See Sharon Begley, "The Science of Doom," *Newsweek* (23 November 1992), 56–60.
5. Hal Lindsey, *The Late Great Planet Earth* (Grand Rapids, MI: Zondervan, [1970] 1971), 137.
6. A.J. Ferris, *When Russia Bombs Germany* (London: Clarendon, [1940] 1941), 58. Postscripts have been added at the end of chapters 2–6. The text of the first edition was left intact. These postscripts attempt to show that the prophecies set out in the September 1940 edition had been fulfilled.
7. Peter Lockwood Rumsey, *Acts of God and the People, 1620–1730* (Ann Arbor, MI: UMI Research, 1986), 103.
8. Rumsey, *Acts of God and the People,* 103.
9. Increase Mather, *Cometographia, A Discourse concerning* COMETS *wherein the nature of* BLAZING STARS *is enquired into: with an Historical Account of all the* COMETS *which have appeared from the Beginning of the World, until this present year,....* (Boston: printed by S.G. for S.S., 1683), 60–61. Quoted in Rumsey, *Acts of God,* 103.
10. A letter from John Richards, a Boston merchant who was serving as Colony agent in London, to Increase Mather (1682). Quoted in Rumsey, *Acts of God,* 103.
11. Hal Lindsey, *The 1980s: Countdown to Armageddon* (King of Prussia, PA: Westgate Press, 1980), 31.
12. Lindsey, *The 1980s,* 31.
13. Lindsey, *The 1980s,* 31.
14. For a discussion of this theme in Lindsey's work, see Timothy Weber, *Living in the Shadow of the Second Coming: American Premillennialism, 1875–1982* (Grand Rapids, MI: Zondervan/Academie, 1983), 218.
15. Lindsey, *The 1980s,* 34–35.

16. Charles C. Ryrie, *The Living End: Enlightening and Astonishing Disclosures about the Coming Last Days of Earth* (Old Tappan, NJ: Fleming H. Revell, 1976), 37.

17. Ryrie, *The Living End,* 45.

18. Erich Von Däniken, *Chariots of the Gods?: Memories of the Future: Unsolved Mysteries of the Past,* trans. Michael Heron (New York: G. Putnam's Sons, 1970) and *Gods from Outer Space: Return to the Stars or Evidence for the Impossible,* trans. Michael Heron (New York: G. Putnam's Sons, 1970). For a helpful treatment of the UFO phenomenon, including an evaluation of Von Däniken, see William M. Alnor, *UFOs in the New Age: Extraterrestrial Messages and the Truth of Scripture* (Grand Rapids, MI: Baker Book House, 1992).

19. Hal Lindsey, *There's a New World Coming* (New York: Bantam Books, [1973] 1984), 124.

20. Hal Lindsey, *Apocalypse Code* (Palos Verde, CA: Western Front Ltd., 1997), 31.

21. Lindsey, *Apocalypse Code,* 33.

22. Notice that John writes that "their faces *resembled* human faces." Lindsey says that they *are* human faces.

23. Lindsey, *Apocalypse Code,* 42.

Chapter Eleven

SUN, MOON, AND STARS

The tribulation described in Matthew 24 took place just prior to the destruction of Jerusalem in A.D. 70 upon the city and the people who rejected the Messiah, the same city that Jesus wept over, and the same people who said, "His blood be on us and on our children!" (Matt. 27:25). It was this Jerusalem, that "kills the prophets and stones those who are sent to her" (23:37), that experienced this "great tribulation."

With this in mind, it's important to notice that verse 29 begins with, "But *immediately after* the tribulation of those days." Whatever verse 29 means, it follows "immediately after" the tribulation described in verses 15–28. "'Immediately' does not usually make room for much of a time gap—certainly not a gap of over 2000 years."[1] Matthew uses "immediately" to mean without delay or gaps in time (Matt. 3:16; 4:20, 22; 8:3; 13:5, 20; 14:22; 20:34; 21:12; 26:74). We should expect the word to have the same meaning in 24:29.

Luke writes that certain signs would occur some time before the end, that is, a number of years before Jerusalem was destroyed in A.D. 70. Jesus warned His disciples not to be "frightened" when they saw these signs (Matt. 24:6). The "end [Jerusalem's destruction] does not follow immediately" after these early signs (Luke 21:9). The early signs that Matthew describes are merely "the *beginning* of birth pangs" (24:8). The events of Luke 21:9 should be placed between verses 6 and 7 of Matthew 24.

When the tribulation of "those days" is completed, the end of the temple and city is near. As the time for Jerusalem's judgment draws ever closer, certain other signs would appear. These later signs are descriptive of the fall of nations and kingdoms. "Jesus is declaring that, immediately after the tribulation of those days surrounding Jerusalem's fall, believers would witness the breakup of all that had seemed most permanent and durable before. This great Day of the Lord would signal the end of the existing dispensation."[2]

"But immediately after the tribulation of those days THE SUN WILL BE DARKENED, AND THE MOON WILL NOT GIVE ITS LIGHT, AND THE STARS WILL FALL *from the sky, and the powers of the heavens will be shaken" (Matt. 24:29).*

As was said above, the darkening of the sun and moon and the falling of the stars occurs "immediately after" the events of verses 15–28. No gap in time is suggested or intimated. But how is it possible that the sun, moon, and stars underwent radical changes in the first century without affecting the earth in any way? Should we be looking for a future cosmic catastrophe or does Jesus have something else in mind?

The Sun, Moon, and Stars

Should we expect the sun literally to be darkened and the moon to cease reflecting the light from the sun? Will literal stars fall from heaven? With God all things are possible; however, since Jesus' disciples did not ask about the end of the world (*kosmos*), and Jesus was not describing the end of the physical world, we would do better to survey how the Old Testament uses and applies this language than to allow our imaginations to run wild. Even those expositors who believe the events described in Matthew 24:29–31 are still future do not maintain that Jesus is describing the end of the world.

The Book of Revelation describes stars falling to the Earth (6:13; notice the cross reference in the New American Standard Version: Matt. 24:29). How can *stars* fall to the Earth and the Earth survive? Revelation 12:4 says that the tail of the "great dragon" (12:3) "swept away a third of the stars of heaven and threw them to the earth." Stars are much larger than Earth. One star would vaporize our planet, let alone "a third of the stars of heaven." John F. Walvoord quotes E.W. Bullinger approvingly: "It is impossible for us to take this as symbolical; or as other than what it literally says. The difficulties of the symbolical interpretation are insuperable, while *no difficulties whatever* attend the literal interpretation."[3] No difficulties whatever?

Stars as Meteorites?

A seemingly plausible explanation for Walvoord is that the "stars" are actually meteorites. But if they are meteorites in Revelation 6:13 and 12:4, then they are meteorites in Matthew 24:29. Again, "a third of the *meteorites* of heaven" would have a devastating effect on our planet. Earth would cease to exist. Scientists have speculated that a single meteorite threw up enough debris upon impact with Earth that it "ended the reign of the dinosaurs.... The colossal energy released in its collision with Earth is now estimated to be equal to the detonation of up to 300 million hydrogen bombs, each some 70 times bigger than the atomic bomb that destroyed Hiroshima."[4] Supposedly these meteorites crash to earth during a seven-year period following the rapture. Jesus would then be ruling over a burned out cinder during the millennium since, according to dispensationalists, the "new heaven and new earth" does not take place until *after* His millennial reign. Additionally, if the "stars" of Revelation 6:13, 12:4 and Matthew 24:29 are meteorites, then this would mean that these passages are not to be interpreted "literally," an interpretive *faux pas* for the literalist. There is a better, more biblical, interpretive solution.

Stars as People and Nations

The language that Jesus uses is typical of Old Testament imagery where stellar phenomena represent people and nations. The people of Israel were represented as stars (Gen. 22:17; 26:4; Deut. 1:10). The flags of many nations include the use of multiple stars (United States, Australia, Brazil, China, Honduras, Iraq, New Zealand, Panama, Papua-New Guinea, Venezuela), a single star (Cameroon, Cuba, Israel, Senegal, Suriname, Vietnam, Yemen, Jordan, North Korea, Liberia), the moon and star (Algeria, Comoros, Mauritania, Pakistan, Singapore, Tunisia, Turkey), the moon and sun (Malaysia), and the sun (Japan, Malawi).

Stars as the Religious and Civil State of Israel

The Old Testament is filled with solar, lunar, and stellar language depicting great political and social upheaval. The rise of kingdoms is compared to the brightness of the sun, moon, and stars. The brightness of these heavenly bodies means that a nation is in ascendancy. When a nation is described as falling—coming under the judgment of God—it is compared to the sun and moon going dark and stars falling from the sky. We describe a person on the way up as a "rising star." When a well-known person is found to have done wrong, we say "his star is tarnished" or "his star has fallen."

Before the advent of speculative exegesis, most Bible commentators who studied the whole Bible understood the relationship of collapsing-universe language with the destruction of the religious and civil state of the Jewish nation.

- "That is, the Jewish heaven shall perish, and the *sun* and *moon* of its glory and happiness shall be darkened—brought to nothing. The *sun* is the religion of the [Jewish] *church*; the *moon* is the government of the [Jewish] *state*; and the *stars* are the judges and doctors of both. Compare Isa. xiii. 10; Ezek. xxxii. 7, 8."[5]
- "The darkening of the sun and moon, the falling of the stars, and the shaking of the powers of the heavens, denote the utter extinction of the light of prosperity and privilege to the Jewish nation; the unhinging of their whole constitution in church and state; the violent subversion of the authority of their princes and priests; the abject miseries to which the people in general, especially their chief persons, would be reduced; and the moral or religious darkness to which they would be consigned."[6]
- "Thus it is that in the prophetic language great commotions and revolutions upon earth, are often represented by commotions and changes in the heavens."[7]
- "Our Saviour goes on, to set forth the calamities that should befall the Jewish nation, immediately after the destruction of Jerusalem. So entire was the subversion of their ecclesiastical and civil state, that it may be metaphorically represented by the sun, moon, and stars, losing their light, and all the heavenly bodies being dissolved...."[8]
- "In ancient Hieroglyphic writings the sun, moon, and stars represented empires and states, with their sovereigns and nobility. The eclipse of

these luminaries was said to denote temporary national disasters, or an entire overthrow of any state. This is still an Eastern mode of writing, and there are some classical examples of it. The Prophets frequently employ it, so that their style seems to be *a speaking hieroglyphic.* Thus Isaiah describes the destruction of Babylon, and Ezekiel that of Egypt— In accordance with this prediction, Josephus gives an account of the persecution and slaughter of the nobility and principal men in the city by the infuriated Zealots, computing their number at twelve thousand."[9]

Is this speculation on the part of these commentators, or does the Bible support their interpretation of stellar imagery?

Stars as Symbols of Kings and Kingdoms

Where in Scripture do we find nations compared to heavenly bodies? As with all Bible study, it is best to start at the beginning. The first chapter of Genesis gives us a clue as to why the Bible compares the sun, moon, and stars to rulers and their kingdoms: The sun ("greater light") and the moon ("lesser light") are said to *"govern* the day" and "night" (Gen. 1:16). Can we find examples of the sun and moon being used as symbols of government? In a dream Joseph saw "the sun and the moon and eleven stars ... bowing down" to him (37:9). The sun, moon, and stars represented Joseph's father, mother, and brothers. Joseph, being only "seventeen years old" (37:2), was under the government of his father, mother, and older brothers. In reality, they ruled over Joseph. Upon hearing about Joseph's dream, Jacob asked him, "What is this dream that you have had? *Shall I and your mother and your brothers actually come to bow ourselves down before you to the ground?"* (37:10). Joseph's father and brothers immediately understood the significance of the images in his dream. They were not looking for the sun, moon, and stars to bow down before Joseph.

Stars are used as symbols of earthly rulers and governments in other places in Scripture. Judges 5:19–20 is a good example. In verse 19 we read that "kings came and fought." In verse 20 we read that "the stars fought from heaven." Both verses are describing the same event in terms of Hebrew parallelism. The stars are symbols of kings and their armies. Stars as we see them in space were not fighting from heaven. Even Bible commentators who insist on interpreting the Bible literally are not always consistent. Consider how the following literalists interpret stellar phenomena:

- "In ancient cultures these astronomical symbols represented rulers."[10]
- "The second dream involved celestial images—the sun, moon, and stars being easily recognized for their significance for rulership."[11]
- "[A]lmost the same symbols appeared in the visions of the apostle John (Revelation 12:1), again probably representing Israel and the twelve tribes."[12]

New Testament Examples

The New Testament picks up on this imagery of Israel being represented by the sun, moon, and stars. In the Book of Revelation we find a descriptive image of a woman dressed in a rather unusual way. There is no mistaking the stellar imagery: "And a great sign appeared in heaven: a woman clothed with the sun, and the moon under her feet, and on her head a crown of twelve stars; and she was with child; and she cried out, being in labor and in pain to give birth" (Rev. 12:1–2). This likeness is a picture of Israel in her glory giving birth to the Messiah, the long-awaited Savior of Israel and the world (Luke 2:29–32; cf. Isa. 54:1–3 and Gal. 4:26; contrast this with rebellious Israel as the harlot in Ezekiel 16 and the "mother of harlots" in Rev. 17). The following commentators (two of whom insist on a "literal interpretation" of Revelation) interpret Revelation 12:1–2 in a non-literal fashion; that is, the sun, moon, and stars *represent* something other than the literal sun, moon, and stars.

- "The **sun, moon,** and **stars** indicate a complete system of government and remind the reader of Genesis 37:9. God had caused royal dignity to rest in Israel in the line of David."[13]
- "The description of the woman as clothed with the sun and the moon is an allusion to Genesis 37:9–11, where these heavenly bodies *represent* Jacob and Rachel, thereby identifying the woman with the fulfillment of the Abrahamic covenant. In the same context, the stars *represent* the patriarchs, the sons of Jacob. The *symbolism* may extend beyond this to *represent* in some sense the glory of Israel and her ultimate triumph over her enemies."[14]
- "[The woman] is not simply Mary, the actual mother of Jesus; nor Mary's ancestress Eve, whose offspring was to be the serpent's great enemy (Gn. 3:15); nor even all mothers in the chosen line between them. For regarded as a 'sign,' she is adorned with the splendour of sun, moon,

and twelve stars, which in a parallel Old Testament dream (Joseph's in Gn. 37:9–11) represent the whole family of Israel…. She is in fact the church: the old Israel [Acts 7:38], 'the human stock from which Christ came' (Rom. 9:5, Knox), and the new Israel, whom he has now left in order to go back to his Father…."[15]

By combining the imagery of the sun, moon, and stars in Matthew 24:29, Jesus describes Israel as a nation, drawing the symbolism from Genesis 37:9. While the passage in Revelation 12 shows Israel in her glory—giving birth to the Messiah—Matthew 24:29 depicts Israel in decline as the nation that rejected her Messiah. The allusion in Matthew 24:29 is unmistakable: Israel's judgment was to take place before that generation passed away.

Lights Out!

In speaking of the sun and moon going dark and stars falling (Matt. 24:29), Jesus describes the nation of Israel under judgment. Here is how one writer depicts it: "The signs in the heavens, the darkening sun and the falling stars, refer to the falling Jewish dignitaries, casting down of authorities and powers, long established, and signifies the darkness that settled upon the Jewish state. The sun of the Hebrew temple was darkened, the moon of the Jewish commonwealth was as blood, the stars of the Sanhedrin fell from their high seats of Authority."[16] Remember, Jesus wept over the city of *Jerusalem* because He foresaw its destruction (Matt. 23:37–39).

The dispute over what this passage means does not center on God's ability to cause the sun and moon to go dark and the stars to fall. Rather, the issue is what Jesus means by the use of this type of language. Only a study of Scripture itself will tell us.

We might fill volumes with extracts showing how exegetes and writers of New Testament doctrine assume as a principle not to be questioned that such highly wrought language as Matt. xxiv, 29–31 … taken almost *verbatim* from Old Testament prophecies of judgment on nations and kingdoms which long ago perished, must be literally understood. Too little study of Old Testament ideas of judgment, and apocalyptic language and style, would seem to be the main reason for this one sided exegesis. It will require more than assertion to convince thoughtful men that the figurative language of Isaiah and Daniel, admitted on all hands to be such in those ancient prophets, is to be literally interpreted when used by Jesus or Paul.[17]

Keep in mind that all the events in Matthew 24:1–34, including those events in verse 29, took place within a generation of Jesus' making the prediction: "This generation will not pass away until *all these things take place"* (24:34).

The downfall of a king and nation is like the darkening of the sun and moon and the falling of stars from the sky. How do we know this? Isn't this "spiritualizing" and "allegorizing"? Aren't we supposed to interpret the Bible literally? Actually, we are to interpret the Bible in the way the Bible interprets itself. A wooden literalism is an impossibility, as nearly every Bible commentator recogniznes.

In each verse of Matthew 24 we have looked to the Bible for our interpretation. In each case the Bible is its own best interpreter, as we would expect. Why should we stop with this method when we come to verses that describe happenings to the sun, moon, and stars? The Bible is still our best hermeneutical manual. How can we avoid seeing every earthquake and astronomical phenomenon as a prelude to the end? Study the Bible and see how it uses the language of the heavens:

> The imagery of cosmic phenomena is used in the Old Testament to describe *this-worldly* events and, in particular, historical acts of judgment. The following passages are significant, not the least because of their affinities with the present context [i.e., Matt. 24]: Isa. 13:10 (predicting doom on Babylon); Isa. 34:4 (referring to "all the nations," but especially to Edom); Ezek. 32:7 (concerning Egypt); Amos 8:9 (the Northern Kingdom of Israel); Joel 2:10 (Judah). The cosmic imagery draws attention to the divine dimension of the event in which the judgment of God is enacted. The use of Joel 2:28–32 in Acts 2:15–21 provides an instance of the way in which such prophetic cosmic imagery is applied to historical events in the present (cf. also Lk. 10:18; Jn. 12:31; 1 Thess. 4:16; 2 Pet. 3:10ff.; Rev. 6:12–17; 18:1). Other Old Testament passages relevant to the interpretation of the present context are Isa. 19:1; 27:13; Dan. 7:13; Deut. 30:4; Zech. 2:6; 12:10–14; Mal. 3:1. In view of this, Mark 13:24–30 may be interpreted as a prophecy of judgment on Israel in which the Son of man will be vindicated. Such a judgment took place with the destruction of Jerusalem, the

desecration of the Temple and the scattering of Israel—all of which happened within the lifetime of "this generation." The disintegration of Israel as the people of God coincides with the inauguration of the kingdom of the Son of man. Such an interpretation fits the preceding discourse and the introductory remarks of the disciples. (Mk. 13:1ff. par.)[18]

The evidence for understanding such language figuratively is overwhelming. To come to any other conclusion is to reject the clear teaching of Scripture and to opt for the wild speculations of those who tout the supposed prophetic mysteries of unidentified flying objects, demons masquerading as aliens, and scientific crackpots who believe they can calculate the second coming of Christ.

Old Testament Parallels

The only written revelation Jesus had and His disciples knew was what we call the Old Testament. There are no secret codes in Scripture, contrary to what books like *The Bible Code* insist.[19] Nothing is hidden to the trained student of the Old Testament Scriptures. When Jesus wanted to define Himself, He pointed His disciples to the only reliable dictionary: "And beginning with Moses and with all the prophets, He explained to them the things concerning Himself in all the Scriptures…. Now He said to them, 'These are My words which I spoke to you while I was with you, that all things which are written about Me in the Law of Moses and the Prophets and the Psalms must be fulfilled'" (Luke 24:27, 44).

The disciples were not left in the dark by Jesus' seemingly cryptic words in Matthew 24. Their hearts burned within them as He spoke to them on the Emmaus road, while He was explaining the Scriptures to them (Luke 24:32). When does your heart burn? When you read the latest prophetic prognosticators and their speculations about the timing of the rapture based on events in Europe, Russia, China, and Isael? Our hearts should burn when we study God's Word for the correct interpretation of prophetic passages: "Let God be found true, though every man be found a liar" (Rom. 3:4).

The language used by Jesus in Matthew 24 was familiar. The disciples had heard it before. They knew what Jesus meant when He described the sun and moon going dark and the stars falling from the sky. The end of a nation was at hand.

"Lights Out" for Babylon

Isaiah wrote that "the day of the LORD is coming," and when it comes,

> The stars of heaven and their constellations will not flash
> forth their light; the sun will be dark when it rises, and the
> moon will not shed its light.
>
> (Isa. 13:9–10)

This is a description of a localized judgment of a world power that existed long ago. Who did God raise up to judge Babylon? "Behold, I am going to stir up the Medes against them" (13:17a). This proves that the Babylon of long ago is the object of judgment. The day of "destruction" which came from "the Almighty" (13:6) is described with graphic expressions: "Hands will fall limp" (13:7); "every man's heart will melt" (13:7); "they will writhe like a woman in labor" (13:8). When the day of the LORD comes, it will be "cruel, with fury and burning anger, to make the land a desolation" (13:9). Even dispensational scholar John Martin interprets Isaiah in a non-literal way:

> The statements in 13:10 about the heavenly bodies (**stars ... sun ...
> moon**) no longer functioning may figuratively describe the total turn-
> around of the political structure of the Near East. The same would be true
> of **the heavens** trembling **and the earth** shaking (v. 13), figures of speech
> suggesting all-encompassing destruction.[20]

The disciples immediately recognized the source and meaning of Jesus' words. They understood that Israel would come under a judgment similar to that of Babylon.[21] *The language is identical.* The interpretation should be equally *identical.* Jerusalem would be treated like the pagan nation of Babylon. This is why Jesus appropriates and applies the Babylon language to Israel and the Book of Revelation characterizes Israel as Babylon (14:8), "the enemy of the true people of the covenant God."[22]

"Lights Out" for Egypt

The destruction of Pharaoh and Egypt is described in a similar way. It is not coincidental that Jerusalem is said to be "Egypt" in Revelation 11:8. Both in Egypt and Jerusalem God's faithful people were persecuted. The

Jerusalem of the first century sought to kill those who taught that Jesus was the promised redeemer.

> And when I extinguish you,
> I will cover the heavens, and darken their stars;
> I will cover the sun with a cloud,
> And the moon shall not give its light.
> All the shining lights in the heavens
> I will darken over you
> And will set darkness on your land.
>
> (Ezek. 32:7–8)

Egypt's conqueror was Babylon (32:11). This language is analogous to the words Jesus used in Matthew 24:29. If the prophecy is not "literal" (using the modern sense of the word) for Babylon and Egypt, then we should not expect it to be "literal" for Jerusalem.

"Lights Out" for Edom

While Scripture describes one nation bringing down the fortunes of another nation, we know that God is behind it all. God is in heaven, but "His sword" finds its way to earth through the terror of other kingdoms. Again, descriptions of happenings in the heavens form the backdrop for national upheaval in the description of the end of a political era.

> And all the host of heaven will wear away,
> And the sky will be rolled up like a scroll;
> All their hosts will also wither away
> As a leaf withers from the vine,
> Or as one withers from the fig tree.
> For My sword is satiated in heaven,
> Behold it shall descend for judgment upon Edom,
> And upon the people whom I have devoted to
> destruction.
>
> (Isa. 34:4–5)

God did not come down *physically* to mete out judgment upon Edom. But the text states that His sword "shall descend for judgment upon Edom."

Did a sword come down from heaven? Did the host of heaven "wear away"? Was the sky "rolled up like a scroll"? Certainly not in literal terms. Again, such language is simply a description of Edom's national judgment.

"Lights Out" for Israel

God had condemned Israel's disdain for things holy by informing the people that He would reject their "festivals" and their "solemn assemblies" (Amos 5:21). "Even though you offer up to Me burnt offerings and your grain offerings, I will not accept them; and I will not even look at the peace offerings of your fatlings" (5:22). In a word, the worship practices of Israel had become an *abomination* in God's sight. Their deeds would bring on "the day of the LORD":

> Alas, you who are longing for the day of the LORD,
> For what purpose will the day of the LORD be to you?
> It will be *darkness and not light.*
>
> (Amos 5:18)

Again, God tells them:

> "And it will come about in that day,"
> declares the LORD GOD, "That I shall make *the sun go down at noon*, and make the earth *dark* in broad daylight."
>
> (Amos 8:9)

While this passage could be describing a solar eclipse, it is more natural and biblical to see it as a description of divine displeasure and judgment. Assyria had put Israel's political lights out while Babylon extinguished the lights of Judah. Rome had eclipsed the political lights of Israel in Jesus' day. Israel could do very little in its ecclesiastical and political courts without Roman permission (John 18:31). Israel was a captive nation that had to live within the confines of Roman law.

What was true in principle would become true in reality. Israel's entire ecclesiastical and political systems were judged when Roman troops sacked, looted, and burned the city.

If these cataclysmic events are correctly interpreted as applying to Israel's defeat, then it is clear that immediately after their national disaster of 70

A.D., the once-exalted, unique theocracy of Israel went into permanent eclipse as God's light-bearers before the nations. (Study Heb. 12:25–29 as commentary on this transition.) Now the Church of Christ occupies this glorious position (Phil. 2:15f.; John 8:12; Matt. 5:14ff.; I Peter 2:9f.). Although Christianity would be established at a time when kingdoms, thrones and religious systems would be thoroughly shaken, it would be a Kingdom that shall never be shaken or replaced by anything better this side of glory (Dan. 2:44; 7:14; Heb. 12:28). From the viewpoint of Jesus' contemporaries, the loss of Judaism's glory would be a world-shaking tragedy indeed, an eclipse. From God's point of view, however, the removal of things that can be shaken in order to establish a Kingdom that cannot be shaken is but to treat the former as obsolete. What, for Him, was already growing old was ready to vanish away even in the first century (Heb. 8:13; 12:27f.).[23]

The Old Covenant order ended in principle at the time of Jesus' death, resurrection, and ascension. Jesus gave the nation forty years after this to gather under God's "wings" by embracing the gospel message (Matt. 23:37). Israel's refusal to repent and embrace its Messiah brought promised judgment. Israel's star had fallen.

Stellar Signs of Blessing

When God wants to demonstrate Israel's obedience and her resultant blessing, He also uses stellar language. But notice the difference: "And the light of the moon will be as the light of the sun, and the light of the sun will be seven times brighter, like the light of seven days" (Isaiah 30:26). This is just the Bible's way of saying that "the LORD binds up the fracture of His people and heals the bruise" (30:26). God's sovereign mercy is poured out on a repentant people. If the language was meant to be taken literally, the earth would be burned to a crisp, especially when we read that the "sun will set no more, neither will your moon wane" (60:20). Again, this type of language is used to reflect God's mercy: "But you will have the LORD for an everlasting light, and the days of your mourning will be finished" (60:20).

We can conclude that "immediately after the tribulation of those days" (Matt. 24:29) national Israel no longer held the place of prominence for the nations (Gen. 37:9; Deut. 4:6; Lam. 1:1; Ezek. 5:5; 16:14; Rev. 12:1; 17:18).

Her brightness was eclipsed by another nation as Jesus had promised: "The kingdom of God will be taken away from you [apostate Israel], and be given to a nation producing the fruit of it [the new Israel of God]" (Matt. 21:43). "A HOLY NATION, A PEOPLE FOR GOD'S OWN POSSESSION" (1 Peter 2:9), arose from the rubble of a desolated Israel.

Notes

1. Paul T. Butler, *The Gospel of Luke* (Joplin, MO: College Press, 1981), 485. Quoted in William R. Kimball, *What the Bible Says About the Great Tribulation* (Grand Rapids, MI: Baker Book House, 1985), 155.

2. Harold Fowler, *The Gospel of Matthew* (Joplin, MO: College Press, 1985), 4:481.

3. E.W. Bullinger, *The Apocalypse* (London: Eyre & Spottiswoode, 1902), 274. Emphasis added. Quoted in John W. Walvoord, *The Revelation of Jesus Christ* (Chicago, IL: Moody Press, 1966), 137.

4. William J. Broad, "New Clue to Cosmic Collision and Demise of the Dinosaurs," *New York Times* (17 September 1993), A8.

5. John Lightfoot, *A Commentary on the New Testament from the Talmud and Hebraica: Matthew—1 Corinthians* (Peabody, MA: Hendrickson Publishers, [1859] 1989), 319–20.

6. Thomas Scott, *The Holy Bible Containing the Old and New Testaments, According to the Authorized Version; with Explanatory Notes, Practical Observations, and Copious Marginal References*, 3 vols. (New York: Collins and Hannay, 1832), 3:110.

7. Thomas Newton, *Dissertations on the Prophecies, Which Have Remarkably Been Fulfilled, and at this Time are Fulfilling in the World* (London: J.F. Dove, 1754), 362.

8. W. Dalton, *An Explanatory and Practical Commentary on the New Testament*, 2 vols. (London: R.B. Seeley and W. Burnside, 1842), 1:118.

9. John Forster, *The Gospel-Narrative* (London: John W. Parker, 1847), 307.

10. Allen Ross, "Genesis," *The Bible Knowledge Commentary: Old Testament*, eds. John F. Walvoord and Roy B. Zuck (Wheaton, IL: Victor Books, 1985), 87.

11. Allen Ross, *Creation and Blessing: A Guide to the Study and Exposition of Genesis* (Grand Rapids, MI: Baker Book House, 1988), 600.

12. Henry M. Morris, *The Genesis Record* (Grand Rapids, MI: Baker Book House, 1976), 537.

13. Charles L. Feinberg, "Revelation," *Liberty Bible Commentary: New Testament*, eds. Jerry Falwell and Edward E. Hindson (Lynchburg, VA: OldTime Gospel Hour, 1982), 820.

14. John F. Walvoord, *The Revelation of Jesus Christ*, 188. Emphasis added.

15. Michael Wilcock, *I Saw Heaven Opened: The Message of Revelation* (Downers Grove, IL: InterVarsity Press, 1976), 118–19.

16. Foy E. Wallace, Jr., *The Book of Revelation* (Fort Worth, TX: Foy E. Wallace Publications, 1966), 354.

17. Milton Terry, *Biblical Hermeneutics: A Treatise on the Interpretation of the Old and New Testaments* (Grand Rapids, MI: Zondervan, [1890] 1974), 596.

18. Colin Brown, "Generation," *The International Dictionary of New Testament Theology,* 3 vols. (Grand Rapids, MI: Zondervan, 1976), 2:38.

19. Michael Drosnin, *The Bible Code* (New York: Simon and Schuster, 1997).

20. John A. Martin, "Isaiah," *The Bible Knowledge Commentary,* 1059.

21. This is further evidence that Jerusalem is "Babylon" in Revelation 17–18, not a revived Roman empire. See Cornelius Vanderwaal, *Hal Lindsey and Biblical Prophecy* (St. Catherines, Ontario, Canada: Paideia Press, 1978).

22. N. T. Wright, *Jesus and the Victory of God* (Minneapolis, MN: Fortress Press, 1996), 354.

23. Fowler, *The Gospel of Matthew,* 4:482.

Chapter Twelve

THE RETURN
OF CHRIST

In *The Daily Oklahoman,* on July 25, 1986, the following advertisement appeared in the "Special Notices" section: "CHRIST IS COMING." The advertisement was not simply stating the *fact* of Jesus' coming. It was a warning that He was coming *soon.* Dates had been set. To back up the claim, the man who placed the advertisement made some peripheral predictions. He predicted that then-President Ronald Reagan was to be in Jerusalem on May 15, 1988. The former president was to be killed in a U.S.S.R. invasion attempt. Last days madness had struck again.

Dave Hunt, a popular end-times writer, asks this question about the future coming of Christ: "How close are we?" He writes that there is "compelling evidence for the soon return of Christ."[1] Hunt's book ignores passages which describe Jesus' coming as being "soon" and "near" for those who read the prophecies, that is, those living in the first-century. He reformulates the Bible's clear statements of nearness into a time frame that makes Jesus' coming an "any moment rapture." Such a position strips the Bible of meaning. "Soon" and "near" cannot mean an undetermined period of time if one claims to interpret the Bible literally.

History is a great teacher if we study and learn its lessons. Speculation on when Jesus will return is a preoccupation that never seems to go away. Conditions for Jesus' return always appear to be favorable. As one failed set of predictions is discarded, a new but no wiser prophet surfaces to take up the banner of prophetic certainty in the belief that past generations did not have the right prophetic key. We are told that as we get nearer to the end the signs become more clear.

Are There Any Signs?

In light of constant date setting, can Christians ever assert that Jesus' return is near in our day? To ask it another way: Can we point to *any* signs that would indicate that Jesus' coming is imminent for us? The answer is no. If you wonder why generation after generation of prophetic speculation has been off the mark, this is it. A series of signs that can be fit together in puzzle-like fashion giving us a picture of when Jesus will return does not exist. All attempts to make predictions, even a generalized prediction that "the antichrist is most certainly alive" somewhere in the world today,[2] or that one "expects the Rapture to occur in his own lifetime,"[3] or that "we live in the generation that will see Armageddon,"[4] are dangerous and unscriptural.

But what about the events described by Jesus in Matthew 24, Mark 13, and Luke 21? As has been demonstrated in previous chapters, the events rehearsed in the Olivet Discourse are signs leading up to and including the destruction of Jerusalem in A.D. 70. These chapters have nothing to do with when Jesus will return at the final judgment.

So, then, when will Jesus return? The only "sign" the Bible gives us is the fullness of the kingdom, "when He has abolished all rule and authority and power. For He must reign until He has put all His enemies under His feet" (1 Cor. 15:24–25). We know that Jesus is presently reigning over the universe from heaven. Heaven is His throne and earth is His footstool (Isa. 66:1). He will continue to reign in this manner until all His enemies are put under His feet (Psalm 110:1; Acts 2:35). When this is accomplished, Jesus will return to judge the living and the dead. It will be at that time when "the dead in Christ shall rise first. Then we who are alive and remain shall be caught up together with them in the clouds to meet the Lord in the air, and thus *we shall always be with the Lord*" (1 Thess. 4:16–17). This verse—a favorite of those who believe in a two-stage coming of Jesus prior to the establishment of an earthly millennium—says nothing about a rapture, either pre-, mid-, or post-tribulational. Not a word is said about an earthly, political millennium ruled by Jews with Jesus reigning from Jerusalem in the midst of a rebuilt temple, a reestablished priesthood, and a bloody sacrificial system. When the event described in 1 Thessalonians 4:16–17 occurs, "we shall always be with the Lord." Nothing else is said to follow this event. The entire futurist scenario is based upon unproven assumptions that are read into this text.

The Coming of the Son of Man

How, then, do we interpret Matthew 24:30 and its reference to the Son of Man coming "on the clouds of glory"? Which event does this verse describe? A future rapture, either pre-, mid-, or post-tribulational? The bodily appearing of Christ with His saints to set up His earthly millennial kingdom? The return of Christ to judge the living and the dead at the end of earthly history just prior to a renovated universe? Jesus stated that the coming described in Matthew 24:30 would occur before that generation passed away; therefore, we are left to conclude that the prophecy has something to do with the destruction of Jerusalem in A.D. 70 and nothing to do with modern speculation about a so-called rapture or the bodily return of Christ.

"And then the sign of the Son of Man will appear in the sky, and then all the tribes of the earth will mourn, and they will see the SON OF MAN COMING ON THE CLOUDS OF THE SKY with power and great glory" (Matt. 24:30).

Part of the difficulty in interpreting this verse lies in the translation, a point we will address below. In addition to translation problems, however, there is a consideration of the direction of Jesus' coming. Is Jesus "coming down" to rapture His church? Is He coming to Earth to set up His thousand-year millennial kingdom? The passage says nothing about a rapture. There is no mention of the establishment of a millennial kingdom after the period of tribulation that was explained in such detail in the preceding verses of Matthew 24. Why the particulars about the Great Tribulation and so few particulars about a so-called rapture or an earthly millennial kingdom if these events immediately follow His coming? Notice that there is no mention of a rebuilt temple or the establishment of a future Israeli state. The silence is deafening.

Jesus' description of His coming in *that* generation differs little from the way Micah describes the coming of Jehovah to judge Samaria and Jerusalem centuries before Jesus' incarnation.

> Hear, O peoples, all of you; listen, O earth and all it contains. And let the Lord GOD be a witness against you, the Lord from His holy temple. For behold, the LORD is coming forth from His place. He will come down and tread on the high places of the earth. The mountains will melt under Him, and the valleys will be split, like wax before the fire, like water poured down a steep place (Micah 1:2–4; compare Zech. 14:4).

The LORD is said to come "forth from His place" to "come down and tread on the high places of the earth."[5] In what way did this take place? Was this a physical/bodily coming so the people actually saw Jehovah? Did the mountains really melt? Did the valleys split? This coming of Jehovah in judgment is directed against the two seats of government in Israel, Samaria in the north and Jerusalem in the south, prior to the Assyrian and Babylonian captivities. The New Testament uses nearly identical language to describe Jesus' judgment-coming on Jerusalem in A.D. 70 (Matt. 24:29).

Coming on the Clouds

The cloud-language of Matthew 24:30 is similar to the imagery of the previous verses and their description of the darkening of the sun and moon and the falling of stars. What is the association of clouds with God? First, God showed Himself by the physical presence of clouds, although no one ever saw Him (*e.g.*, Ex. 13:21; 14:24; 19:9; 20:21; 24:15; 33:9; 34:5; 1 Kings 8:12). Second, God's abode is described as a canopy of clouds (Psalm 97:2). Third, God's mode of transportation is figuratively described as a cloud chariot (104:3). Fourth, when God speaks, "He causes the clouds to ascend from the end of the earth" (Jer. 10:13; 51:16). Fifth, the "day of the LORD ... will be a day of clouds" (Ezek. 30:3; Joel 2:2). Sixth, God's judgment of the wicked is described as the upheaval of the created order: "In whirlwind and storm is His way, and clouds are the dust beneath His feet" (Nahum 1:3). In each of the above examples, clouds are symbols of God's presence.

In addition, there are verses which describe God "*coming* on the clouds": "Behold, the LORD is riding on a swift cloud, and is about to come to

Egypt" (Isa. 19:1; cf. Psalm 104:3). This is no more "literal" than God riding a cloud chariot, abiding in a cloud canopy, or clouds moving when God speaks. The image of God riding on a swift cloud depicts His sovereignty over the nations.[6]

> He makes the clouds His chariot;
> He walks upon the wings of the wind;
> He makes the winds His messengers;
> Flaming fire His ministers.
>
> (Psalm 104:3–4)

God does not physically appear on clouds, using them as "chariots." Neither does He literally walk upon "wings of the wind" or make "the winds His messengers." The language describes judgment and retribution. Why should anyone think it unusual to find similar language in the New Testament being interpreted in the same way?

Exaltation to Kingly Power

There is a third cloud motif in Scripture. The reference is found in Daniel 7:13–14, the passage that Jesus quotes in Matthew 24:30. Notice that the coming of the Son of Man in Daniel 7 is not *down* but *up!* The Son of Man, Jesus, comes *up* "with the clouds of heaven" *to* "the Ancient of Days and was presented before Him."

> In Daniel's vision, coming on the clouds means that the Son of Man was coming onstage, into the scene. It is not a coming toward Daniel or toward earth, but a coming seen from the standpoint of God, since Daniel uses three verbs that all indicate this: "coming … approached … was led to" the Ancient of Days. This is no picture of the Second Coming, because the Son of man is going the wrong way for that. His face is turned, not toward earth, but toward God. His goal is not to receive His saints, but to receive His kingdom (Cf. 1 Peter 3:22; Luke 19:12; Acts 2:32–36; 3:22; 5:31; Col. 3:1; Rev. 3:21.).[7]

Jesus had Daniel 7 in mind as He described His enthronement: "The key verse in Daniel 7:13 that predicts the triumph of the Son of Man represents

Him as coming into the presence of the Ancient of Days 'with the clouds *of heaven,*' a phrase that is repeated in Matthew 26:64; Mark 14:62; Revelation 14:14. Clouds are much more closely associated with the glory and throne of God than they are connected with the earth."[8]

Being familiar with the Hebrew Scriptures, Jesus' disciples understood the context of His words and grasped their meaning. Jesus spoke against the backdrop of the Old Testament.

> Our discussion of the meaning of Daniel 7:13 in its Old Testament context led us to the conclusion that its keynote is one of vindication and exaltation to an everlasting dominion, and that the "coming" of verse 13 was a coming to God [the Ancient of Days] to receive power, not a "descent" to earth. When we studied Jesus' use of these verses, we found that in every case this same theme was the point of the allusion, and, in particular, that nowhere (unless here) was verse 13 [in Dan. 7] interpreted of his coming to earth at the Parousia. In particular, the reference to Mark 14:62, where the wording is clearly parallel to that in the present verse [Mark 13:26], was to Jesus' imminent vindication and power, with a secondary reference to a manifestation of that power in the near future. Thus, the expectation that Jesus would in fact use Daniel 7:13 in the sense in which it was written is amply confirmed by his actual allusions. He saw in that verse a prediction of his imminent exaltation to an authority which supersedes that of the earthly powers which have set themselves against God.... Jesus is using Daniel 7:13 as a prediction of that authority which he exercised when in AD 70 the Jewish nation and its leaders, who had condemned him, were over-thrown, and Jesus was vindicated as the recipient of all power from the Ancient of Days.[9]

At His trial, Jesus told Caiaphas the high priest and the Sanhedrin that *they* would *see* "the Son of Man sitting at the right hand of power and coming on the clouds of heaven" (Matt. 26:64). When would this take place? "The phrase . . . 'from now on' means exactly what it says . . ., and refers not to some distant event but to the imminent vindication of Jesus which will shortly be obvious to those who have sat in judgement over him."[10] What did they "see"? Certainly not an event that was thousands of years in the future. Caiaphas will not look out of the window one day and observe a human figure flying downwards on a cloud. It is absurd to imagine either Jesus, or Mark, or anyone in between, supposing the words to mean that. Caiaphas will witness the strange events which follow Jesus' crucifixion: the rise of a group of disciples claiming that he has been raised from the dead, and the events which accelerate towards the final clash with Rome, in which, judged according to the time-honoured test, Jesus will be vindicated as a true prophet. In and through it all, Caiaphas will witness events which show that Jesus was not, after all, mistaken in his claim, hitherto implicit, now at last explicit: he is the Messiah, the anointed one, the true representative of the people of Israel, the one in and through whom the covenant God is acting to set up his kingdom.[11]

At His ascension, Jesus had come up to the Ancient of Days "with the clouds of heaven" to receive the kingdom from His Father (Mark 16:19; Acts 1:9). Jesus' reception of the kingdom gave Him possession so that He could do with it as He pleased. He had earlier stated that the kingdom would be "taken away from" those who rejected Him and would "be given to a nation producing the fruit of it" (Matt. 21:43). The church—made up initially of believing Jews and later of believing Gentiles—is described by Peter as a "holy nation" (1 Peter 2:9). It is this "nation" that is in possession of the kingdom by right of transfer. This covenant transfer is confirmed for us at the stoning of Stephen (Acts 7:54–56). Stephen's murderers objected to being called "stiff-necked and uncircumcised in heart and ears" (7:51). His words of condemnation had put them outside the covenant community because they, too, persecuted and killed the prophets by publicly denouncing the gospel message (7:52).

> So Stephen saw Him, before his death by stoning (Acts 7:56), and thus prophesied judgment on his murderers, at the very moment when he prayed for their forgiveness. The priesthood stood on trial that day, although the execution of their sentence was yet to come, on that awful day in AD 70 when the priests were cut down at the altar as they steadily continued their sacrifices.[12]

The church was persecuted by Jewish opposition for forty years after Jesus' death, once again confirming what Jesus had prophesied. With the destruction of Jerusalem in A.D. 70, the truth was comprehended by the tribes of Israel (Rev. 1:7). The generation that Jesus said would not pass away until all these things came to pass finally came to understand the implications of their rebellion: Jesus is the one who was given "[D]ominion, Glory and a kingdom, that all the peoples, nations, and men of every language might serve Him" (Dan. 7:14). They were not to look for another (Matt. 24:26).

A Heavenly Throne

Jesus' coming to judge Jerusalem represented the passing of the Old Covenant. Jerusalem would no longer be the center of worship (John 4:20–24) because Jesus fulfilled all that the temple and its glory represented (2:19). When the high priest heard Jesus identify Himself as the "Son of Man" of Daniel 7:13–14, he "tore his robes, saying, 'He has blasphemed!'" (Matt. 26:65). Jesus had made it clear that He was the one who would occupy David's throne *in heaven!* (Psalm 110:1; Matt. 22:44–45; Acts 2:30–36).

God the Father raised Jesus "from the dead, and seated Him at His right hand *in the heavenly places,* far above all rule and authority and power and dominion, and every name that is named, not only in this age, but also in the age to come. And He put all things in subjection under His feet, and gave Him as head over all things to the church, which is His body, the fullness of Him who fills all in all" (Eph. 1:20–23). The earthly temple in Jerusalem was made obsolete by Jesus in His death, resurrection, and ascension. It seems that the unbelieving high priest had a better understanding of Bible prophecy than many present-day prophetic soothsayers.

The "coming of the Son of Man" is a depiction of the exaltation and enthronement of Jesus in heaven. Matthew 24:30 has nothing to do with the rapture or any end-time scenario. Each time Jesus used the phrase, "the Son of Man coming on the clouds," the reference had contemporary application. N. T. Wright's summary puts the biblical imagery in perspective:

> The Daniel text [quoted by Jesus in Matt. 24:30]. . . has nothing to do with a figure 'coming' *from* heaven *to* earth. Despite the widespread opinion that this is what it 'must' mean in the gospels, there is no reason to suppose that on the lips of Jesus, or in the understanding of the earliest traditions, it means anything other than vindication. It speaks of exaltation: of one who, representing 'the people of the saints of the most high',

is raised up from suffering at the hands of the beasts and given a throne to sit on, exercising royal power.[13]

A direct quotation from the Old Testament must be interpreted in terms of its original context. Daniel 7:13–14 depicts the Son of Man going up, approaching the Ancient of Days. Nothing could be more clear, contrary to what prophetic sensationalists maintain.[14]

The Sign in Heaven

At first reading, many assume that Matthew 24:30 teaches that we should expect to see Jesus "appear in the sky ... coming on clouds." Unfortunately, we are working with a poor translation. Let's look at a word-for-word translation from the Greek: "And then will appear the sign of the Son of Man in *heaven*, and then will mourn all the *tribes of the land* and they [i.e., the tribes] will see the Son of Man coming on the clouds of heaven with power and great glory." The *sign* is that the Son of Man is enthroned *in heaven* (Heb. 9:24).

Jesus was not telling His disciples that *He* would appear in the *sky*. The Greek word that is translated "sky" is best translated "heaven." Because of this ambiguous translation, some early commentators believed that a visible sign would appear as a foreshadowing of what they believed to be the soon return of Christ. They did not believe the sign itself was Jesus.

Jesus told His disciples that they would see a sign that proved He was in heaven, sitting at His Father's right hand (Acts 2:30–36).

When the temple was destroyed, the localized place of worship went with it. Jesus told the Samaritan woman that "an hour is coming when neither in this mountain, nor in Jerusalem, shall you worship the Father" (John 4:21). All Christians look to "the Jerusalem above" (Gal. 4:26) where Jesus was "exalted to the right hand of God" (Acts 2:33). He now occupies David's throne in the heavenly Jerusalem.

The fulfillment of the prophecies regarding a descendant of David sitting on David's throne forever was realized in Jesus, David's Son (Matt. 1:1; Luke 3:31; Acts 2:22–36). Isn't this similar to what Stephen saw? "Behold, I see the heavens opened up and the Son of Man *standing at the right hand of God*" (Acts 7:56). Stephen saw Jesus enthroned in heaven. All Israel would know it when the temple and holy city came under judgment, a judgment that would take place in their generation. It would take forty years for the rest of Israel to figure it out.

The Land or the Earth?

The "coming" of "the Son of Man" is most often taught as a worldwide event since Jesus states that "all the tribes of the *earth* will mourn" (Matt. 24:30). Again, most Bible translations do not capture the true meaning of the Greek. A better translation is "tribes of the land," indicating that the event is restricted to Israel since Israel is the topic of discussion. The Greek word often translated "earth" can also be translated "soil" (Matt. 13:5, 8, 23), "ground" or "dirt" (25:25), "land" (countryside: 27:45), "Earth" (world: 16:10), or the "land of Israel" (2:6, 20–21), depending on the context. Since "tribes" is used in conjunction with land in Matthew 24:30, "land [of Judea]" is the best translation. If Matthew 24:30 refers to a future second coming of Christ "the translation *all the tribes of the earth, i.e.,* 'all the people of the world', is right. But if . . . the reference is to the conditions prevailing when Jerusalem was being attacked, the translation should be 'all the tribes of the land' (so Knox), *i.e.* the land of Judaea (cf. Zc. xii. 12)."[15] The New Testament pattern follows the Old Testament pattern. The meaning of the Hebrew word *eretz*

> is simply "the land" and not "the earth" as in most English translations. For the most part, it refers to a specific stretch of land in a local, geographical, or political sense. Often it means simply "the ground" upon which one stands. As such, it is frequently used interchangeably with another common Hebrew word *adamah* (that is, "arable ground"). . . . Not only does the Hebrew term *eretz* normally mean "land" as opposed to "the earth," but it usually refers specifically to the land promised to Abraham (Genesis 15:18). Certainly the term doesn't always denote "the promised land." It may be "the land" of Egypt (Exodus 1:7) or simply the place of one's birth, the "homeland" (Genesis 12:1). But most often in Genesis and throughout the Pentateuch the term *eretz* refers to the promised land.[16]

Earlier in Matthew 24, Jesus warned His audience to flee "Judea" (24:16) when they saw the "abomination of desolation" (24:15), or as Luke describes it, "Jerusalem surrounded by armies" (Luke 21:20). Only those near enough to the temple would be able to see the "abomination of desolation . . . standing in the holy place." The Olivet Discourse was not a message to the world (*kosmos*); it was a warning to the tribes of Israel that dwelled in the land as part of that first-century generation.

The warning to all the tribes of the land that their city and sanctuary were about to be reduced to rubble caused great mourning because they understood that judgment was near. They must either repent and embrace the Messiah or perish in the conflagration. The Jewish Christians left when they saw "Jerusalem surrounded by armies" (Luke 21:20). No escape was available to those determined to stay. We should remember that many of the Jews rejected Jesus because He was not a political savior. They still believed that a redeemer would come to deliver them from Roman oppression and that if they forced the Romans into a confrontation, God would intervene and save them. They were wrong. More than a million Jews died at the hands of the Roman army. Their Savior had come, and they had crucified Him forty years earlier. Again, the language of judgment is familiar to students of the Old Testament: "And I will pour out on the house of David and on the inhabitants of Jerusalem, the Spirit of grace and supplication, so that they will look on Me whom they have pierced; and they will mourn for Him, as one mourns for an only son, and they will weep bitterly over Him, like the bitter weeping over a first-born" (Zech. 12:10).

How do we know that this is a reference to a first-century fulfillment? Zechariah describes Messiah the King as "coming" to the "daughter of Zion": "He is just and endowed with salvation, humble, and mounted on a donkey, even on a colt, the foal of a donkey" (Zech. 9:9). This was fulfilled during Jesus' earthly ministry (Matt. 21:5; John 12:15). Zechariah's prophecy in 9:9 *precedes* the prophecy in 12:10. The price of Jesus' betrayal as well as the potter's field where Judas was buried are described in Zechariah 11:13. These prophecies were also fulfilled during Jesus' earthly ministry (Matt. 27:3–10; Acts 1:1, 9), and they *follow* the prophecy of the mourning of those who pierced Him. In addition, there is a description of what happens when "the Shepherd" is struck: "the sheep" will be "scattered" (Zech. 13:7; cf. Matt. 26:31). Sandwiched between Zechariah 9:9, 11:13, and 13:7 are the references that predict that those who pierced Him will mourn over their misdeed (12:10). "Jesus' time connection is highly revealing: when *the sign of the Son of Man in heaven appears, then* will Israel mourn, as if the cause of their desperation and sorrow were the appearing of the sign. The connection is clear: those who assassinated God's Son would live to see the day when He would be gloriously vindicated and the resultant heinousness of their crime against Him appropriately exposed and punished."[17]

Seeing the Son of Man

Those who pierced Jesus lived in the first century. This helps explain Revelation 1:7 where the same wording is used. Those who "see" Him are "those who pierced Him" (cf. John 19:7). John is telling us that those who pierced Jesus experienced His covenant wrath. Revelation 1:7 must refer to a pre-A.D. 70 fulfillment, before that generation passed away (Matt. 16:27–28; 24:34). Nineteenth-century commentator James Glasgow explains it this way:

> *"Every eye, and those who pierced Him, shall see Him."*—The subject of the text is "the people of the land," viz. Judea; and it would be a direct misinterpretation, as well as false logic, to strain a term beyond its subject, by applying it to the final judgment of all. That all men shall see Him, we learn from other scriptures [2 Cor. v. 10]; but we must deal faithfully with the text, and not force any word in order to make out a case. Truth never requires this. That the land of Judea, in the prophetic sense, is the subject, is evident from Zech. xii. 10; from which the words are taken, both here and in John xix. 37.
>
> *"Those who pierced Him"* are obviously those who had a hand in His death. The text declares they shall see Him, employing for seeing the verb *optomai*, already noticed, as not limited to ocular seeing. Though those who pierced Him saw not His person after His ascension, yet they saw His power bringing judgment on them, and making His cause prevail in despite of their persecution, and they speedily saw their kingdom terminated.[18]

Equating "seeing" with "understanding" is a common biblical metaphor. In John 12:40 Jesus quotes Isaiah 6:10 to explain why some have not believed His message. Notice how "seeing" is equivalent to "understanding":

> Render the hearts of this people insensitive, their ears dull, and their eyes dim, lest they *see with their eyes*, hear with their ears, *understand* with their hearts, and repent and be healed (Isaiah 6:10).[19]

In quoting Isaiah, Jesus states that Jehovah "has blinded their eyes" (John 12:40). This is not a physical blinding. The blinding is spiritual. To be blind is not to understand; to see is to understand and believe. "To open their eyes" is an expression used by the biblical writers to describe recognition and understanding (Acts 26:18; cf. 1 Kings 8:29, 52; 2 Kings 2:16; 6:20; 19:16; Isa. 35:5; 42:7, 16). The eyes of the disciples "were opened" by Jesus and "they recognized Him" (Luke 24:31) is another example of equating "seeing" with "understanding." David Chilton summarizes the text for us: "The crucifiers would **see Him** coming in judgment—that is, they would *understand* that His coming would mean wrath on the land (cf. the use of the word *see* in Mark 1:44; Luke 17:22; John 3:36; Rom. 15:21)."[20]

Notes

1. Dave Hunt, *How Close Are We?: Compelling Evidence for the Soon Return of Christ* (Eugene, OR: Harvest House, 1993), cover copy.
2. Dave Hunt, *Global Peace and the Rise of Antichrist* (Eugene, OR: Harvest House, 1990), 5.
3. John Walvoord quoted in "The Final Days Are Here Again," *Newsweek* (18 March 1991), 55. John Walvoord believes that he will live to see the rapture.
4. Hal Lindsey as quoted in Brad Miner, *National Review* (19 November 1990), 49.
5. Like the Greek word for earth (*ge*), the Hebrew word for earth (*eretz*) can also mean land, specifically the land of Israel.
6. Edward J. Young, *The Book of Isaiah,* 3 vols. (Grand Rapids, MI: Eerdmans, 1969), 2:14.
7. Harold Fowler, *The Gospel of Matthew*, 4 vols. (Joplin, MO: College Press, 1985), 4:487.
8. Gleason L. Archer, Jr., "Response to the Posttribulation Rapture Position," *The Rapture: Pre-, Mid-, or Post-Tribulational?,* Richard R. Reiter, *et al.,* (Grand Rapids, MI: Zondervan, 1984), 215–16.
9. R.T. France, *Jesus and the Old Testament* (Grand Rapids, MI: Baker Book House, [1971] 1982), 235, 236. Emphasis added.
10. R.T. France, *Matthew: Evangelist and Teacher* (Downers Grove, IL: InterVarsity Press, [1989] 1998), 315.
11. N. T. Wright, *Jesus and the Victory of God* (Minneapolis, MN: Fortress Press, 1998), 525.
12. R.A. Cole, *The Gospel According to Mark: An Introduction and Commentary* (Grand Rapids, MI: Eerdmans, 1961), 229.
13. Wright, *Jesus and the Victory of God,* 524.
14. Gary Hedrick, "Distress of Nations with Perplexity," *Foreshadows of Wrath and Redemption,* William T. James, editor (Eugene, OR: Harvest House, 1999), 117.
15. R.V.G. Tasker, *The Gospel According to St. Matthew* (Grand Rapids, MI: Eerdmans, 1961), 230.
16. John Sailhamer, *Genesis Unbound: A Provocative New Look at the Creation Account* (Sisters, OR: Multnomah, 1996), 50.
17. Fowler, *The Gospel of Matthew,* 4:485.
18. James Glasgow, *The Apocalypse Translated and Expounded* (Edinburgh: T. & T. Clark, 1872), 126–27.

19. John 12:40 reads: "He has blinded their eyes, and He hardened their heart; lest they see with their eyes, and perceive with their heart, and be converted, and I heal them."
20. David Chilton, *The Days of Vengeance: An Exposition of the Book of Revelation* (Tyler, TX: Dominion Press, 1987), 66.

Chapter Thirteen

GATHERING
THE ELECT

Immediately after the destruction of the temple and the judgment of Jerusalem, the Old Covenant age came to an end. The New Covenant was realized in all its fullness. The author of Hebrews writes that God had promised "Yet once more" to "shake not only the earth, but also the heaven" (Heb. 12:26). "'Yet once more' . . . denotes the removing of those things which can be shaken, as of created things, in order that those things which cannot be shaken remain" (12:27). God did this house cleaning in His judgment coming in A.D. 70. The temple, priesthood, and animal sacrificial system—"as of created things"—were gone forever. While the stones of the temple were cast down, a new temple would be raised made of "living stones . . . being built up as a spiritual house for a holy priesthood, to offer up spiritual sacrifices acceptable to God through Jesus Christ" (1 Peter 2:5). This new spiritual edifice would consist of Jews and Gentiles "brought near through the blood of Christ" (Eph. 2:13). Both groups (Jews and Gentiles) "are no longer strangers and aliens" but "are fellow-citizens with the saints, and are of God's household, having been built upon the foundation of the apostles and prophets, Christ Jesus Himself being the corner stone, in whom the whole building, being fitted together is growing into a holy temple in the Lord" (2:19–21). No longer is Jesus' message directed only to the "lost sheep of Israel" (Matt. 10:6; 15:24); it now includes "the children of God who are scattered abroad" (John 11:52). The nations began to recognize Christ as King, not only of Israel but of the world. In context, Matthew 24:31 does not refer to the end of the world. Rather, it speaks of the spread of the gospel to the nations and their eventual discipleship (28:18–20).

"And He will send forth His angels WITH A GREAT TRUMPET and THEY WILL GATHER TOGETHER His elect from the four winds, from one end of the sky to the other" (Matt. 24:31).

On Wings of Angels

Dispensationalists, taking a wooden literalism, teach that angels will pick up Jews from around the world and bring them to Jerusalem. The note in the *Believer's Study Bible* reads: "At the intervention of Christ from heaven, the elect will be gathered by the angels from the ends of the earth" (1380). J. Dwight Pentecost takes a similar position:

> During the Tribulation Israel will be scattered out of the land by military invasions (Rev. 12:14–16), and the Israelites will flee and find refuge among Gentile nations. Supernaturally God will bring people back to the land through the instrumentality of angels, which will be the final restoration anticipated in the Old Testament (Deut. 30:1–8).[1]

Thomas Ice also believes "that our Lord . . . will use the agency of angels to accomplish this task (rather than El Al airline!)."[2] While with God "all things are possible" (Mark 10:27), it is highly improbable that Jesus had this interpretation in mind. Using the Old Testament as our guide, we learn that when God "gathers His elect," angelic beings are not in view (Deut. 30:1–4; Isa. 11:12).

Angels as Gospel Messengers

The Greek word translated "angels" is the common word used for "messengers." God's prophets, messengers, and ministers, both in the Old and

New Testament, are described as angels. Even dispensational prophecy writer Ed Hindson recognizes this. "The term *angel* (Greek, *angelos*) means 'messenger.' God's angels are His divine messengers (Heb. 1:14; Rev. 1:1), and His true prophets and preachers are called angels of the churches (Rev. 2:1, 8, 12, 18; 3:1, 7, 14)."[3] In the Greek version of the Old Testament (Septuagint or LXX), the Greek word *angelos* is translated numerous times as "messenger": "And the LORD, the God of their fathers, sent word to them again and again by His *messengers*, because He had compassion on His people and on His dwelling place" (2 Chron. 26:15). The people continually "mocked the messengers of God, despised His words and scoffed at His prophecies, until the wrath of the LORD arose against His people, until there was no remedy" (26:16). These verses parallel the events leading up to the destruction of Jerusalem in A.D. 70. Haggai is described as "the messenger [*angelos*] of the LORD (Hag. 1:13). The priest in Malachi is designated a messenger [*angelos*] of the LORD of hosts" (Mal. 2:7). John the Baptist is an "angel," a messenger of God (Matt. 11:10; Mark 1:2; Luke 7:24, 27; cf. Mal. 3:1). Jesus "sent messengers [*angeloi*] ahead of Him" (Luke 9:52). The spies Joshua sent to Jericho are called "messengers" (James 2:25).

The Four Winds

These messengers in Matthew 24:31 call together God's people "from the four winds," a reference to the four corners of the earth (Zech. 2:6; 13:29), and from one end of the sky to the other. This is a reference to the entire horizon of the world (Psalm 22:27; Deut. 4:32; Matt. 28:18–20). We should not be pressed to interpret "four winds" in a scientific fashion. "Four winds" suggests a square world, as does "four corners of the earth" or "land of Israel" (Isa. 11:12; Ezek. 7:2; Rev. 7:1; 20:8). The Bible, speaking in theological terms, depicts the earth as a house. Heaven is described in a similar fashion (John 14:2). None of this language suggests that the earth is flat or a cube, something that a wooden literalism would demand. The Bible alludes to the earth's circularity in Isaiah 40:22: "'It is he that sits upon the circle of the earth'—'circle' being the translation of the Hebrew *khug*, sphere."[4] By using this metaphor of the four winds, Jesus is telling us that the elect are gathered from everywhere, not limited to the land, or house (Matt. 15:24), of Israel (8:11).

We notice that the story in Acts begins in Jerusalem and ends in Rome. To the Jew, Jerusalem was the centre, while Rome was the "ends of the earth" (see Acts 1:8; cf. Ps. of Solomon 8:15). To the Gentile, as one suspects Theophilus (Acts 1:1) was, Rome was the hub of the inhabited world. The author recounts how the gospel broke out of Jerusalem into Judaea and from Judaea to Samaria and from Samaria to the Gentiles and ultimately to Rome.[5]

The Old Testament description of Elam's judgment uses similar language. "And I shall bring upon Elam the four winds from the four ends of heaven, and shall scatter them to all these winds" (Jer. 49:36; also see Dan. 7:2; 8:8; Rev. 7:1).

The Great Trumpet

The "great trumpet" of verse thirty-one is the call of the gospel. It refers to Numbers 10:1–10 where silver trumpets were made to call the people together for worship and to set them on their march. It also alludes to the year of Jubilee, the year when the world reverts to its original owners, the year when Satan is dispossessed and Christ reclaims the world (Acts 3:19–21). "Now is THE ACCEPTABLE TIME" (2 Cor. 6:2). The Jubilee year was announced by trumpets and signified the coming of Christ's kingdom (Lev. 25:8–17; Luke 4:16–21; Isa. 61:1–3). The voice of the messengers of the gospel is similar to the sound of a trumpet calling the people to repentance: "Cry loudly, do not hold back; raise your voice like a trumpet, and declare to My people their transgression, and to the house of Jacob their sins" (Isa. 58:1; see Jer. 6:17; Ezek. 33:3–6; Rom. 10:18).

The gospel began to go out to the world at Pentecost, but throughout the Book of Acts the gospel went "to the Jew first" (Rom. 1:16). With the destruction of Jerusalem the gospel went out to the Gentiles in new fullness and with the expectation that the *nations*—Gentiles—would be discipled (Matt. 28:18–20).

Matthew 24:31 draws on Old Testament imagery: trumpet, four winds, from one end of the sky to another. The trumpet is symbolic of a great work about to commence, the great gathering of God's people into one new *spiritual* nation. The word for "gather" is the Greek word *sunagogue*. A gathering of Jews met in a synagogue. Judaism, in its rejection of Christ, had become a

"synagogue of Satan" (Rev. 2:9; 3:9). The true synagogue of God—the church—
is made up of believing Jews and Gentiles. The elect are scattered around the
world, "from the four winds, from one end of the sky to the other" (cf. Matt.
28:18–20). God heralds the great ingathering of His elect from every tribe,
tongue, and nation by sending His gospel messengers into the world (John
11:51–52; Rev. 7:9). History attests to the fact that Jesus' elect have been and
even now are being "gathered together" (Matt. 24:31) as "a chosen race, a
royal priesthood, a holy nation, a people for God's own possession. . . for you
once were not a people, but now you are the people of God . . ." (1 Peter 2:9–
10). Tasker offers a helpful summary of Matthew 24:31:

> It was in fact only after the old order ended with the destruction of the
> Temple that world evangelism by the Christian Church, now entirely
> separate from Judaism, could be conducted in earnest. Not till then could
> the *trumpet* of the gospel be sounded throughout the world. Not till then
> could the Son of man, having 'visited' the old Israel in judgment, *send his*
> *angels* (i.e. His messengers) to *gather together his elect from the four winds, from*
> *one end of heaven to the other*, a result which could be obtained only when
> the gospel had been preached to the whole world (29–31).[6]

"Now learn the parable from the fig tree: when its branch has already be-
come tender, and puts forth its leaves, you know that summer is near; even so
you too, when you see all these things, recognize that He is near, right at the
door" (Matt. 24:32–33).

Hal Lindsey, author of *The Late Great Planet Earth*, believes these verses
refer to the 1948 national rebirth of Israel.

> The most important sign in Matthew has to be the restoration of the
> Jews to the land in the rebirth of Israel. Even the figure of speech "fig
> tree" has been a historic symbol of national Israel. When the Jewish people,
> after nearly 2,000 years of exile, under relentless persecution, became a
> nation again on 14 May 1948 the "fig tree" put forth its first leaves.
> Jesus said that this would indicate that He was "at the door," ready to
> return. Then He said, "Truly I say to you, *this generation* will not pass away
> until all these things take place" (Matthew 24:34, NASB).

What generation? Obviously, in context, the generation that would see the signs—chief among them the rebirth of Israel. A generation in the Bible is something like forty years. If this is a correct deduction, then within forty years or so of 1948, all these things could take place. Many scholars who have studied Bible prophecy all their lives believe that this is so.[7]

Lindsey was not alone in coming to this conclusion. Chuck Smith, pastor of Calvary Chapel and founder of the worldwide Calvary Chapel system of churches, went a step further than Lindsey: "That generation that was living in May 1948 shall not pass away until the second coming of Jesus Christ takes place and the kingdom of God established upon the earth. How long is a generation? Forty years on average in the Bible. . . . Where does that put us? It puts us right out at the end. We're coming down to the wire."[8]

Without this interpretive keystone, the predictive elements in Lindsey's prophetic blueprint are nothing more than scattered bricks on an unorganized building site.

Hal Lindsey times the events of Matthew 24 on his belief that the "fig tree" illustration in verses 32–33 refers to the restored nationhood of Israel. If the "fig tree" is a figure of a restored national Israel, then Lindsey might have a case for a future fulfillment, although one must still deal with the meaning of "this generation." On the other hand, if the fig tree illustration has nothing to do with the re-establishment of national Israel, then Lindsey and all who adopt his position are left with little support for their position, especially in light of the rest of the New Testament which makes no mention of restored covenantal status for the nation of Israel. John Walvoord, a dispensationalist, does not believe the fig tree represents Israel.

Actually, while the fig tree could be an apt illustration of Israel, it is not so used in the Bible. In Jeremiah 24:1–8, good and bad figs illustrate Israel in the captivity, and there is also mention of figs in 29:17. The reference to the fig tree in Judges 9:10–11 is obviously not Israel. Neither the reference in Matthew 21:18–20 nor that in Mark 11:12–14 with its interpretation in 11:20–26, gives any indication that it is referring to Israel, any more than the mountain referred to in the passage.[9] Accordingly, while this interpretation is held by many, there is no clear scriptural warrant.

A better interpretation is that Christ was using a natural illustration. Because the fig tree brings forth new leaves late in the spring, the budding of the leaves is evidence that summer is near. In a similar way, when those living in the great tribulation see the signs predicted, they will know that the second coming of Christ is near. The signs in this passage, accordingly, are not the revival of Israel, but the great tribulation.[10]

The parallel passage in Luke 21:29 shows that Jesus referred not only to the fig tree but to "all the trees": "And He told them a parable: 'Behold the fig tree, *and all the trees*; as soon as *they* put forth leaves, you see it and know for yourselves that the summer is now near. Even so you, too, when you see these things happening, recognize that the kingdom of God is near'" (Luke 21:29–30). Thus, it's not just the fig tree but trees in general whose leaves herald the nearness of summer. The parable of the fig tree is used as an analogy. When you see leaves on a fig tree, and for that matter, when you see leaves on *all* the trees, you know that summer is near. In a similar way, when you see certain signs, then know that Jesus is near, "right at the door" (Matt. 24:33). Near to what? Near to fulfilling the promise He made about coming within a generation to destroy the temple.

Dispensationalists like to speak of the *"generation* of the fig tree." This distorts the time indicators that are inherent in the parable of the fig tree. Leaves come out in spring. This is an indicator that summer is near. A single season is in view, not forty or fifty seasons. The leaves are the signs that manifested themselves in the spring of A.D. 70. This can have nothing to do with Israel's nationhood in 1948, the Six-Day War of 1967, or the first steps toward Israel and Palestinian peace efforts in 1993.

The New Testament makes it very clear that the preferred symbols for spiritual Israel are the vine (John 15:1–11), the olive tree (Rom. 11:16–24), the lump of dough (11:16), and the flock (Isa. 40:11; Jer. 23:2; Matt. 26:31; Luke 12:32; John 10:16; 1 Peter 5:2).

If, as Hal Lindsey and Chuck Smith claim, *the* sign that we should be looking for is the re-establishment of Israel as a nation, why is its meaning hidden in the cryptic fig-tree reference since Jesus used such detail to describe what His disciples should *not* view as signs of the nearness of the "end" (Matt. 24:4–14)? Furthermore, as the time was about to draw near for the temple's destruction, Jesus was specific as to what they were to look for in the way of signs: "Therefore when *you see* the ABOMINATION OF DESOLA-

TION which was spoken of through Daniel the prophet, standing in the holy place (*let the reader understand*)" (24:15). Why would Jesus all of a sudden use a non-defined symbol to be *the most important sign* in determining the time when the events of the Olivet Discourse are to take place?

Notes

1. J. Dwight Pentecost, *Thy Kingdom Come: Tracing God's Kingdom Program and Covenant Promises Throughout History* (Wheaton, IL: Victor Books, 1990), 255.

2. Thomas Ice, "The Great Tribulation is Past: Rebuttal," in Thomas Ice and Kenneth L. Gentry, Jr., *The Great Tribulation: Past or Future?—Two Evangelicals Debate the Question* (Grand Rapids, MI: Kregel, 1999), 158.

3. Ed Hindson, "False Christ's, False Prophets, Great Deception," *Foreshadows of Wrath and Redemption*, William T. James, ed. (Eugene, OR: Harvest House, 1999), 33.

4. Samuel Eliot Morison, *The European Discovery of America: The Northern Voyages* (New York: Oxford University Press, 1971), 6.

5. Paul Barnett, *Is the New Testament Reliable?: A Look at the Historical Evidence* (Downers Grove, IL: InterVarsity Press, [1986] 1993), 139.

6. R. V. G. Tasker, *The Gospel According to St. Matthew: An Introduction and Commentary* (Grand Rapids, MI: Eerdmans, 1961), 227.

7. Hal Lindsey, *The Late Great Planet Earth* (Grand Rapids, MI: Zondervan, 1970), 53–54.

8. Chuck Smith, *Snatched Away* (Costa Mesa, CA: Maranatha Evangelical Association of Calvary Chapel, 1976), 21. Quoted in Richard Abanes, *EndTime Visions: The Road to Armageddon?* (New York: Four Walls Eight Windows, 1998), 442, note 81.

9. Walvoord is clearly wrong about this. First-century Israel is the object of Jesus' judgment discourse in Matthew 21:18–20 and Mark 11:12–14.

10. John F. Walvoord, *Matthew: Thy Kingdom Come* (Chicago, IL: Moody, [1974] 1980), 191–92.

Chapter Fourteen

THIS GENERATION
OR THIS RACE?

Several interpretive models are offered to avoid the inescapable conclusion that "this generation" of Matthew 24:34 refers to the generation to whom Jesus was speaking. Translating "this generation" as "this Jewish race" has been a popular interpretation for many years. Adam Clarke in his commentary on Matthew, first published in 1810 as part of a larger work on the entire Bible, takes the position that the Greek word for "generation" (*genea*) should be translated "race." He offers no exegetical support for his opinion. Not one cross-reference is listed. Even so, Clarke still maintains that all the events prophesied by Jesus in Matthew 24 were fulfilled in the events leading up to and including the destruction of Jerusalem in A.D. 70.

> This chapter contains a prediction of the utter destruction of the city and temple of Jerusalem, and the subversion of the whole political constitution of the Jews; and is one of the most valuable portions of the new covenant Scriptures, with respect to the *evidence* which it furnishes of the *truth* of Christianity. Every thing which our Lord foretold should come on the temple, city, and people of the Jews, has been fulfilled in the most correct and astonishing manner....[1]

"Truly I say to you, this generation will not pass away until all these things take place" (Matt. 24:34).

With this verse we are brought full circle. In a straightforward manner, Jesus makes it clear that all the events outlined in the preceding verses would be fulfilled before the passing away of that first-century generation.

[T]he Saviour uttered these words in connection with the prophesied distress of the Jewish people and the destruction of Jerusalem, His words mean that, before the generation then living should have died out, these things would occur. And this is what actually happened. Towards the end of A.D. 70 (*i.e.*, some forty years after Jesus uttered these words) everything predicted by Him in verses 10–24 [of Luke 21] in connection with the events before and during the destruction of Jerusalem was already fulfilled—the temple was destroyed to the last stone, all Jerusalem was a ruin, the Jewish people were slain by hundreds of thousands ... and carried off into captivity.[2]

Matthew 24:34 is, in the words of J. Marcellus Kik, "the key to Matthew Twenty-four."[3] Luke's account of the Olivet Discourse confirms that the generation Jesus had in mind was the generation to whom He was speaking: "But keep on the alert at all times, praying in order that *you* may have strength to escape all these things that *are about to take place*, and to stand before the Son of Man" (Luke 21:36). Once we determine the meaning of "you," we can resolve the meaning of "this generation." Clearly, Luke 21:36 refers to those to whom Jesus spoke, the same group Jesus told to "keep on the alert" and to pray. Jesus confirmed the nearness of the unfolding of the events by telling His listeners that the cataclysm was "about to take place." Without a proper understanding of this key time text, prophetic forecasters will always find Matthew 24 fertile ground for wild speculation.

Generation as "Race"

One way out of the time problem is to translate the Greek world *genea* as "race" instead of "generation." Contemporary writers who translate *genea* as "race" invariably support their view by claiming that the events described in

Matthew 24 were not fulfilled in A.D. 70. Arno C. Gaebelein writes: "Verse 34 has been a difficulty for many. The word generation does not mean the people who were then living; it has the meaning of 'this race.' The Jewish race cannot pass away till these things be fulfilled."[4] In a footnote on "this race," Gaebelein writes: "Same as 1 Pet. ii:9, 'a chosen generation,' *i.e.*, class of peoples." A comparison of the Greek in 1 Peter 2:9 will show that *genos* (race) is used, not *genea* (generation). Peter speaks of a chosen "race," not of a chosen "generation."

There are still some commentators who assert that *genea* should be translated "race" but offer little or no exegetical evidence to support their claim. J. Dwight Pentecost, a dispensational premillennialist, calls the translation of *genea* as "race" the "best explanation" without offering any exegetical defense.[5] William Hendriksen, an amillennialist, puts up a weak exegetical argument for *genea* being translated "race." The most serious flaw in Hendriksen's method is that he does not compare the use of *genea* in Matthew 24:34 with how *genea* is used elsewhere in Matthew's gospel.[6]

Translating "this generation" as "this race of people" gained popularity through the notes of the *Scofield Reference Bible*. The *New Scofield Reference Bible* (1967), retains a modified version of the note of the first edition. Since millions of Bible students have used the Scofield notes in their study of the Bible, it is necessary that we make a thorough study of the position.

Following Scofield's lead, the text would read, the "nation or family of Israel will be preserved 'till all these things be fulfilled.'" For Scofield, the Greek word *genea* has the "primary definition" of "race, kind, family, stock, breed." If this is the proper translation and interpretation, Matthew 24:34 would be the only place in the Bible where *genea* has this meaning. To support his position, Scofield claims that all Greek lexicons agree that *genea* means "race." Scofield writes:

> The Greek word *genea*, translated "generation," means primarily (as does indeed the English word), "race, kind, family, stock, breed" (Webster); "An age, race or generation of men" (Greenfield); "Men of the same stock, a family" (Thayer). To so interpret, therefore, the passage in question is but to give it its natural unforced meaning.[7]

Not all lexicons agree. Scofield lists Thayer's *Greek-English Lexicon of the New Testament* as an authority in support of his contention that *genea* in

Matthew 24:34 should be translated "race." Thayer, contrary to Scofield, puts forth the following definition for *genea*: "*the whole multitude of men living at the same time*: Mt. xxiv. 34; Mk. xiii. 30; Luke i. 48."[8] Thayer cites Matthew 24:34 and Mark 13:30 in support of translating *genea* as "generation." Thayer does not apply the "race" translation to Matthew 24:34. A check of other lexicons and theological dictionaries will show that *genea* is translated "generation"—"those living at the same time"—not "race."

- "This generation is to be understood temporally."[9]
- "In Matt. it has the sense of *this generation*, and according to the first evangelist, Jesus expected the end of this age ... to occur in connection with the judgment on Jerusalem at the end of that first generation (see Mk. 9:1 and Matt. 16:18)."[10]
- "'Generation' is the most probable translation of *genea*."[11]
- "The meaning *nation* is advocated by some in Mt 24:34; Mk 13:30; Lk 21:23; but s[ee] also 2. **2.** basically, the sum total of those born at the same time, expanded to include all those living at a given time *generation, contemporaries*."[12] In this lexicon, the most widely used today, Matthew 24:34 is employed as a reference in support of translating *genea* as "generation," not "race."

The Greek word *genos* rather than *genea* is best translated "race" (see Mark 7:26; Acts 4:36; 7:19; 13:26; 17:28; 18:24; 2 Cor. 11:26; Gal. 1:14; Phil. 3:5; 1 Peter 2:9). "It seems unlikely that all three evangelists would have failed to use this word if this was the idea they meant to convey."[13]

Even after considering all of this contrary evidence, some still claim that *genea* should be translated "race." For example, Acts 2:40 is offered as support: "And with many other words he [Peter] solemnly testified and kept on exhorting them, saying, 'Be saved from this perverse generation!'" Peter, a Jew, is telling his fellow Jews to come to Christ because it is "this generation," the generation of which he is a part, that will encounter God's wrath when the temple and city are destroyed. Why would Peter, a Jew, call his own race "perverse"? There was nothing perverse about Jews as a race of people. Peter remained an ethnic Jew after He became a Christian. As Matthew 24:22 and 24 state, only the elect—most of whom were Jews—would be saved from the tribulation that was to occur before their generation passed away.

Hebrews 3:10 is sometimes used in support of translating *genea* as "race," but it actually refers to the single generation of Jews who wandered in the wilderness for forty years: "Where your fathers tried Me by testing Me, and saw My works for forty years. Therefore I was angry with *this generation.* . . ." This verse fits very well with *genea* being translated "generation" instead of "race," especially in light of the fact that a generation is forty years, the amount of time that transpired between the Olivet Discourse in A.D. 30 and Jerusalem's destruction in A.D. 70.

Nearly all Bible translations render *genea* as "generation." The King James, American Standard (1901), New English Bible, Revised Standard, New King James, New Berkeley Version, the Jerusalem Bible, New International,[14] and the New American Standard translate *genea* as generation. If *genea* should be translated "race," then why don't translators translate it as "race"? Even Hal Lindsey admits that *genea* should not be translated "race."

> **ETERNITY**: You don't think it would mean simply the *race of people?*
> **LINDSEY**:   No, because the context is not talking about a race but about time. The context, and I've debated this with many people including Earl Radmacher, is dealing with a general time or else it would have no meaning at all. Only the third meaning of the word in the Greek lexicon is "race." That's a very remote usage of that word.[15]

Generation does not mean "race" in English, as Scofield insists. Noah Webster's 1828 *American Dictionary of the English Language* defines "generation" as "a single succession in natural descent, as the children of the same parents; hence an age. Thus we say, the third, the fourth, or the tenth *generation.* Gen xv. 16. The people of the same period, or living at the same time: 'O faithless and perverse *generation.*' Luke ix." Noah Webster lists "race" as the sixth possible meaning. *The Shorter Oxford English Dictionary* (1968 edition) lists "race" last as a possible meaning. Contemporary usage also mitigates against using "generation" as a synonym for race. When we speak of a "generation gap," we do not mean a gap between races. A "generation gap" is an interval of time that exists between two groups of people raised in different eras. The Greek word *genea*, in its "natural unforced meaning," when comparing Scripture with Scripture, means "generation." And in the case of Matthew 24:34, the generation to whom Jesus was speaking. This means that the prophecy delivered by Jesus on the Mount of Olives is now history.

Notes

1. Adam Clarke, *Clarke's Commentary*, 3 vols. (Nashville, TN: Abingdon Press, [1810] n.d.), 3:225.

2. Norval Geldenhuys, *Commentary on the Gospel of Luke* (Grand Rapids, MI: Eerdmans, 1951), 538–39.

3. J. Marcellus Kik, *An Eschatology of Victory* (Nutley, NJ: Presbyterian and Reformed, 1971), 59.

4. Arno C. Gaebelein, *The Gospels and the Book of Acts* in *The Annotated Bible: The Holy Scriptures Analyzed and Annotated* (New York: Our Hope, 1917), 52.

5. J. Dwight Pentecost, *Things to Come: A Study in Biblical Eschatology* (Grand Rapids, MI: Zondervan, [1958] 1987), 281.

6. See William Hendriksen, *Matthew: New Testament Commentary* (Grand Rapids, MI: Baker Book House, 1973), 867–69.

7. *C.I. Scofield's Question Box* (Chicago, IL: The Bible Institute Colportage Association, n.d.), 72.

8. Joseph Henry Thayer, *A Greek-English Lexicon of the New Testament*, rev. ed. (New York: American Book Co., 1889), 112.

9. Friedrich Buchsel, "Genea," *Theological Dictionary of the New Testament*, ed. Gerhard Kittel, trans. Geoffrey W. Bromiley, 10 vols. (Grand Rapids, MI: Eerdmans, 1964), 1:665.

10. R. Morgenthaler, "Generation," *New International Dictionary of New Testament Theology*, ed. Colin Brown, 3 vols. (Grand Rapids, MI: Zondervan, 1976), 2:37–38.

11. Colin Brown, "Generation," *New International Dictionary*, 2:38.

12. William F. Arndt and F. Wilbur Gingrich, *A Greek-English Lexicon of the New Testament and Other Early Christian Literature* (Chicago, IL: University of Chicago Press, 1957), 153.

13. David J. Palm, "The Signs of His Coming: An Examination of the Olivet Discourse from a Preterist Perspective" (Deerfield, IL: Trinity Evangelical Divinity School, 1993), 21.

14. The New International Version, like the New American Standard, cites "race" as an alternative translation with "generation" as the preferred translation.

15. Stephen Board interviews Hal Lindsey, "The Great Cosmic Countdown: Hal Lindsey on the Future," *Eternity* (January 1977), 20.

Chapter Fifteen

THE PASSING AWAY OF HEAVEN AND EARTH

When Jesus' disciples heard His frightening prediction about the destruction of the temple and the judgment of Jerusalem in their generation (Matt. 23:36–39), they asked when this cataclysm would take place, what signs would precede the event, and what sign would signify His coming "and of the end of the age" (24:3). It is quite obvious that the disciples connected Jesus' "coming" with the "end of the age." The "coming" of Matthew 24:3 refers to the coming of Jesus in judgment upon Jerusalem in A.D. 70. James, as well as other New Testament writers, is clear about the nearness of Jesus' coming: "the coming of the Lord is at hand" (James 5:8), at hand for those who first read the epistle.

The destruction of the temple, and with it the priesthood and sacrificial system, inaugurated a new era in which "the blood of Christ" cleanses our "conscience from dead works to serve the living God" (Heb. 9:14). Therefore, the expression "end of the age" refers "to the end of the 'Jewish age,' *i.e.,* the time of transference from a national to an international people of God,"[1] what the Apostle Paul describes as the "ends of the ages." The "end" had come upon the first-century church (1 Cor. 10:11).

A similar phrase is used by the author of Hebrews: "But now once at the *consummation of the ages* He has been manifested to put away sin by the sacrifice of Himself" (Heb. 9:26). Jesus was manifested, not at the beginning, but "at the consummation of the ages." The period between A.D. 30 and 70 is, as the apostle Peter describes it, "these last times" (1 Peter 1:20). As time drew near for Jerusalem's destruction, Peter could say that "the end of all things was at hand" (4:7). Milton Terry offers the following as a summary of the meaning of the "end of the age":

> It is the solemn termination and crisis of the dispensation which had run its course when the temple fell, and there was not left one stone upon another which was not thrown down. That catastrophe, which in Heb. xii, 26, is conceived as a shaking of the earth and the heaven, is *the end* contemplated in this discourse; not "the end of the world," but the termination and consummation of the pre-Messianic age.[2]

Notice that the disciples did not ask about the dissolution of the physical heaven and earth or the judgment of the "world" (*kosmos*), ideas foreign to the Bible. After hearing Jesus pronounce judgment on the temple and city of Jerusalem (Matt. 23:37–39), His disciples ask about the end of the "age" (*aion*). When did the "end" occur? The only proximate eschatological event that fits the "end of the age" framework is the destruction of Jerusalem in A.D. 70. The disciples knew that the fall of the temple and the destruction of the city meant the end of the Old Covenant order and the inauguration of a new order. As Jews who were familiar with Old Testament imagery, the disciples recognized the meaning of this restructuring language. Jesus nowhere corrects or modifies their multi-faceted question.

The numerous New Testament time indicators demonstrate that Jesus did not have a distant "end" in mind when He spoke of the "end of the age." Charles Wright, in his commentary on Zechariah, offers the following helpful discussion of the meaning of the "end of the age":

> The passing away of the dispensation of the law of Moses, which as limited in great part to Israel after the flesh, might well be called the Jewish dispensation, was justly regarded as "the end of the age" (... Matt. xxiv. 3). The Messiah was viewed as the bringer in of a new world. The

period of the Messiah was, therefore, correctly characterised by the Synagogue as "the world to come." In this signification our Lord used that expression when he uttered the solemn warning that the sin against the Holy Ghost would be forgiven "neither in this world (the then dispensation), neither in the world to come" (Matt. xii. 32), or the new dispensation, when, "having overcome the sharpness of death," Christ "opened the kingdom of heaven to all believers."[3]

The "age to come," therefore, is simply a designation for the Christian era, an era that was long ago prophesied by the prophets. Abraham, for example, "rejoiced in order to see [Jesus'] day; and he saw it, and was glad" (John 8:56). The old covenant with its attendant animal sacrifices and earthly priesthood passed away when God's lamb, Jesus Christ, took away the sins of the world.

Among Reformed preterist adherents, there is a great deal of agreement with the above interpretation and the application of Matthew 24:1–34 to the destruction of Jerusalem in A.D. 70. Among these same preterists, however, a debate arises over a proposed shift in topics and eras with verses 35 and 36 being *time transition* verses. Numerous commentators claim that Jesus redirects His discussion from the Great Tribulation of A.D. 70 (Matt. 24:1–34) to a distant coming that will result in the passing away of our present physical "heaven and earth" (24:35).

J. Marcellus Kik writes in his highly regarded and influential commentary on Jesus' Olivet Discourse, *An Eschatology of Victory*, that "many have recognized that with verse 36 a change in subject matter occurs. [Charles H.] Spurgeon indicates this in his commentary on verse 36 [of Matt. 24]: 'There is a manifest change in our Lord's words here, which clearly indicates that they refer to His last great coming to judgment.'"[4] Kenneth L. Gentry, author of many helpful works on prophecy, takes a similar view.[5] While I respect the work of these men, I do differ with them on their analysis of Matthew 24:35 and following.

The Passing Away of Heaven and Earth

Jesus does not change subjects when He assures the disciples that "heaven and earth will pass away." Rather, He merely affirms His prior predictions which are recorded in Matthew 24:29–31. Verse 36 is a summary and confirmation statement of these verses.[6] Keep in mind that the central focus of the Olivet Discourse is the desolation of the "house" and "world" of apostate Israel (23:36). The old world of Judaism, represented by the earthly temple, is taken apart stone by stone (24:2). James Jordan writes, "each time God brought judgment on His people during the Old Covenant, there was a sense in which an old heavens and earth was replaced with a new one: New rulers were set up, a new symbolic world model was built (Tabernacle, Temple), and so forth."[7] The New Covenant replaces the Old Covenant with new leaders, a new priesthood, new sacraments, a new sacrifice, a new tabernacle (John 1:14), and a new temple (John 2:19; 1 Cor. 3:16; Eph. 2:21). In essence, a new heaven and earth.

The darkening of the sun and moon and the falling of the stars, coupled with the shaking of the heavens (24:29), are more descriptive ways of saying that "heaven and earth will pass away" (24:35). In other contexts, when stars fall, they fall to the earth, a sure sign of temporal judgment (Isa. 14:12; Dan. 8:10; Rev. 6:13; 9:1; 12:4). So then, the "passing away of heaven and earth" is the passing away of the old covenant world of Judaism led and upheld by those who "crucified the Lord of glory" (1 Cor. 2:8).

John Owen (1616–1683) maintained that the "passing of heaven and earth" in 2 Peter 3:5–7 had reference, "not to the last and final judgment of the world, but to that utter desolation and destruction that was to be made of the Judaical church and state" in A.D. 70.[8] John Brown (1784–1858), commenting on Matthew 5:18, follows the same methodology.

> "Heaven and earth passing away," understood literally, is the dissolution of the present system of the universe; and the period when that is to take place, is called the "end of the world." But a person at all familiar with the phraseology of the Old Testament Scriptures, knows that the dissolution of the Mosaic economy, and the establishment of the Christian, is often spoken of as the removing of the old earth and heavens, and the creation of a new earth and new heavens.[9]

After surveying how this language is used throughout the Bible and in Jewish literature, John Lightfoot applies the "passing away of heaven and earth" to the "destruction of Jerusalem and the whole Jewish state…as if the whole frame of this world were to be dissolved."[10]

This and That

Commentators often argue that Matthew 24 contains both a discussion of the A.D. 70 destruction of religious, social, and political Judaism as well as a reference to a yet-future return of Christ. This supposed distinction is drawn by contrasting "*this* generation" and "*that* day and hour." Gentry writes that "there seems to be an intended contrast between that which is *near* (in verse 34) and that which is *far* (in verse 36): *this* generation vs. *that* day. It would seem more appropriate for Christ to have spoken of 'this day' rather than 'that day' if He had meant to refer to the time of 'this generation.'"[11] Not at all. We should expect to see "that" used for a time still in the speaker's future, whether that event is forty years or four thousand years in the future. "This generation" refers to the present generation Jesus was addressing. "This" is therefore the appropriate word for something *present* while "that" is the most appropriate word for something *future*. Arndt and Gingrich agree: "*[T]his*, referring to something comparatively near at hand, just as *ekeinos* [that] refers to something comparatively farther away."[12] "That day" would come in the final destruction of the Jews who rejected their Messiah, a time still in the future for Jesus' audience. John Gill writes:

> *But of that day and hour knoweth no man, &c.]* Which is to be understood, not of the second coming of Christ, the end of the world, and the last judgment; but of the coming of the son of man, to take vengeance on the Jews, and of their destruction; for the words manifestly regard the date of the several things going on before, which only can be applied to that catastrophe, and dreadful desolation.[13]

Gill assumes that the previous context of the chapter governs the meaning of "that day." As was pointed out above, Matthew 24:29 is a familiar Old Testament description of the "passing away of heaven and earth," that is, the end of a social, religious, and political system.

Adam Clarke offers a similar interpretation: "Verse 36. *But of that day and hour]* [The Greek word] *Ora* is translated *season* by many eminent critics, and is used in this sense by both sacred and profane authors. As the *day* was not known, in which Jerusalem should be invested by the Romans, therefore our Lord advised his disciples to pray that it might not be on a *Sabbath*; and as the *season* was not known, therefore they were to pray that it might not be in the *winter*; ver. 20. See on Mark xiii 32."[14]

John Lightfoot's comments show that the only possible reference was to the destruction of Jerusalem in A.D. 70: "That the discourse is of the day of the destruction of Jerusalem is so evident, both by the disciples' question, and by the whole thread of Christ's discourse, that it is a wonder any should understand these words of the *day and hour* of the last judgment."[15]

The Absence of Signs

Another reason offered in support of dividing the chapter at 24:35 is that the signs that follow are of a general nature compared to specific signs detailed in 24:1–34. There are two very good reasons for the absence of signs. First, the signs have already been given. All the signs that were necessary to understand the general timing of Jesus' return in judgment were specified. Second, the topic changes from signs leading up to the temple's destruction to watchfulness and expectation during the interim.

Those Days and That Day

Gentry writes that "we should notice the pre-transition emphasis on plural 'days' in contrast to the focus on the singular 'day' afterwards. 'This generation' involves many 'days' for the full accomplishment of the protracted (Matt. 24:22) Great Tribulation." He states that in contrast to the "many 'days'" of the Great Tribulation, "'that day' of the future Second Advent will come in a moment, in the twinkling of an eye (cp. 1 Cor. 15:52)." Notice, however, that the Great Tribulation of Matthew 24:15–28 does not include either the dissolution of the social, political, and religious world of the Jews (24:29) or the "coming of the Son of Man" (24:30). The events of 24:29–30 (the coming of Jesus in judgment before that first-century generation passes away) follow "immediately after the tribulation of those *days*" (24:29). Such a distinction indicates that Jesus was pointing towards a certain day when the temple and the city of Jerusalem would fall.

The description of the Great Tribulation leads up to the heart of the discourse which is found in 24:29–31. This is why Matthew describes the "coming of the Son of Man" as following the "days" of the Great Tribulation. The "coming of the Son of Man" in 24:30 parallels the "Son of Man" who comes up "to the Ancient of Days" in Daniel 7:13. This "coming" was not a multi-day event; it happened on a certain day known only to the Father. The collapse of the social, religious, and political world of Israel (Matt. 24:29)—witnessed by tens of thousands as they saw their beloved city and sanctuary turn to ashes amidst the flames—was evidence that the Son of Man had come "up to the Ancient of Days and was presented before Him" (Dan. 7:13; cp. Matt. 24:30).

Just Like the Days of Noah

To help His listeners better understand the timing and circumstances of the events leading up to and including the destruction of the temple before their generation passed away, Jesus draws on a familiar Old Testament judgment event—the flood. Jesus, teaching by analogy, shows how the coming of the flood waters and His own coming are similar. In Noah's time we read about "*those days* which were before the flood" and "*the day* that NOAH ENTERED THE ARK" (Matt. 24:38). Similarly, there were *days* before the coming of the Son of Man and the *day* of the coming of the Son of Man. The same people were involved in both the "days before" and "the day of" the Son of Man. Those who "were eating and drinking" and "marrying and giving in marriage" were the same people who were shut out on "the day that Noah entered the ark." Noah entered the ark on a single day similar to the way Jesus as the Son of Man came on the "clouds of the sky with power and great glory" (24:30), a day and hour known only to the Father (24:36). "Some shall be rescued from the destruction of Jerusalem, like Lot out of the burning of Sodom: while others, no ways perhaps different in outward circumstances, shall be left to perish in it."[16]

Jesus says that His coming "will be just like the days of Noah" (24:37). The people were doing normal things—"eating and drinking" and "marrying and giving in marriage." Jesus is telling his audience that life will be going on as usual when He returns in judgment. People had no thought of a coming judgment in Noah's day since there were no signs. Noah was told to prepare for "things *not yet seen*" (Heb. 11:7). Jesus is not describing evil behavior like drunkenness and sexual sins like "'exchanging mates' or 'wife swapping,'" contrary to what M. R. DeHaan and Jack Van Impe claim.[17] "Marrying and given in marriage" is a phrase to describe, well, "marrying and giving in marriage" (see Matt. 22:30). Families do it every day. Men and women marry and parents give their daughters away in marriage. D. A. Carson's comments are helpful:

[T]hat the coming of the Son of Man takes place at an unknown time can only be true if in fact life seems to be going on pretty much as usual— just as in the days before the flood (v. 37). People follow their ordinary pursuits (v. 38). Despite the distress, persecutions, and upheavals (vv. 4–28), life goes on: people eat, drink, and marry. There is no overt typological usage of the Flood as judgment here, nor any mention of the sin of that generation.[18]

Support for Carson's interpretation can be found in Luke's account of the time just before Sodom's destruction: "It was the same as happened in the days of Lot: they were eating, they were drinking, they were buying, they were selling, they were planting, they were building; but on the day that Lot went out from Sodom it rained fire and brimstone from heaven and destroyed them all" (Luke 17:28). Buying, selling, planting, and building describe life going on as usual without any regard to an impending judgment. Are dispensationalists willing to say that these activities "connote moral corruption"? Darrell L. Bock attempts this interpretation even though he admits that the idea of "moral corruption . . . is not emphasized in Luke's description."[19] No one disputes that Noah and Lot lived in a time of moral corruption that brought judgment. Jesus' point is that the people in Noah and Lot's day went on with their lives as if the promise of imminent judgment was a lie (see 2 Peter 3:3–4). The same is true of those who were told that Jesus would return in judgment within a generation.

No Rapture Here!

Many futurists claim that the phrase "took them all away" (24:39) refers to a rapture that is still in our future. On the contrary. "In the context of 24:37–39, 'taken' presumably means 'taken to judgment' (cf. Jer. 6:11 NASB, NRSV)."[20] The phrase ties the judgment of the world in Noah's day with the judgment of the Jews' world in Israel's day that took place with the destruction of the city of Jerusalem and the temple. Who was taken away in the judgment of the flood? Not Noah and his family. They were left behind to carry on God's work. John Gill writes in his commentary on this passage: "the whole world of the ungodly, every man, woman, and child, except eight persons only; Noah and his wife, and his three sons and their wives...." were taken away in judgment. And what does Gill say about those in the field?: They shall be taken away "by the eagles, the Roman army, and either killed or carried captive by them." The Bible gives its own commentary on the meaning of "took them all away" in Luke 17:27, 29: "Destroyed them all" is equivalent to "took them all away." Consider the meaning that dispensationalist John Walvoord gives "took them away."

> An argument advanced by Alexander Reese and adopted by [Robert] Gundry is that the references in Matthew 24:40, 41 should be interpreted as referring to the rapture. These verses state, "Then shall two be in the field; the one shall be taken, and the other left. Two women shall be grinding at the mill; one shall be taken and the other left."
>
> Here both Gundry and Reese violate the rule that the context should determine the interpretation of a passage. Both Gundry and Reese concede that the context deals with judgment such as characterized the time of Noah. According to Matthew 24:39 those living at that time "knew not until the flood came, and took them all away, so shall also the coming of the Son of Man be." Those taken away were taken away in judgment.
>
>   * * * * *
>
> Claiming that those taken in verses 40 and 41 are taken away in the rapture, Gundry in discussing the parallel passage in Luke 17:34–37 ignores verse 37. There two are pictured in the same bed, with one taken and the other left. Two are grinding together, and one is taken and the other left. Two are in the field, one is taken and the other left. Then, in verse 37, the question is asked, "Where, Lord?" The answer is very dramatic: "And He said unto them, Wherever the body is, there will the eagles be gathered together." It should be very clear that the ones taken are put to death and their bodies are consumed by the vultures. If the ones taken are killed, then verses 40, 41 of Matthew 24 speak of precisely the same kind of judgment as occurred in the flood where the ones taken were taken in judgment.[21]

But like Reese and Gundry, Walvoord ignores the time texts that run throughout Matthew 24–25, claiming that they refer to a distant coming of Christ. Since there was a judgment where Jews were in fact "taken away in judgment," it makes much more sense to place the timing of such an event to the closest event, Jerusalem's destruction in A.D. 70.

Mix and Match

Luke 17:22–37 describes five Olivet-Discourse prophetic events that are identical to those found in Matthew 24. The difference between Matthew 24 and Luke 17 is in the order of the events, a characteristic of the passages that few commentators can explain. Ray Summers writes:

> This is a most difficult passage. The overall reference appears to be to the coming of the Son of Man—Christ—in judgment at the end of the age. Some small parts of it, however, are repeated in Luke 21 in reference to the destruction of Jerusalem (A.D. 70), and larger parts of it are in Matthew 24, also in reference to the destruction of Jerusalem. The entire complex cautions one against dogmatism in interpreting.[22]

Taking Matthew 24 as the standard, Luke places the Noah's ark analogy (Matt. 24:37–39) before the events of Matthew 24:17–18 ("let him who is on the housetop not go down"), verse 27 ("for just as the lightning comes from the east"), and verse 28 ("wherever the corpse is, there the vultures will gather"). If the five prophetic events of Matthew 24 that are found in Luke 17:22–37 are numbered 1–2–3–4–5, Luke's numbering of the same events would be 2–4–1–5–3.[23] While this is not positive proof of an A.D. 70 fulfillment for chapters 24 and 25, it certainly adds credibility to the position.

After A Long Time

Another line of evidence offered by those who believe that events following Matthew 24:34 refer to the personal and physical return of Jesus is the meaning given to "after a long time" (24:48; 25:19) and the "delay" by the bridegroom (25:5). On the surface these examples seem to indicate that two different events are in view, one near (the destruction of Jerusalem) and one distant (the second coming of Christ). This is the view of Stephen F. Hayhow.

> Both parables, the parables of the virgins (vv. 1–13), and the parable of the talents (vv. 14–30), speak of the absence of the bridegroom/master, who is said to be "a long time in coming" (v. 5) and "After a long time the master of the servants returned..." (v. 19). This suggests, not the events of A.D. 70 which were to occur in the near future, in fact within the space of a generation, but a distant event, the return of Christ.[24]

Notice that the evil slave says, "My master is not coming for a long time" (Matt. 24:48). The evil slave then proceeds to "beat his fellow-slaves and eat and drink with drunkards" (24:49). But to the surprise of the "evil slave" the master returned when he least expected him (24:50). The master did not return to cut the evil slave's distant relatives in pieces (24:51); he cut *him* in pieces. The evil slave was alive when the master left, and he was alive when the master returned. In this context, a "long time" must be measured against a person's lifetime. In context, two years could be a long time if the master usually returned within six months.

The same idea is expressed in the parable of the "talents." A man entrusts his slaves with his possessions (25:14). The master then goes on a journey (25:15). While the master is gone, the slaves make investment decisions (25:16–18). We are then told that "after a long time the master of *those slaves* came and settled accounts *with them*" (25:19). In this context "a long time" is no longer than an average lifetime. The settlement is made with the same slaves who received the talents. In every other New Testament context, "a long time" means nothing more than an extended period of time (Luke 8:27; 23:8; John 5:6; Acts 8:11; 14:3, 28; 26:5, 29; 27:21; 28:6). Nowhere does it mean centuries or multiple generations.

The delay of the bridegroom is no different from the "long time" of the two previous parables. The bridegroom returns to the same two groups of virgins (25:1–13). The duration of the delay must be measured by the audience.

This brief analysis helps us understand the "mockers" who ask, "Where is the promise of His coming?" (2 Peter 3:3–4). Peter was aware that Jesus' coming was an event that would take place before the last apostle died (Matt. 16:27–28; John 21:22–23). The doctrine of the soon return of Christ was common knowledge (Matt. 24:34; 26:64; Phil. 4:5; Heb. 10:25; 1 John 2:18; Rev. 1:1, 3). It is not hard to imagine that the passage of several decades would lead some to doubt the reliability of the prophecy, especially as the promised generation of destruction was coming to a close. The horrendous events of A.D. 70 silenced the mockers.

Different Comings?

Is the "coming of the Son of Man" in Matthew 24:37 different in time and kind from the "coming of the Son of Man" in verses 27 and 30? There is no indication that Jesus is describing two comings separated by an indeterminate period of time. What would have led the disciples to conclude that Jesus was describing a coming different from the one He described moments before when He uses identical language to describe both of them? Jesus does not say "*this* coming of the Son of Man" or "*that* coming of the Son of Man" to distinguish two comings as He does with "*this* generation" and "*that* day."

Similarly, there is little evidence that the "coming of the Son of Man" in Matthew 24:27, 30, 39, and 42 is different from the "coming of the Son of Man" in 25:31. Compare 25:31 with 16:27, a certain reference to the destruction of Jerusalem in A.D. 70:

> "For the Son of Man is going to come in the glory of His Father with His angels; and will then recompense every man according to his deeds" (Matt. 16:27).
> "But when the Son of Man comes in His glory, and all the angels with Him, then He will sit on His glorious throne" (Matt. 25:31).

These verses are almost identical. The timing of Matthew 16:27 is tied to verse 28: "Truly I say to you, there are some of those who are standing here who shall not taste death until *they see the Son of Man coming in His kingdom*." "Recompensing every man according to his deeds" corresponds with "He will sit on His glorious throne" to execute judgment among the nations (25:32). But how was this universal judgment fulfilled in A.D. 70?

There is no indication that Matthew 25:31–46 describes a single event. Rather, the passage describes a judgment over time, related to Jesus' dominion as an "everlasting dominion" (Dan. 7:14). Jesus was "exalted to the right hand of God" where He rules until all His enemies are made a "footstool for [His] feet" (Acts 2:33, 35). Paul writes that Jesus "must reign until He has put all of His enemies under His feet" (1 Cor. 15:25). Milton Terry writes that "the ideal of judgment presented in Matt. xxv, 31–46, is therefore no single event, like the destruction of Jerusalem."[25] Terry continues:

> The Old Testament doctrine is that "the kingdom is Jehovah's, and he is ruler among the nations" (Psalm xxii, 28). "Say ye among the nations, Jehovah reigneth; he shall judge the peoples with equity. He cometh, he cometh to judge the earth; he shall judge the world in righteousness, and

the peoples in his truth" (Psalm xcvi, 10–13). The day of judgment for any wicked nation, city, or individual is the time when the penal visitation comes; and the judgment of God's saints is manifest in every signal event which magnifies goodness and condemns iniquity.[26]

The King of glory is continually judging and reigning among the nations, and He will not cease from this work until "He has abolished all rule and all authority and power" (1 Cor. 15:24).

Finding a Solution

The solution in determining when certain prophetic events take place is the presence of time indicators in context. The phrase "long time" has been made to stretch over several millennia even though there is no indication of such an extended period of time in Matthew 24:48 and 25:19. While all admit that time indicators are present in Matthew 24–25, few are willing to allow the words and the context to set the limits on how long a "long time" is. The use of "long time" has no eschatological significance in other New Testament contexts (Luke 8:27; 20:9; 23:8; John 5:6; Acts 8:11; 14:3, 28; 26:5, 29; 27:21; 28:6). For example, Herod "had wanted to see Jesus for a long time" (Luke 23:8). The same can be said for the New Testament use of "delay" (Luke 1:21; 18:7; Acts 9:38; 22:16; 25:17; Heb. 10:37; Rev. 10:6).

The parables of Matthew 24–25 are clear on the duration of the delays—the two masters who go on a journey return to the same people they left. There is no need to allegorize these parables to force them to depict a distant coming of Christ. In addition, the delay of the bridegroom in the parable of the ten virgins is not very long, unless the virgins are related to Rip Van Winkle. The virgins get drowsy at dusk, and the bridegroom returns at midnight (Matt. 25:6). How can this "delay" be turned into a span of time nearly two thousand years in length?

Notes

1. R. T. France, *The Gospel According to Matthew: An Introduction and Commentary* (Grand Rapids, MI: Eerdmans, 1985), 337.

2. Milton S. Terry, *Biblical Apocalyptics: A Study of the Most Notable Revelations of God and of Christ* (Grand Rapids, MI: Baker Book House, [1898] 1988), 225.

3. Charles Henry Hamilton Wright, *Zechariah and His Prophecies* (Minneapolis, MN: Klock and Klock, [1879] 1980), 449.

4. J. Marcellus Kik, *An Eschatology of Victory* (Phillipsburg, NJ: Presbyterian and Reformed, 1975), 158.

5. Kenneth L. Gentry, Jr., "An Encore to Matthew 24," *Dispensationalism in Transition* (May 1993).

6. Henry Alford, *The New Testament for English Readers* (Chicago, IL: Moody Press, n.d.), 169.

7. James B. Jordan, *Through New Eyes: Developing a Biblical View of the World* (Brentwood, TN: Wolgemuth & Hyatt, 1988), 167.

8. John Owen, *The Works of John Owen*, 16 vols. (London: The Banner of Truth Trust, 1965–68), 9:134.

9. John Brown, *Discourses and Sayings of Our Lord*, 3 vols. (Edinburgh: The Banner of Truth Trust, [1852] 1990), 1:170.

10. John Lightfoot, *Commentary on the New Testament from the Talmud and Hebraica: Matthew—1 Corinthians*, 4 vols. (Peabody, MA: Hendrickson Publishers, [1859], 1989), 3:454.

11. Gentry, "An Encore to Matthew 24," 2.

12. William F. Arndt and F. Wilbur Gingrich, *A Greek-English Lexicon of the New Testament and Other Early Christian Literature,* 4th ed. (Chicago, IL: The University of Chicago Press, 1952), 600.

13. John Gill, *An Exposition of the New Testament*, 3 vols. (Paris, AR: The Baptist Standard Bearer, [1809] 1989), 1:296.

14. Adam Clarke, *Clarke's Commenatary: Matthew–Revelation* (Nashville, TN: Abingdon Press, [1824] n.d.), 234.

15. Lightfoot, *Commentary on the New Testament from the Talmud and Hebraica*, 2:442.

16. Thomas Newton, *Dissertations on the Prophecies, Which Have Remarkably Been Fulfilled, and at This Time are Fulfilling in the World* (London: J.F. Dove, 1754), 379.

17. Jack Van Impe, *The Great Escape: Preparing for the Rapture, the Next Event on God's Prophetic Clock* (Nashville, TN: Word, 1998), 127.

18. D. A. Carson, "Matthew," *The Expositor's Bible Commentary*, gen. ed., Frank E. Gaebelein (Grand Rapids, MI: Zondervan, 1984), 8:509. Also see N. T. Wright, *Jesus and the Victory of God* (Minneapolis, MN: Fortress Pess, 1996), 365–66.

19. Bock, *Luke: Baker Exegetical Commentary on the New Testament*, 2 vols. (Grand Rapids, MI: Baker Books, 1996), 2:1432–33.

20. Craig S. Keener, *The IVP Bible Background Commentary: New Testament* (Downers Grove, IL: InterVarsity Press, 1993), 115.

21. John F. Walvoord, *The Blessed Hope and the Tribulation: A Historical and Biblical Study of Posttribulationism* (Grand Rapids, MI: Zondervan, 1976), 89, 90. Walvoord writes in another place: "Because at the rapture believers will be taken out of the world, some have confused this with the rapture of the church. Here, however, the situation is the reverse. The one who is taken, is taken in judgment. This is in keeping with the illustration of the time of Noah when the ones taken away are the unbelievers." (John F. Walvoord, *Matthew: The Kingdom Come* [Chicago, IL: Moody Press, 1974], 193).

22. Ray Summers, *Commentary on Luke: Jesus, the Universal Savior* (Waco, TX: Word Books, 1972), 202.

23. See the helpful chart in Edward E. Stevens, *What Happened in A.D. 70?* (Bradford, PA: Kingdom Publications, 1997).

24. Stephen F. Hayhow, "Matthew 24, Luke 17 and the Destruction of Jerusalem," *Christianity and Society* 4:2 (April 1994), 4.

25. Terry, *Biblical Apocalyptics*, 251.

26. Terry, *Biblical Apocalyptics*, 251.

Chapter Sixteen

AVOIDING RAPTURE FEVER

The pretribulational rapture of the church has been described as the next great eschatological event in God's prophetic timetable, an event so significant that all Bible prophecy is dependent upon it taking place. But Dave Hunt has called it "The Late Great Rapture Theory."[1] He is lamenting the fact that many Christians are beginning to question whether the Bible actually teaches that the church will be "caught up" prior to the Great Tribulation.

Of course, as I hope to demonstrate, there is good reason to question this relatively new doctrine. Hunt writes that "in the early 1970s the Rapture was the most-talked-about topic in the church. [Hal] Lindsey had captured the attention and imagination of his generation. Pastors preached about heaven and Christians eagerly anticipated being caught up at any moment to meet the Lord in the air."[2] Hunt fails to make a distinction between teaching about heaven and teaching about the rapture. The church knew nothing about a pre-tribulational rapture prior to 1830. Are we to assume, using Hunt's logic, that for eighteen hundred years the church was not preaching about heaven? Hunt intimates the newness of the pre-tribulational rapture theory. He says that J.N. Darby and C.I. Scofield "helped to make the pretribulation rapture belief dominant for 100 years."[3] What he does not say is that the doctrine began in Darby's lifetime!

Why had Lindsey "captured the attention and imagination of his generation"? There is one simple answer: He set a date for the rapture, placing it sometime between 1981 and 1988. Hunt tries to get Lindsey off the hook by claiming that Lindsey did not intend for his readers to come to this conclusion. Hunt states, "*The Late Great Planet Earth* had only suggested that Christ's statement concerning 'this generation' might possibly indicate a fulfillment within 40 years from Israel's rebirth."[4] Why did Lindsey's readers think that he had set a date? Lindsey made the calculations. Hunt himself has entered the Jesus-will-rapture-His-church-soon game.

In his book on the nearness of the pre-tribulational rapture, *How Close Are We?*,[5] Hunt offers what he believes is "compelling evidence for the soon return of Christ." While he has not set a date for the rapture, he has made it clear that he believes that it is "near." This in itself is a remarkable admission. Futurists like Hunt have been telling us that the biblical terms "near," "shortly," and "quickly" are not to be interpreted literally, that these words do not mean what they seem to mean. They maintain that terms relating to the timing of prophetic events only mean that Jesus could come at any moment. Since nearly two thousand years have passed, and the rapture has not taken place, can we not assume that Hunt's use of "soon" as he applies it to *this* present generation should have a similar abstract meaning?

No Fear of the Bible

Tim LaHaye has been called a "prophecy expert." In his defense of the pretribulational rapture in *No Fear of the Storm*, LaHaye writes that the "Bible teaches that Jesus Christ is coming soon."[6] Those who believe in a pretribulational rapture teach that Jesus' could come at any moment. This is nonsense. "Soon" means "near in time," before the generation of the apostles who were with Jesus passed away (Matt. 24:34). Sound Bible interpretation cannot maintain that "near" (Matt. 24:32–33; Mark 13:28–29; Luke 10:9, 11; 21:31; Rev. 1:3; 22:10), "shortly" (Acts 25:4; Phil. 2:19, 24; 3 John 14; Rev. 1:1; 22:6),[7] and "quickly" (Matt. 5:25; 28:7–8; Luke 15:22; 16:6; John 11:29, 31; 13:47; Acts 12:7; 22:18; Rom. 9:28; Gal. 1:6; 2 Tim. 2:2; Rev. 2:16; 3:11; 11:14; 22:7, 12, 20) can mean "any moment" when nearly two thousand years have passed. Try substituting

LaHaye's interpretation of "any moment" in these texts whenever "near," "shortly," and "quickly" are used in the Bible.

LaHaye wants to uphold "a belief in an authoritative, Holy Spirit-inspired, inerrant Bible."[8] This is certainly a worthwhile goal in an age of unbelief. But this goal cannot be attained by asserting that what Jesus really meant when He said He would come before that first-century generation passed away was that He "could come for His church at any time"[9] in a pre-tribulational rapture, even after the passage of nearly two millennia. Such a position is impossible to hold for anyone who believes "in an authoritative, Holy Spiritinspired, inerrant Bible." For LaHaye, anyone who does not believe that the Bible teaches a pre-tribulational rapture is interpreting the Bible "figuratively or as an allegory."[10] This is a harsh accusation, especially coming from an advocate of a position that was not taught until 1830. Moreover, it seems rather presumptuous to advocate a doctrine that does not have a single verse to support it, something LaHaye and other dispensationalists willingly admit!

> One objection to the pre-Tribulation Rapture is that no one passage of Scripture teaches the two aspects of His Second Coming separated by the Tribulation. This is true. But then, no one passage teaches a post-trib or mid-trib Rapture, either.[11]

There is a very good reason for this lack of biblical support for *any* future rapture view: The entire futuristic scenario as concocted by pre-, mid-, and post-tribulationalists is based on verses that have already been fulfilled! None of these attempts to predict the proximity of the rapture is new. In 1970, Hal Lindsey's *The Late Great Planet Earth* hit the bookstores and shook the Christian publishing industry. It has been described as "the bestselling non-fiction book of the decade, selling more than 18 million copies worldwide." Since 1970 "more than 25 million copies have been printed in 30 languages."[12] The book continues to sell well.[13] "Things sensational" would be a more appropriate description.

What made *The Late Great Planet Earth* so successful? First, it was written in a popular style, much like a work of fiction. Second, it got into the prediction game, "interpreting" current events in the light of Bible prophecy with rock-solid certainty. Third, it took a "crystal ball" approach to interpretation by giving readers a sense of being able to gaze into the future. In fact, the final chapter in *The Late Great Planet Earth* is "Polishing the Crystal Ball."

"This Generation"

Lindsey's date for the rapture is tied to the meaning he gives "this generation" in Matthew 24:34. For Lindsey, "a generation is something like forty years."[14] By adding forty years to 1948, the year Israel regained nationhood status, he arrives at 1988. But Lindsey believes in a *pretribulational* rapture.[15] and thus believes that the rapture occurs seven years *before* Jesus returns to set up His earthly millennial kingdom. This means that the rapture should have occurred, using Lindsey's calculations, sometime around 1981 with 1988 being the year of the Second Coming and the establishment of Jesus' earthly millennial reign. If Lindsey calculated that the rapture was to occur at the very end of the forty-year generation, then he was still wrong, since 1988 has come and gone.

Just in case his prediction proved to be wrong, Lindsey covered himself with phrases like "*if* this is a correct deduction," "*something like* forty years," "forty years *or so*," and "*could take place*" (emphasis added). Lindsey's prophetic guesses, however, were not considered guesses by his readers. Many took the rebirth of Israel and the forty-year generation scenario as date setting. They set their sights on what they believed to be the assured return of Christ sometime before 1988. Now that 1988 has passed, prophetic readjusting has taken place.

A Clouded Crystal Ball

Gary Wilburn, in his review of the film version of *The Late Great Planet Earth,* agrees that the 1948–88 scenario is the keystone to Lindsey's multimillion best-seller. "The world," as Wilburn evaluates Lindsey's logic, "must end within one generation from the birth of the State of Israel. Any opinion of world affairs that does not dovetail with this prophecy is dismissed."[16] In *The 1980s: Countdown to Armageddon,* Lindsey leads his readers to a pre-1990 climax of history, although he continues to evade certainty: "I believe many people will be shocked by what is happening right now and what will happen in the very near future. *The decade of the 1980s could very well be the last decade of history as we know it.*"[17] The rapture did not occur as Lindsey said it would, based on the 1948–88 timetable and a forty-year generation. The decade of the '80s is over.

"Hero or Bum"?

While Lindsey did not assure his readers that we would not see the nineties, his intimations led many Christians to believe that the rapture was near and the Battle of Armageddon was around the corner. In an interview published in *Christianity Today* in April 1977, Ward Gasque asked Lindsey, "But what if you're wrong?" Lindsey replied: "Well, there's just a split second's difference between a hero and a bum. I didn't ask to be a hero, but I guess I have become one in the Christian community. So I accept it. But if I'm wrong about this, I guess I'll become a bum."[18]

Lindsey has since revised his thinking on the length of a generation. Subsequent to the publication of *The Late Great Planet Earth*, Lindsey wrote that he did not know "how long a Biblical generation is. Perhaps somewhere between sixty and eighty years. The state of Israel was established in 1948. There are a lot of world leaders who are pointing to the 1980s as being the time of some very momentous events. Perhaps it will be then. But I feel certain that it will take place before the year 2000."[19] In an article entitled "The Eschatology of Hal Lindsey," published in 1975, Dale Moody wrote, "If the 'Great Snatch,' as Lindsey repeatedly calls the rapture, does take place before the Tribulation and by 1981, I will beg forgiveness from Lindsey for doubting his infallibility as we meet in the air."[20] It is Lindsey who needs to apologize, and yet he continues to speak and write on the topic of eschatology. Moreover, many Christians consider him to be an authority on the subject. His views remain the standard in many churches, Bible schools, and seminaries.

Rapture—Again!

When the crisis in the Middle East began with Saddam Hussein's invasion of Kuwait in 1990, the prophecy pundits shifted into high gear once again with a barrage of new books psyching up the church with their assured belief that the rapture was near. Millions of Christians began to suffer the ravages of last days madness. Iraq, under the leadership of Saddam Hussein, was seen by one writer to be the ancient empire of Babylon restored.[21] John Walvoord revised his *Armageddon, Oil and the Middle East* to address what he believed was "a scenario leading to the world's final war."[22] Brad Miner, a writer for *National Review*, asked Hal Lindsey, "Is the end of history beginning in the Gulf?"

Lindsey replied, "That's what everybody wants to know. I've never named a day or time, but I can tell you this: Prophecy is on fast forward. I do believe we live in the generation that will see Armageddon."[23]

Newspaper Exegesis

We are living in a heightened era of what Greg L. Bahnsen has described as "newspaper exegesis," that is, reading the Bible through the lens of current events. "The newspaper has no prerogative to challenge God's word of truth. Nor do those who read the newspapers."[24] Of course, prophetic prognosticators try to convince their supporters that current events are being read in light of the Bible. But this claim has often been made with less than satisfactory results:

> All the scripture texts claimed as proof that the coming of Jesus Christ must now be close at hand have also been confidently so used in former generations. Not a few Christians in the past have been erroneously convinced that their age must witness the end. When the Teutonic barbarians overturned Rome and reduced a stable world to chaos in the fifth century A.D., many in the Church despairingly drew the wrong conclusion that the world could have no future. Even larger numbers did so at the approach of the year 1000, believing that the closing millennium would end the world. In the gloom of the fourteenth century such tracts appeared as *The Last Age of the Church,* and in terms very similar to that old title a great number have written since.[25]

Predicting the end (or the pre-tribulational rapture) based on current events is a risky business, as history surely attests and the Bible warns against. The typical Christian appeals to current events to support his belief that the rapture is near. But past failed predictions also were tied to current events, events which were read back into the Bible. Each time the end was predicted with confidence.

What Saith the Scriptures?

Marvin Rosenthal, a prominent and respected advocate for evangelizing the Jews, states that he could no longer hold to a belief in a pre-tribulational rapture because he could *not* find biblical support for the position. What saith the Scriptures? Rosenthal observed that in John Walvoord's *The Rapture Question* fifty arguments for pre-tribulationalism were offered, but no biblical text was given that explicitly taught the position:

> Not once, among fifty arguments, does this godly Christian leader cite one biblical text that explicitly teaches pretribulation rapturism—not once. This was not an oversight. The reason for the omission of any pretribulation Rapture texts is clear. There are none. Walvoord's own comment helps substantiate that fact. He wrote, "It is therefore not too much to say that the Rapture question is determined more by ecclesiology [the doctrine of the Church] than eschatology [the doctrine of the last things]." In other words, he is saying that verses which deal with the church must be used to prove an issue that relates to the prophecy. There simply is no explicit exegetical evidence for pretribulation rapturism.[26]

This is a bombshell. There is not one explicit verse to support a position that millions of Bible-believing Christians hold with unbending reverence. In the first edition of *The Rapture Question,* John Walvoord had to confess that evidence for either a pre-tribulational or a post-tribulational rapture was not explicitly taught in the Bible. "He deleted this statement in later editions of the book."[27] Why? It certainly was not because he found a verse that without question supported either position.

Rapture or Resurrection?

Dispensationalists take Bible passages that refer to the general resurrection and apply them to what they call "the rapture." Dave Hunt states that "Christ's promise to take His own to heaven [in the rapture] has no significant place in [the] future plans" of those who believe that the world that God created is important.[28] The "promise" that Hunt has in mind is the pretribulational rapture. But the rapture is not the Bible's blessed hope. Instead, the clear teaching of Scripture is that Christians find hope in the promise that when they die they will go to heaven to be with the Lord (Phil. 1:21).

The resurrection, not the rapture, is the hope of the church. Paul was on trial "for the resurrection of the dead" (Acts 24:21), not the rapture of the church. Paul is emphatic: "But if there is no resurrection of the dead, not even Christ has been raised; and if Christ has not been raised, then our preaching is vain, your faith also is vain" (1 Cor. 15:13–14). No such defense is made of a supposed pretribulational, mid-tribulational, post-tribulational, or pre-wrath rapture.

The error of rapture fever has obscured the Bible's focus: the resurrection of Jesus and the resurrection of the saints. Paul's goal was to "attain to the resurrection from the dead" (Phil. 3:11), not the rapture of the church. The Christian message hinges on the reality of the resurrection, not the rapture of the church. The unbiblical pre-tribulational rapture doctrine obscures and distorts this message. Without the resurrection the Christian message is just one religious point of view among countless others. The pre-trib rapture doctrine is an unnecessary, unbiblical, and unhistorical diversion from the central truth of the Christian faith.

Notes

1. Dave Hunt, *Whatever Happened to Heaven?* (Eugene, OR: Harvest House, 1988), chapter 3. A more appropriate title for this book would be, *Whatever Happened to the Pretribulational Rapture?* No one is disputing the reality of heaven.

2. Hunt, *Whatever Happened to Heaven*, 63.

3. Hunt, *Whatever Happened to Heaven*, 64.

4. Hunt, *Whatever Happened to Heaven?*, 67.

5. Dave Hunt, *How Close Are We?: Compelling Evidence for the Soon Return of Christ* (Eugene, OR: Harvest House, 1993).

6. Tim LaHaye, *No Fear of the Storm: Why Christians Will Escape All the Tribulation* (Sisters, OR: Multnomah Press, 1992), 10.

7. Philippians 2:19, 24 and 3 John 14 are interesting. Paul writes in Philippians 2:19: "I *hope* in the Lord Jesus to send Timothy to you *shortly*." "Shortly" obviously means "soon." But Paul is not sure if it will happen as he plans, so he qualifies the expectation with "I hope." Similar qualifiers are found in Philippians 2:24 and 3 John 14. No such qualifiers accompany Revelation 1:1 and 22:6. In fact, God states that "the things" outlined in Revelation "*must* shortly take place" (1:1).

8. LaHaye, *No Fear of the Storm*, 16.

9. LaHaye, *No Fear of the Storm*, 16.

10. LaHaye, *No Fear of the Storm*, 17.

11. LaHaye, *No Fear of the Storm*, 69.

12. Gary Friesen, "A Return Visit," *Moody Monthly* (May 1988), 30.

13. Books with doomsday themes began selling well in 1990 due to fears that Saddam Hussein would drag the world into a fiery Armageddon. "Zondervan Publishing House announced that sales of Hal Lindsey's 1970 multimillion seller 'The Late Great Planet Earth,' now in its 108th printing, shot up 83 percent between August and September [1990]. 'Often times we see during a crisis that people more actively turn toward God and things spiritual,' Zondervan executive Paul Van Duinen said" (*National & International Religion Report* [22 October 1990], 1).

14. Hal Lindsey, *The Late Great Planet Earth* (Grand Rapids, MI: Zondervan, 1970), 54.

15. For a discussion of the various rapture theories, see Richard R. Reiter, *et al.*, *The Rapture: Pre-, Mid-, or Post-Tribulational?* (Grand Rapids, MI: Zondervan, 1984).

16. Gary Wilburn, "The Doomsday Chic," *Christianity Today* (27 January 1978), 22.

17. Hal Lindsey, *The 1980s: Countdown to Armageddon* (King of Prussia, PA: Westgate Press, 1980), 8.

18. W. Ward Gasque, "Future Fact? Future Fiction?," *Christianity Today* (15 April 1977), 40.

19. Gasque, "Future Fact? Future Fiction?," 40.

20. Dale Moody, "The Eschatology of Hal Lindsey," *Review and Expositor* (Summer 1975), 278.

21. Charles H. Dyer, *The Rise of Babylon: Sign of the End Times* (Wheaton, IL: Tyndale, 1991). Notice that no question mark follows the subtitle. This is a book of prediction.

22. Cal Thomas, "Time for Armageddon?" *Marietta Daily Journal* (January 1991).

23. *National Review* (19 November 1990), 49.

24. Greg L. Bahnsen, "The *Prima Facie* Acceptability of Postmillennialism," *The Journal of Christian Reconstruction*, Symposium on the Millennium, ed. Gary North, 3:2 (Winter 1976–77), 53–55.

25. Iain Murray, *The Puritan Hope: Revival and the Interpretation of Prophecy* (London: Banner of Truth Trust, 1971), xix.

26. Marvin Rosenthal, *The Pre-Wrath Rapture of the Church: A New Understanding of the Rapture, the Tribulation, and the Second Coming* (Nashville, TN: Thomas Nelson, 1990), 280.

27. William Sanford LaSor, *The Truth About Armageddon: What the Bible Says About the End Times* (Grand Rapids, MI: Baker Book House, 1982), 134.

28. Hunt, *Whatever Happened to Heaven?*, 44.

Chapter Seventeen

NO EVIDENCE
FOR A RAPTURE

O bjections to a pre-tribulational rapture are certainly not unique to this writer. The doctrine has been criticized since its inception in the early part of the nineteenth century. As you consider some of the texts used to support the doctrine, ask yourself this question: Is it self-evident that these texts teach a pre-tribulational rapture, that is, that the church will be taken off the earth prior to a future great tribulation? The arguments used by adherents of the pre-tribulational rapture position are complex, since no single verse actually teaches the doctrine. The complexity of these arguments requires that we consider the strongest texts in support of the position. It should be kept in mind that the entire pre-tribulational scheme is based on a faulty interpretation of Daniel 9:24–27. The dispensationalist maintains that the last seven years (the seventieth "week") is still future and that the rapture will inaugurate this final week (seven years) of the seventy weeks (490 years). This supposedly will give God the opportunity to deal exclusively with Israel as a nation again.

Revelation 4:1

Let's begin our study of the pre-tribulational rapture doctrine by taking a close look at Revelation 4:1:

After these things I looked, and behold, a door standing open in heaven, and the first voice which I had heard, like the sound of a trumpet speaking with me, said, 'Come up here, and I will show you what must take place after these things.'"

John Walvoord, an ardent believer in the pre-tribulational rapture, imports an already-constructed pre-tribulational rapture theory into texts that say nothing about the church being taken to heaven. His exposition of Revelation 4:1 is evidence of this:

> It is clear from the context that this is not an explicit reference to the Rapture of the church, as John was not actually translated [raptured]; in fact he was still in his natural body on the island of Patmos. He was translated into scenes of heaven only temporarily. Though there is no authority for connecting the Rapture with this expression, there does seem to be a typical representation of the order of events, namely, the church age first, then the Rapture, then the church in heaven.[1]

If one takes Walvoord's position, then Rosenthal is correct: There is no verse that explicitly teaches the doctrine![2] *All* of the texts used to support the rapture theory *presuppose* the validity of the theory, a theory that does not have a single text to support it. The doctrine has been constructed before texts have been evaluated.

This unsound approach to Bible interpretation has done little to dissuade the adherents of the various rapture theories. Grant R. Jeffrey, for example, begins with Revelation 4:1 as one of the *"five definitive indications* supporting the pretribulation Rapture."[3] Here's how the argument goes for those who see the rapture of the church in this verse:

- The voice that John heard was "like the sound of a trumpet speaking."
- When Jesus returns to rapture His church, He will do so "with the trumpet of God" (1 Thess. 4:16).
- Since a trumpet is used just prior to the rapture in 1 Thessalonians 4:16, we should assume that a rapture is in view when "a door [is] standing open in heaven," presumably to receive the raptured church (Rev. 4:1–2).

- The church is no longer mentioned in the Book of Revelation; therefore, the church must have been raptured.
- John's being directed to "Come up here" is a depiction of the rapture in the same way that the church will be "caught up" at the time of the pretribulational rapture. Jeffrey writes, "When John was *'in the Spirit'* ... he was 'Raptured up' to Heaven...."[4]

This is absurd exegesis to be sure, but it is standard dispensational teaching.[5]

As has been noted, the pre-tribulational rapture doctrine assumes that the seventieth week of Daniel is separated from the sixty-ninth week and is yet to be fulfilled. The dispensational interpretation also assumes that the Book of Revelation was written about a time period in the remote future rather than for the people for whom events were to happen "shortly" (Rev. 1:1). For the readers of the prophecy in the first century, "the time is near" (1:3). The Book of Revelation was written before A.D. 70. Its purpose was to describe events leading up to and including the destruction of Jerusalem. The evidence for a pre-A.D. 70 date is overwhelming.[6] For one thing, the temple was still standing when John received the Revelation and wrote it down for the "seven churches" (Rev. 11:1–2), churches that were in existence in John's day. Jesus assured the first readers of Revelation that He would be coming "quickly" (2:16; 3:11; 22:7, 12, 20). Those who claim to hold a literal interpretation want to avoid the obvious conclusion of these verses—the prophecy is describing events that refer to the first-century church. This does not mean that the Book of Revelation has no meaning for today's church. The crucifixion occurred before the destruction of Jerusalem in A.D. 70, and no one claims that Christ's death has no meaning for today. Numerous events in the Old Testament are history, but they have meaning and application for our day as well: "Now these things happened to them as an example, and they were written for *our instruction*, upon whom the ends of the ages have come" (1 Cor. 10:11).

But let's get back to the supposed evidence for a pre-tribulational rapture in Revelation 4:1. First, John didn't hear a trumpet. He heard a *voice "like* the *sound* of a trumpet speaking." Second, it is fallacious to argue that the absence of a reference to the church indicates its rapture (absence from the earth). Hal Lindsey states, "Since the Church is mentioned nineteen times in the first three chapters under divine outline of 'the things which are,' and since the Church is not mentioned or implied as being on earth even once after the statement 'Come up here, and I will show you what must take place *after these things*,' I conclude that it is the end of the Church age that is meant here, and that the Church is in heaven thereafter until it returns as the bride of Christ in Revelation 19:7–14."[7] Notice that no text states this. These are Lindsey's conclusions.

Let's test Lindsey's hypothesis. The first three chapters of Revelation deal with churches, assemblies of saints in Asia Minor in the first century: the church *in* Ephesus (2:1), the church *in* Smyrna (2:8), the church *in* Pergamum (2:12), the church *in* Thyatira (2:18), the church *in* Sardis (3:1), the church *in* Philadelphia (3:7), and the church *in* Laodicea (3:14). After chapter three, Jesus (1:1) deals with those who make up the church—the "saints" (5:8; 8:3, 4; 11:18; 13:7, 10; 14:12; 16:6; 17:6; 18:24; 19:8). In the first three chapters, local churches are addressed, not the church generally. After chapter three the "saints," individuals who make up the seven churches in Asia Minor and elsewhere, are referred to. Is there exegetical evidence for this interpretation? Yes. "To the *church of God which is at Corinth,* to those who have been sanctified in Christ Jesus, *saints by calling,* with all who in every place call upon the name of our Lord Jesus Christ, their Lord and ours" (1 Cor. 1:2; cf. 6:1–6; 14:33; 2 Cor. 2:1). Is Paul describing two groups of people? No! The saints constitute the church.

It takes amazing hermeneutical manipulation to create a doctrine where none exists. Lindsey's view must be read into the text. He begins with his pretribulational rapture theology (still not documented by arguments from Scripture) and forces it on a verse that must be twisted to prove what he claims it teaches. Nothing like what Lindsey believes can be found in Revelation 4:1.

Let's continue by applying Lindsey's hermeneutical logic to other passages. The words *church* and *churches* appear just once in the Book of Hebrews (12:23) and twice in 2 Corinthians (1:1 and 2:14): "The church is not mentioned as such in Mark, Luke, John, 2 Timothy, Titus, 1 Peter, 2 Peter, 1 John, 2 John, or Jude, and not until chapter 16 of Romans. Unless we are prepared to relegate large chunks of the NT to a limbo of irrelevance to the Church, we cannot make the mention or omission of the term 'church' a criterion for determining the applicability of a passage to saints of the present age."[8]

Is Bible interpretation based on word counts? The same reasoning process has been taken with the Book of Esther by liberal scholars: "There can be no doubt that the historicity and canonicity of Esther has been the most debated of all the Old Testament books. Even some Jewish scholars questioned its inclusion in the Old Testament because of the absence of God's name."[9] If word counts are to be so heavily relied upon then Lindsey refutes his own argument. He finds the Antichrist all over the Book of Revelation, but the word is nowhere to be found.

If chapters 4–19 are not about the church, then what group of people would Jesus as the true author of Revelation have in mind? The dispensationalist believes that these passages describe the time of the great tribulation, when Israel, not the church, is in view. But word-count exegesis leaves us in something of a dilemma since the word *Israel* only appears once after the supposed rapture of the church, and not until Revelation 7:4! One would think that if the church is in view in the first three chapters because the words *church* and *churches* are used nineteen times, then shouldn't we expect to find the word *Israel* used more than once after chapter three if this entire seven-year period is about Israel? The word *Israel* does appear in 21:12, but the word *churches* appears in 22:16. Revelation 22:16 demonstrates that the entire book is "for the churches," not just the first three chapters.

A glaring inconsistency can be found in Tim LaHaye's defense of an any-moment rapture based on Revelation 4:1. He states that the "first-century church believed in the imminent return of Christ, possibly during their lifetime."[10] He means by this that first-century Christians and Christians thereafter believed that Jesus could come at any moment. But later in the same book he writes, "Chapter 1 is the introduction; chapters 2 and 3 [of Revelation] *cover the church age,* using seven historical churches to describe the entire age. (For example, the church in Ephesus is the only one that refers to apostles because the first-century church alone included apostles.)"[11] Chuck Smith, another popular prophcy writer, pushes the same idea while maintaining that Jesus' coming is always imminent, that is, that He could come at any moment. But like LaHaye, he contradicts himself when he writes that "each of these seven churches . . . represents a particular period of Church history. For instance, the church at Smyrna represents the Church of the second through fourth centuries—a time when persecution was horrible and as many as six million Christians were executed for their faith. The church at Pergamum represents the beginning of the church-state system that developed under Constantine. And so on."[12]

How could Christians believe that Jesus could come at any moment and also believe that He would not come until the last of the seven representative churches (Laodicea) appeared? This destroys the dispensationalist's doctrine of imminency, the any-moment rapture of the church. It also destroys literalism since the seven churches are purported to *represent* seven distinct periods of the church age, not individual churches. William Hendriksen comments on the seven churches/seven ages view:

> The notion that these seven churches describe seven successive periods of Church history hardly needs refutation. To say nothing about the humorous—if it were not so deplorable—exegesis which, for example, makes the church of Sardis, which was dead, refer to the glorious age of the Reformation; it should be clear to every student of Scripture that there is not one atom of evidence in all the sacred writings which in any way corroborates this thoroughly arbitrary method of cutting up the history of the Church and assigning the resulting pieces to the respective epistles of Revelation 2 and 3.[13]

According to dispensationalists, the rapture is a two-stage event: Jesus comes *for* His saints before the seven-year tribulation period and *with* His saints at the end of the tribulation period to defeat antichrist and set up the millennial kingdom (Revelation 19). But there is no mention of the church in Revelation 19 following Jesus on His "white horse" (19:11). The "armies of heaven," not the church, follow Jesus on their "white horses" (19:14). If dispensationalists maintain that the "armies of heaven" are the church or saints, then this only shows that the word church does not have to appear for it to be present. A final point needs to be made. Dispensationalists teach that Jesus coming on "a white horse" in Revelation 19 is the second coming. Robert L. Thomas is a representative of this popular position:

> This picture climaxes the NT emphasis on the second coming of Christ as the fulfillment and vidication of the Christian hope (e.g., Matt. 13:41–42; 25:41; Rom. 2:5; 2 Thess. 1:7–8, 9–10; 2:8) . . . . It answers specifically to the theme verse of Rev. 1:7 which tells of the worldwide audience this event will have (cf. Matt. 24:27–31). . . . In fact, this is the only event in Revelation that corresponds to that coming narrowly construed to refer to Christ's personal coming.[14]

In Acts 1:9–11 we are told that "a cloud received Him out of their sight" (1:9). No horse was involved. "This Jesus, who has been taken up from you into heaven, *will come in just the same way as you have watched Him go into heaven"* (1:11). Jesus did not go into heaven on a horse, and He will not return on a horse.

Like the dispensational hermeneutical methodology in general, the pre-tribulational rapture doctrine is a gigantic hoax. Because the pretribulational rapture is a pillar of the dispensational system, we should expect to find proof of its existence in clear texts. Even one text would suffice. There is not a single passage that clearly and dogmatically supports a pretribulational rapture. If so many people believe the pre-tribulational rapture doctrine, why is it that no verse can be appealed to that explicitly teaches it? Most pre-tribulationists have never been challenged to produce a verse.

1 Thessalonians 4:16–17 *Read Page 277-280*

In a debate on eschatology with Dave Hunt, I challenged him to point to one verse that taught a pre-tribulational rapture. He immediately appealed to 1 Thessalonians 4:16–17. Read it for yourself. The idea of a pre-tribulational rapture must be *assumed* by the reader and imposed on the text. Sound biblical interpretation, however, requires textual proof before a doctrine can be formulated.

Most postmillennialists and amillennialists see 1 Thessalonians 4:16–17 as relating to the general resurrection of the saints. The text simply describes the raising of those who are "in Christ." No mention is made of the church being raptured either before or after a tribulation period. Nothing in the text even points to a tribulation period. Anthony Hoekema, an amillennialist, rejects the idea that the Apostle Paul was teaching a pre-tribulational rapture:

> What this passage clearly teaches is that at the time of the Lord's return all the believing dead (the "dead in Christ") will be raised, and all believers who are still alive will be transformed and glorified (see 1 Corinthians 15:51–52); then these two groups will be caught up to meet the Lord in the air. What these words do not teach is that after this meeting in the air the Lord will reverse his direction and go back to heaven, taking the raised and transformed members of the church with him. The passage does not breathe a word of this. To be sure, verse 17 ends with the words, "and so we shall always be with the Lord." But Paul does not say *where* we shall always be with the Lord. The idea that after meeting the Lord in the air we shall be with him for seven years in heaven and

later for a thousand years in the air above the earth is pure inference and nothing more. Everlasting oneness with Christ in glory is the clear teaching of this passage, not a pretribulational Rapture.[15]

Non-premillennialists do not deny the rapture as such (even though the word is not found in Scripture); they only deny the dispensationalists' version of it. Not only is the Bible on the side of those who view the rapture as the general resurrection, so are eighteen hundred years of church history: "As an established view, it can be traced back to J.N. Darby and the Plymouth Brethren in the year 1830. Some scholars, seeking to prove error by association, have attempted (perhaps unfairly) to trace its origin back two years earlier to a charismatic, visionary woman named Margaret MacDonald."[16] Even pretribulational dispensationalists admit the novelty of the position:

> It is scarcely to be found in a single book or sermon through the period of 1600 years! If any doubt this statement, let them search ... the remarks of the so-called Fathers, both pre and post Nicene, the theological treatises of the scholastic divines, Roman Catholic writers of all shades of thought, the literature of the Reformation, the sermons and expositions of the Puritans, and the general theological works of the day. He will find the "mystery" conspicuous by its absence.[17]

Here is a dispensationalist admitting that there is "scarcely" any historical evidence to support the position. He's too generous. There is *no* evidence. So where does a dispensationalist get this doctrine? Tommy Ice, a fervent proponent of dispensationalism, writes that the theory is based on "deduction":

> A certain theological climate needed to be created before premillennialism would restore the Biblical doctrine of the pretrib Rapture. Sufficient development did not take place until after the French Revolution. The factor of the Rapture has been clearly known by the church all along; therefore, the issue is the *timing* of the event. Since *neither pre nor posttribs have a proof text for the time of the Rapture* (unless the promise made to the church in Rev. 3:10 is an exception which promises deliverance— the Rapture—from the future tribulation before the seven-year period begins),[18] then it is clear that this issue is the product of a deduction from one's overall system of theology, *both for pre and posttribbers.*[19]

What an admission! A pillar doctrine of dispensationalism does not have a single text to prove it.[20] Dispensationalism's process of "deducing" the rapture theory is this: First, create the system; second, create the doctrines to make the system work; third, claim to have restored "the Biblical doctrine of the pretrib Rapture," which is based on a "deduction from one's overall system of theology" because there are no verses that teach it; fourth, imply that the early church, the apostles of the apostles, knew nothing of this foundational doctrine. Bizarre. Millions of Christians today hold to a system of interpretation (dispensationalism) that does not have one verse to prove one of its foundational doctrines, the pre-tribulational rapture of the church, the concept that makes dispensationalism dispensational. This system of interpretation is a theological house of cards.

Hoping to seek historical validation for the pre-tribulation rapture, dispensationalists have turned to an obscure and questionable source, Pseudo-Ephraem (probably a seventh-century composition). While the sermon *On the Last Times, the Antichrist, and the End of the World* claims to be authored by Ephraem of Nisibis (306–73), no one really knows who wrote it or when it was written. Even so, pre-tribulationists believe that it contains "two proto-rapture statements."[21] An appeal to Pseudo-Ephraem is an act of desperation by those in need of historical support since they have no biblical support for their position.

Titus 2:13

Dave Hunt, in *How Close Are We?*, maintains that "Paul called the Rapture 'that blessed hope'" (Titus 2:13).[22] There is no mention of a rapture, either pre-, mid-, or post-tribulational in this passage. Hunt, as a pre-tribulationist, asserts that "the appearing of the glory of our great God and Savior" is a description of Jesus' coming at the end of the seven-year tribulation period while the "blessed hope" is the rapture of the church prior to the tribulation period. The belief that Titus 2:13 describes two comings must be read into the passage. Paul was "awaiting our blessed hope" *which was* "the appearing of the glory of our great God and Savior, Jesus Christ." Even John Walvoord believes that Titus 2:13 describes only one event.[23]

What is this "blessed hope"? It was the "appearing of the glory" of Jesus. We have come across this language before in Matthew 16:27: "For the Son of Man is going to *come in the glory of His Father* with His angels..." (Matt. 16:27; cf. Mark 8:38). When did this happen? "Truly I say to you, there are some of those standing here who shall not taste death until they see the Son of Man coming in His kingdom" (Matt. 16:28). Jesus had His generation in mind, not a distant generation.

Notice that Titus 2:13 describes the "appearing of *the glory* of our great God and Savior, Jesus Christ." Paul does not say that Jesus will appear, only that "the glory" will appear. There is a significant difference in meaning. Peter writes in a similar fashion:

> Beloved, do not be surprised at the fiery ordeal among you, which comes upon you for your testing, as though some strange thing were happening to you; but to the degree that you share the sufferings of Christ, keep on rejoicing; so that at the *revelation of His glory*, you may rejoice with exultation (1 Peter 4:12–13).

First, Peter writes that his readers were personally involved in a "fiery ordeal." This was not some future event. Second, not only were they experiencing a "fiery ordeal," but they would "rejoice with exultation" at the "revelation of His glory." There is no indication that a long period of time exists between their "fiery ordeal" and the "revelation of His glory." In this same chapter Peter writes that "the end of all things is *at hand*" (1 Peter 4:7), at hand for those reading his letter in the first century. What was this "end" that was "at hand"? Jay Adams' comments summarize the argument:

> [First] Peter was written before A.D. 70 (when the destruction of Jerusalem took place).... The persecution (and martyrdom) that these (largely) Jewish Christians had been experiencing up until now stemmed principally from unconverted Jews (indeed, his readers had found refuge among **Gentiles** as resident aliens).... [H]e refers to the severe trials that came upon Christians who had fled Palestine under attack from their unconverted fellow Jews. **The end of all things** (that had brought this exile about) was **near.**
>
> In six or seven years from the time of writing, the overthrow of Jerusalem, with all its tragic stories, as foretold in the Book of Revelation and in the Olivet Discourse upon which that part is based, would take place. Titus and Vespasian would wipe out the old order once and for all. All those forces that led to the persecution and exile of these Christians in Asia Minor—the temple ceremonies (outdated by Christ's death),

Pharisaism (with its distortion of O.T. law into a system of works-righ-
teousness) and the political stance of Palestinian Jewry toward Rome—
would be erased. The Roman armies would wipe Jewish opposition from
the face of the land. Those who survived the holocaust of A.D. 70 would
themselves be dispersed around the Mediterranean world. "So," says Peter, "hold on; the end is near." The full **end** of the O.T. order (already
made defunct by the cross and the empty tomb) was about to occur.[24]

Third, if the "revelation of His glory" were a depiction of a pre-tribulational
rapture that is yet to occur, how would this distant event comfort those who
were involved in a "fiery ordeal" nearly two thousand years ago? In death
they saw Jesus "face to face" (1 Cor. 13:12; 2 Cor. 5:8). Did they not behold
the *fullness* of His glory at that time? In another context, the Apostle Paul
writes, "For I consider that the sufferings of this present time are not worthy
to be compared with the *glory* that is to be revealed to us" (Rom. 8:18). The
New American Standard translation does not catch the full meaning of this
passage. Following Robert Young's *Literal Translation of the Bible*, we read,
"For I reckon that the sufferings of the present time are not worthy to be
compared with the glory *about to be revealed in us.*" Whatever the glory is, it
was "about to be revealed" (see Rev. 2:10; 3:2, 10; 10:4; 12:4; 17:8). Peter
tells his readers that the "Spirit of glory and of God rests upon you" (1 Peter
4:14). This was a *present* condition, not something that the people in Peter's
day would have to wait for in a future rapture.

If the "appearing of *the glory* of our great God and Savior, Jesus Christ"
(Titus 2:13) is neither a distant event nor the bodily return of Christ, then
what is it? The "appearing of the glory" is the coming of the fullness of
the New Covenant promises as outlined in the gospel. The Old Covenant
came with glory "which fades away" (1 Cor. 3:7, 10–11, 13). The New
Covenant has come with even more glory (3:8). "For if the ministry of
condemnation has glory, much more does the ministry of righteousness
abound in glory. For indeed what had glory, in this case has no glory on
account of the glory that surpasses it. For if that which fades away was
with glory, much more that which remains is in glory" (3:9–11).

With the destruction of Jerusalem in A.D. 70 the Old Covenant that had
faded in glory was obliterated. The gospel is the new glory which those
who are still attached to the fading glory of the Old Covenant do not see.
"And even if our gospel is veiled, it is veiled to those who are perishing, in

whose case the god of this world [lit., *age*] has blinded the minds of the unbelieving, *that they might not see the light of the gospel of the glory of Christ, who is the image of God*" (2 Cor. 4:3–4).

The blessed hope, therefore, is the coming of the fullness of the gospel in the "glory of Christ." This fullness was accomplished with the obliteration of the symbols of the Old Covenant: the temple, priesthood, and sacrificial system.

1 Corinthians 15

This section of Scripture falls into the same category as 1 Thessalonians 4:16–17. Again, no one denies that Christians are going to be raised; the dispute is over when the event happens. The passage makes no mention of a "secret rapture," or Jesus coming "for His saints" before a future great tribulation and then later returning "with His saints" after the great tribulation. Nowhere in 1 Corinthians 15 will you find a discussion of the great tribulation or an earthly millennial reign of Christ. The pre-tribulational rapture must be read into 1 Corinthians 15. The chapter deals with resurrection not rapture: first, the resurrection of Jesus; second, the resurrection of Christians. Without the resurrection of Jesus there will be no resurrection of Christians. The resurrection of believers comes just before the end: "But each in his own order: Christ the first fruits, after that those who are Christ's at His coming, then comes the end, when He delivers up the kingdom to the God and Father, when He has abolished all rule and all authority and power" (15:23–24). This "resurrection of the dead" occurs *after* the period of the kingdom (there must be something to deliver up) and just before "the end."

How do premillennialists fit an earthly millennium into these two verses? You guessed it. There are gaps inserted to divide the passage into three events: the pre-tribulational rapture, the coming of Christ seven years later, and the resurrection of unbelievers a thousand years after the end of the Millennium. Again, these "gaps" or "intervals" must be read into the text. John 5:28–29 states very clearly that believers and unbelievers will be raised at the same time, not separated by a thousand years.

Christians must refuse to be guided by the latest interpretive trends or to be swayed by current events. The Bible is the Christian's guide, not the conjectures of self-appointed prophecy "experts," the latest newspaper headlines, or the movements of national boundaries. The Bible is our starting point regardless of what we think is going on in the world.

The only question is *whether* the *Bible* actually teaches these things. If it does, then "let God be true but every man a liar" (Rom. 3:4). The newspaper has no prerogative to challenge God's word of truth. Nor do those who read the newspapers. As faithful disciples of Christ, we are to trust God as the sovereign controller over human history, "who works all things after the counsel of His own will" (Eph. 1:1), declaring the end from the beginning and from ancient times things not yet done, saying, "My counsel shall stand, and I will accomplish all my purpose" (Isa. 46:10), so that "none can stay his hand" (Dan. 4:35). With the Psalmist we should declare, "Whatever the Lord pleases, he does, in heaven and on earth" (115:3).[25]

Returning to a true understanding of the Bible and its application to presentday conditions will bring about great revival and reformation to a world languishing in the pit of despair and darkness. Jesus is the answer. It is in the world that God calls sinners to Himself.

Notes

1. John F. Walvoord, *The Revelation of Jesus Christ* (Chicago: Moody, 1966) 103.

2. For a critique of Walvoord's position of John's "translation" as a type of rapture, see Robert H. Gundry, *The Church and the Tribulation* (Grand Rapids, MI: Zondervan, 1973), 68–9.

3. Grant Jeffrey, *Armageddon: Appointment with Destiny* (Toronto: Frontier Research, 1988), 135.

4. Jeffrey, *Armageddon,* 136.

5. See Hal Lindsey, *The Rapture* (New York: Bantam Books, 1983), 88–91.

6. See Kenneth L. Gentry, Jr., *Before Jerusalem Fell: Dating the Book of Revelation,* 2nd ed. (Atlanta, GA: American Vision, 1999).

7. Hal Lindsey, *The Rapture,* 90.

8. Gundry, *The Church and the Tribulation,* 78. Also see Gundry's *First the Antichrist* (Grand Rapids, MI: Baker Book House, 1997), 84–87.

9. Edward G. Dobson, "Esther," *Liberty Bible Commentary,* eds. Edward E. Hindson and Woodrow M. Kroll (Lynchburg, VA: The Old-Time Gospel Hour, 1982), 909.

10. Tim LaHaye, *No Fear of the Storm: Why Christians Will Escape All the Tribulation* (Sisters, OR: Multnomah Press, 1992), 65.

11. LaHaye, *No Fear of the Storm,* 74.

12. Chuck Smith with David Wimbish, *Dateline Earth: Countdown to Eternity* (Old Tappan, NJ: Chosen Books, 1989), 28–29.

13. William Hendriksen, *More Than Conquerors: An Interpretation of the Book of Revelation,* 2nd ed. (Grand Rapids, MI: Baker Book House, [1940] 1982), 60. In his *Dateline Earth,* Chuck Smith identifies the Church of Sardis with the Protestant Reformation because the Protestant Church celebrated Christmas. "Should Christians stop celebrating on December 25?," Smith asks. "Not at all. We enjoy glorious liberty as children of God to celebrate or not to celebrate, as we choose" (33). So why wasn't this true for those who started celebrating Christmas on December 25?

14. Robert L. Thomas, *Revelation 8–22: An Exegetical Commentary* (Chicago, IL: Moody Press, 1995), 382.

15. Anthony A. Hoekema, *The Bible and the Future* (Grand Rapids, MI: Eerdmans, 1979), 168.

16. Marvin Rosenthal, *Pre-Wrath Rapture of the Church: A New Understanding of the Rapture, the Tribulation, and the Second Coming* (Nashville, TN: Thomas Nelson, 1990), 54. For a study on the preDarbyite source of the pre-tribulational

rapture, see Dave MacPherson, *The Incredible Cover-Up* (Medford, OR: Omega, [1975] 1980 and *The Rapture Plot* (Simpsonville, SC: Millennium III Publishers, 1995). John L. Bray disputes the Darbyite and MacDonald sources. He has traced its origin to Morgan Edwards, *Two Academical Exercises on Subjects Bearing the Following Titles: Millennium, and Last-Novelties* (Philadelphia, PA: Dobson and Lang, 1788). See Bray's *Morgan Edwards and the Pre-Tribulation Rapture Teaching (1788)*, Lakeland, FL: John L. Bray Ministries, 1995) for documentation on this theory.

17. H.A. Ironside, *The Mysteries of God* (New York: Loizeaux Brothers, 1908), 50.

18. Notice what Revelation 3:10 says: "Because you have kept the word of My perseverance, I also will keep you from the hour of testing, that hour *which is about to come upon the whole world, to test those who dwell on the earth.*" This passage was written nearly two thousand years ago. The "hour of testing" was "about to come upon the whole world [Greek, *oikoumene: the inhabited earth*]." This means not long after the time it was spoken. That hour of testing was the conflagration leading up to the destruction of Jerusalem in A.D. 70, the tribulation period from which Christians were warned to "flee," which they did (Matt. 24:16).

19. Thomas D. Ice, "The Origin of the Pretrib Rapture: Part II," *Biblical Perspectives* (March/April 1989), 5. Emphasis added.

20. Ice and Demy attempt to get around this admission in *The Truth About the Rapture* (Eugene, OR: Harvest House, 1996).

21. Timothy J. Demy, "Pseudo-Ephraem," *Dictionary of Premillennial Theology*, gen. ed. Mal Couch (Grand Rapids, MI: Kregel, 1996), 329. Also see Demy and Thomas D. Ice, "The Rapture and an Early Medieval Citation," *Bibliotheca Sacra* (July/September 1995), 306–17 and Grant R. Jeffrey, "A Pretrib Rapture Statement in the Early Medieval Church," gen. eds. Thomas Ice and Timothy Demy, *When the Trumpet Sounds* (Eugene, OR: Harvest House, 1995), 105–125. For a refutation of Demy, Ice, and Jeffrey, see Gundry, "'Pseudo-Ephraem' on Pretrib Preparation for a Posttrib Meeting with the Lord" in *First The Antichrist*, 161–88.

22. Hunt, *How Close Are We?*, 199.

23. John F. Walvoord, *The Prophecy Knowledge Handbook: All the Prophecies of Scripture Explained in One Volume* (Wheaton, IL: Victor Books, 1990), 496–97.

24. Jay E. Adams, *Trust and Obey: A Practical Commentary on First Peter* (Phillipsburg, NJ: Presbyterian and Reformed, 1978), 129–30.

25. Greg L. Bahnsen, "The *Prima Facie* Acceptability of Postmillennialism," *The Journal of Christian Reconstruction*, Symposium on the Millennium, ed. Gary North, 3:2 (Winter 1976–77), 54.

Chapter Eighteen

WHO'S GOT
THE NUMBER?

The attempt to identify the number of the Beast has entered the computer age. No longer does one need a keen mathematical mind to make the calculations. A computer program has been developed so we can all learn who the Beast is in the privacy of our own homes. Any number of people, places, or events can receive the dreaded number. Here's how it works: Place the diskette into the floppy disk drive. Type "666" at the "A" prompt. Press the "Enter" key. A screen appears with these words: ENTER WORD OR PHRASE TO DECODE. Who or what is cursed with the dreaded number 666? "New York" is 666. "A War in Iraq" is 666. "Bush's War" is 666. Millions of children around the world will be heartbroken to learn that "Santa Claus" is also 666. This is no joke. A computer program called "666: Ancient Mystery Code Revealed!" exists. There's a book that goes with it: *666: The Final Warning!*[1] The author's conclusion?

Again, the goal of this book was to share with the readers what I personally feel the Lord has shown me over a period of twelve years as I studied His Word regarding the *End-Time* events and the *possible key players* involved. Does this "prove" that Ronald Wilson Reagan is the predestined *Antichrist,* and that Pope John Paul II will become the *False Prophet?* In my opinion, the *"evidence"* shown in this book is *overwhelmingly in favor* of their being *"history's prime candidates"* for these *"unholy"* positions.[2]

This book identifies Ronald Reagan as the Beast and Pope John Paul II as the false prophet of Revelation 13. Of course, the author leaves his speculations open to adjustment. If Reagan stays in retirement "at what was formerly *666* Saint Cloud Road, and only speaks at 'after lunch and after dinner' events, then he can not be the fulfillment of the *Antichrist.*"[3] Will Reagan's "fatal wound" (Alzheimer's Disease) be healed (Rev. 13:3, 12, 14) in order for him to qualify for beast status? This is the way speculative prophecy always seems to work. A person is the Antichrist until it is proved that he is not the Antichrist. When an Antichrist candidate does not turn out to be *the* Antichrist, "adjustment theology" takes over. For example, "in a pamphlet on Armageddon theology, Jimmy Swaggart notes that all the world's dictators—Genghis Khan, Attila the Hun, Hitler, Stalin—acted in the *spirit* of the Antichrist but could not rival his supreme evil."[4]

In *666: The Final Warning!* we learn that television will be used by Satan to "tell us" his "good news," thus setting the stage for Antichrist. Here's how the theory is developed:

> Did you ever notice that the symbol *Te,* and the words *Levi* and *Sion* are found in the word *television?* *Te* is the chemical symbol for *tellurium* which is "a rare, white nonmetallic chemical element." The Latin word is *tellus,* which means the *earth!*[5] Satan comes to the earth as an *Angel of Light,* and he will *tell* (tellus) his "good news" (his gospel); the same lie that *Levi* said would bring the Messiah back to earth upon *Mount Sion! Sion* is the Greek word for the Hebrew name *Zion* where Jesus, the real Messiah, will touch down upon his return to earth. This will usher in the real *NEW AGE* ... THE LORD'S KINGDOM ON EARTH! Television is a means of "mind control" as well as an *image converter.* Many, at the threat of death under this instrument of Satan, will worship the *image of the Beast! Will Satan use TeLevi-Sion to usher in his kingdom* on earth? *There is no doubt about it!*[6]

The sad fact is that there are probably many people who will fall for this "logic." Using a similar line of argumentation, we can make a few deductions of our own. When Jesus came down from the Mount of Transfiguration, He told His disciples, "*Tell the vision* to no one until the Son of Man has risen from the dead" (Matt. 17:9). So, prior to the resurrection, television was prohibited, but now that Jesus "has risen from the dead," television is permitted. As you know, television is made up of two words—the Greek word *têle* (far) and the Latin word *vision* (to view)—meaning "viewing from afar" or "viewing at a distance."

Speaking of television, it seems that Barney is the Beast of Revelation 13. Literary scholar Kathryn Lindskoog sent the following to her friends via the Internet to show how almost anyone or anything can be made to read 666.[7]

> Given: Barney is a cute purple dinosaur
> Prove: Barney is really the Antichrist in disguise
>
> 1. Start with the given:
>   CUTE PURPLE DINOSAUR
>
> 2. Change all the U's to V's (which is proper Latin anyway):
>   CVTE PVURPLE DINOSAVR
>
> 3. Extract all Roman numerals in the phrase:
>   CVVLDIV
>
> 4. Convert these into Arabic values:
>   100 5 5 50 500 1 5
>
> 5. Add all the numbers:
>   666

This is why it is important to pay attention to time texts and theological context when interpreting the Bible. The significance of 666 is found in the Bible, not in television or newspapers.

The Candidates

Keep in mind that many today mistakenly use *Antichrist* and *Beast* interchangeably. Generally, a Christian hears the word *Antichrist* and thinks of the Beast in the Book of Revelation. Ed Hindson lists ten titles that he says identify the Antichrist, eleven if you count his inclusion of "false Christ" (Greek, *pseudochristos*).[8]

For centuries the papacy was the unanimous Antichrist candidate.[9] The papal system was identified as "both the 'man of sin' and the Babylonian whore of which Scripture forewarns (2 Thess. 2; Rev. 19). In the conviction of the sixteenth-century Protestants, Rome was the great Anti-Christ, and so firmly did this belief become established that it was not until the nineteenth century that it was seriously questioned by evangelicals."[10] Why was the Roman Church, best represented by the papal leadership, identified as the Antichrist? First, such an identification is based on a faulty reading of 2 Thessalonians 2:4, where Paul said that the "man of lawlessness" would set himself up in the "temple of God," which was seen as a reference to the church (1 Cor. 3:16–17; 6:19; Eph. 2:20; 1 Tim. 3:15; 1 Peter 2:5). The Roman Catholic Church, since prior to the Reformation, was considered to be a false church and its religious leaders impostors. The Antichrist was a religious charlatan who would rule over an apostate church. The best candidate, it seemed, was the papacy.

Second, individual popes (e.g., Leo X) and the papal succession (papacy) were thought to be viable candidates because of the various Latin titles (e.g., *Vicarius Filii Dei* = "in place of the Son of God") used to describe them and their offices. There are two possible meanings for the prefix *anti:* "against" and "in the place of." The papal leadership, as the "vicar of Christ," was viewed as a counterfeit Christ, a religious leader who took an authority position "in the place of Christ."[11]

Third, Irenaeus (A.D. 130–200) put forth the view that the name of the first ruler of the Roman Catholic church was Latinus. In Greek his name is spelled *lateinos*. "In the Greek letter evaluation system the following works out nicely: l=30, a=1, t=300, e=5, i=10, n=50, o=70, s=200. The total is 666. The mark of the Beast is the Latin church; the Roman Catholic system which is opposed to true Christianity."[12]

Even an enemy of the papacy like Martin Luther came in for a numerical drubbing. Here's how it's done: "Take the name Martin Luther and Latinize the surname to get MARTIN LUTERA. Now let the letters from *A* to *I* represent the numbers from 1 to 9 (considering *I* and *J* interchangeable, as was the custom then), the letters *K* to *S* represent the numbers from 10 to 90 (by multiples of 10) and the letters from *T* to *Z* represent the numbers from 100 to 700 (by multiples of 100)."[13] The result? M(30) + A(1) + R(80) + T(100) + I(9) + N(40) + L(20) + U(200) + T(100) + E(5) +R(80) + A(1) = 666.

As one might suspect, political figures from the time of Nero have been easy targets of the dreaded triple six. Napoleon was always a favorite:

> There were plenty of people … [in the 1800s] who took Napoleon to be Antichrist. Mrs. [Hester Thrale] Piozzi noted that many were saying that he was "the Devil incarnate, the Appollyon mentioned in Scripture." She believed that his name in the Corsican dialect was N'Apollione, "the Destroyer," and "he does come forwards [sic] followed by a Cloud of Locusts from ye bottomless Pit." She learned from the ladies of her village in Wales that Napoleon's titles, translated into Roman numerals, totaled 666.[14]

In our own century we have been assured on numerous occasions of the identity of the Beast. Hitler's hatred of the Jews and his numbering of them made him a prime candidate. Hitler, however, did not mark the Jews with 666; rather, each Jew was given a different number similar to a serial number. The next step was to determine if Hitler's name fit the 666 designation. Lo and behold, it did! By converting the English alphabet into numerical equivalents starting with A=100, B=101, C=102, etc., we get the following: H=107, I=108, T=119, L=111, E=104, R=117. The result is 666. But why not start with A=1, B=2, C=3, etc., as in Hebrew and Greek?

Hitler may be dead, but he has been resurrected recently as a candidate for the Beast/Antichrist. Robert Van Kampen believes there are two possible Antichrist candidates—Nero and Hitler.[15] Since Van Kampen believes that the Book of Revelation was written in A.D. 95, nearly thirty years after the death of Nero, he dismisses Nero as a viable candidate for the Beast. In his dismissal of Nero, Van Kampen does not discuss those texts which describe the events in Revelation as taking place "shortly" (1:1).[16] He jumps two thousand years in the future in search of a person who Revelation tells us was "near" in John's day (1:3).

> Without question, Hitler best meets all the requirements to be the Antichrist … and he certainly was the historical embodiment of Antichrist's supremely evil nature although the early church was convinced that Nero was the Antichrist.[17]

According to Van Kampen, Hitler will be "resurrected" to serve Satan as the Beast/Antichrist: "Who is Antichrist? Can we in fact identify who he actually is, or will be? Perhaps the most startling fact concerning Antichrist is that he is (or will be) a dead man brought back to life, whose 'fatal wound was healed' (Rev. 13:3)."[18] Van Kampen hedges a bit by asserting that "we cannot be dogmatic about" Hitler being the Beast of Revelation 13, but "it would be hard to imagine that any other man could better fit the Scripture's description of this diabolical world leader."[19]

A booklet published in 1940 identified Mussolini as the Antichrist. The author stated that he fulfilled forty-nine prophecies of the Antichrist.[20] "Many will recall widespread preaching during the World War II era that Mussolini or Hitler was the Antichrist. Since the slogan VV IL DUCE was widely used by Mussolini, and because the Roman numeral value of the slogan/title is 666, many were sure of positive identification."[21] Henry Kissinger,[22] Anwar Sadat,[23] and, as we saw, even Ronald (6) Wilson (6) Reagan (6). There was passing speculation that the attempted assassination of Reagan and the wound to the head of James Brady might be the prelude to the fulfillment of the prophecy of Revelation 13:3 where one of the heads of the Beast "had been slain, and his fatal wound was healed." If you followed the newscasts after the assassination attempt, you will recall that Dan Rather of CBS actually reported that Brady was dead. He then asked for a moment of silence. "Miraculously," Brady was reported to be alive. This story of prophetic fulfillment never got very far once people realized that Brady suffered severe brain damage.

Mikhail Gorbachev still serves as a strong candidate.[24] Since Antichrist supposedly makes a covenant with Israel, the belief that Gorbachev could be the Antichrist was reinforced by newspaper stories that showed him being welcomed to Jerusalem by Prime Minister Yitzhak Shamir. Gorbachev was talking like a man of peace, another attribute of Antichrist. At Ben-Gurion International Airport Gorbachev said: "I won't hide that I have deep feelings and honor toward this nation." Foreign Minister David Levy made the following Antichrist-like statement: "We have been waiting for the day we could receive a great man whose actions and struggle have left their imprint on the entire world arena."[25]

In the January 4, 1993, issue of *Time* magazine many readers noticed that *Time*'s "Man of the Year," Bill Clinton, had horns. By covering up the "T," the "I," and the "E," one could see the then President-elect with a neatly cropped set of horns made from the points of the "M." One caller to *Time's* news desk "pointed out that Clinton is the 66th 'Man of the Year,'" just short by 600. As all Bible students know, the number of the Beast is 666, not three 6s (Rev. 13:18). This shows, as *Time* spokesman Robert Pondiscio tells it, that "*Time* is in league with the devil."[26]

There is nothing new in any of this. "David Brady ... gives well over a hundred varying interpretations of the number 666, some based on Hebrew, some on Greek, some on Latin, which have been confidently proposed."[27] And Brady was only dealing with British writers between 1560 and 1830![28]

"Newton's Gift"

The number 666 has long fascinated theologians and mathematicians. Maybe the interest in the number has something to do with the attainment of wisdom and understanding since to "calculate the number of the Beast" will reward the diligent (Rev. 13:18).

Wallace John Steinhope is the physicist in Paul Nathan's fictional "Newton's Gift." In this story Steinhope has an intense desire to travel back in time to help Isaac Newton with the tedium of calculations by putting a modern calculator in his hands. Steinhope invents a knapsack-sized time machine and travels to England in 1666 to bestow on Newton a pocket calculator.

> Newton, however, is afraid of the calculator, particularly its glowing red digital display: "As the Lord is my savior, is it a creation of Lucifer? The eyes of it shine with the color of his domain."
>
> "You cannot deny your own eyes," Steinhope responds. "Let me *show* you it works. I'll divide two numbers for you with just the punch of a few buttons." Steinhope entered, at random, 81,918 divided by 123. When the answer lit up, Newton fell to his knees and started to pray. Then he got up, grabbed a hot poker from the fireplace, and swung it at Steinhope, who barely escaped back to the space-time coordinates of today.[29]

Why the violent reaction? Steinhope had made an unfortunate choice of numbers: 81,918 divided by 123 happens to be 666, the number of the Beast. This fictional story of superstition unfortunately seems to describe many people today. For example, Mary Stewart Relfe teaches that we are presently using the 666 system in monetary transactions. The 666 prefix, according to Relfe, is attached to credit cards like VISA and MasterCard.[30] However fallacious her reasoning,[31] she maintains that the mark of the Beast is just around the corner.

Number, Number, Who *Had* the Number?

But what meaning would any of these theories have had for Christians reading the Book of Revelation in the first century? The first readers were to have "understanding" to "calculate the number of the Beast" (Rev. 13:18). The Beast must have been a contemporary of the first-century readers. We can have the same "understanding" by studying the history of the period. We don't have to speculate on the identity of some future Beast. While Dave Hunt, Hal Lindsey, Salem Kirban, and others believe that the Antichrist is alive somewhere in the world today, the Bible says that he is buried somewhere in the world today.

Notes

1. Gary D. Blevins, *666: The Final Warning!* (Kingsport, TN: Vision of the End Ministries, 1990).

2. Blevins, *666*, 460. Emphasis in original.

3. Blevins, *666*, 461.

4. Ed Dobson and Ed Hindson, "Apocalypse Now?: What Fundamentalists Believe About the End of the World," *Policy Review* (Fall 1986), 20.

5. *Terra* is the Latin word for "earth."

6. Blevins, *666*, 394.

7. Robert G. Clouse, Robert N. Hosack, and Richard V. Pierrard, *The New Millennium Manual: A Once and Future Guide* (Grand Rapids, MI: Baker Books, 1999), 171.

8. Ed Hindson, *Approaching Armageddon: The World Prepares for War With God* (Eugene, OR: Harvest House, 1997), 202–203. An antichrist is someone who denies that Jesus has come in the flesh (1 John 2:22; 2 John 7). A false Christ is someone who claims to be the Messiah. The terms are not necessarily synonymous.

9. Samuel J. Cassels, *Christ and Antichrist or Jesus of Nazareth Proved to be the Messiah and the Papacy Proved to be the Antichrist* (Philadelphia, PA: Presbyterian Board of Publication, 1846) and Christopher Hill, *Antichrist in Seventeenth-Century England* (New York: Oxford University Press, 1971), 1–40.

10. Iain Murray, *The Puritan Hope: Revival and the Interpretation of Prophecy* (London: Banner of Truth Trust, 1971), 41.

11. For some, the Pope remains a candidate for the Antichrist. Pope John Paul II has been called the "man of sin" and "the Beast." See J.P. Slavin, "Pope runs into hostility in Jamaica," *Atlanta Journal/Constitution* (11 August 1993), A2. Dave Hunt attempts to revive this view in his *A Woman Rides the Beast: The Roman Catholic Church and the Last Days* (Eugene, OR: Harvest House, 1994).

12. Ray Summers, *Worthy is the Lamb: An Interpretation of Revelation* (Nashville, TN: Broadman, 1951), 176.

13. Paul Hoffman, *Archimedes' Revenge: The Joys and Perils of Mathematics* (New York: Norton, 1988), 22.

14 Clarke Garrett, *Respectable Folly: Millenarians and the French Revolution in France and England* (Baltimore, MD: Johns Hopkins University Press, 1975), 211.

15. Robert Van Kampen, *The Sign of Christ's Coming and the End of the Age* (Wheaton, IL: Crossway Books, 1999), 223–225.

16. Van Kampen cites portions of Revelation 1:1 and 3. He conveniently leaves out the words "shortly" and "near", the crucial time texts. See Van Kampen, *The Sign of Christ's Coming and the End of the Age*, 32.

17. Van Kampen, *The Sign*, 224–25.

18. Van Kampen, *The Sign*, 201.

19. Van Kampen, *The Sign*, 208.

20. See Ralph Woodrow, *Great Prophecies of the Bible*, (Riverside, CA: Ralph Woodrow Evangelistic Association, 1971), 148.

21. David A. Lewis, "The Antichrist: Number, Number, Who's Got the Number?" (no publishing information). For another attempt at identifying Mussolini as the Antichrist, see the discussion of the works of Leonard Sale-Harrison in Robert G. Clouse, "The Danger of Mistaken Hopes," in *Handbook of Biblical Prophecy*, eds. Carl E. Armerding and W. Ward Gasque (Grand Rapids, MI: Baker Book House, [1977] 1978), 33–36.

22. Salem Kirban, *Kissinger: Man of Peace?* (Huntingdon Valley, PA: Salem Kirban, 1974).

23. Mary S. Relfe, *When Your Money Fails...the "666 System" Is Here* (Montgomery, AL: Ministries, 1981), 143–45.

24. Robert W. Faid, *Gorbachev! Has the Real Antichrist Come?* (Tulsa, OK: Victory House, 1988).

25. "Gorbachev hailed as friend of Israel," *Atlanta Constitution* (15 June 1992), A5.

26. For a humorous treatment of the *Time* cover, see Gary DeMar, "Here-We-Go-Again Eschatology," *Biblical Worldview* (February 1993), 10–11.

27. Philip Edgcumbe Hughes, *The Book of Revelation* (Grand Rapids, MI: Eerdmans, 1990), 154 note 3.

28. David Brady, *The Contribution of British Writers between 1560 and 1830 to the Interpretation of Revelation 13:16–18 (the Number of the Beast): A Study in the History of Exegesis* (Mohr: Siebeck, Tübingen, 1983).

29. Hoffman, *Archimedes' Revenge*, 18.

30. Mary Stewart Relfe, *When Your Money Fails* and *The New Money System* (Montgomery, AL: Ministries, 1982).

31. For a helpful analysis of Relfe's 666 madness, see William M. Alnor, *Soothsayers of the Second Advent* (Old Tappan, NJ: Fleming H. Revell, 1989), 82–86.

Chapter Nineteen

TECHNOLOGY AND THE MARK OF THE BEAST

In the February 12, 1994 issue of the *San Jose Mercury News*, Richard Scheinin reported on the "Red Lion Bible Conference" in Southern California. Speakers included Hal Lindsey, John Walvoord, Peter and Paul Lalonde, and a group of lesser known prophetic speculators. Scheinin does a good job in explaining Peter Lalonde's beliefs about Bible prophecy and its tenuous link with the computer age:

> Never before has electronic technology existed to assist the anti-Christ—"the beast" of Scripture—to rise to power by instantaneously spreading his false messages and causing "the Earth and them which dwell therein to worship" him, as Revelation says.
>
> And never before, insists Lalonde, has technology existed to create the cashless economy that many Christians believe is described in Revelation: a prediction borne out in credit cards, smart cards and proposals for national identification cards. Or to allow the anti-Christ to imprint the dreaded "mark of the beast" in the right hands or foreheads of all people, "both small and great, rich and poor, free and slave," as Revelation predicts.

According to Lalonde, the "mark of the beast" is now possible because of "technological feasibility" since microchips can now be implanted in animals to monitor their locations if they stray from home. Will implants be accepted, Lalonde muses, to thwart child abductions? Lalonde wants us to believe that before the advent of computer chips, the Book of Revelation remained a closed book.

On or Under?

Peter and Paul Lalonde spell out their views on technology and Bible prophecy in *Racing Toward the Mark of the Beast*. When the authors deal with the way technology can be misused, the book is worthy of our attention. Unfortunately, the Lalondes force Revelation 13:17–18 into a modern context by trying to make it conform to the latest technological advances. They write: "As always, God is way ahead of the latest biometric engineers, smart card developers, and global communication systems planners. . . . For the first time in history, the technology to easily fulfill this incredible prophecy exists."[1] Nonsense. The technology existed in the first century to accomplish what literalists maintain is required to fulfill the prophetic particulars of Revelation 13:16–18. A simple mark, for example, a tattoo or a brand, could easily be made on the forehead and hand. Branding has been used for centuries to identify slaves, idolaters, and property.

> We read in 3 Macc. ii. 29, of Ptolemy Philopater, that he ordered the Jews of Alexandria to be forcibly enrolled, and when enrolled, to be marked with a red-hot brand on their body, with the sign of Bacchus the Ivy-weaver. And Philo mentions idolaters who confessed their idolatry by branding themselves with indelible marks.[2]

A "certain man clothed in linen with a writing case" went through the city of Jerusalem to "put a mark on the foreheads of the men who sigh and groan over all the abominations which are being submitted in its midst" (Ezek. 9:4). There's nothing high-tech about this. The mark was given for divine protection, similar to the marks given in the Book of Revelation (7:3; 9:4; 14:1).

Adding to the Bible

The Lalondes, in an attempt to make Revelation 13:16–18 conform to the latest advances in technology, must add to the text. In an advertisement for their *This Week in Bible Prophecy* television program, they write: "**The Mark of the Beast**—it's one of the clearest and most dramatic prophecies in the Bible. It states simply that in the last days that no man will be able to buy or sell unless he has the mark IN his right hand or forehead." The "IN" apparently refers to an embedded microchip or something similar placed *under* the skin. Their emphasis is on the word "IN."

The Greek preposition *epi* is used in Revelation 13:13, not *ev*, to describe where the mark was to be placed. *Epi* is best translated as "on" or "upon." This is why the passage states that the mark is to be given "*on* their right hand, or *on* their forehead" (13:16), not "*in* their right hand, or *in* their forehead." If Jesus had wanted to say "in," He would have used the Greek preposition *en*.

The Lalondes prey on the ignorance of Christians who have not studied the Bible for themselves. Their sensationalistic rhetoric serves as a substitute for sound hermeneutics. Their interpretation of Revelation 13:18 forces us to believe that the message of the "mark of the beast" has been unintelligible for nearly two thousand years since computer chips and scanning technology are late-twentieth century innovations. Those who teach this foolishness ignore some very clear biblical realities.

- The time texts indicate that the events recorded in the Book of Revelation "must shortly take place" (1:1). In addition, those who first read the prophecy were assured that "the time is near," near for them (1:3).
- Those who first read "the words of the prophecy" are said to be "blessed" (1:3). What kind of blessing comes to people who cannot understand what they are reading because the prophecies describe conditions in a super-technological society?
- How high-tech does a society have to be for people "to be given a mark on their right hand or on their forehead" (13:16)? Either you have the mark or you don't. Who needs a computer or laser technology for this? Low-tech methods of screening a population can be quite effective, as the men of Gilead found out (Judges 12:4–7). During the reign of Caesar Augustus Rome was able to tax the entire empire (Luke

2:1–4). There was nothing high-tech about the numbering system Hitler used on the Jews to identify and "catalog" them.

Is It Visible?

A more fundamental question needs to be asked, however: Is the "mark of the beast" a visible mark? Consider that none of today's prophetic techno-sensationalists compare the mark that is given to the 144,000 by the "Lamb" in Revelation 14:1 with the mark given by the "beast" in 13:16. The marks have to be the same. Will Jesus implant a micro-chip in the foreheads of the 144,000? There are other considerations as well. Are the "beast" and the "lamb," that is, are literal animals doing the numbering? Should we look for a beast that literally comes "up out of the sea, having ten horns and seven heads" (13:1)? Is there a literal land beast that has "two horns like a lamb" and speaks "as a dragon" (13:11)? Those who insist on literalism are very selective in what they choose to interpret literally. Insisting that the "mark of the beast" is actually a "computer chip" is not a literal interpretation.

> It is not at all clear that John is thinking of a literal brand visible on the person of the worshippers of the beast. The seal of God placed on the forehead of the 144,000 (7:3) is surely not meant to be a visible mark; it is a symbolic way of expressing divine protection (see Isa. 44:5). The mark of the beast may be intended to be a parody on the mark of God.[3]

John D. Hannah, Chairman and Professor of Historical Theology at Dallas Theological Seminary, offers a similar perspective on Exodus 13:9:

> Like the Passover ([Exodus] 12:26-27), the Feast of Unleavened Bread had great educational value in the home (13:8-9). The feast was **like a sign on** their **hand** or **forehead**, that is, it was a continual reminder of God's mighty deliverance from **Egypt**. Some orthodox Jews today interpret that passage (and Deut. 6:8; 11:18) literally and bind passages of the Law (viz., Ex. 13:2-10; Deut. 6:4-9; 11:13-21) on their arms and foreheads in small pouches, so-called phylacteries, though this was probably not God's intention.[4]

John J. Davis writes that "Many feel that the expressions found in [Exodus 13]:9, 16 are not to be interpreted literally but refer alone to symbolic action."[5] Not a single commentator I consulted thought the actions were to be taken literally.[6] Similar commentary is offered by Elmer Towns, also a dispensationalist, on Deuteronomy 6:8 where he states that "these verses are still carried out literally by many orthodox Jews. . . . The intent of this passage," Towns continues, "is that the Word of God should be hidden in a person's heart and should constantly be a source of devotion and obedience to the Lord."[7] The comments of Keil and Delitzsch are especially helpful: "The line of thought referred to merely expresses the idea, that the Israelites were not only to retain the commands of God in their hearts, and to confess them with the mouth, but to fulfill them with the hand, or in act and deed, and thus to show themselves in their whole bearing as the guardians and observers of the law."[8]

A Symbolic Mark

Every Jew would have understood that a mark on the hand or the forehead was an identification of loyalty, ownership, and heart-felt allegiance to Jehovah. This is made clear when we read the instructions that were given to the Israelites as they were about to depart from Egypt: "And it shall serve as a sign to you on your hand, and as a reminder on your forehead, that the law of the LORD may be in your mouth; for with a powerful hand the LORD brought you out of Egypt" (Exodus 13:9; see Deut. 6:8).

> These signs were not literal marks on the skin—one cannot literally wear the observance of a festival on one's body—but were spiritual, visible only to God. (The phylacteries of the Jews in a later period were based on a materialistic interpretation of this passage.) As His Old Testament people were marked on hand and head as a sign of their covenant with the Lord who brought them out of slavery and made them a nation, so are those who give allegiance to the beast marked with his name.[9]

Throughout the Book of Revelation marks given on the hand and head are symbolic. Commentators do not usually claim that when God gives a mark to set apart His people that the mark is visible to the eye. For example, in Revelation 3:12 we read: "He who overcomes, I will make him a pillar in the temple of My God, and he will not go out from it any more; and I will write upon him the name of My God, and the name of the city of My God, the New Jerusalem, which comes down out of heaven from My God, and My new name."

Is writing God's name and the name of the New Jerusalem an external tattoo or brand of those who overcome? Is being a "pillar in the temple" of God to be understood literally as well? Robert Thomas concludes correctly that the "pillar" language is "clearly metaphorical."[10] Thomas intimates that writing God's name on "he who overcomes" is also metaphorical. "To have 'the name of My God,'" Thomas writes, "was equivalent to belonging to God, being endowed with divine power (Moffatt). This sets the overcomer in utter contrast with the assumptions of the present Jewish persecutors (Beckwith)."[11] Having the "name of the city of My God" written upon the overcomer meant the right of citizenship in the new Jerusalem. "Christ's 'new name' symbolizes the full revelation of His character promised to the overcomer at Christ's second advent."[12]

What then is the solution to this seemingly enigmatic passage? Like much of Revelation, its *familiar* symbols are meant to *represent* familiar concepts. This is why Revelation must be read against the backdrop of the Old Testament. As Ferrel Jenkins writes: "The book of Revelation is the most thoroughly Jewish in its language and imagery of any New Testament book. This book speaks not the language of Paul, but of the Old Testament prophets Isaiah, Ezekiel, and Daniel."[13] The beasts, both sea and land, the mark on the hand or head, and the number 666 should be interpreted in light of the Old Testament, similar to the way Sodom (11:8), Egypt (11:8), Jezebel (2:20), Balaam (2:14), and Babylon (14:8; 16:19; 17:5; 18:2, 10, 21) are interpreted. Understanding the way the Old Testament uses and applies marks, it is not that difficult to determine what John is describing in Revelation 13. Whoever carried the mark of the beast would be protected by Satan, and whoever carried the mark of the Lamb would be protected by God. Those who identified with Rome against Jesus Christ died in the destruction of Jerusalem when Titus and his army swept in to destroy the temple and the city.

Bar Codes and the Mark of the Beast

If not computer chips, why not bar codes? Since 1973 bar codes have been used to identify products for pricing, controlling inventory, tracking baggage at airports, and making the check-out line at the local supermarket move faster. In fact, the bar code is ubiquitous, an ever-present reminder that technology has invaded every area of our life. But is the bar code the dreaded numbering system outlined in Revelation 13? Gary H. Kah thinks so: "It will only be a matter of time before humans are tattooed with a similar mark to the codes in the supermarket."[14] Others believe that it is a precursor to a more ominous computer chip implant.

Before evaluating the Bar Code=666 theory, we should spend some time explaining the function of the bar code. The technical name for the bar code is the Universal Product Code, or UPC for short. The symbol is designed to be read by an *optical scanner*, a device that measures and interprets reflected light patterns.

The UPC symbol does not contain the price of a product purchased. The price is actually in the computer that corresponds to the code on a product. This allows a store to change the price without changing the code. When a store wants to change a price of a product, a computer operator simply calls up the Item Number in the computer and changes the corresponding price. Every time a product with the code is processed, the cash register logs the new price. Before the advent of the UPC symbol a store employee would have to change the price on every item, a very time consuming, inefficient, expensive, and messy job.

The UPC bar code consists of twelve digits grouped into four numbers separated by Guard Bars (more about these later). When used to identify merchandise to be purchased the first digit identifies the product. A 3, for example, means drug and certain health-related products. The next five digits are the Manufacturer ID Number. The following five digits are assigned by the manufacturer to represent the product, the Item Number. The final digit is the check digit. It signals the computer if one of the other digits is incorrect.

How It Works

The logic of the UPC bar code follows the logic of the computer, a binary rather than the base-ten Arabic system. The computer reads yes/no, on/off, commands. The bars on the UPC bar code, both black and white, represent 1s (black) and 0s (white), the essence of the binary numbering system. The 1s and 0s are converted into Arabic numbers based on where they are placed in a series. Any base-ten number can be converted into a binary number of 1s and 0s and vice versa. Here's how it works. Beginning with the number 1, each subsequent number is doubled: 1, 2, 4, 8, 16, 32, 64, 128, 256, 512, 1,024, 2,048, *ad infinitum*. Different places represent different powers of two. For example, the binary number for 4 would be 001 (0+0+4). The binary number for 12 would be 0011 (0+0+4+8). The 0 is an "off" switch while the 1 is an "on" switch. The binary number for 666 would be 0101100101 (0+2+0+8+16+0+0+128+0+512).

The UPC bar code is a visual representation of the binary numbering system. The light that reads the black and white bars reads them as *binary* 1s and 0s which in turn converts them to Arabic numerals for the cash register receipt. The UPC bar code has adapted the binary system to fit its particular needs. The binary code for the Manufacturer ID Number and the Item Number are different from the standard binary numbering system explained above, although they operate on the same principle of on/off bar readings. For example, the Manufacturer ID Number three is 0111101 while the Item Number three is 1000010, converse images of one another. As you can see by the manufacturer's number three with its four 1s in a row, the thickness of the black line representing the number is wide. The three on the product side has two very thin black lines separated by a wide white bar, the four 0s.

But where does 666 come in? The Manufacturer ID Number and the Item Number are bound and divided by three longer bars of two lines each called "Guard Bars." The Left-Hand Guard Bar separates the Number System Character from the Manufacturer ID Number. The Right-Hand Guard Bar separates the Item Number from the Check Character. The Tall Center Pattern separates the Manufacturer ID Number from the Item Number. It is these three bars that are said to register as 6–6–6. There are a number of problems with this theory. The Guard Bars are not 6s. The Manufacturer ID Number for 6 is 0101111 while the Product item Number is 1010000. The Left Guard Bar and the Right Guard Bar are 101. The Tall Center Bar is 01010.

Those who maintain that the UPC symbol is a clever way of marking all of us with 6–6–6 have confused the Item Number 6 with the Guard Bars because they look identical to the eye. But they are not identical to the machine. The machine also reads white spaces. Notice that the Tall Center Bar separating the manufacturer's ID Number from the Item Number has two extra white bars. Even if the Left and Right Guard Bars are 6s (101), the Center Bar is a different number (01010). It is impossible to get 666 out of this configuration. But let's suppose that the three Guard Bars are 6s. How does this fit with Revelation 13:18 where the number is six-hundred and sixty-six, not simply three consecutive 6s?

Attempts to force the Bible to speak of nuclear detonation, UFOs, Cobra helicopters, computer chips, and bar codes are an exercise in futility. Moreover, such approaches demean the character of the Bible by turning it into a crystal ball rather than a revelation of God's character and His special word to His people.

Buying and Selling

The control of economic transactions drives modern claims of a one-world government controlled by the antichrist during the great tribulation. This sensationalistic but popular view is outlined by Thomas Ice and Timothy Demy in their *The Coming Cashless Society*:

> Using every means at his disposal, including the technology of a cashless society, the Antichrist and his demands will bring the world into its greatest-ever moral and economic turmoil. Such chaos will make the stock market crash of 1929 look like a minor economic adjustment.
>
> Revelation 13:16, 17 is the biblical point of entry for discussion of the cashless society, a one-world governement, global economics, and biblical prophecy.[15]

Having gone out on a limb with this prediction, the authors come back to biblical reality and write, "The Bible does not specifically predict computers, the Internet, credit cards, or any of the other trimmings that facilitate the modern electronic banking system."[16] In fact, Revelation 13:16–17 is not describing the control of financial transactions but rather access to the temple controlled by the Jewish anti-Christian religious establishment. The key to interpreting the passage is the prohibition "to buy or to sell" (13:17) if a worshipper does not have the mark of the beast.

Buying and selling are controlled by the temple leadership and are used to regulate access to the temple (Matt. 21:12). Buying and selling, properly understood, are worship-related rituals (Isa. 55:1). "This is established in [Revelation] 3:18 (and compare 21:6). When those who refuse the mark of the Beast are not allowed to buy and sell, it means that they are expelled from the synogogue and Temple. The merchants of the land in Revelation 18 are those who worshipped at the Temple and synagogue."[17] Jesus foretold this: "They will make you outcasts from the synagogue; but an hour is coming for everyone who kills you to think that he is offering service to God" (John 16:2).

Early in the church's history the disciples went to the temple to preach the gospel (Acts 5:20–21, 24, 42; 24:12). At first, they were welcomed (Acts 2:46). Peter and John frequented the temple during "the hour of prayer" (Acts 3:1). Jewish Christians continued to use the temple, even participating in some of its rituals (Acts 21:26). After the temple officials learned that these Jews were preaching that Jesus was the Messiah—the lamb of God who takes away the sin of the world—they were shut out of the temple (21:26–30).

These events help explain the theological meaning of buying and selling in Revelation 13:17. During Jesus' ministry, the temple officials were "selling" and worshippers were "buying" access to the temple (Matt. 21:12). Their "buying and selling" turned "God's house" into a "robbers' den" (21:12–13). Only those Jews who aligned themselves with the priests, the sacrificial system, and the temple would be allowed to enter the temple for worship. If they did not have the mark of the beast, that is, if they did not align themselves with what the temple now represented, they could not "buy or sell" in order to offer the appropriate sacrifices. To take the "mark of the beast" meant a person denied that Jesus was the Messiah, the true temple of God, the only sufficient sacrifice. Of course, Christian Jews avoided the mark of the beast and showed their true allegiance to Jesus, "having His name and the name of his father written on their foreheads" (Rev. 14:1).

The "World Wide Web" and the Mark of the Beast

It was only a matter of time before the Internet became an apocalyptic feature in modern-day prophetic speculation. Zola Levitt writes in his April 1999 ministry newsletter that after attending a prophecy conference that he "started looking into the Hebrew language and certain computer designations." Levitt is correct about the Hebrew language, and I would add, the Hebrew Bible. The New Testament cannot be understood without understanding the Old Testament, especially Revelation. But like any interpretive key, it can be misused. Levitt attempts to make a link between the World Wide Web and 666:

To begin with, the familiar symbol for the Internet, World Wide Web or "www", would be rendered in Hebrew as *vav, vav, vav* (the Hebrew alphabet does not have a "w" and Hebrew speaking people us the *vav*, or "v", in place of our "w"). The interesting part is that since Hebrew letters also have numerical values (Hebrew speakers do not prefer Arabic numerals), we have a number of the letter *vav*. Since it is the sixth letter of the alphabet, the expression "www", in Hebrew, is 666.

Like the majority of prophecy writers who claim to be experts on the subject, Levitt, who should know better, seemingly is unaware that the number for the mark of the beast is six hundred and sixty-six, not three sixes.

Dispensationalists are notorious for playing the interpretive game of "sounds like." The Hebrew word "Rosh" in Ezekiel 38–39 is said to be modernday Russia since Rosh sounds like Russia. What should we make of the "wilderness of Sin" (Ex. 16:1; 17:1; Num. 33:11) since sin sounds like Sin?

Yahoo Hermeneutics

Levitt doesn't stop with identifying the World Wide Web as the Beast of Revelation. Step two in sound-alike exegesis is to identify the popular search engine Yahoo! as the Antichrist. Levitt reasons:

> Finally, the popular search engine, Yahoo, is an important Hebrew word repeated often in the Scriptures. The name *Yahweh* is shortened to *Yah* in names; and *hu*, in Hebrew, stands for the pronoun "he." Thus, "Yahoo" on the end of a name in Hebrew, such as *Netanyahu*, means "he . . . God" in English. In the case of Netanyahu, since *netan* means "gift," his entire name means "He is the gift of God." The prophets Isaiah (Yeshayahu) and Jeremiah (Yirmeyahu) also had *yahu* on the ends of their names. These were meant in complimentary terms, but in the case of the Antichrist, yahoo by itself expresses exactly his counterfeit: "he is God."

As in both cases (www) and (Yahu), Hebrew is being used as the bridge language. Unlike Latin and Greek, there are not many Hebrew words that make up the English language. Words which do make it into English are most often given their proper singular Hebrew definition, for example, kosher and kibbutz. These words mean what they mean in Hebrew because the design of the language is so different in structure from that of English. Hebrew words are not used as prefixes and suffixes as are Latin and Greek words (e.g., anti, ante, post, contra, bene, etc.).

The same can be said for a language like Chinese. Low Mein is a Chinese dish served in most Chinese restaurants. You won't find a Chinese equivalent of High Mein. The Chinese word Low does not mean what low means in English even though their sounds are identical. The same is true of Hebrew. There are probably numerous Hebrew words that sound a lot like English words, but there is no meaningful association. Even English has words that are pronounced alike but have different meanings (homophones):

- to, too, two
- reign, rain, rein
- sea, see, sí

Then there are words that are spelled the same way but have different meanings (homonym):

- bat (animal and wooden club)
- ball (sphere and dance)

Yahoo! has at least two meanings in English: a western expression of excitement and Jonathan Swift's designation of a race of brutes in his satirical *Gulliver's Travels* (1726). You can decide which fits Zola Levitt's interpretive idiosyncracies.

Notes

1. Peter Lalonde and Paul Lalonde, *Racing Toward the Mark of the Beast: Your Money, Computers, and the End of the World* (Eugene, OR: Harvest House, 1994), 87 and 103.

2. Henry Alford, *The New Testament for English Readers* (Chicago, IL: Moody Press, n.d.), 1889.

3. George Eldon Ladd, *A Commentary on the Revelation of John* (Grand Rapids, MI: Eerdmans, [1972] 1987), 185.

4. John Hannah, "Exodus," *The Bible Knowledge Commentary: Old Testament*, eds. John F. Walvoord and Roy B. Zuck (Wheaton, IL: Victor Books, 1985), 130.

5. John J. Davis, *Moses and the Gods of Egypt: Studies in Exodus*, 2nd ed. (Grand Rapids, MI: Baker Book House, 1986), 163.

6. John I. Durham, *Word Biblical Commentary: Exodus* (Waco, TX: Word, 1987), 178; W.H. Gispen, *Bible Student's Commentary: Exodus* (Grand Rapids, MI: Zondervan, 1982), 133, 135; R. Alan Cole, *Tyndale Old Testament Commentaries: Exodus* (Downers Grove, IL: InterVarsity Press, 1973), 114; James G. Murphy, *A Critical and Exegetical Commentary on The Book of Exodus with a New Translation* (Minneapolis, [1866] 1979), 141; C.F. Keil and F. Delitzsch, *Biblical Commentary on the Old Testament: Pentateuch*, trans. James Martin, 3 vols. (Grand Rapids, MI: Eerdmans 1951), 2:36-37; Philip C. Johnson, "Exodus," *The Wycliffe Bible Commentary*, eds. Charles F. Pfeiffer and Everett F. Harrison (Chicago, IL: Moody Press, 1962), 63; Hywel R. Jones, "Exodus," *The New Bible Commentary: Revised*, eds. Donald Guthrie and J.A. Motyer (Grand Rapids, MI: Eerdmans, 1970), 128.

7. Elmer L. Towns, "Deuteronomy," *Liberty Bible Commentary: Old Testament*, eds. Edward E. Hindson and Woodrow Michael Kroll (Lynchburg, VA: The Old-Time Gospel Hour, 1982), 338.

8. Keil and Delitzsch, *Biblical Commentary on the Old Testament: Pentateuch*, 2:37.

9. J. E. Leonard, *Come Out of Her, My People: A Study of the Revelation to John* (Chicago, IL: Laudemont Press, 1991), 105.

10. Robert L. Thomas, *Revelation 1–7: An Exegetical Commentary* (Chicago, IL: Moody Press, 1992), 292.

11. Thomas, *Revelation 1–7*, 293.

12. Thomas, *Revelation 1–7*, 293.

13. Ferrel Jenkins, *The Old Testament in the Book of Revelation* (Grand Rapids, MI: Baker Book House, 1976), 22.

14. Gary H. Kah, *En Route to Global Occupation* (Lafayette, LA: Huntington House, 1991), 12.

15. Thomas Ice and Timothy Demy, *The Coming Cashless Society* (Eugene, OR: Harvest House, 1996), 69–70.

16. Ice and Demy, *The Coming Cashless Society*, 85.

17. James B. Jordan, *A Brief Reader's Guide to Revelation* (Niceville, FL: Transfiguration Press, 1999), 19.

Chapter Twenty

IDENTIFYING
THE BEAST

If the Beast of Revelation is a historical figure with a past, then it should not be too difficult to discover who he was once we survey the biblical evidence. But this is exactly what present-day date setters say they do. There is a difference, however. It's not enough to come up with a *plausible* solution to the identity of 666; what is required is *"a relevant solution."*[1]

First, the Book of Revelation was written before the destruction of Jerusalem, which all of history attests happened in A.D. 70. Revelation makes it clear that the events described therein were to happen "shortly" (Rev. 1:1). In verse 3 Jesus states that "the time is near." John is said to be a "fellow-partaker in the tribulation and kingdom and perseverance which are in Jesus" (1:9). John is told to write "the things which [he has] seen, and the things which are, and the things which shall take place after these things" (1:19). The things which "shall take place" follow on the heels of "the things which are," that is, events that were going on in John's day. Many commentators want to project "the things which shall take place" into the far distant future. This is an untenable position because the text literally should read, "the things which *are about to occur* after these things." Furthermore, the Book of Revelation *ends* with these words: "'These words are faithful and true'; and the Lord, the God of the spirits of the prophets, sent His angel to show to His bond-servants *the things which must shortly take place"* (22:6). Again, the angel tells John that "the time is near" (22:10). Jesus says that He is "coming quickly" (3:11 and 22:20). The book begins and ends with statements that the time was near for those who first read the Revelation.[2]

Second, when Revelation was written the temple was still standing. John is told to measure "the temple of God, and the altar, and those who worship in it" (11:1). It is highly unlikely that this is a description of a future rebuilt temple since the New Testament, including the Book of Revelation, says nothing about a rebuilt temple. The Old Testament describes plans to rebuild the temple (Ezra 1:2–4; 3:7–13), and it also mentions its completion and dedication 515 B.C. (5:1–6:22). This temple was still operating when Herod gained control of Jerusalem in 37 B.C. Herod dismantled this rebuilt temple so he could build a new one that would be associated with his name and reign. Work began around 20 B.C., and while it was operating within a decade, it was not completed until A.D. 64, only six years before it was destroyed by the Romans.

Futurists claim that when the New Testament describes an event taking place in the temple sometime in the future it is speaking of a rebuilt temple. They cannot produce a single verse to prove their case. While it is impossible to be certain of the exact date when Revelation was written, it is clear that it was written before A.D. 70:

> All that can be asserted is that the book was written before the destruction of Jerusalem, and the burning of the Temple. This is clear from the beginning of the eleventh chapter. The Temple is there spoken of as still standing, in language which closely resembles, and indeed directly refers to, the language of our Lord in his great eschatological discourse [Matthew 24]. Such language, and the whole sequel of it, would have been unreal and misleading if, at the time when it was penned, nothing remained of the Temple and city of Jerusalem but heaps of bloodstained stones.[3]

The temple that John sees is not a heavenly temple because "the court which is outside the temple ... has been given to the nations" (Rev. 11:2; see Luke 21:24). There is no temple in heaven (Rev. 21:22). Flesh and blood worshipers occupy the temple. The holy city "will be tread under foot ...

for forty-two months" (11:2), the precise time the Romans occupied Jerusalem. The "temple" resides in the "holy city." The holy city is Jerusalem.

Third, the judgment visions of Revelation 4–19 apply "to the historical turmoil which came to a head shortly after John wrote. The fulfillment of the majority of its prophecies would then apply to the very beginning of Christianity, rather than to its conclusion."[4] This turmoil would include the first Roman persecution of Christianity (A.D. 64–68), the Jewish War with Rome (A.D. 67–70) as described in detail by the Jewish historian for the Romans, Flavius Josephus, the death of Christianity's most infamous persecutor, Nero Caesar, in A.D. 68, the Roman Civil Wars (A.D. 68–69), and the destruction of Jerusalem and the temple in A.D. 70.

Two First-Century Candidates

The time parameters of Revelation limit who the Beast can be. Since the events of Revelation were "near" (Rev. 1:3) for those who first read the prophecy, the list of Beast candidates must also be near in time to the original audience. Revelation 13 describes two beasts: a sea beast (Rome) and a land beast (Israel).

A Political Candidate: Nero

The enigmatic 666 fits very well with the construction of Nero's name, his beastly character, the time in which he ruled, and his anti-Christian edicts leveled against the church. Keep in mind that we need more than a plausible candidate; we need a relevant candidate. The first readers of Revelation were told to "calculate the number of the Beast, for the number is that of a man; and his number is six hundred and sixty-six" (13:18). Since the Book of Revelation was written to a first-century audience, we should expect the first-century readers to be able to calculate the number with relative ease. They would have had few candidates from which to choose. The Roman emperor would have been their most likely political choice.

As was explained earlier, ancient numbering systems use an alpha-numeric method. This is true of the Latin (Roman) system that we still use today: I=1, V=5, X=10, L=50, C=100, D=500, M=1000. The same is true of Greek and Hebrew. Since the Book of Revelation is written in a Hebrew (Aramaic) context by a Jew with numerous allusions to the Old Testament, we should expect the solution to deciphering the meaning of 666 to be Hebraic. "The reason clearly is that, *while he writes in Greek, he thinks in Hebrew,* and the thought has naturally affected the vehicle of expression."[5]

Is there anything in the Bible, especially in Revelation, that hints at this use of both Greek and Hebrew? The "angel of the abyss" is described in two ways: "His name in Hebrew is Abaddon, and in the Greek he has the name Apollyon" (Rev. 9:11). Something similar is done with "Har-Mageddon" (Hill of Megiddo) or "Ar-Mageddon" (City of Megiddo) (16:16). In John's gospel, the place where Pilate sat down to judge Jesus was called "The Pavement." John calls attention to its Hebrew name "Gabbatha" (John 19:13). In the same chapter, John writes how Pilate had an inscription placed on the cross above Jesus' head written in "Hebrew, Latin, and in Greek" (19:20). Going from Greek to Hebrew was normal. Americans who try to find a contemporary solution to the 666 problem invariably use English.

When Nero Caesar's name is transliterated into Hebrew, we get *Neron Kesar* (*nrwn qsr*: Hebrew has no letters to represent vowels). "It has been documented by archaeological finds that a first century Hebrew spelling of Nero's name provides us with precisely the value of 666. Jastrow's lexicon of the Talmud contains this very spelling."[6] When we take the letters of Nero's name and spell them in Hebrew, we get the following numeric values: n=50, r=200, w=6, n=50, q=100, s=60, r=200 = 666. "Every Jewish reader, of course, saw that the Beast was a symbol of Nero. And both Jews and Christians regarded Nero as also having close affinities with the serpent or dragon.[7] ... The Apostle writing as a Hebrew, was evidently thinking as a Hebrew.... Accordingly, the Jewish Christian would have tried the name as he *thought* of the name—that is *in Hebrew letters.* And the moment that he did this the secret stood revealed. No Jew ever thought of Nero except as '*Neron Kesar.*'"[8] Those who read John's account of the Beast probably had come to this conclusion even before they made their calculation.

Subsequent Christian history supports the view that Nero was the Beast. "All the earliest Christian writers on the Apocalypse, from Irenaeus down to Victorinus of Pettau and Commodian in the fourth, and Andreas in the fifth, and St. Beatus in the eighth century, connect Nero, or some Roman Emperor, with the Apocalyptic Beast."[9]

There is a curious variation on 666. Some manuscripts read 616. Why would a copyist make such a number change? "Perhaps the change was intentional, seeing that the Greek form Neron Caesar written in Hebrew characters (*nrwn qsr*) is equivalent to 666, whereas the Latin form Nero Caesar (*nrw qsr*) is equivalent to 616."[10] Keep in mind that there were no copy machines in the first century. If you wanted a copy of a book, you had to copy it by hand. No matter how carefully a scribe worked, mistakes were inevitable. Some mistakes occurred when a scribe was making a copy of a known copy. He might have thought the copy was mistaken and that it was up to him to correct it. A Greek or Latin copyist might have thought that 666 was an error because Nero Caesar did not add up to 666 when transliterated into Latin. He then changed 666 to 616 to conform to the Latin rendering since it was generally accepted that Nero was the Beast. In either case, a Hebrew transliteration nets 666, while a Latin spelling nets 616. Nero was the "man" and 666 was his number.

A Religious Candidate: Jewish Priesthood

Following the methodology of letting Scripture interpret Scripture, there is another possible solution in identifying the number "six hundred and sixty-six" (Rev. 13:18). The number is found in three places in the Old Testament: 1 Kings 10:14; 2 Chronicles 9:13; Ezra 2:13. For our purposes, the references in 1 Kings 10:14 and 2 Chronicles 9:13—parallel accounts—shed some light on the choice of 666 for the "beast coming up out of the earth" (Rev. 13:11). The land beast, Israel, promotes the efforts of the sea beast and can only operate under the direction and authority of the sea beast. We are told that the land beast "had two horns like a lamb, and he spoke as a dragon" (13:11). The land beast is not the dragon, but he speaks "as a dragon." We learn from Jesus that the religious leaders who opposed Him were in league with the devil, the dragon: "You are of your father the devil, and you meant to do the desires of your father. He was a murderer from the beginning, and does not stand in the truth, because there is no truth in him. Whenever he speaks a lie, he speaks from his own nature; for he is a liar, and the father of lies" (John 8:44). The apostate Jews are described as a "synagogue of Satan" (Rev. 2:9; 3:9). The land beast is in league with the sea beast against the Christians of the first century. The land beast wants the sea beast to protect its corrupt religion against the religion of the lamb.

There is nothing new in this scenario since the apostate Jews turned to the Roman civil state to have Jesus put to death (John 18:31). In a final denouncement of their promised Messiah, the Jewish religious leaders cried out, "We have no king but Caesar" (John 19:15). Acts tells a similar story of

Jewish collaboration with the Romans to persecute the Bride of Christ, the church (e.g., Acts 24:1–9).

Solomon's Number

The Jews had seen six hundred and sixty-six before. Prior to Solomon's slide into apostasy, a description of his reign is given. One of the things said about him is that "the weight of gold which came in to Solomon in one year was 666 talents of gold" (1 Kings 10:14). From the number of shields (300) to the price of a horse imported from Egypt (150 shekels), we find round numbers, except when the number of gold talents is mentioned.

From the point where 666 talents of gold is mentioned, we read of Solomon's apostasy. First, Solomon violates the law regarding the accumulation of horses, chariots, wives, and gold (1 Kings 10:26; see Deut. 17:16-17).

> The law of Deuteronomy 17 forbad the king to multiply gold, women, and horses, but here we see Solomon do all three. In Revelation, the religious rulers of the "land" are called kings, the "kings of the land." The apostasy of the High Priest, and of the religious leaders of Israel, is thus linked to Solomon's sin. As Solomon lost his kingdom when the northern tribes rebelled after his death, so the Land Beast will lose his kingdom permanently when Jerusalem is destroyed.[11]

Second, Solomon sells himself to foreign interests. It is here that we see a parallel with Revelation 13. In their rejection of their Messiah, the Jews committed spiritual adultery with the nations (Rome) in the way that Solomon committed adultery with the nations surrounding him: "Now Solomon loved many foreign women along with the daughter of Pharaoh: Moabite, Ammonite, Edomite, Sidonian, and Hittite women, from the nations concerning which the LORD had said to the sons of Israel, 'You shall not associate with them, neither shall they associate with you, for they will surely turn your heart away after their gods.' Solomon held fast to these in love. And he had seven hundred wives, princesses, and three hundred concubines, and his wives turned his heart away" (1 Kings 11:1–3). James Jordan sums up the connection between Solomon and the apostate character of the Church's enemy in Revelation 13:

The number of the name (character) of the Sea Beast, then, means "apostate Solomon; apostate Jew." It is Solomon, not free under Yahweh's rule, but enslaved to Gentiles through illicit trade, the idol worshipping wiles of his women, and his lust for gold.[12]

So which is it, Nero or Solomon? It's possible that the number refers to both since the Sea Beast (Rome under Nero) and the Land Beast (Israel as the "synagogue of Satan") cooperate in their desire to see the Church destroyed. Those Jews who rejected Jesus—the heir to David's throne—embraced the apostasy of Solomon who did not follow after his father David.

While this interpretation does not answer all the questions we might have concerning this passage, it gets us started in terms of biblical theology rather than newspaper exegesis. The luxury that pre-tribulationalists have in their interpretive system is that the Beast and his mark do not appear until *after* the so-called rapture. They can speculate all they want as to the Beast's identity since they can never be proven wrong because, according to their theory, we will not be here. Popular dispensational author John Hagee writes: "This information about how to identify the Antichrist [Beast] is of no practical value to the Church since we will be watching from the balconies of heaven by the time he is revealed."[13] This means that *all* dispensational prophecy books are pure speculation because they can never be tested against the events of history.

If an event does not transpire as predicted, these writers can always say that the prophecy will not be fulfilled until after the rapture, an event that is always near. While this is a convenient way to interpret the Bible, the approach in no way deals honestly with texts that clearly describe prophetic events as happening within the lifetime of those who first read the prophecy.

Preterists, those who believe certain prophecies have already been fulfilled because of the incidence of time indicators, must defend their position against the events of history. Futurists, unless they predict a specific date or identify a specific person, can never be judged as false prophets. They usually mask their predictions with words like "could be" and "might take place."

While turning to 1 Kings 10 may seem unusual in trying to derive the meaning of 666, it is no more unusual than those who assert that the Beast (Antichrist) is alive somewhere in the world today. At least 1 Kings 10 is God's Word. Christians have more assurance of getting something right by appealing to the Bible than reading a daily newspaper.

Notes

1. Milton Terry, *Biblical Apocalyptics: A Study of the Most Notable Revelations of God and of Christ* (Grand Rapids, MI: Baker Book House, [1898] 1988), 401.

2. On the dating issue, see Kenneth L. Gentry, Jr., *Before Jerusalem Fell: Dating the Book of Revelation*, 2nd ed. (Atlanta, GA: American Vision, 1999). One reviewer of *Before Jerusalem Fell* wrote: "Anyone wishing to date Revelation late must answer some of the excellent arguments which Gentry has advanced. He has given late-date advocates a challenge for future study" (Thomas D. Lea, *Criswell Theological Review* [1992], 115). For a similar opinion, see Steve Gregg, ed. *Revelation: Four Views—A Parallel Commentary* (Nashville, TN: Thomas Nelson, 1997), 15, 18.

3. F.W. Farrar, *The Early Days of Christianity* (New York: E.P. Dutton, 1882), 412.

4. Kenneth L. Gentry, Jr., *The Beast of Revelation* (Tyler, TX: Institute for Christian Economics, 1989), 85.

5. R.H. Charles, *A Critical and Exegetical Commentary on the Revelation of St. John,* 2 vols. (New York: Charles Scribner's Sons, 1920), 1:cxliii.

6. Gentry, *The Beast of Revelation*, 34. See Charles, *A Critical and Exegetical Commentary on the Revelation of St. John*, 1:367.

7. "The Sibyllists had already spoken of Caligula as Beliar (*Carm.* iii. 63), and as a serpent. The stories of the serpent which had crawled from Nero's cradle, and of his serpent-amulet ... would add significance to the symbolism" (Farrar, *Early Days of Christianity*, 471, note 1).

8. Farrar, *Early Days of Christianity*, 471. In a footnote, Farrar writes: "I am not sure that a Jew would not have tried Hebrew letters at once" (471, note 2).

9. Farrar, *Early Days of Christianity*, 472.

10. Bruce M. Metzger, *A Textual Commentary on the Greek New Testament* (London: United Bible Societies, 1971), 751–52.

11. James B. Jordan, *A Brief Reader's Guide to Revelation* (Niceville, FL: Transfiguration Press, 1999), 36.

12. James B. Jordan, "The Beasts of Revelation (4)," *Studies in the Revelation* (April 1996), 2.

13. John Hagee, *Beginning of the End: The Assassination of Yitzhak Rabin and the Coming of Antichrist* (Nashville, TN: Thomas Nelson, 1996), 135. This does not stop the author from making a prediction: "This so-called man of peace, this Son of Satan, this false messiah, the Antichrist, is probably alive right now and may even know his predestined demonic assignment."

Chapter Twenty-One

IDENTIFYING ANTICHRIST

H al Lindsey wrote in 1970 that he believed that the antichrist was alive somewhere in the world. He repeated this belief in 1977 when he wrote that it was his "personal opinion" that "he's alive somewhere now. But he's not going to become this awesome figure that we nickname the Anti-Christ until Satan possesses him, and I don't believe that will occur until there is this 'mortal wound' from which he's raised up."[1] In 1980 he re-stated this conviction by writing that "this man [antichrist] is alive today—alive and waiting to come forth."[2] Although Lindsey believes the antichrist is alive somewhere in the world today, and actually has been since at least 1970, he has stated that "we must not indulge in speculation about whether any of the current world figures is the antichrist."[3] Anyway, determining the identity of the antichrist does not really matter since Lindsey and others believe "that Christians will not be around to watch the debacle brought about by the cruelest dictator of all time."[4]

Not to be outdone, Dave Hunt voices a similar opinion: "Somewhere, at this very moment, on planet Earth, the antichrist is almost certainly alive—biding his time, awaiting his cue. Banal sensationalism? Far from it! That likelihood is based upon a sober evaluation of current events in relation to Bible prophecy. Already a mature man, he is probably active in politics, perhaps even an admired world leader whose name is almost daily on everyone's lips."[5] Salem Kirban wrote in 1977 that "those of us familiar with Scriptures can easily see the handwriting on the wall as the way is prepared for the coming Antichrist."[6]

Lindsey, Hunt, Kirban, and many others share a belief that is strikingly similar to that of fortuneteller Jeane Dixon. Dixon claimed to have received a divine vision on February 5, 1962, about a coming world religious-political ruler; her "prophecy" resembles the modern doctrine of antichrist: "A child, born somewhere in the Middle East shortly before 7 A.M. (EST) on February 5, 1962, will revolutionize the world. Before the close of the century he will bring together all mankind in one all-embracing faith. This will be the foundation of a new Christianity, with every sect and creed united through this man who will walk among the people to spread the wisdom of the Almighty Power."[7] "Mrs. Dixon claims that this man's influence will be felt in the early 1980s and that by 1999, the ecumenical religion will be achieved."[8] Why should we believe present-day prophetic prognosticators when we have been offered assurances of the identity of the antichrist numerous times over the centuries?

Saint Martin of Tours, who died in A.D. 397, wrote of the coming antichrist whose reign would signify the last days. His prediction sounds strangely familiar. "*Non est dubium, quin antichristus....* There is no doubt that the antichrist has already been born. Firmly established already in his early years, he will, after reaching maturity, achieve supreme power."[9] Now go back and reread the quotations of Lindsey and Hunt. Christians should repudiate the writings of anyone who speculates that the antichrist is a contemporary figure. Such speculation is biblically unsound, as will become evident as we survey the passages used to make the identification.

Why all the confusion over who the antichrist is? The confusion arises because of two misconceptions: (1) treating divergent biblical references as if they all refer to the same person thereby creating a composite figure that is not found in Scripture; and (2) mistaking the time period in which these divergent figures are to appear.

The Composite Modern-Day Antichrist

Before we begin to sort through this confusion, let's first establish what generally passes as the modern understanding of antichrist. The antichrist of today's speculative theology combines the characteristics of Daniel's "prince who is to come" and other features from the Book of Daniel (9:26; 7:7–8, 19–26; 8:23–25); elements from Matthew and Daniel's "abomination of desolation" (Matt. 24:15; Dan. 9:27); Paul's "man of lawlessness" (2 Thess. 2:3); John's "antichrist" language (1 John 2:18, 22; 4:3; 2 John 7); and John's "beast" (Rev. 13:11–18).

This futurized composite antichrist supposedly will make himself known after the rapture of the church during the seven-year tribulation. It is speculated that he will arise out of Europe since he arises out of the midst of the "ten horns" on the head of the "fourth beast" (Dan. 7:7–8, 19–26). Others believe that he is Jewish.[10] This "fourth beast" with its "ten horns" is said to be a revived Roman Empire. This is the same beast that rises out of the sea of Revelation 13 (verses 1–10). Some believe the beast or antichrist must be a Jew since he will come "up out of the earth" or land (Rev. 13:11). Others believe that since he arises out of the sea, a designation for Gentile nations, he must be a Gentile (cf. Isaiah 57:20).

The modern antichrist is pictured as a charismatic political figure, the perfect media man. In the 1960s John F. Kennedy seemed to fit all the criteria for a modern-day antichrist, and his mortal head wound clinched it for many gullible Christians. The antichrist purportedly will have the eloquence of a Winston Churchill (Rev. 13:5) and the raw emotion and crowd appeal of an Adolf Hitler (Dan. 7:20; 8:23).

The conjecture which surrounds this figure continues with amazing detail based on scant biblical evidence. The antichrist will come to prominence as part of a ten-nation confederation approximating the land area of the old Roman Empire. Initially he will gain control through war, subduing three of the powers in the confederation. Some speculate that the ten-nation confederation will begin with thirteen. Once he secures power, he will pursue avenues of peace like Adolf Hitler (Dan. 8:25). His talk of peace will be attractive to an apostate Christianity (1 Thess. 5:3). As with Hitler who made peace with the "Holy See" of Rome, these overtures of peace will act like sedatives on the people.

> In his speech of March 23, 1933, to the Reichstag when the legislative body of Germany abandoned its functions to the dictator, Hitler paid tribute to the Christian faiths as "essential elements for safeguarding the soul of the German people," promised to respect their rights, declared that his government's "ambition is a peaceful accord between Church and

State" and added—with an eye to the votes of the Catholic Center Party, which he received—that "we hope to improve our friendly relations with the Holy See."[11]

As a man of peace, the antichrist will make a covenant with the Jews guaranteeing them peace and security in their own land. In the middle of the covenant period, he will break the covenant and turn on the Jews. He will then make war with the Jewish saints and will overcome them (Rev. 13:17; Dan. 7:21). Of course, during this three-and-one-half year period of time twothirds of the Jews living in Palestine will be killed (Zech. 13:8–9). Since he hates God, the antichrist will blaspheme God and His tabernacle (Rev. 13:6).

As a counterfeit Christ, the antichrist will be given great powers by the devil to try to duplicate Jesus' work. He will even seek to match the resurrection; the antichrist will seem to have suffered a mortal blow to the head but will then be miraculously resurrected. Lindsey says that he "does not believe it will be an actual resurrection, but it will be a situation in which this person has a mortal wound. Before he has actually lost life, however, he will be brought back from this critically wounded state. This is something which will cause tremendous amazement throughout the world."[12] This is highly doubtful. The world would not be amazed. A vast majority would consider it a trick. They've seen too much of the magician David Copperfield. The antichrist will immediately become an object of worship (Rev. 13:3–8) and will set himself up as God in the temple in Jerusalem (2 Thess. 2:4). The false prophet will erect an image or idol to the antichrist. He will then cause the statue to come alive and to speak (Rev. 13:14–15).

According to this elaborate scenario, the world will be living under a tyranny directed by Satan through his beast-antichrist and false prophet. Each and every person will be stamped with the dreaded 666! This recipe for disaster will eventually lead to Armageddon where all the nations of the world will be brought against Israel. Only the return of Christ will save Israel and the world.

When tested against sound biblical interpretation, will such a theory hold up? The issue of timing invalidates the entire modern antichrist theory. Is it possible that what was prophecy is now history? Could the beast of Revelation 13 and his attendant number 666 be referring to a well-known historical figure who played a prominent role during the time in which the Book of Revelation was written?

As we will see, the modern doctrine of antichrist is an amalgamation of biblical concepts and events that either are unrelated or find their fulfillment in past events. This is why confusion persists. Modern antichrist hunters are pursuing a figure who no longer exists. Let's look at the biblical evidence.

The Biblical Antichrist

First, we must find a *biblical* definition of antichrist. The word "antichrist" appears only in John's epistles (1 John 2:18, 22; 4:3; 2 John 7). "What is taught in these passages constitutes the whole New Testament doctrine of Antichrist."[13] John's description of antichrist is altogether different from the modern image. John's antichrist is

- Anyone "who denies that Jesus is the Christ" (1 John 2:22).
- Anyone who "denies the Father and Son" (1 John 2:23).
- "Every spirit that does not confess Jesus" (1 John 4:3).
- "Those who do not acknowledge Jesus Christ as coming in the flesh. This is the deceiver and the antichrist" (2 John 7).

None of what John writes relates to the modern doctrine of the antichrist as previously outlined. John's antichrist doctrine is a theological concept related to an apostasy that was fomenting in his day. John did not have a particular individual in mind but rather *individuals* who taught that Jesus Christ is not who the Bible says He is:

> In one word, "Antichrist" meant for John just denial of what we should call the doctrine, or let us rather say the fact, of the Incarnation. By whatever process it had been brought about, "Christ" had come to denote for John the Divine Nature of our Lord, and so far to be synonymous with "Son of God." To deny that Jesus is the Christ was not to him therefore merely to deny that he is the Messiah, but to deny that he is the Son of God; and was equivalent therefore to "denying the Father and the Son"—that is to say, in our modern mode of speech, the doctrine—in fact—of the Trinity, which is the implicate of the Incarnation. To deny

that Jesus is Christ come—or is the Christ coming—in flesh, was again just to refuse to recognize in Jesus Incarnate God. Whosoever, says John, takes up this attitude toward Jesus is Antichrist.[14]

Is this interpretation possible? Aren't we supposed to look for a future apostasy out of which *the* antichrist will arise? As the New Testament makes clear, apostasy was rampant almost from the church's inception. The apostasy about which John wrote was operating in his day. Paul had to counter a "different gospel" that was "contrary" to what he had preached (Gal. 1:6–9). He had to battle "false brethren" (2:4, 11–21; 3:1–3; 5:1–12). He warned the Ephesian church leadership that "men will arise, speaking perverse things, to draw away the disciples after them" (Acts 20:28–30). Theological insurrection came from within the Christian community.

Many people prior to Jerusalem's destruction in A.D. 70 questioned and disputed basic Christian doctrines like the resurrection (2 Tim. 2:18); some even claimed that the resurrection was an impossibility (1 Cor. 15:12). Strange doctrines were taught. Some "Christians" prohibited marriage (1 Tim. 4:1–3). Others denied the validity of God's good creation (Col. 2:8, 18–23). The apostles found themselves defending the faith against numerous false teachers and "false apostles" (Rom. 16:17–18; 2 Cor. 11:3–4, 12:15; Phil. 3:18–19; 1 Tim. 1:3–7; 2 Tim. 4:2–5). Apostasy increased to such an extent that Paul had to write letters to a young pastor who was experiencing these things firsthand (1 Tim. 1:19–20; 6:20–21; 2 Tim. 2:16–18; 3:1–9, 13; 4:10, 14–16). In addition, entire congregations fell to apostasy:

> One of the last letters of the New Testament, the Book of Hebrews, was written to an entire Christian community on the very brink of wholesale abandonment of Christianity. The Christian church of the first generation was not only characterized by faith and miracles; it was also characterized by increasing lawlessness, rebellion, and heresy from within the Christian community—just as Jesus foretold in Matthew 24.[15]

The Book of Revelation recounts such heretical teachings: "evil men" (2:2), "those who call themselves apostles" but who are found to be "false" (2:6), a revival of "the teaching of Balaam" (2:14), those "who hold the teaching of the Nicolaitans" (2:15), the toleration of the "woman Jezebel ... who leads" God's "bond-servants astray, so that they commit acts of immorality and eat things sacrificed to idols" (2:20). *The* apostasy was alive and well on planet earth in the *first* century (2 Thess. 2:3).

Antichrist is simply any belief system that disputes the fundamental teachings of Christianity, beginning with the person of Christ. These antichrists are "religious" figures. The antichrist, contrary to much present-day speculation, is not a political figure, no matter how *anti-* (against) Christ he might be. The modern manufactured composite antichrist is not the antichrist of 1 and 2 John: "Putting it all together, we can see that *Antichrist* is a description of both *the system of* apostasy and *individual apostates*. In other words, antichrist was the fulfillment of Jesus' prophecy that a time of great apostasy would come, when 'many will fall away and will betray one another and hate one another. And many false prophets will arise, and will mislead many' (Matt. 24:10–11)."[16]

In addition, you will not find the word antichrist in the Book of Revelation. This is significant since the John who defines antichrist for us in his first two letters is the same John who penned the Book of Revelation.

> It is remarkable that a word so "characteristic of the School of John" does not appear in the Apocalypse, where it might have served the writer's purpose in more than one passage. That the conception of a personal Antichrist existed among the Christians in Asia in the first century is certain from I John ii. 18.[17]

Second, according to the Bible antichrist is not a single individual. John wrote, "Children, it is the last hour; and just as you heard that antichrist is coming, even now *many* antichrists have arisen; from this we know that it is the last hour" (1 John 2:18). "He calls them just 'Antichrists,' and he sets them over against the individual Antichrist of which his readers had heard as the reality represented by that unreal figure."[18] It is possible that the early church "heard" that one man was to come on the scene who was to be *the* antichrist. John seems to be correcting this mistaken notion: "John is adducing not an item of Christian teaching, but only a current legend—Christian or other— in which he recognizes an element of truth and isolates it for the benefit of his readers. In that case we may understand him less as expounding than as openly correcting it—somewhat as, in the closing page of his Gospel, he corrects another saying of similar bearing which was in circulation among the brethren, to the effect that he himself should not die but should tarry till the Lord comes [John 21:18–23]."[19] In a similar manner, the people in Jesus' day had "heard" certain things that were only partially true. Jesus corrected them in their misreading of the Bible (Matt. 5:21, 27, 33, 38, 43).[20]

Third, whether there was to be only one or many antichrists, John made it clear that "it is the last hour" for those who *first* read his letters (1 John 2:18). How do we know this? John said, "Even *now* many antichrists have arisen." And in case you did not get his point, he repeated it: "From *this* we know that it *is* the last hour." John did not describe a period of time thousands of years in the future. It was the "last hour" for *his contemporaries.* Keep in mind that Jesus had told His disciples years before, John among them, that their generation would see the destruction of the temple and Jerusalem (Matt. 24:1–34). John, writing close to the time when this prophecy was to be fulfilled, described its fulfillment in the rise of "many antichrists," that is, many who preach and teach a false religious system, the denial that Jesus had come in the flesh (2 John 7). The apostle's knowledge about coming antichrists was probably taken from Matthew 24:24: "For false Christs and false prophets will arise and will show great signs and wonders, so as to mislead, if possible, even the elect."

They had heard that "the spirit of antichrist" was coming. For them, "*now* it is *already* in the world" (1 John 4:3). Antichrists had arrived. It is inappropriate to look for a contemporary rising political leader and describe him as *the* antichrist. Such a designation cannot be supported from Scripture. Does this mean that the *spirit* of antichrist cannot be present in our day? Not at all. It does mean, however, that a figure called *the* antichrist cannot be alive somewhere in the world today. Having said this, we still must conclude that John had the time prior to Jerusalem's destruction in mind when he described the theological climate surrounding the concept of the antichrist.

An antichrist, therefore, is *anyone* who "denies that Jesus is the Christ" and *anyone* "who denies the Father and the Son" (1 John 2:22). "*Every* spirit that does not confess Jesus is not from God; and *this* is the spirit of antichrist" (1 John 4:3). "For *many* deceivers have gone out into the world, *those* who do not acknowledge Jesus Christ as coming in the flesh. *This* is the deceiver and the antichrist" (2 John 7).

Notes

1. "The Great Cosmic Countdown: Hal Lindsey on the Future," *Eternity* (January 1977), 80.

2. Hal Lindsey, *The 1980s: Countdown to Armageddon* (King of Prussia, PA: Westgate Press, 1980), 15.

3. Hal Lindsey, *The Late Great Planet Earth* (Grand Rapids, MI: Zondervan, 1970), 113.

4. Lindsey, *The Late Great Planet Earth*, 113.

5. Dave Hunt, *Global Peace and the Rise of Antichrist* (Eugene, OR: Harvest House, 1990), 5.

6. Salem Kirban, *Countdown to Rapture* (Irvine, CA: Harvest House, 1977), 181.

7. Quoted in Robert Glenn Gromacki, *Are These the Last Days?* (Schaumburg, IL: Regular Baptist Press, 1970), 90.

8. Gromacki, *Are These the Last Days?*, 90.

9. Quoted in Otto Friedrich, *The End of the World: A History* (New York: Coward, McCann and Geoghegan, 1982), 27.

10. Jerry Falwell believes that when the antichrist appears during "the tribulation period he will be a full-blown counterfiet of Christ. Of course, he'll be Jewish. Of course he'll pretend to be Christ." (Quoted in Sonja Barisic, "Jewish Leaders Say Falwell Evokes Anti-Semitism," *Atlanta Journal/Constitution* [16 January 1999], A4).

11. William L. Shirer, *The Rise and Fall of the Third Reich: A History of Nazi Germany* (New York: Simon and Schuster, 1960), 234.

12. Lindsey, *Late Great Planet Earth,* 108.

13. Benjamin B. Warfield, "Antichrist," in *Selected Shorter Writings of Benjamin B. Warfield,* John E. Meeter, ed. (Nutley, NJ: Presbyterian and Reformed, 1970), 1:356.

14. Warfield, "Antichrist," 360–61.

15. David Chilton, *Paradise Restored: A Biblical Theology of Dominion* (Tyler, TX: Institute for Christian Economics, 1985), 108.

16. Chilton, *Paradise Restored*, 111.

17. Henry Barclay Swete, *The Apocalypse of St John: The Greek Text with Introduction, Notes, and Indices* (New York: The Macmillan Company, 1906), lxxv.

18. Warfield, "Antichrist," 359.

19. Warfield, "Antichrist," 357.

20. Gary DeMar, *"You've Heard It Said"* (Atlanta, GA: American Vision, 1991).

Chapter Twenty-Two

THE MAN OF LAWLESSNESS (I)

M any believe that 2 Thessalonians 2 describes the end times leading up to the rapture of the church, the revealing of antichrist, and the second coming. Tim LaHaye, a representative of this perspective, writes: "Second Thessalonians 2:1–12 contains the rapture, Tribulation, and Glorious Appearing all in one chapter, the only time I find this in the Bible."[1] While LaHaye claims to be certain, there are many who have gone before him who are not quite so confident.

Augustine was one of the first to admit that parts of 2 Thessalonians 2 are perplexing: "I frankly confess I do not know what [Paul] means."[2] New Testament Greek scholar Marvin Vincent was puzzled enough to give the chapter only a cursory study: "I attempt no interpretation of this passage as a whole, which I do not understand. The varieties of exposition are bewildering."[3] The renown Greek linguist A.T. Robertson finds that "the whole subject is left by Paul in such vague form that we can hardly hope to clear it up."[4] P.J. Gloag, in his comments on the "Man of Sin" in the *Pulpit Commentary*, acknowledges that "there is an obscurity in the language" that "could not have been so great to those to whom the apostle wrote, for he had previously instructed his readers in the nature of the occurrence (ch. ii. 5, 6);

but our ignorance of these instructions renders the passage to us enigmatical and difficult to understand."[5] Gary W. Demarest writes that 2 Thessalonians 2:1–12, "is undoubtedly one of the most difficult in all of Paul's writings. It has given rise to more speculative and diverse interpretations than any other section of Paul's letters."[6]

While there are some things in 2 Thessalonians that we do not know, there is a great deal we can figure out by putting the pieces together. By comparing Scripture with Scripture, Paul's man of lawlessness will be revealed.

The Coming of the Lord

Is "the coming of our Lord Jesus Christ" a reference to the Second Coming, that is, an event that is still in our future, or is it a coming in judgment upon first-century Jerusalem that would be the event to bring the "last days" to a close (2 Thess. 2:1)?[7] The word translated "coming" in verse 1 is the Greek word *parousia*, best translated as "presence" in other contexts (2 Cor. 10:10; Phil. 2:12). "The term itself does not mean 'return' or 'second' coming; it simply means 'arrival' or 'presence.' Applying it to Christ's coming from heaven in a sense changes what the word connotes."[8] N. T. Wright agrees:

> The word 'parousia' is itself misleading, anyway, since it merely means 'presence'; Paul can use it of his being present with a church, and nobody supposes that he imagined he would make his appearance flying downwards on a cloud. . . . The church expected certain events to happen within a generation and happen they did, though there must have been moments between AD 30 and 70 when some wondered if they would and in consequence took up the Jewish language of delay. Jerusalem fell; the good news of Jesus, and the kingdom of Israel's God, was announced in Rome, as well as in Jerusalem and Athens.[9]

Translating *parousia* as "coming" is not at all improper, however, since the Bible's use of "coming" does not always mean bodily presence, as so many Old and New Testament passages make clear. In addition, we know that the Bible clearly states that "the coming [*parousia*] of the Lord" was said to be "at hand," that is, "near" to Christians living prior to the destruction of Jerusalem in A.D. 70 (James 5:8). How could James have told his readers to "be patient ... *until* the "coming of the Lord" if the Lord's coming was not "near" for them? James bases his call for patience upon the fact that the Lord's coming *was near*, near for those who first read his letter. "James clearly believed, as others of his time did, that the Coming of Christ was imminent. Since, then, there is not long to wait, his plea for patience is greatly reinforced."[10]

So then, our understanding of 2 Thessalonians 2:1 must be considered within the time frame of the *parousia* which was said to be "near" for the first-century church. As we will see, Paul was not countering the belief that the Thessalonians were under a false impression that Jesus' coming was near. The nearness of Jesus' coming—a coming in judgment upon Jerusalem—was an accepted New Testament doctrine. Rather, Paul was correcting their misconception that the Day of the Lord *had already taken place.*

Confusion exists over the meaning of the New Testament doctrine of "coming" because Bible readers have been taught that "coming" always means the bodily return of Jesus. James Macknight's comments are helpful:

In the prophetic writings of the Jews (2 Sam. xxii. 10, 12; Psalm xcvii. 2–5; Isa. xix. 1) great exertions of the Divine power, whether for the salvation or destruction of nations, are called *the coming, the appearance, or the presence of God.* Hence it was natural for the apostles, who were Jews, to call any signal and evident interposition of Christ, as Governor of the world, for the accomplishment of his purposes, *his coming* and *his day.* Accordingly, those exertions of his power and providence, whereby he destroyed Jerusalem and the temple, abrogated the Mosaic institutions, and established the Gospel, are called by the apostles *his coming* and *day*; not only in allusion to the ancient prophetic language, but because Christ himself, in his prophecy concerning these events, recorded [in] Matt. xxiv., has termed them *the coming of the Son of Man,* in allusion to the ... prophecy of Daniel, of which his own prophecy is an explication; Dan vii. 13. 'I saw in the night visions, and behold, one like the Son of Man came with the clouds of heaven, and came to the Ancient of Days. And they brought him near before him. 14. And there was given him dominion, and glory, and a kingdom, that all people, nations, and languages should serve him. His dominion is an everlasting dominion, which shall not pass away, and his kingdom that which shall not be destroyed.' This prophecy, the Jewish doctors with one consent interpreted of their Messiah, and of

that temporal kingdom which they expected was to be given him. Farther, they supposed he would erect that temporal kingdom by great and
visible exertions of his power for the destruction of his enemies. But they
little suspected, that [they] themselves were of the number of those enemies whom he was to destroy, and that his kingdom was to be established upon the ruin of their state. Yet that was the true meaning of 'the
coming of the Son of man in the clouds of heaven.' For, while the Jewish
nation continued in Judea, and observed the institutions of Moses, they
violently opposed the preaching of the Gospel, by which the Messiah
was to reign over all people, nations, and languages. Wherefore, that the
everlasting kingdom might be effectually established, it was necessary
that Jerusalem and the Jewish state should be destroyed by the Roman
armies. Now, since our Lord foretold this sad catastrophe in the words of
the Prophet Daniel, Matthew xxiv. 30, 'And they shall see the Son of man
coming in the clouds of heaven with power and great glory;' and after
describing every particular of it with the greatest exactness, seeing he
told his disciples, ver. 34 'This generation shall not pass till all these
things be fulfilled;' can there be any doubt that the apostles (who, when
they wrote their epistles, certainly understood the true import of this
prophecy), by 'their master's coming' and by 'the end of all things,' which
they represent as at hand, meant his coming to destroy Jerusalem, and put
an end to the institutions of Moses?[11]

Macknight cites numerous New Testament passages to support his view
that verses referring to the "near" coming of Christ point to His coming in
judgment upon Jerusalem in A.D. 70 and the establishment of "his spiritual
kingdom over all people, nations, languages, and not his coming to put an
end to this mundane system" (Matt. 16:28; 1 Cor. 10:11; Phil. 4:5; Heb.
9:26; 10:25; James 5:7–8; 1 Peter 4:7; 1 John 2:18).[12]

The Presence of the Lord in the New Testament

God's presence was a sign of blessing because of Israel's special covenantal status (Isa. 55:3; Jer. 1:19). God's departure was a sign of judgment. For
the nations, God's presence was a sign of judgment because of their wickedness. Because of Israel's abominations, God's presence left the temple
(Ezek. 5–11). Israel was then treated like the nations and would hide from
and lament His presence in the future.

In similar fashion, because of Israel's rejection of the Messiah and the persecution of His church, Christ's bride, God would make His presence known to Israel in the form of judgment. God rejected His once-covenanted people and their temple of stone because of the nation's rejection of the promised Son of Man (Matt. 23:38; 24:1). Like Ezekiel (Ezek. 8), Jesus inspected the temple, found it filled with abominations (Matt. 21:12–13), and left it desolate (23:38). He returned in A.D. 70 to inspect the temple for a final time and found it full of abominations. His presence now abides with a new people of God constructed as a "spiritual house," the true temple of God (1 Peter 2:4–10; cf. 2 Cor. 6:14–18).

In effect, Christ's *parousia* in 2 Thessalonians 2:1 is the fulfillment of the promise that the presence of Christ will reside with the true Israel forever (Rom. 2:28–29; 9:6; 10:12; Gal. 6:15–16; Phil. 3:3; Col. 3:11; Heb. 8:8, 10). Remember, during His earthly ministry Jesus "came out from the temple" (Matt. 24:1), foretold its destruction (24:15–34), and returned in A.D. 70 to destroy it (22:7). A new covenant nation arose from the ashes of the temple: "Therefore I say to you [speaking to the chief priests and the elders], the kingdom of God will be taken from you, and be given to a nation producing the fruit of it. And he who falls on this stone will be broken to pieces; but on whomever it falls, it will scatter him like dust" (21:43–44).

There is no doubt that Jesus' "coming" in 2 Thessalonians 2:1 should be attributed to the first century since the time indicators ("has come," "now," "already") leave no room in this passage for a coming in the distant future (*e.g.,* Matt. 16:27–28; 24:29–31; 26:64; Heb. 10:37; James 5:7–8; Rev. 2:5, 16; 3:11). Jesus' coming in A.D. 70 was a coming in judgment upon an apostate nation.

"Our Gathering Together"

Tim LaHaye states, "The 'gathering together to Him' refers to the Rapture, the event when He welcomes His church to be with Him."[13] The Greek word for "gather" (*episunagogue*) is not a word employed by Paul to indicate the rapture (1 Thess. 4:17). For those who claim that it is, we must ask why Paul would use a different word in his second letter to clear up a supposed misunderstanding about what the Thessalonians thought he meant concerning "our being caught up" in his first letter? Why didn't Paul write,

"With regard to *our being caught up* to Him"? The answer is quite obvious: Paul is discussing two separate events.

Episunagogue is used in only one other place in the New Testament (Heb. 10:25), although cognates are found elsewhere (Matt. 23:37; Mark 13:37; Luke 17:37). In Hebrews 10:25 the word clearly refers to an assembly of Christians on earth, not a "catching up" (rapture) to heaven. Why should the word suddenly change meaning in 2 Thessalonians 2:1? The gathering together of God's people has a specific meaning.

> Ever since the time of Isaiah xi. 11 and xxvii. 13 Israelites had cherished the hope that their brethren who had been led away in captivity or were dispersed in foreign lands would be gathered together into Palestine to share in the glories of the Messianic Kingdom.... The idea had passed over into Christian Apocalyptic. In Heb. x.25 the word is used for the ordinary gathering on the Lord's Day.[14]

The related Greek word *sunagogue*, from which we get the word synagogue, is used frequently in the New Testament and means to assemble in a group. "For where two or three have *gathered together* in My name, there I am in their midst" (Matt. 18:20; cf. 2:4; 3:12; John 6:13; 11:47; 11:52; 20:19; Acts 4:27, 31; 14:27; 15:30; 20:8; 1 Cor. 5:4; Rev. 16:14, 16; 19:17, 19; 20:8). There is no indication that the rapture is in view in any of these passages.

The gathering is horizontal and earthly, not vertical and heavenly. Jesus wanted to "gather" the children of Israel "together the way a hen gathers her chicks under her wings" (Matt. 23:37). This is not a description of a rapture. God will "gather" together those who embrace Him as the Messiah and "scatter" those who reject Him (21:44). This is done in terms of the call of the gospel.[15] The process of this "gathering" was made possible after the death of Jesus and the gospel's embrace of the nations (28:18–20). A commentary on this use of the meaning of "gather" can be found in Jesus' encounter with the chief priests and Pharisees:

> Therefore the chief priests and the Pharisees convened a council, and were saying, "What are we doing? For this man is performing many signs. If we let Him go on like this, all men will believe in Him, and the Romans will come and take away both our place and our nation." But a certain one of them, Caiaphas, who was high priest that year, said to them, "You

know nothing at all, nor do you take into account that it is expedient for you that one man should die for the people, and that the whole nation should not perish." Now this he did not say on his own initiative; but being high priest that year, he prophesied that Jesus was going to die for the nation; and not for the nation only, *but that He might gather together into one the children of God who are scattered abroad* (John 11:47–52).

Notice the relationship between "scattered abroad," "gather together," and "one." Those "scattered abroad" are the "other sheep"—Gentiles—Jesus spoke of in John 10:16. A full exposition on this new covenant idea is found in Ephesians 2:11–22. Gentiles were *"separate* from Christ, *excluded* from the commonwealth of Israel, and *strangers* to the covenants of promise" (2:12). Those who are "in Christ," who "formerly were *far off* have been *brought near*" (2:13). Jesus has "made *both* groups *one"* (2:14), making "the *two* into *one* new man" (2:15), reconciling "them *both* in *one body* to God through the cross" (2:16). Jesus "CAME AND PREACHED PEACE TO YOU WHO WERE *FAR AWAY,* AND PEACE TO THOSE WHO WERE *NEAR"* (2:17). *"Both"* have access in *"one* Spirit to the Father" (2:18). Gentile Christians are "no longer *strangers* and *aliens* but are *fellow-citizens* with the saints, and are of God's household" (2:19). There is "one new man," "one body," and a new "holy temple in the Lord" in Christ (2:21). The new "household" is the "church of the living God, the pillar and support of the truth" (1 Tim. 3:15).

Those who deny Christ are "members" of the "household" of Beelzebul (Matt. 10:25). A similar reference is made in the Book of Revelation where a gathering of apostate Jews is described as a "synagogue of Satan" (Rev. 2:9; 3:9). Their synagogues were false gathering places since the redemptive work of Messiah Jesus nullified the Old Covenant order.

With the coming destruction of Jerusalem and the Temple, Christians would henceforth be "gathered together" in a *separate* and *distinct* "assembly" (*episunagoge*; the Church is called a *synagogue* in James 2:2). After the Temple's destruction, God would no longer tolerate going up to the Temple to worship (it would be impossible!), as Christians frequently did prior to A.D. 70.[16]

Prior to the destruction of the temple and its services, the synagogues (Acts 13:5, 14; 14:1; 15:21) and temple (21:26–36) were still frequented by Christians. The period between A.D. 30 and 70 was a transitional time for the transference from the Jewish exclusive Old Covenant to the inclusive New Covenant comprised of Jews *and* Gentiles. There had to be a new synagogue, a new gathering of the people of God made up solely of believers in the Messiah where "in Christ neither circumcision nor uncircumcision means anything" (Galatians 5:6). Peter describes this new group of believers in terms previously reserved for Old Covenant Israel: "But you are a CHOSEN RACE, A ROYAL PRIESTHOOD, A HOLY NATION, A PEOPLE FOR God's OWN POSSESSION, that you may proclaim the excellencies of Him who has called you out of darkness into his marvelous light; for you once were NOT A PEOPLE, but now you are THE PEOPLE OF GOD; you had NOT RECEIVED MERCY but now you have RECEIVED MERCY" (1 Peter 2:9–10).

Such a future gathering had been predicted in the Old Testament: "The LORD GOD, who gathers the dispersed of Israel, declares, 'Yet others I will gather to them, to those already gathered'" (Isaiah 56:8). This gathering began immediately after the ascension of Jesus and continues throughout the church era. With the destruction of the temple in Jerusalem in A.D. 70 there no longer would be any confusion as to the makeup of the new temple, the "new people of God."

The Time Element

In his description of the man of lawlessness, Paul makes it clear that he had a contemporary figure in mind. First, he tells the Thessalonians that "the mystery of lawlessness *is already at work*" (2 Thess. 2:7).

Second, the Thessalonians knew what was presently restraining the man of lawlessness: "And *you know* what restrains him *now*" (2:6). Paul does not write, "You know what *will* restrain him." In addition, Paul affirms that "only he who *now* restrains will do so until he is taken out of the way" (2:7). While there is a great deal of speculation on the identity of the restrainer, from these time-text passages we know that he was restraining in Paul's day. Without ever being able to identify the man of lawlessness we can conclude that he appeared and disappeared in the first century.

It is highly unlikely, if we take the futurist position, that the restrainer could have been active in Paul's day and throughout history, since the restraint was only necessary when the man of lawlessness was alive. If the man of lawlessness was not alive when Paul wrote, then why did he clearly state that the Thessalonians knew what and who was restraining the man of lawlessness? Benjamin B. Warfield summarizes this section of 2 Thessalonians 2 for us:

> The withholding power is already present. Although the Man of Sin is not yet revealed, as a mystery his essential "lawlessness" is already working—"only until the present restrainer be removed from the midst." He expects him to sit in the "temple of God," which perhaps most naturally refers to the literal temple in Jerusalem, although the Apostle knew that the out-pouring of God's wrath on the Jews was close at hand (I Thess. ii. 16). And if we compare the description which the Apostle gives of him with our Lord's address on the Mount of Olives (Mt. xxiv), to which, as we have already hinted, Paul makes obvious allusion, it becomes at once in the highest degree probable that in the words, "he exalteth himself against all that is called God, or is worshipped, so that he sitteth in the sanctuary of God showing himself that he is God," Paul can have nothing else in view than what our Lord described as "the abomination of desolation which was spoken of by Daniel the prophet, standing in the holy place" (Mt. xxiv. 15); and this our Lord connects immediately with the beleaguering of Jerusalem (cf. Luke xxi. 20).[17]

Third, the Thessalonians thought that the day of the Lord had come. Paul exhorts his readers: Do not be "quickly shaken from your composure or be disturbed either by a spirit or a message or a letter as if from us, *to the effect that the day of the Lord has come*" (2 Thess. 2:2).

Paul was not correcting a belief of the Thessalonians that the day of the Lord was "near" or "at hand," as some translations have it (*e.g.,* KJV and ASV). If so, Paul would have been contradicting himself and the rest of the New Testament since they state that the day of the Lord was near (*e.g.,* Rom. 13:12; James 5:8; Rev. 1:1, 3). "All the Apostles believed that the day was near (1 Cor. xv. 51; James v. 8, 9; 1 Pet. iv. 7; 1 John ii. 18; Rev. xxii. 20), and their watchword was 'Maranatha,' 'the Lord is *near.*'"[18] Those who hold a futurist perspective understand the implications of what Paul writes concerning the nearness of the day of the Lord. This is why a number of them force the text to read "is near" instead of the more accurate "is present." The Greek word translated "is present" is found in six places in the New Testament in addition to 2 Thessalonians 2:1. In each case, "present" and not "near" is the best translation (Rom. 8:38; 1 Cor. 3:22; 7:26; Gal. 1:4; 2 Tim. 3:1; Heb. 9:9. "Is near," therefore, is not in keeping with the meaning of the word.

> Some commentators hold the meaning to be that the day of the Lord was on the very point of occurring. The verb, however, does not mean "to be at hand" but rather "to be present." It is sometimes contrasted to verbs expressing the future idea (*e.g.,* Rom. 8:38; 1 Cor. 3:22). Moreover, Paul could, and did, say that the Parousia was "at hand" (with a different Greek expression, Phil. 4:5). It seems that the verb ought to be given its usual sense here, rather than to have the idea of imminence imported into it.[19]

E.J. Bicknell writes that "*'is now present'* ... is the only possible translation of the Greek.... Attempts are made to soften down the translation because of the difficulty of seeing how any one could suppose that the Day of the Lord had actually arrived."[20] This means that LaHaye and other dispensationalists are incorrect when they identify 2 Thessalonians with the pre-tribulational rapture ("our gathering together to Him") since *not one Christian at Thessalonica had been raptured!* Remember, the Thessalonians believed that the day of the Lord *had come.* It was believed to be a *past* event (2:2).

Furthermore, the passage cannot be describing the Second Coming since the Thessalonians believed they had received "a message or a letter" that had been sent to them by Paul informing them, to repeat the point, that "the day of the Lord *has come*" (2:2). If they had thought that either the rapture or the Second Coming had taken place—as per Paul's supposed message or letter—would they not have asked themselves why Paul had not been raptured? How could Paul have written a letter after the rapture or the Second Coming if he was no longer on the earth?[21]

The Day of the Lord

The Bible describes numerous "days of the Lord," not all of which refer to the Second Coming of Christ or the dissolution of the physical heavens and earth. Isaiah wrote, "Wail, for the day of the LORD is near!" (Isaiah 13:6). He continues with, "Behold, the day of the LORD is coming, cruel, with fury and burning anger, to make the land a desolation; and He will exterminate its sinners from it" (13:9). This was "the oracle concerning

Babylon," the Babylon of the Old Testament, the Babylon that suffered divine retribution (13:1). For Babylon, the "day of the LORD" is past.

The "day of the LORD" was to draw "near on all the nations" (Obad. 1:15), all the nations then in existence. Zephaniah states that "the day of the LORD is near" (Zeph. 1:7). This is restated in verse 14: "Near is the great day of the LORD, near and coming very quickly." For those of us who read this, this particular "day of the LORD" is past. The "day of the LORD" came to Israel in the sacking of Jerusalem by Babylon in 586 B.C. John Walvoord, a futurist, makes a valuable comment about the multi-faceted character and application of the "day of the Lord":

> The "Day of the Lord" is an expression frequently used in both the Old and New Testaments to describe any period of time during which God exercises direct judgment on human sin. The Old Testament records a number of times when Israel endured a day of the Lord, lasting a few days or, in some cases, several years.[22]

The "day of the Lord" was a day of God's judgment and vengeance. As a result, there could be many such days. Luke describes the destruction of Jerusalem in A.D. 70 as "days of vengeance" (Luke 21:22), the fulfillment of Isaiah 61:2: "The day of vengeance of our God" (also see 63:4). In the case of 2 Thessalonians 2 the "day of the Lord" that the Thessalonians thought had already come was God's judgment upon the Old Covenant order localized in Jerusalem that occurred in A.D. 70 (John 4:21; Gal. 4:25). John Lightfoot writes that "the Scripture and the apostle had spoken of 'the day of the Lord's coming;' when he should come to take vengeance of the Jewish nation, for their wickedness and unbelief."[23] Paul described this coming judgment in his first letter to the Thessalonians. He reminded them that it was the apostate Jews who "killed the Lord Jesus and the prophets.... They are not pleasing to God, but hostile to all men, hindering us from speaking to the Gentiles that they might be saved; with the result that they always fill up the measure of their sins. But wrath has come upon them to the utmost" (1 Thess. 2:15–16; cf. Matt. 23:31–32, 35–36; John 3:36).

This was a first-century indictment of a single generation of Jews. God's wrath was vented in A.D. 70. "We have no right to lay the sins of the Jews of the first century or any other century on Jewish people today."[24] Unfortunately, those who believe that these passages address a future Jewish holocaust during a so-called Great Tribulation inadvertently keep the fires of anti-semitism alive.[25] Paul's "day of the Lord" is past (1 Thess. 5:2). "While they are saying, 'Peace and safety!' then destruction will come upon them suddenly like birth pangs upon a woman with child; and they shall not escape" (5:3; cf. Matt. 24:15–25). The Thessalonians had been warned of this coming judgment: "But *you*, brethren, are not in darkness, that the day should overtake *you* like a thief" (5:4). Paul had told the Thessalonians that certain indicators were available to them that would prepare them for the "day of the Lord" that was fast approaching.

If the "day of the Lord" refers to the dissolution of the physical heavens and earth, again, how could the Thessalonians have thought that it had already come? There is no way they could have missed it. Supposedly the end of the world will occur when the physical "elements will be destroyed with intense heat, and the earth and its elements will be burned up" (2 Peter 3:10), events that will be impossible to ignore. In fact, no one will be on earth to witness these events since, according to dispensationalists, they follow the earthly millennium. Dispensationalists try to get around this timing factor by giving a specialized meaning to the "day of the Lord." Literalism is once again abandoned for the sake of a preconceived system of theology. When Paul "speaks of a coming day of the Lord (2 Thess. 2.2), the passage cannot be referring to the end of the space-time universe. It envisages the possibility that the Thessalonians might hear of the great event by *letter*."[26]

Dispensationalists have a difficult time reconciling the diverse ways "day of the Lord" is used by Paul in 1 Thessalonians 5:2, 2 Thessalonians 2:2 and by Peter in 2 Peter 3:10. They tell us that while the Thessalonian "day of the Lord" refers to events *prior* to the thousand years of Revelation 20:4, Peter's "day of the Lord" refers to events *following* the thousand years. How can these "days" be reconciled? Consider this improbable solution: "That day begins immediately after the Rapture of the church and ends with the conclusion of the Millennium."[27] Dispensationalists insist on interpreting the Bible *literally*. What happened here?

The "day of the Lord" has now become a thousand years using dispensational hermeneutics! Does this mean that the "thousand years" of Revelation 20 constitute a single day? It is obvious that Paul (1 Thess. 5:2) and Peter (2 Peter 3:10) are speaking of the same day since they both use the metaphor "like a thief in the night."[28] Using 2 Peter 3:8—where it is said that "*with the Lord* one day is *as* a thousand years, and a thousand years *as* one day" —

every time we do not like the implications of clear time texts is nothing less than irresponsible.

A final question must be asked: Why would the Thessalonian church have been concerned that the destruction of Jerusalem (the "day of the Lord") had occurred? The answer is quite simple. The Thessalonians were concerned about fellow Christians who they believed had gone through a terrible tribulation. While they rejoiced that their persecutors would be taken out of the way, "they had cause to 'rejoice with trembling,' as their Lord had plainly intimated that it was to be a season of severe trial to his friends, as well as fearful vengeance against his enemies."[29] They themselves had experienced tribulation (1 Thess. 1:6), so they had some idea what Christians in Jerusalem might experience during "a great tribulation, such as has not occurred since the beginning of the world until now, nor ever shall" (Matt. 24:22). The churches showed concern for one another (1 Cor. 16:1–3). It is even possible that the Thessalonians, many of whom were Jews (Acts 17:1–9), had relatives living in Jerusalem at the time. The only word they had was a false report that the day of the Lord, that is, the destruction of Jerusalem, had come. They heard nothing further about the fate of their fellow Christians. They were understandably concerned. Paul assures them that the day of the Lord had not come, Jerusalem was still standing, and certain events had to transpire before the city and temple would be destroyed.

Notes

1. Tim LaHaye, *No Fear of the Storm: Why Christians Will Escape All The Tribulation* (Sisters, OR: Multnomah/Questar, 1992), 73.
2. Augustine (354–430), *The City of God* in *A Select Library of the Nicene and Post-Nicene Fathers of the Christian Church*, ed. Philip Schaff, vol. 2 (Grand Rapids, MI: Eerdmans, 1983), Book XX, chap. 19, page 437.
3. Marvin R. Vincent, *Word Studies in the New Testament*, 4 vols. (Peabody, MA: Hendrickson Publishers, [1887] n.d.), 4:67, note.
4. A.T. Robertson, *Word Pictures in the New Testament*, 6 vols. (Nashville, TN: Broadman Press, 1930), 4:51.
5. P.J. Gloag, "II Thessalonians," *The Pulpit Commentary*, eds. H.D.M. Spence and Joseph S. Exell (New York: Funk & Wagnalls, n.d.), 50.
6. Gary W. Demarest, *The Communicator's Commentary: 1, 2 Thessalonians; 1, 2 Timothy; and Titus* (Dallas, TX: Word, 1984), 116.
7. For a brief survey of those who hold that 2 Thessalonians 2 describes events leading up to and including the destruction of Jerusalem in A.D. 70, see Henry Alford, *The Greek Testament*, 4 vols. (5th ed.; Cambridge, England: Deighton, Bell, and Co., 1871), 3:62–63.
8. Ben Witherington III, *Jesus, Paul and the End of the World: A Comparative Study in New Testament Eschatology* (Downers Grove, IL: InterVarsity Press, 1992), 152.
9. N. T. Wright, *The New Testament and the People of God* (Minneapolis, MN: Fortress Press, 1992), 463.
10. C. Leslie Mitton, *The Epistle of James* (Grand Rapids, MI: Eerdmans, 1966), 186–87. See Matt. 24:32; 26:18; John 2:13; 6:4; 7:2; 11:55 for the way "near" is used.
11. James Macknight (1721–1800), *A New Literal Translation from the Original Greek of all the Apostolical Epistles with Commentary, and Notes, Philological, Critical, Explanatory, and Practical* (New York: M.W. Dodd, [1795] 1850), 423.
12. Macknight, *A New Literal Translation*, 560.
13. LaHaye, *No Fear of the Storm*, 73.
14. E.J. Bicknell, *The First and Second Epistles to the Thessalonians* (London: Methuen and Co., 1932), 73.
15. Bob Gundry, *First the Antichrist: Why Christ Won't Come before the Antichrist Does* (Grand Rapids, MI: Baker Book House, 1997), 176–84.

16. Kenneth L. Gentry, *He Shall Have Dominion* (Tyler, TX: Institute for Christian Economics, 1992), 386–87.

17. Benjamin B. Warfield, "The Prophecies of St. Paul," in *Biblical and Theological Studies,* ed. Samuel G. Craig (Philadelphia, PA: Presbyterian and Reformed, 1968), 472.

18. F.W. Farrar, *Texts Explained or Helps to Understand the New Testament* (Cleveland, OH: F.M. Barton, 1899), 178.

19. Leon Morris, *The First and Second Epistles to the Thessalonians,* rev. ed. (Grand Rapids, MI: Eerdmans, 1991), 216. Geerhardus Vos writes: "The rendering 'is at hand' seems a compromise due to doctrinal motives" (*The Pauline Eschatology* [Grand Rapids, MI: Eerdmans, 1952], 95, note 1).

20. Bicknell, *The First and Second Epistles to the Thessalonians,* 74.

21. For a similar discussion of this point, see N. T. Wright, "Jerusalem in the New Testament," P.W.L. Walker, ed., *Jerusalem Past and Present in the Purposes of God* (Grand Rapids, MI: Baker, 1994), 64.

22. John F. Walvoord, *Prophecy: 14 Essential Keys to Understanding the Final Drama* (Nashville, TN: Thomas Nelson, 1993), 114–15.

23. John Lightfoot, *The Whole Works of the Rev. John Lightfoot,* ed. John Rogers Pitman, 13 vols. (London: J.F. Dove, 1822), 3:231.

24. Demarest, *The Communicator's Commentary,* 62.

25. Hal Lindsey falls into this trap. See his poorly reasoned *The Road to Holocaust* (New York: Bantam Books, 1989), 220, where he describes the Jewish holocaust in A.D. 70 as a "picnic" compared to a supposed super holocaust that will kill billions of people, including two-thirds of the Jews living in Israel during the tribulation period.

26. N. T. Wright, *The New Testament and the People of God* (Minneapolis, MN: Fortress Press, 1992), 460.

27. Constable, "1 and 2 Thessalonians," *The Bible Knowledge Commentary,* 705. Extending the "day of the Lord" over a thousand years seems to be a standard feature of dispensationalism. See J. Dwight Pentecost, *Things to Come: A Study in Biblical Eschatology* (Grand Rapids, MI: Zondervan, [1958] 1987), 230–31.

28. Some commentators apply 2 Peter 3:10—the passing away of "heaven and earth"—to the destruction of Jerusalem in A.D. 70. See John Owen, *Works,* 16 vols. (London: The Banner of Truth Trust, 1965–68), 9:134–38; John Brown, *Expository Discourses on the First Epistle of the Apostle Peter,* 3 vols. (Edinburgh: William Oliphant, 1866), 3:84–85; John Brown, *The Discourses and Sayings of*

Our Lord, 3 vols. (London: Banner of Truth Trust, [1852] 1967), 1:171–74; John Lightfoot, *A Commentary on the New Testament from the Talmud and Hebraica: Matthew—1 Corinthians*, 4 vols. (Peabody, MA: Hendrickson Publishers, [1859], 1989), 3:451–54.

29. Brown, *Expository Discourses on the First Epistle of the Apostle Peter*, 3:86.

Chapter Twenty-Three

THE MAN OF LAWLESSNESS (II)

The Reformers, almost without exception, believed that the papal system was the antichrist, with the individual popes reflecting the spiritual application of Paul's description of the Man of Lawlessness of 2 Thessalonians 2.[1] The papal antichrist view was written into the confessions of that era. The Westminster Confession of Faith (1643–47) declared that "There is no other head of the Church but the Lord Jesus Christ; nor can the Pope of Rome in any sense be head thereof; but is that Antichrist, the son of perdition, that exalteth himself in the Church against Christ, and all that is called God" (25.7). Some who dared to make their views known were burned at the stake. Leroy Froom writes:

> In the centuries just preceding the Reformation an ever-increasing number of pious persons began openly to express the conviction that the dire prophecies concerning Antichrist were even then in the process of fulfillment. They felt that the "falling away" had already taken place. They declared that Antichrist was already seated in the churchly temple of God, clothed in scarlet and purple. Numerous individuals of influence spoke mysterious things about seven-hilled Rome, and solemnly pointed the

finger at the Roman church as the predicted Man of Sin, which had now become a historical reality.[2]

While the Reformers were correct in their judgment of Roman Catholic doctrine, they, too, ignored the time indicators outlined by Paul in 2 Thessalonians 2. The time texts, the present restraining, and the "mystery of lawlessness already at work," restricts the passage's time of fulfillment to the first century. Since the destruction of Jerusalem is in view, the papacy cannot be in the picture. Nisbett's comments are important:

> Various are the interpretations of the learned, concerning the man of sin and the son of perdition, &c. some referring to Simon Magus [Acts 8:9–24],[3] some to Mahomet [*i.e.,* Muhammad], and some to the Popes of Rome and their clergy. But if it be allowed, that the Apostle is speaking of the destruction of Jerusalem; the supposition of the two last, cannot be admitted, as being wholly foreign to the purpose, and in many other respects highly improbable.[4]

There are at least three possible first-century, pre-A.D. 70 candidates: a political figure (Nero or a representative of the Roman government), a religious figure (Phannias or another member of the priesthood), or a zealot (John Levi Gischala).

Political Man of Lawlessness

Some conjecture that the man of lawlessness was a political figure, possibly Nero, or a representative of Rome, Titus. Titus did in fact enter the temple area. The deification of the Roman emperors was well known to the Jews of the first century. Reservations about using the tribute coin were tied to deification of the emperors (Matt. 21:15–22).

> The emperor's image on the coin was contrary to the second commandment.... [T]he inscription on Tiberius' coin read 'TI[berius] CAESAR DIVI AUG[usti] F[ilius] AUGUSTUS,' or, in translation, "Tiberius Caesar Augustus, son of the deified Augustus." The inscription was virtually an ascription of deity to the reigning emperor, which would insult the religious conviction of any Jew that no man could claim to be God.[5]

Caligula (A.D. 37–41) proposed that Tiberius should be deified. In A.D. 40 Caligula began to seek worship for himself. Caligula ordered that a statue of Zeus with his own features be placed in the Temple in Jerusalem, and demanded also that he be worshipped at Rome.[6] A national revolt was averted at the last moment by his own death. Caligula openly sat in the Temple of Jupiter. During the reign of Claudius (A.D. 41–54), writers often referred to him as "our god Caesar." In Book 12 of the Sibylline Oracles, Nero (A.D. 54–68) is called "terrible and frightful," "a terrible snake," one engaged in "making himself equal to God."[7] Nero "styled himself 'divi Claudi filius' [son of the deified Claudius]."[8] Some believe that Nero was the man of lawlessness and Claudius the "restrainer."[9] Nero never sat in the temple.

Titus, as a representative of the Roman Emperor, was acclaimed *imperator*—victorious commander—by the Roman soldiers while Jerusalem went up in flames. The act of destroying the "temple of God" would have given him delusions of power and status never dreamed of by mortal men. Moreover, pagan worship took place on the temple grounds. "When the temple area was taken by the Romans, and the sanctuary was still burning, the soldiers brought their legionary standards into the sacred precincts, set them up opposite the eastern gate, and offered sacrifices to them there...."[10] This act of worship might have been a prelude to a more specific fulfillment. There are examples of Old Testament civil leaders assuming the role of "gods" (Isa. 14:4, 12–14, 22; Ezek. 28:2, 6, 11–12; Dan. 11:36).

Some commentators believe that Paul's use of enigmatic language was designed to hide references to a Roman man of lawlessness, and thus is further evidence that a Roman is in view. Supposedly Paul feared Roman reprisals so he wrote in cryptic terms so as not to turn the Empire against the congregation at Thessalonica. Rome would have had little interest in the affairs of a small congregation of Jews in Asia Minor. Moreover, Paul had no fear of Rome. He spoke boldly in the presence of Rome's representatives (Acts 25:11). As a Jew, Paul would have styled himself after the godly prophets of the Old Testament. These prophets leveled judgments against specific nations without fear: Babylon (Isaiah 13), Moab (15–16), Edom, Syria, Damascus (17), Ethiopia (18) Egypt (19), Tyre (23), to cite a few examples. Many paid the ultimate price for boldness and faithfulness (Heb. 11:35–40), as did Peter (John 21:18–19) and Paul.

A Priestly Man of Lawlessness

While a Roman political figure is a plausible solution, I believe it fails to account for Paul's methodology: He always wrote against the backdrop of the Old Testament. What seems to be mystery and enigma are actually restatements of Old Testament themes often missed by readers who are unfamiliar with the Old Testament. Since Paul, "a Hebrew of Hebrews" (Phil. 3:5), was living in the "last days" of the Old Covenant (1 Cor. 10:11), we should expect him to use Old Covenant terminology when speaking of its dissolution. When 2 Thessalonians 2 is compared with the Old Testament a number of literary similarities can be found: "presence of our Lord" (Lev. 10:2; 16:1; Deut. 29:15), "coming" (Isa. 13:9), "gather" (Isa. 40:11; Jer. 31:8; Micah 2:12; Zeph. 3:20; Zech. 10:8), "day of the Lord" (Isa. 13:6, 9; Lam. 2:22; Ezek. 7:19; 13:5; 30:3; Joel 1:15), "apostasy" (Jer. 2:19; 5:6; 8:5; 14:7), "breath of his mouth" (Isa. 11:14), "deluding influence" (1 Kings 22:19–22), etc. In addition, as was suggested previously, we should expect Paul's perspective to fall in line with the prophecies outlined by Jesus in the Olivet Discourse (Matt. 24; Mark 13; Luke 21). Moreover, the theological setting suggests a Jewish "falling away" that was already in operation in the first century (Heb. 3:12–15; 4:11; 6:4–8; 10:26–31, 37–39; 12:25–29).

The Jewish converts and "God-fearing Greeks" of Thessalonica (Acts 17:1–4) would have immediately picked up these Old Covenant allusions and their application to the present Jewish apostasy. "The apostasy here described is plainly not of a civil, but of a religious nature; not a revolt from the government, but a defection from the true religion and worship, 'a departing from the faith,' (1 Tim. iv. 1,) 'a departing from the living God,' (Heb. iii. 12) as the word is used by the apostle in other places."[11]

Jewish Opposition to the Gospel

The apostles were persecuted by the Jews soon after Pentecost (Acts 4:1–31; 5:17–42; 7:54–60). After his conversion, Paul experienced similar persecution at the hands of the Jews (9:29; 13:50; 14:2, 19), especially by the Jews of Thessalonica (17:1–15). Some of the Jews who heard Paul's message became "jealous and taking along some wicked men from the market place, formed a mob and set the city in an uproar" (17:5).

The Jews were everywhere the jealous, malignant and energetic enemies of the Gospel. At Antioch, Thessalonica, Corinth, and in every principal city, they kindled opposition and persecution. In one of the latest of his epistles Paul writes: "Beware of the dogs, beware of the evil workers, beware of the [circumcision]" (Phil. 3:2). At first it was not the empire, nor Paganism that made deliberate, organized opposition to Christianity. As Pilate would have released the Saviour but for the Jewish hierarchy, so the imperial authorities regarded the church with indifference and contempt, except when its industrious Jewish enemies succeeded in exciting their suspicion or their fear.... During our Lord's ministry it was the Jews who were primarily "his adversaries" (Luke 13:17); it was the same during the ministry of the apostles.[12]

This opposition came from three groups: (1) those Jews who denied that Jesus was the Messiah; (2) those Jews who were "zealous for the law," that is, the Mosaic ceremonial ordinances (Acts 21:20), insisting that these Old Covenant customs should be retained as a condition for salvation; and (3) those Jews who neglected "the commandment of God" while keeping their man-made "tradition" (Mark 7:8–9). Jews who had rejected their Messiah outright had apostatized from the one true faith (Ephesians 4:5). They had rejected the faith of believing Israelites such as Mary, Joseph, Elizabeth, Zacharias, Simeon (Luke 2:34–35), Anna (2:36–38), Nicodemus (John 3; 19:39), Joseph of Arimathea (John 19:38), the apostles, the disciples, the "three thousand" (Acts 2:41), the "five thousand" (Acts 4:4), and Paul himself (Acts 9). They were vocal antagonists of the gospel. The man of lawlessness is akin to a traitor, a Judas. A synonym for the "man of lawlessness" is the "son of destruction" (2 Thess. 2:3), the title given to describe Judas (John 17:12).

Jewish Apostasy

The Greek word *apostasia* has two meanings in biblical literature: political revolt and religious defection. The Septuagint, the Greek translation of the Hebrew Scriptures, uses *apostasia* to describe both a political revolt (Ezra 4:12, 15, 19; Neh. 2:19; 6:6) and a religious defection (Joshua 22:22; Jer. 2:19; 2 Chron. 29:19; 33:19). H. Wayne House attempts to prove that *apostasia* means a "departure from earth," *i.e.*, a rapture.[13] House does admit, however, that "the case is not conclusive" (286). If *apostasia* does mean a "physical or spatial departure," then it best fits an A.D. 70 scenario. Jesus told His first-century audience that when they saw the abomination of desolation, they were to "flee to the mountains" (Matt. 24:16). We could then interpret Paul in this way: "Let no one in any way deceive you, for the judgment on Jerusalem will not come until Christians living in Judea flee to the mountains first, and the man of lawlessness is revealed. . ." (2 Thess. 2:3).

Josephus uses *apostasia* to characterize the Jewish revolt against the Roman government.[14] If Paul in 2 Thessalonians 2:3 is using *apostasia* to describe a political revolt, then this also neatly fits the historical context of the Jewish rebellion against Roman authority that is known in history as the "Jewish War."

The New Testament also uses *apostasia* to describe a religious rebellion. For example, Jews who questioned the sufficiency of Jesus' death to pay the penalty for sin believed that forsaking the customs of Moses—especially circumcision—was "apostasy" (Acts 21:21). Unfortunately, most translations do not translate the Greek word *apostasia* in Acts 21:21 as "apostasy." Here is a literal rendering of Acts 21:21:

> Now the [believing Jews] have heard reports about you, how you teach all the Jews who live among the Gentiles *to commit apostasy against Moses*, telling them to stop circumcising their children and not to follow the customs [of Moses].

For the Judaizers apostasy was a rejection of the customs of Moses which they believed were a condition for salvation even if one embraced Jesus as the Messiah. It was this controversy that was settled at the first church council in Jerusalem (Acts 15:1–35). For Paul, apostasy was following the customs of Moses as a condition for salvation. Of course, Paul's definition of apostasy is the correct one. Paul told Timothy that "in later times some will fall away [apostasontai] from the faith" (1 Tim. 4:1). These apostates would reject the counsel of the apostles and claim that Gentiles who embrace Jesus as the Messiah must be circumcised and directed "to observe the Law of Moses" (Acts 15:5). These "doctrines of demons"—apostasies—had already shown themselves in the first-century church (Col. 2:16, 23; cf. 1 Tim. 4:3). F.F. Bruce writes that the first-century Christians "must withstand the temptation to return to Judaism; that was the sin of apostasy which by its very nature was irremediable, for (as they had already acknowledged) there was no other name in the world but the name of Jesus in which salvation could be found. Not only was such apostasy sin; it was folly."[15]

Jesus warned about an approaching apostasy that His disciples would have to confront (Matt. 7:15, 22; 24:5, 10–12, 24). Paul cautioned the church at Ephesus, that after his departure, "savage wolves will come in among *you*, not sparing the flock; and *from among your own selves* men will arise, speaking perverse things, to *draw away* the disciples after them" (Acts 20:29–30). This adds another dimension to the apostasy—Jews who were first attracted to the gospel, but after learning that it did not maintain Old Covenant ceremonials, rejected it (Heb. 6:4–8). Notice that Paul warns the Ephesians that this departure from the faith will affect them. The apostates will come "from among your own selves," Paul warns.

The Corinthian church is warned about "false apostles, deceitful workers" who "disguise themselves as apostles of Christ" (2 Cor. 11:13). Paul describes them as "servants" of "Satan" (11:14–15). Those in Galatia were disturbed by those who "want to distort the gospel of Christ" (Gal. 1:7). The entire church was disturbed by "false brethren" who were desirous to bring Christians "into bondage" to the law (2:4).

The church at Rome was warned to keep an eye "on those who cause dissensions and hindrances contrary to the teaching which" they had learned. Paul's admonition is to "turn away from them." Through their "smooth and flattering speech they deceive the hearts of the unsuspecting" (Rom. 16:17–18). Paul becomes more specific when he tells the Philippians to "beware of the dogs, beware of the evil workers; beware of the false circumcision" (Phil. 3:2). They are "enemies of the cross of Christ, whose end is destruction" (3:18).

Personal counsel was given to Timothy to "instruct certain men not to teach strange doctrines, nor to pay attention to myths and endless genealogies, which give rise to speculation rather than furthering the administration of God which is by faith" (1 Tim. 1:3–4). Again, Paul has unbelieving Jews in mind since they are those who want "to be teachers of the Law" (1:7). Even by Timothy's day some had "suffered shipwreck in regard to their faith" (1:19). Of course, apostasy had been predicted by the Holy Spirit who explicitly said "that in later times some will fall away from the faith, paying attention to deceitful spirits and doctrines of demons" (4:1). Deceit and unsound doctrine were present in Timothy's day: "O Timothy, guard what has been entrusted to you, avoiding worldly and empty chatter and the opposing arguments of what is falsely called 'knowledge'—which some have professed and thus gone astray from the faith" (6:20–21).

Timothy was given further instructions to "preach the word; be ready in season and out of season; reprove, rebuke, exhort, with great patience and instruction. For the time will come when they will not endure sound doctrine; but wanting to have their ears tickled, they will accumulate for themselves teachers in accordance to their own desires; and will turn away their ears from the truth, and will turn aside to myths" (2 Tim. 4:2–4). Who are these people who distort the faith? "For there are many rebellious men, empty talkers and deceivers, *especially those of the circumcision,* who must be silenced because they are upsetting whole families, teaching things they should not teach.... This testimony is true. For this cause reprove them severely that they may be sound in the faith, *not paying attention to Jewish myths and commandments of men who turn away from the truth....* They profess to know God, but by their deeds they deny Him, being detestable and disobedient, and worthless for any good deed" (Titus 1:10–11, 13–14, 16).

Peter describes a similar apostasy: "But false prophets also arose among the people, just as there will also be false teachers among *you,* who will secretly introduce destructive heresies, even denying the Master who bought them, bringing swift destruction upon themselves" (2 Peter 2:1).

John's epistles describe a contemporary apostasy, those who denied that Jesus had come in the flesh (1 John 2:22). False prophets were prevalent in John's day (4:1). "For many deceivers have gone out into the world, those who do not acknowledge Jesus Christ as coming in the flesh. This is the deceiver and the antichrist" (2 John 7). John makes it clear that for the first-century church it was the "last hour" (1 John 2:18). He offers the following evidence to support his claim: "They went out from us, but they were not really of us; for if they had been of us, they would have remained with us; but they went out, in order that it might be shown that they all are not of us" (2:19).

Jude warns the "beloved" (verse 1) to "contend earnestly for the faith.... For certain persons have crept in unnoticed, those who were long beforehand marked out for this condemnation, ungodly persons who turn the grace of our God into licentiousness and deny our holy Master and Lord, Jesus Christ" (verses 3–5). Jude then recounts several judgment periods in

Israel's history (verses 5–17). These "certain persons" are those who "were spoken beforehand by the apostles of our Lord Jesus Christ" (verse 17). Their appearance in Jude's day is evidence that it was "the last time" (verse 18). The "mockers" who "crept in unnoticed" were alive in Jude's day. They would meet the same fate as those mockers described in verses 5–17. When would this take place? The judgment had to be leveled against them personally since Jude compares their fate to Old Covenant "mockers" (verses 5–17). This means the judgment had to be near.

> [I]n this interpretation, the apostasy is obviously the great apostasy of the Jews, gradually filling up all these years and hastening to its completion in their destruction. That the Apostle certainly had this rapidly completing apostasy in his mind in the severe arraignment that he makes of the Jews in I Thess. ii. 14–16, which reached its climax in the declaration that they were continually filling up more and more full the measure of their sins, until already the measure of God's wrath was prematurely … filled up against them and was hanging over them like some laden thunder-cloud ready to burst and overwhelm them,—adds an additional reason for supposing his reference to be to this apostasy—above all others, "the" apostasy—in this passage.[16]

Taking into account the way these Jews aligned themselves with Rome to crucify Jesus (John 19:12–15) and their relentless persecution of the early church (Acts 13:50; 14:1–7), there does not seem to be a more prominent example of apostasy anywhere else in the annals of history. "The 'falling away' then refers to that of Jews after the ascension of Christ, rather than that of the Church in the end of this age."[17]

Jesus did not bring a new way of salvation; therefore, any Jew who rejected Him as the Messiah was an apostate (Galatians 1:6–24). Jesus was the fulfillment of all that the Jews had read about and hoped for (Luke 24:44). Therefore, those Jews who rejected Jesus made up the great apostasy. "To be more definite, the *principle* denounced by the apostle is that of Pharisaic Judaism; its historic *embodiment* we are to find in the Jewish hierarchy and religious leaders of the century following the crucifixion…. No other historic embodiment of sin … so fully and accurately answers to the terms of the prophetic description."[18]

Prevalence of Jewish Lawlessness

If the "apostasy" arose from the midst of Judaism, is it not possible that the man of lawlessness is also a Jewish figure of the first century?[19] A number of indicators in the text give us reason to believe that a particular man is in view. First, as we have already observed, Paul's language is pulled directly from Jesus' prophetic pronouncements, biblical vocabulary, and theological themes from the Old Testament. All of these suggest a covenantal interpretation. Jesus had dealt with the "mystery of lawlessness" during His ministry:

- *"Neglecting the commandment of God*, you hold to the tradition of men" (Mark 7:8).
- "You nicely *set aside the commandment of God* in order to keep your tradition" (7:9).
- *"Invalidating the word of God* by your tradition which you have handed down; and you do many things such as that" (7:13).
- "Now the *chief priests* and the whole Council kept trying to obtain *false testimony* against Jesus, in order that they might put Him to death" (Matt. 26:59).

While the Jews purported to be keepers of the law, these texts and many more like them show that their deeds were contrary to the law, the very essence of lawlessness, for "sin is lawlessness" (1 John 3:4).

Second, the Thessalonians were Jews and "God-fearing Greeks" (Acts 17:1–4). They would have understood and applied the covenantal language to their era since "the mystery of lawlessness *was already at work*" (2 Thess. 2:7). The Thessalonians would have been looking for a contemporary figure. In fact, they knew who it was since Paul writes: "And you know what restrains him now" (2:6).

Third, persecution came by way of the Jews, stirred up by the priests (Acts 9:14; 22:30; 25:2, 15; 26:10, 12). When Paul was struck by the high priest Ananias, Paul called him a "whitewashed wall," accusing him of lawlessness: "And do you sit to try me according to the Law, and in *violation of the Law* order me to be struck?" (Acts 23:3).

The Bible records the blasphemous expression of lawlessness uttered by the priests in rejecting Jesus and turning Him over to the pagan State of Rome to be crucified: "We have no king but Caesar," the religious leaders cried out (John 19:15). They also demonstrated their perverted application of the law in the stoning of Stephen and showed their rejection of the New Covenant as they took their places of false authority in the temple (Acts 7:54–60). Prior to his conversion, Paul participated in this "lawlessness" with full support of "the high priest" (22:5). John Lightfoot writes that "'The mystery of iniquity was already working,' when the apostle wrote this Epistle, which cannot possibly be understood but of the Jewish nation; and so it is explained again and again [1 John, ii.18, and iv.3, and 2 John, ver. 7, &c.]."[20] Paul must have spoken about this many times when he described his experiences with the Jews.

Fourth, lawlessness must be understood in covenantal terms. Jesus inaugurated "the new covenant in" His "blood" (Luke 22:20; 1 Cor. 11:25; Heb. 12:25). Any deviation from New Covenant precepts is apostasy. An Old Covenant example will demonstrate this point. Nadab and Abihu, the sons of Aaron, "offered strange fire before the LORD, which He had *not commanded* them" (Lev. 10:1). Fire was an integral part of the sacrifice (2:2). Their lawless deed was that they offered a type of fire that was contrary to the law. This means that the priests were "men of lawlessness." They did what God "had not commanded them." Their judgment was by fire that "came out from the *presence* of the LORD" (10:2; cf. 2 Thess. 2:8). Jerusalem was destroyed by "fire" (Matt. 22:7) that was sent by the "king" (cf. Luke 3:9; 2 Thess. 1:7; Heb. 12:29; Rev. 8:5).

Similarly, the high priest who served in the temple prior to its destruction in A.D. 70 offered "strange" sacrifices that violated the provisions of the New Covenant that is now defined by Jesus' blood and no longer by the blood of "bulls and goats" (Hebrews 10:4). The sin of the high priest was akin to that of Nadab and Abihu. He was the man of lawlessness as defined by the provisions of the New Covenant. Animal sacrifices were detestable to God in light of the sacrifice of His only begotten Son (cf. Isa. 1:11; 65:1–11). The following is a description of God's attitude to continued animal sacrifices in light of the finished work of Jesus:

> He who kills an ox is like one who slays a man; he who sacrifices a lamb is like the one who breaks a dog's neck; he who offers a grain offering is like one who offers swine's blood; he who burns incense is like the one who blesses an idol. As they have chosen their own ways, and their soul delights in their abominations, so I will choose their punish-

ments, and I will bring on them what they dread. Because I called, but no one answered; I spoke, but they did not listen. And they did evil in My sight, and chose that in which I did not delight (Isa. 66:3–4).

The priests who continued to offer sacrifices in the temple were acting like Nadab and Abihu. Their fire was "strange" and their sacrifices detestable because Jesus was God's sacrificial lamb whom they scorned and later slaughtered by turning Him over to the Romans to be crucified. When Jesus came in judgment upon Jerusalem and the temple and put an end to the system of sacrifices that the Jews sought to maintain, He brought it all "to an end by the appearance of His coming" (2 Thess. 2:8).

Fifth, prior to Jesus' description of events leading up to the destruction of the temple in A.D. 70 (Matt. 24), He denounced the lawless religious leaders who "*seated* themselves in the chair of Moses" (23:2). Paul did the same (Acts 23:3). Of course, there is no "chair of Moses." To sit in Moses' chair is to assume the authority of Moses. When Jesus sat at the right hand of His Father (Acts 2:34; Heb. 1:13; 8:1), He assumed a position of authority equal to His Father.

The idea that rulers, either ecclesiastical or civil, are described as "god" or "gods" has a rich Old Testament history.

> Then the anger of the LORD burned against Moses, and He said, "Is there not your brother Aaron the Levite? I know that he speaks fluently. And moreover, behold, he is coming out to meet you; when he sees you, he will be glad in his heart. And you are to speak to him and put the words in his mouth; and I, even I, will be with your mouth and his mouth, and I will teach you what you are to do. Moreover, *he shall speak for you to the people; and it shall come about that he shall be as a mouth for you, and you shall be as God to him*" (Ex. 4:14–17; cf. Psalm 82:1, 6; John 10:34).

The Hebrew term for "gods" (*elohim*) in Psalm 82:6, for example, is a reference to those who *exercise judicial authority in God's name.* "The passage refers to the judges of Israel, and the expression 'gods' is applied to them in the exercise of their high and God-given office."[21] To be brought before a judge was like being brought before God because the judge *represented* God. The word translated "God" in Exodus 21:6 (from the Hebrew *elohim*) is referring to a judge who acts in God's name. This can be seen in Ex. 22:8–

9. The word translated "judge" is actually *elohim*, the same Hebrew word often translated as "god" or "gods."

With this background in mind, it is clear that in Matthew 23:2, Jesus is describing the way the religious leaders used their "*legislative seat*"[22] to distort the law and to enslave the people (23:4, 15). In effect, they were renegade "gods," serving as corrupt magistrates (John 10:34–35; cf. Psalm 82:6). As the gospels make clear, the religious leaders of Jesus' day declared themselves to be gods in a humanistic sense, determining the meaning of the law without regard to the Word of God (cf. Isa. 14:4, 12–14, 22; Ezek. 28:2, 6, 11–12; Dan. 11:36).[23] They set up their traditions above the commandments of God, thus nullifying God's law (Matt. 12:2, 10–12; 15:1–14; 23:23; Mark 3:4; John 7:19). Jesus describes them as those who "outwardly appear righteous to men, but inwardly [they] are full of hypocrisy and *lawlessness*" (Matt. 23:28).

The religious leaders, led by the high priest, had so perverted the law that they despised the "objects of worship," in effect, exalting themselves "above every so-called god or object of worship" (2 Thess. 2:4): "Woe to you blind guides, who say, 'Whoever swears by the temple, *that is nothing;* but whoever swears by the gold of the temple, he is obligated.... And 'Whoever swears by the altar, *that is nothing,* but whoever swears by the offering upon it, he is obligated'" (Matt. 23:16, 18). Is this language not similar to what Paul says about the man of lawlessness as he is described in 2 Thessalonians 2:4?: "He takes his *seat* in the temple of God, displaying himself as being God." Lightfoot comments that this happened

> to the very letter; their scribes, in the temple of God itself, sitting and setting up their traditions above the commands of God [Matt. xv.6]. But how they exalted themselves against every thing called God, or the magistracy, and those that were set over them, we may observe in such passages as these,—"They despise government" [2 Pet. ii.10], "They despise dominion, and speak evil of dignities" [Jude, ver. 8], and in their own stories to endless examples.[24]

The *man* of lawlessness was the principal religious leader of Israel—the high priest who officiated over Jewish law and did not concern himself with using the law in a God-honoring way (Matt. 26:57–68). All of the lawless deeds of those priests who sent Jesus to His death and persecuted

His bride, the church, had reached their climax by the time the temple was destroyed in A.D. 70 (23:32–36). In addition, the defilement of the temple was the result of their lawless acts.

> The zealots had got possession of the Temple at an early stage in the siege, and profaned it by these and other like outrages; they made the Holy Place (in the very words of the historian [Josephus]) "a garrison and stronghold" of their tyrannous and lawless rule; while the better priests looked on from afar and wept tears of horror. The mysterious prediction of 2 Thess. ii.4 may point, in the first instance, to some kindred "abomination."[25]

Josephus describes how the Zealots dismantled the biblically prescribed method of choosing priests and "ordained certain unknown and ignoble persons for that office." Their choice for high priest was Phannias. "Yet did they hail this man, without his own consent, out of the country, as if they were acting a play upon the stage, and adorned him with a counterfeit face; they also put upon him the sacred garments, and upon every occasion instructed him what he was to do. This horrid piece of wickedness was sport and pastime with them, but occasioned the other priests, who at a distance saw their law made a jest of, to shed tears, and sorely lament the dissolution of such a sacred dignity."[26] William Whiston, the translator of Josephus's *Works*, writes that we do not "meet with any other so much as pretended high priests after Phannias, till Jerusalem was taken and destroyed."[27]

John Bray offers another first-century candidate who fits Paul's description of the man of lawlessness. John Levi of Gischala, Bray writes, "was the key man in the destruction of Jerusalem, the greatest instigator of the tribulation upon the Jews in the city, and an 'abomination' himself as he 'sat' in power in the Temple itself. And he was the cause of the ceasing of the daily sacrifices there and one half years after Vespasian came against the city. So far as the people were concerned, he had taken the place of God in the Temple!"[28] Following Josephus, Bray offers compelling historical evidence for his opinion, everything from murder to defilement of the temple. Mireille Hadas-Lebel recounts John's lawless deeds:

> Crimes against men were accompanied by what Josephus considered crimes against God. John of Gischala was especially guilty of these latter. Early in the siege he had used timber intended for the Temple to con-

struct war machines. Next, he had all the sacred vessels melted down, including precious vases offered by the emperor Augustus and his wife. Then he had dipped into the Temple reserves of oil and wine.[29]

John Levi of Gischala is a likely candidate since the people living in Jerusalem followed his every move. His occupation of the temple followed the surrounding of Jerusalem by armies. Those who believe that Paul is describing an event that requires a rebuilt temple miss the simple fact that the Thessalonians would have had no such notion in mind as they read Paul's letter.

Whether the man of lawlessness was Phannias, John of Gischala, or some other first-century personage, we know that he was alive when Paul wrote his epistle because the Thessalonians knew who and what restrained him *in their day.*

The Restrainer

Paul refers to "*what* restrains" the man of lawlessness (2 Thess. 2:6) and "*he* who now restrains" him (2:7). The Thessalonians were certainly aware of the what and the who of this restraint, but for us they remain a mystery. We can only offer an educated guess. The futurists are left with a similar puzzle, as Gregory P. Allen's list of possible candidates indicates: The Roman Empire, orderly human government, gentile dominion, the Jewish state, contemporary eschatological speculation, the Roman emperor, Satan, the gospel, the church, the Holy Spirit, the archangel Michael. Allen's choice is the archangel Michael.[30] As I hope to demonstrate, the first-century Roman government was the likely restrainer of Jewish persecution against Christians (Acts 22–28). The restraint was in operation for decades. The Jews, for example, were "not permitted to put anyone to death" (John 18:31). We know that the restraint had to be in geographical proximity to the temple, and thus the restrainer resided in Jerusalem.

The "What"

The "what" is likely the Roman civil government that, for the most part, kept the Jewish hierarchy from persecuting the infant Jewish Christian church. Roman restraint meant that the high priest could no longer use his judicial authority to call for imprisonment, persecution, and death of Christians

(Acts 4:1–22; 5:17–42; 7:54–60). In time, however, the disturbances in-
cited by the Jews at the directive of the high priest were affecting the Roman social order. Rome began to step in to halt the civil unrest (22:22–30;
23:1–22). When the Sanhedrin met to council to put James the brother of
Jesus to death, King Agrippa "wrote in anger to Ananus, and threatened that
he would bring him to punishment for what he had done; on which king
Agrippa took the high priesthood from him."[31] Here we see that Agrippa is
restraining the excesses of the priesthood in protection of the church.

The Romans foiled a plot to assassinate Paul by restraining the Jews and
providing safe passage for him to be moved to Caesarea (23:12–22). Claudius
Lysias sent the following letter to "governor Felix": "When this man [Paul]
was arrested by the Jews and was about to be slain by them, I came upon
them with the troops [using them as a restraining force] and rescued him,
having learned that he was a Roman" (Acts 23:27).

At this point in time Rome insisted that the Jews make all charges against
the Christians in Roman courts (23:30). Paul makes his defense before Felix
(24), Festus (25), Agrippa (26), and eventually Caesar (27–28), all Roman
authorities. The Jews are forced to comply with the Roman edict: "And after
five days the high priest Ananias came down with some elders, with a certain attorney named Tertullus; and they brought charges to the *governor*
against Paul" (24:21). Here is a direct reference as to how Rome was acting
as a civil restrainer. The remarks of F.F. Bruce on the role Rome may have
played are helpful:

[I]f Paul had the imperial power and the emperor in mind, he was
not thinking necessarily of Claudius [Caesar] himself, although some
have envisaged a play on the idea of 'restraint' and the name Claudius.[32]
And he was certainly not looking forward to Nero, Claudius's stepson
and eventual successor, as the 'man of lawlessness', for Nero at this time
was only thirteen years old. Paul was thinking much more of his own
experience of Roman justice, which encouraged him to think of the
empire as being—temporarily, at any rate—a safeguard against the un-
ruly forces which endeavored to frustrate the progress of the gospel.
On the strength of this experience he could write of the imperial authorities several years later— when Nero had already been emperor
two years and more—as 'ministers of God' [Rom. 13:4, 6]; on the
strength of this experience, too, he confidently appealed towards the

end of A.D. 59 to have his case transferred from the jurisdiction of the procurator of Judaea to the emperor's court in Rome.[33]

F.W. Farrar makes a similar observation when he writes, "Up to the tenth year of Nero's reign the Christians had many reasons to be grateful to the power of the Roman Empire. St. Paul, when he wrote from Corinth to the Thessalonians, had indeed seen in the fabric of Roman polity, and in Claudius, its reigning representative, the 'check' and the 'checker' which must be removed before the coming of the Lord."[34] He continues by describing how the "Roman politarchs of Thessalonica had treated him with humanity. He had been protected from the infuriated Jews in Corinth by the disdainful justice of Gallio."[35] Bicknell offers this helpful summary:

> We may point to the encouragement and protection afforded to St. Paul at Paphos by the proconsul (Acts xiii) and by his Roman citizenship at Philippi (Acts xvi. 37–9). Soon after writing this Epistle he was acquitted by Gallio at Corinth (Acts xviii. 12–17). All this suggests that at the moment he had every ground for regarding the Roman empire as well disposed to himself and to Christianity, and as willing to protect him against the hostility both of the Jews and of pagan mobs stirred up by the Jews, in whom he may well have seen evidence of the working of Satan.[36]

Since Scripture is our guide, and the Book of Acts continually puts the local agencies of the Roman Empire forward as the consistent restrainer of Jewish aggression against the church, and Paul writes to the Thessalonians that "*you* know what restrains him *now*," Rome is the likely candidate.

The "Who"

If the force of Roman authority is *what* restrains, then *who* is the restrainer? This question is much more difficult to answer since we have to single out an individual with a name. The following is merely suggestive of a possible solution.

If the restrainer (neuter) is the force of Roman civil authority, then it is most likely that the restrainer (masculine) is a representative of that authority. Someone like King Agrippa would fit the requirements since he was the one who stopped the Jews from further bloodletting after the death of James, the brother of Jesus. It was Agrippa who "had the prerogative of appointing the Jewish high priests. He did his best to prevent the outbreak of the Jewish war against Rome in AD 66."[37] When his attempt to stop the revolt failed, he became a staunch supporter of the Romans throughout the war.[38] Was it at this point that King Agrippa was removed as the restrainer of the "man of sin," the high priest?

Putting forth Herod Agrippa as the restrainer is an opinion based on the available historical evidence. We may never know who Paul had in mind. What we do know, however, is that the people in Thessalonica knew who he was (2 Thess. 2:6).

The End of the Man of Lawlessness

When "that lawless one" is revealed, "the Lord will slay" him "with the breath of His mouth and bring [him] to an end by the appearance of His coming" (2 Thess. 2:9). Paul uses descriptive language from the Old Testament to describe the judgment of this usurper of God's authority. Paul's language is reminiscent of Isaiah 11:4: "And He will strike the earth with the rod of His mouth, and with the breath of His lips He will slay the wicked." Notice that in its Old Testament context that Jehovah does not appear in bodily form. The language is obviously meant to be interpreted figuratively since God does not have a mouth or lips. Similar language is found in Hosea 6:5: "Therefore I have hewn them in pieces by the prophets; I have slain them by the words of My mouth." Corresponding language is found in Isaiah 30 as a description of the coming judgment on Assyria. Notice that God's "lips," "tongue," and "breath" are connected with real judgment:

> Behold, the name of the LORD comes from a distant place;
> Burning is His anger, and dense is His uplifting;
> His lips are filled with indignation,
> And His tongue is like a consuming fire;
> And His breath is like an overflowing torrent, Which
> reaches to the neck,
> To shake the nations back and forth in a sieve, And to put
> in the jaws of the peoples the bridle which leads to ruin.
> ★ ★ ★ ★ ★
> And the LORD will cause His voice of authority to be heard.
> And the descending of His arm to be seen in fierce anger,

And in the flame of a consuming fire,
In cloudburst, downpour, and hailstones.

* * * * *

The breath of the LORD, like a torrent of brimstone, sets
it afire.

(Isa. 30:27–28, 30, 33)

The Lord's arm is said "to be seen" (30:30) and the Lord's "breath" causes a "fire" (30:33). Isaiah's figurative language is little different from the way Paul describes the judgment-end of the man of lawlessness in 2 Thessalonians 2:8.

Signs and False Wonders

What do we make of the activity of Satan that manifests itself "with all power and signs and false wonders" (2 Thess. 2:9)? There is certainly enough evidence to support the view that false Christs had made their appearance with numerous "signs and wonders" during the period before Jerusalem's fall (Matt. 24:24). Paul warned Timothy to be on the lookout for those who used "false wonders" to deceive the people, men like "Jannes and Jambres," the Egyptian high priests who "opposed Moses" (2 Tim. 3:8). Remember, God had identified Jerusalem with "Egypt," the place "where their Lord was crucified" (Rev. 11:8). It seems likely that any number of the corrupt Jews adopted Egyptian pagan practices. These religious impostors were said to "oppose the truth, men of depraved mind, rejected as regards the faith" (2 Tim. 3:8). This language is similar to that used by Paul in 2 Thessalonians 2:12: They "did not believe the truth, but took pleasure in wickedness." In both cases Paul has unbelieving Jews in mind.

Is there any historical evidence that the Jews used "signs and wonders" to deceive the people? Josephus writes:

> And now these impostors and deceivers persuaded the multitude to follow them into the wilderness, and pretended that they would *exhibit manifest wonders and signs*, that should be performed by the providence of God.... Moreover, there came out of Egypt about this time to Jerusalem, one that said he was a prophet, and advised the multitude of the common people to go along with him to the Mount of Olives.... He said farther, that he would show them from hence, how, at his command, the walls of Jerusalem

would fall down; and he promised that he would procure them an entrance into the city through those walls, when they were fallen down.[39]

In another place Josephus tells of a false prophet "who had made a public proclamation in the city … that God commanded them to get up upon the temple, and that there they should receive miraculous signs of their deliverance."[40] Josephus writes of "a star resembling a sword, which stood over the city, and a comet that continued a whole year." There was "a heifer, as she was led by the high priest to be sacrificed, brought forth a lamb in the midst of the temple."[41]

Eschatological expectation intensified as Jerusalem's war with Rome came to a head. Many believed that the Messiah would return to deliver them. False prophets took advantage of this spurious expectation and deceived many. God had sent them "a deluding influence so that they might believe what is false in order that they all may be judged who did not believe the truth, but took pleasure in wickedness" (2 Thess. 2:11–12). This passage parallels 1 Kings 22:19–22 where Ahab is enticed to go up and fall at Ramoth-Gilead. In like manner, first-century Israel was enticed to go up and fight against the Romans and fall at Jerusalem.

Conclusion

Based on this brief survey of 2 Thessalonians 2, we can conclude that Paul is not describing a future Antichrist who will make a covenant with the Jews during a period popularly described as the Great Tribulation. Such a view is pure speculation that has no basis in *biblical* fact. Paul's man of lawlessness was revealed in his day, and, in B. B. Warfield's words, God *has* "blown him away."[42]

Notes

1. Christopher Hill, *Antichrist in Seventeenth-Century England* (London: Oxford University Press, 1971), 1–40.

2. Leroy Froom, *The Prophetic Faith of Our Fathers: The Historic Development of Prophetic Interpretation,* 4 vols. (Washington, D.C.: Review and Herald, 1948), 2:66. See Ralph Woodrow, *Great Prophecies of the Bible* (Riverside, CA: Ralph Woodrow Evangelistic Assoc., 1971) for an able defense of this position.

3. This is the view of Henry Hammond, *A Paraphrase, and Annotations Upon all the Books of the New Testament, Briefly Explaining all the Difficult Places thereof,* 7th ed. (London: John Nicholson, [1653] 1702), 609.

4. N. Nisbett, *An Attempt to Illustrate Various Important Passages in the Epistles, &c. of the New Testament from Our Lord's Prophecies of the Destruction of Jerusalem, and from some Prophecies of the Old Testament* (London: Simmons and Kirby, 1787) 88–89. Nisbett's book has been reprinted as *The Prophecy of the Destruction of Jerusalem* (Lakeland, FL: John L. Bray Ministry, Inc., 1992), 27.

5. Merrill C. Tenney, *New Testament Times* (Grand Rapids, MI: Eerdmans, 1965), 152.

6. Tenney, *New Testament Times,* 115.

7. Quoted in Kenneth L. Gentry, *Before Jerusalem Fell: Dating the Book of Revelation,* 2nd ed. (Atlanta, GA: American Vision, 1999), 77.

8. Miriam T. Griffin, *Nero: The End of a Dynasty* (New Haven, CT: Yale University Press, 1984), 96.

9. Kenneth L. Gentry, Jr., *He Shall Have Dominion* (Tyler, TX: Institute for Christian Economics, 1992), 383–93.

10. F.F. Bruce, *Israel and the Nations: From the Exodus to the Fall of the Second Temple* (Grand Rapids, MI: Eerdmans, 1963), 224.

11. Thomas Newton, *Dissertations on the Prophecies, Which Have Remarkably Been Fulfilled, and at this time are Fulfilling in the World* (London: J.F. Dove, 1754), 389.

12. William Arnold Stevens, "The Man of Sin," *Baptist Quarterly Review* (July 1889), 340.

13. See "Apostasia in 2 Thessalonians 2:3: Apostasy or Rapture?," eds. Thomas Ice and Timothy Demy, *When the Trumpet Sounds* (Eugene, OR: Harvest House, 1995), 262–96.

14. Flavius Josephus, "The Life of Flavius Josephus," in *The Works of Josephus,* trans. William Whiston (Peabody, MA: Hendrickson Publishers, 1988), 4.

15. F.F. Bruce, *The Spreading Flame: The Rise and Progress of Christianity from its First Beginnings to the Conversion of the English* (Grand Rapids, MI: Eerdmans, 1958), 152.

16. Benjamin B. Warfield, "The Prophecies of St. Paul," in *Biblical and Theological Studies*, ed. Samuel G. Craig (Philadelphia, PA: Presbyterian and reformed, 1968), 474.

17. Bruce E. Hoyt, "What About the Antichrist?" *The Presbyterian Journal* (17 May 1978), 8.

18. William Arnold Stevens, "Commentary on the Epistles to the Thessalonians," *An American Commentary on the New Testament*, ed. Alvah Hovey (Philadelphia, PA: American Baptist Publication Society, 1887), 92. For a description of the growing first-century rift between the Jewish church and Pharisaic Judaism, see Paul Barnett, *Behind the Scenes of the New Testament* (Downers Grove, IL: InterVarsity Press, 1990), 162–63, 181, 189, 208–9.

19. Some who see the apostasy as being Jewish in nature understand the man of lawlessness to represent the Jewish nation, especially its religious leaders. While this interpretation has some merit, it does not satisfy the way "man" is used in the Bible.

20. John Lightfoot, *The Whole Works of the Rev. John Lightfoot*, ed. John Rogers Pitman, 13 vols. (London: J.F. Dove, 1822), 3:232.

21. Leon Morris, *The Gospel According to John* (Grand Rapids, MI: Eerdmans, 1971), 525.

22. John Lightfoot, *A Commentary on the New Testament from the Talmud and Hebraica: Matthew—1 Corinthians*, 4 vols. (Peabody, MA: Hendrickson Publishers, [1859] 1989), 2:289. Emphasis in original.

23. For a discussion of how the Bible uses "gods" as judges, see Gary DeMar and Peter Leithart, *The Reduction of Christianity: A Biblical Response to Dave Hunt* (Atlanta, GA: American Vision, 1988), 77–83.

24. Lightfoot, *Whole Works*, 3:233.

25. Edward Hayes Plumptre, "The Gospel According to St. Matthew," *A New Testament Commentary for English Readers*, ed. Charles John Ellicott, 3 vols. (London: Cassel and Company, 1897), 3:147.

26. Flavius Josephus, *Wars of the Jews* in *The Works of Josephus*, 4:3:6–8, 671.

27. William Whiston in Josephus, *The Wars of the Jews*, 671, note *b*.

28. John Bray, *The Man of Sin of II Thessalonians 2* (Lakeland, FL: John Bray Ministries, 1997), 26. See Paul L. Maier, *Josephus: The Essential Writings* (Grand Rapids, MI: Kregel, 1988), 347–54 for a discussion of John Levi.

29. Mireille Hadas-Lebel, *Flavius Josephus: Eyewitness to Rome's First-Century Conquest of Judea*, trans. Richard Miller (New York: Macmillan, [1989] 1993), 165.

30. Gregory P. Allen, "The Identity of the Restrainer in 2 Thessalonians 2:2–7" (Multnomah School of the Bible, n.d.).

31. Josephus, *The Antiquities of the Jews* in *The Works of Josephus*, 20:9:1, 538.

32. If there is an enigmatic reference to Claudius in the Latin *claudere*, is it possible that Paul had "Claudius Lysias" in mind (Acts 23:26)? It was Claudius Lysias who restrained the Jews and kept them from completing their assassination plot.

33. F. F. Bruce, *New Testament History* (Garden City, NY: Anchor Books/ Doubleday, [1969] 1972), 310. Also see F.F. Bruce, *The Defence of the Gospel in the New Testament* (Grand Rapids, MI: Eerdmans, 1959), 65.

34. F.W. Farrar, *The Early Days of Christianity* (New YorK: E.P. Dutton, 1882), 12.

35. Farrar, *The Early Days of Christianity*, 12.

36. Bicknell, *The First and Second Epistles to the Thessalonians*, 76.

37. F.F. Bruce, "Herod," *The New Bible Dictionary*, ed. J.D. Douglas (Grand Rapids, MI: Eerdmans, [1962] 1973), 523. Also see Bruce, *The Spreading Flame*, 154.

38. Harold W. Hoehner, "Herod, Herodian Family," *Baker Encyclopedia of the Bible*, ed. Walter A. Elwell, 2 vols. (Grand Rapids, MI: Baker Book House, 1988), 1:972.

39. Josephus, *The Antiquities of the Jews*, 20:8:6, 536. Emphasis added.

40. Josephus, *Wars of the Jews*, 6:5:2, 741.

41. Josephus, *Wars of the Jews*, 6:5:3, 742.

42. Warfield, "The Prophecies of St. Paul," 471.

Chapter Twenty-Four

ARMAGEDDON THEOLOGY

A rmageddon! The name is synonymous with mass destruction, carnage, and unrivaled bloodshed. Talk of Armageddon and the assurance of its imminency is not new. S.D. Baldwin wrote about the coming of Armageddon in his day in *Armageddon: or the Overthrow of Romanism and Monarchy; the Existence of the United States Foretold in the Bible.* This was in 1854![1] Baldwin believed that events in his day proved that Armageddon was near.

Speculation over Armageddon theology was a topic of discussion during the presidency of Ronald Reagan: "I sometimes believe we're heading very fast for Armageddon," Reagan told Jerry Falwell in 1981.[2] The political left shuddered when they read about Reagan's "Armageddon theology," thinking he might believe himself to be God's instrument to make prophecy come true by unleashing a military attack against the "evil empire" of the former Soviet Union. According to today's prophecy pundits, there will be, there *must* be, a "Battle of Armageddon" culminating in the near-destruction of Israel and the rest of the human race. Former President Reagan made it clear that he was familiar with the popular books on the subject, as the following quotations demonstrate:

- In 1981 Reagan discussed Armageddon with Senator Howell Heflin and said, "Russia is going to get involved in it."[3]
- In the December 6, 1983, issue of *People* magazine, Reagan said, "[T]theologians have been studying the ancient prophecies—what would portend the coming of Armageddon—and have said that never, in the time between the prophecies up until now, has there ever been a time in which so many of the prophecies are coming together. There have been times in the past when people thought the end of the world was coming, but never anything like this."[4]
- In October 1983, Reagan told Tom Dine of the American-Israel Public Affairs Committee: "You know, I turn back to your ancient prophecies in the Old Testament and the signs foretelling Armageddon, and I find myself wondering if we're the generation that's going to see that come about. I don't know if you've noted any of those prophecies lately, but believe me, they certainly describe the times we're going through."[5]
- "This may be the generation that sees Armageddon."[6]

In his second debate with Walter Mondale, however, Reagan gave a rather vague response when Marvin Kalb asked about Armageddon. "Reagan acknowledged a 'philosophical' interest in Armageddon, and noted that 'a number of theologians' believed 'the prophecies are coming together that portend that.'"[7] Talk of Armageddon cooled as East-West relations thawed. Any change in the political status of Israel, the Palestinians, and the Arab nations could renew talk about the rapture and Armageddon.

An entire book has been written on the subject of modern prophetic speculation and the Armageddon scenario. Grace Halsell takes on the TV evangelists and their talk of Armageddon and their belief in the inevitability of nuclear war. She claims these men "preach that only a nuclear war will bring Christ back to earth. Convinced that God has fore-ordained that precisely those of us living in this generation must wage the battle of armageddon, they tell their millions of listeners that we can do nothing to prevent the ultimate holocaust. Arms negotiations, they insist, are useless and any talk of peace is 'heresy.'"[8] This is not an accurate picture of the Armageddon scenario since Christians will not be around when the supposed Battle of Armageddon ensues. The theory is that Christians will be "raptured" before the "Great Tribulation" period commences. If this is true, then why all the speculation about this supposed end-time battle?

Dispensationalists have always taught that there are no prophetic events *prior* to the rapture. This means that current events are irrelevant when it comes to speculating when the rapture will occur. But if they can produce evidence that Armageddon might be near, then the rapture must be imminent. John F. Walvoord, former professor of systematic theology and president of Dallas Theological Seminary until 1986, "is sincerely convinced that many current events have fulfilled the necessary prophecies on the 'Armageddon Calendar' so that the Rapture of the saints is imminent."[9] While dispensationalists say no one can predict the timing of the rapture, they seem to go out of their way to speculate on Armageddon.

- "The prophecies of the Bible indicate why mankind is facing this present crisis, the events which will culminate in the final Battle of Armageddon and the tremendous promises of the Messianic Age which await fulfillment at the return of Christ."[10] This author evaluates current events ("this present crisis") and concludes that Armageddon is around the corner. If Armageddon is around the corner, then the rapture must be just ahead.
- "I do not want to linger here on the who, what, why, how, or when of Armageddon. I will simply state my own belief that it is near."[11]
- Ed Hindson asserts that we are "approaching armageddon" while telling us that "there are no specific time indicators of when" the event will take place.[12] If this is true, then how do we know that we are approaching armageddon?

What sort of time frame is "near"? If you recall how dispensationalists interpret "near," "soon," and "quickly," Armageddon could be two thousand years away.

The Illusion of Peace

Not to be outdone, there are those who see peace as the great enemy. While books on the Armageddon theme flood the market, there are a few authors who concern themselves with talk of peace by world leaders: "And now, at long last, the prospect of a peace such as the world has never known before seems to have metamorphosed from an impossible dream to a realistic hope. In fact, the nations of the world will indeed establish an unprecedented international peace, and probably fairly soon.[13] Of this we are certain, because it has been foretold in the Bible for thousands of years that it would occur in the 'last days.'"[14]

So which is it? Should we be concerned about war or peace? On one hand, we hear people addressing the Armageddon issue. On the other hand, concern is voiced over the New World Order with its promises of peace and security. Should we fight the New World Order by clamoring for war? Or should we fight the machine of war by calling for peace? What is a Christian to do? The solution for many is an imminent rapture that will take the church out before a decision has to be made either way. Convenient, but certainly not biblical.

Most people are concerned about the prospects for war. This is why Armageddon talk puts many on edge, especially when such talk is tied to prophetic inevitabilities. If war is in fact a prophetic inevitability, then what can anyone possibly do to avert it? Could we be messing with God's prophetic timetable by sending soldiers to force combatants to consider avenues of peace? But when all the signs seem to point toward an Armageddon showdown, at the last minute some adjustment has to be made to explain why the rapture or Armageddon did not come as promised.

- "God is sovereign and may accelerate or postpone 'the appointed time.'" Here Grant Jeffrey seems to be saying that we really don't know anything about timing because ultimately all these decisions are God's to make. But he does not leave well enough alone when he postulates that "the year A.D. 2000 is a probable termination date for the 'last days.'" Jeffrey goes out even further on the prophetic limb by claiming that Jesus may begin His kingdom on October 9, 2000.[15]
- In *Magog 1982 Canceled,* David A. Lewis claims that while Russia had set a date for the invasion of Israel and had stockpiled two billion dollars' worth of arms in Lebanon, it was Israel that "saved the whole world from a bloodbath" through its invasion of Lebanon in 1982.[16]

Like every other prediction, speculations about the nearness of Armageddon have been wrong time and time again. Some unforeseen set of circumstances always forces the prognosticators to make periodic adjustments. Why? The Armageddon scenario is fraudulent from start to finish. There is no future Armageddon battle.

Har-Mageddon or Ar-Mageddon?

The word "Armageddon" appears only once in the Bible as *Har-Mageddon* or *Ar-Mageddon* (Rev. 16:16). This is why it's surprising to read one prominent Bible teacher write that "the prophets have described it more specifically as the final suicide battle of a desperate world struggle centered in the Middle East."[17] This author makes it seem as if the Battle of Armageddon is a doctrine about which all the prophets wrote. The term is absent from the Old Testament, and, as I hope to demonstrate, so is the modern conception of the doctrine. Yet most Christians are convinced that the Bible has much to say about this future cataclysmic battle.

Armageddon has reference to a place: The mount or mountain (*har*) of Megiddo or the city (*ar*) of Megiddo. The "city of Megiddo" may be the better translation. This is the position taken by John Albert Bengel in his *Gnomon of the New Testament* (1742) and other New Testament commentators.[18] A number of battles were fought at Megiddo: Barak and Deborah overthrew the armies of the Canaanite king, Jabin, and the Midianites (Judges 5:19), and King Josiah was killed by Pharaoh Neco (2 Kings 23:29). Modern advocates of the Armageddon doctrine have combined these and other Megiddo battles into one great future "Great Tribulation" conflict where the Antichrist will bring all the nations of the world into a final war against Israel. While this interpretation of Revelation 16:16 is popular, a close look at Scripture will show that it is an untenable doctrinal position. Revelation is describing a past battle between first-century Rome and Israel: "The notion that Armageddon refers to some great cataclysm of the world's affairs in the future is hardly warranted."[19]

Megiddo: Israel's Waterloo

It is useless to try to understand Revelation 16:16 (or any passage for that matter) until we first determine how the Old Testament applies to the New Testament text. Megiddo is a symbol of war between rival kings and kingdoms. In one case, Israel is the victor (Judges 5:19). In another instance, Israel is the vanquished (2 Kings 23:29). To which battle does Revelation 16:16 refer? It depends on the identity of the guilty party. Since apostate Israel is the object of God's wrath in Revelation, the Josiah incident is more appropriate. God had warned King Josiah not to go to battle against the Egyptians. The king refused to heed God's warning, and at the battle of Megiddo Josiah was mortally wounded (2 Chron. 35:20–25). It is this Megiddo event that was burned into Israel's collective memory (Jer. 25:10).

Following Josiah's death, Judah's downward spiral into apostasy, destruction, and bondage was swift and irrevocable (2 Chronicles 36). The Jews mourned for Josiah's death, even down through the time of Ezra (see 2 Chronicles 35:25), and the prophet Zechariah uses this as an image of Israel's mourning for the Messiah.[20]

Israel remembered Megiddo as a place where God vented His divine wrath against rebellion, whether exhibited by Israel or a foreign power. God brought the nations of the world against first-century Jerusalem as He had promised (Matt. 22:7; 24:34). Rome, as an "empire of nations" (Syria, Asia Minor, Palestine, Gaul, Egypt, Britain, and others)[21] representing all the nations of the world (see Luke 2:1), came up against Jerusalem and destroyed her:

By the time of Christ, the Caesars ruled a territory so vast that they could almost equate it with the known world. Spreading outward in all directions from the sea that the Romans called Mare Nostrum, it extended roughly two thousand miles from Scotland south to the headwaters of the Nile and about three thousand miles from the Pillars of Hercules eastward to the sands of Persia. Its citizens and subject peoples numbered perhaps eighty million. One of the last and least important acquisitions of the giant empire was the coastal strip sometimes known as Palestine or Israel, actually the four disparate territories of Judea, Samaria, Galilee and Peraea.[22]

There were those in Israel who actually attempted to fight against this world empire and, like King Josiah, met their "Waterloo." This great battle was fought by Rome (the Beast) against the "great city," Jerusalem, where the Bible tells us Israel crucified her Lord (Rev. 11:8). This may explain why the battle is described as the "City [Heb: ar] of Megiddo." The battle does not take place on the plains of Megiddo but in the city of Jerusalem.

Similar to the way Old Testament figures are used in Revelation to describe Israel (Jezebel: 2:20; Sodom: 11:8; Egypt: 11:8; and Babylon: 14:8), Megiddo represents God's decisive battle against the city that rejected and killed His Son (Matt. 21:38–39; 22:7). It no more takes place in Megiddo than Jerusalem is *literally* Sodom, Egypt, and Babylon. Jerusalem had taken on the characteristics of these wicked cities. "This figure in the text of the apocalypse was employed not for the physical location but for the battle imagery. The deepest affliction of Jerusalem could be symbolized in no stronger terms of mourning, as prophesied by Zechariah in chapter 12:11: 'In that day shall there be a great mourning in Jerusalem, as the mourning of Hadadrimmon in the valley of Megiddon.'"[23]

A study of the context of Rome's battle with Israel indicates that the plain of Megiddo was in view as was the city of Jerusalem. This only reinforces an A.D. 70 fulfillment.

> Josephus tells us that when Titus left Egypt with orders from his father [Vespasian] to subdue the Jews that he returned "to Caesarea, having taken a resolution to gather all his other forces together at that place." Bear in mind that Caesarea was within sight of Mt. Carmel, the mountain of Megiddo, and that those armed forces coming from the northern regions must pass through Megiddo before reaching the appointed place of gathering. Titus stayed in the regions around Caesarea until most of the forces from the north arrived, and then moved on to Jerusalem for the "battle of the great day of God Almighty."[24]

So then, whether we understand this battle to be a symbolic war with Israel, using the Megiddo imagery to show God's covenantal judgment, or to be another literal Megiddo battle, the war is over.

How do we know that Israel met her "Waterloo" at this juncture in history? First, Jesus told His disciples that the tribulation period would occur within their lifetime (Matt. 24:1–34). Second, the Book of Revelation describes events in the first century. The time was "near" (1:1, 3; 3:11; 22:7, 10, 12, 20). Third, Jesus had warned the representatives of Israel that judgment would come upon the city and sanctuary. Many in Israel had "disowned the Holy and Righteous One, and asked for [the] murderer [Barabbas] ... and put to death the Prince of life" (Acts 3:14–15). For this, Israel received her just punishment: "His blood be on us and on our children," the Jews cried out to Pilate (Matt. 27:25). The armies of Rome came "and destroyed those murderers, and set their city on fire" at the symbolic battlefield of Megiddo (Matt. 22:7).

Notes

1. S.D. Baldwin, *Armageddon* (Cincinnati, OH: Applegate and Company, 1854). Like today's dispensationalists, Baldwin insisted on a "literal" interpretation, except, of course, when a text was "symbolic" (13).

2. *Boston Globe,* 2 May 1982. Quoted in F.H. Knelman, *Reagan, God and the Bomb: From Myth to Policy in the Nuclear Arms Race* (Buffalo, NY: Prometheus, 1985), 179. The article originally appeared in the *Los Angeles Times* (4 March 1981). See Jim Castelli, *A Plea for Common Sense: Resolving the Clash Between Religion and Politics* (San Francisco, CA: Harper and Row, 1988), 74.

3. Quoted in Castelli, *A Plea for Common Sense,* 74.

4. Quoted in Castelli, *A Plea for Common Sense,* 75.

5. Wolf Blitzer, *Jerusalem Post* (28 October 1993), A28.

6. Candidate Ronald Reagan on the "PTL Club," 1980. Quoted in Gary North, "The Armageddon Button," *Remnant Review* (19 December 1986), 5.

7. Paul Boyer, *When Time Shall Be No More: Prophecy Belief in Modern American Culture* (Cambridge, MA: The Belknap Press of Harvard University Press, 1992), 142.

8. Grace Halsell, *Prophecy and Politics: Militant Evangelists on the Road to Nuclear War* (Westport, CT: Lawrence Hill, 1986), dust-jacket copy.

9. Edwin Yamauchi, "Updating the Armageddon Calendar," *Christianity Today* (29 April 1991), 50.

10. Grant R. Jeffrey, *Armageddon: Appointment with Destiny* (Toronto: Frontier Research, 1988), 8.

11. Billy Graham, *Storm Warning* (Dallas, TX: Word, 1992), 294.

12. Ed Hindson, *Approaching Armageddon: The World Prepares for War with God* (Eugene, OR: Harvest House, 1997), 36.

13. What does Hunt mean by "fairly soon"?

14. Dave Hunt, *Global Peace and the Rise of Antichrist* (Eugene, OR: Harvest House, 1990), 13.

15. Jeffrey, *Armageddon,* 193, 191.

16. See Dwight Wilson, "Foreword," *Armageddon Now!: The Premillenarian Response to Russia and Israel Since 1917* (Tyler, TX: Institute for Christian Economics, [1977] 1991).

17. John F. Walvoord, *Armageddon, Oil and the Middle East Crisis: What the Bible Says About the Future of the Middle East and the End of Western Civilization* (Grand Rapids, MI: Zondervan, 1990), 23.

18. See James Glasgow, *The Apocalypse Translated and Explained* (Edinburgh, T & T Clark, 1872), 419; Alfred Plummer, "Revelation," *The Pulpit Commentary*, eds. H.D.M. Spence and Joseph S. Spence (New York: Funk & Wagnalls, 1913), 396; and R. H. Charles, *A Critical and Exegetical Commentary on The Revelation of St. John*, 2 vols. (New York: Scribner's Sons, 1920), 2:50.

19. David S. Clark, *The Message from Patmos: A Postmillennial Commentary on the Book of Revelation* (Grand Rapids, MI: Baker Book House, 1989), 103.

20. David Chilton, *The Days of Vengeance: An Exposition of the Book of Revelation* (Ft. Worth, TX: Dominion Press, 1987), 411–12.

21. Kenneth L. Gentry, Jr., "The Preterist Interpretation of the Kingdom," in Greg L. Bahnsen and Kenneth L. Gentry, Jr., *House Divided: The Break-Up of Dispensational Theology* (Tyler, TX: Institute for Christian Economics, 1989), 273.

22. Otto Friedrich, *The End of the World: A History* (New York: Coward, McCann and Geoghegan, 1982), 28.

23. Foy E. Wallace, Jr., *The Book of Revelation: Consisting of a Commentary on the Apocalypse of the New Testament* (Fort Worth, TX: Foy E. Wallace Jr. Publications, 1966), 335.

24. Arthur M. Ogden, *The Avenging of the Apostles and Prophets: Commentary on Revelation*, 2nd ed. (Somerset, KY: Ogden Publications, [1985] 1991), 320.

Chapter Twenty-Five

DANIEL'S SEVENTY WEEKS

If Armageddon is a past event, then why do many Christians look for a future all-out battle between the nations of the world and Israel? As we just saw, understanding the timing (first century versus distant future) and theme (first-century Rome and Israel versus a distant revived Roman Empire and modern Israel) of the event is crucial. There remains, however, a hermeneutical anomaly called dispensationalism that takes the seventieth week (representing seven years) of Daniel's prophecy in Daniel 9:24–27, separates it from the other sixty-nine weeks, and projects it far into the future. Just before the resumption of the seventieth week, the rapture of the church supposedly occurs. Following this, the antichrist is revealed, and near the end of the seven-year period, the battle of Armageddon takes place.

According to this way of interpreting Scripture, between the sixty-ninth and seventieth weeks of Daniel's prophecy there exists a period of time called the "church age," now nearly two thousand years in duration, more than five times longer than the span of the original prophecy. This phantom time period (also known as a "gap" or "parenthesis") supposedly separates the first sixty-nine weeks (483 years) from the last week (seven years). This imaginary parenthesis pushes the seven-year interval further and further into the future for as long as the Church remains on the earth. While Daniel writes that "seventy weeks have been decreed" (Dan. 9:24), dispensationalists believe that seventy weeks and a *gap* or *parenthesis* of indeterminate length have been decreed. It is surmised that during this future seven-year period the events in Revelation 4–19 will take place with the rise of antichrist, a rebuilt temple, the mark of the Beast, and the Battle of Armageddon. Anthony Hoekema describes it this way:

> During this seven-year period, while the church remains in heaven [having just been raptured, Rev. 4:1], a number of events will occur on earth [Rev. 4–19]: (1) the tribulation predicted in Daniel 9:27 now begins, the latter half of which is the so-called *great tribulation*; (2) the Antichrist now begins his cruel reign—a reign which culminates in his demanding to be worshipped as God; (3) terrible judgments now fall on the inhabitants of the earth; (4) during this time the "Gospel of the Kingdom" will be preached—a gospel having as its central content the establishment of the coming Davidic kingdom, but including the message of the cross and the need for faith and repentance; (5) at this time a remnant of Israel will turn to Jesus the Messiah—the 144,000 sealed Israelites of Revelation 7:3–8; (6) through the witness of these 144,000 an innumerable multitude of Gentiles will also be brought to salvation (Revelation 7:9); (7) the kings of the earth and the armies of the beast and the false prophet now gather together to attack the people of God in the Battle of Armageddon.[1]

While nearly all Bible scholars agree that the first sixty-nine weeks of Daniel's prophecy refer to the time up to Jesus' crucifixion, only dispensationalists believe that the entire seventieth week is yet to be fulfilled. Without a futurized seventieth week, the dispensationalist system falls apart. There can be no pretribulational rapture, great tribulation, or rebuilt temple without the gap. How do dispensationalists find a gap in a text that makes no mention of a gap?

Dispensationalism's Clock of Prophecy

Dispensationalists believe that when the Jews rejected Jesus as their King and Messiah, God postponed His kingdom program for Israel. The prophetic time clock stopped for Israel at the end of the sixty-ninth week

(483 years from the decree to build the temple as described in Daniel 9:24). The prophetic time clock supposedly will not start ticking again for Israel until the rapture of the church, a future event. Because the prophecy clock has stopped, according to dispensationalism, *there are no prophetic events prior to the rapture*; therefore, all talk about the antichrist being alive somewhere in the world today, the "present crisis" that is leading us to Armageddon, and the role of national Israel in prophecy, becomes irrelevant. At the end of the seven years, God will have fulfilled His covenantal commitment to national Israel. It is during the final seven-year period of Daniel's seventy weeks that Israel and the world experience a great tribulation, with untold suffering to the Jews and billions of others, ending with the Battle of Armageddon. Is there biblical support for this view? Let's look at what the Bible says.

Created Out of Necessity

It's been said that necessity is the mother of invention. The "gap" that has been placed between the sixty-ninth and seventieth weeks of Daniel's prophecy was created because it was needed to make the dispensational hermeneutical model work. Nothing in the text of Daniel 9:24–27 implies a "gap." This isn't the first place in the Bible where dispensationalists find a gap where none is specifically indicated.

A widely held opinion among fundamentalists is that the primeval creation of Genesis 1:1 may have taken place billions of years ago, with all the geological ages inserted in a tremendous time gap between Genesis 1:1 and 1:2. The latter verse is believed by these expositors to describe the condition of the earth after a great cataclysm terminated the geological ages. This cataclysm, which left the earth in darkness and covered with water, is explained as a divine judgment because of the sin of Satan in rebelling against God. Following the cataclysm, God then "recreated" the world in the six literal days described in Genesis 1:3–31.

Most popularly known as the "gap theory," this idea has also been called the "ruin-and-reconstruction theory" and the "pre-Adamic cataclysm theory." . . . [I]t has been widely popularized by the notes in the Scofield Reference Bible and has been taught in most of the Bible institutes and fundamentalist seminaries of the United States for the past century.[2]

Those who hold to the Genesis gap theory cannot be called six-day creationists. At best, they should be described as six-day *recreationists*.[3] The gap theory was designed "to harmonize the Biblical chronology with the accepted system of geological ages which was becoming prominent" in the nineteenth century.[4]

In a similar way, dispensationalists need to insert a period of time between the feet and the toes of Nebuchadnezzar's statue (Dan. 2:40–43) and between the sixty-ninth and seventieth week of the prophecy outlined in Daniel 9:24–27 in order to make the dispensational system work. A reading of both passages will show that there are no gaps of time. What we find in dispensational writers is a hermeneutical method whereby the theological system determines what a text *should* say to support the theological system. Dispensationalists are trapped in an endless loop of circular reasoning.

One dispensational writer, offering no exegetical evidence for the inclusion of a gap between the feet and toes of the colossus of Daniel 2—a gap that indicates a period between the sixty-ninth and seventieth weeks of Daniel 9:24–27—states, "At some point in this symbolism [of Nebuchadnezzar's statue] an extended gap in time *must be fixed,* because by verse 44 the interpretation describes the future day of Christ's millennial reign, as will be seen."[5] Again, no such gap is intimated by a reading of the text, nor by subsequent New Testament interpretative evidence.

So what makes this dispensational writer postpone the kingdom for two thousand years to "the future day of Christ's millennial kingdom" when the Bible clearly states that it was set up "in the days of those kings" (Dan. 2:44)?[6] There are no exegetical reasons to postpone the kingdom of Daniel 2. No gap is mentioned. The fifth stone-kingdom follows the fourth kingdom of the statue with no interruption in time. The statue comprises four kingdoms, one following another, with God's kingdom supplanting the kingdoms of men.

An Inspired Prophetic Calendar

J. Barton Payne shows that Daniel's prophecy does not require a "gap" to force it to fit with biblical history. If taken literally, the passage is a beautiful description of the extraordinary reliability of predictive prophecy found in the Bible:

The most noteworthy feature of Daniel's prophecy is the inspired prophetic calendar that accompanies it. Daniel predicted a lapse of "seventy weeks [of years]," or 490 years, for the accomplishing of the redemptive work (Dan. 9:24). The beginning point would be indicated by the commandment to restore Jerusalem (v. 25), an event that was accomplished, a century after Daniel, in the reign of the Persian, Artaxerxes I (465–424 B.C.), under Nehemiah (444 B.C.). But there had been an earlier attempt, in the same reign, to restore the city's walls, which had been thwarted by the Samaritans (Ezra 4:11–12, 23). This attempt seems to have been made under Ezra (458 B.C.; cf. 9:9), on the basis of the extended powers granted him in Artaxerxes' decree (7:18, 25, even though nothing explicit is said about restoring Jerusalem). Daniel then went on to predict that from this commandment, to the Messiah, would be "seven weeks, and three score and two weeks" (9:25), or 69 weeks of years, equaling 483 years. From 458 B.C. this brings one to A.D. 26, the very time which many would accept for the descent of the Holy Spirit upon Jesus Christ and the commencement of His incarnate ministry. Verses 26 and 27 then describe how, in the midst of the final week (that is, of the last seven year period, and therefore in the spring of A.D. 30), He would bring to an end the Old Testament economy by His death. There could hardly have been a more miraculously accurate prediction than was this! The 490 years then conclude with the three and a half years that remained, during which period the testament was to be confirmed to Israel (cf. Acts 2:38). It terminated in A.D. 33, which is the probable date for the conversion of Paul. At this point the Jews, by their stoning of Stephen, in effect cut themselves off from the eternal blessings of inheritance under the newer testament (cf. Rev. 12:6, 14); and shortly thereafter, within that generation, the Romans destroyed Jerusalem, A.D. 70.[7]

Stephen was probably martyred the same year Jesus was crucified and Paul was converted. Paul writes in Galatians 1:18 that he met with Peter "three years later" in Jerusalem "to become acquainted with Cephas." It was at this same time that Peter was given instructions that the gospel was to go to the Gentiles (Acts 10–11). This means that Paul's meeting with Peter and Peter's instructions concerning the Gentiles occurred 3.5 years after the crucifixion, marking the end of the seventy weeks "for Israel."

This has been the standard interpretation for centuries, except for minor differences in details.[8] John Nelson Darby and others changed all this with their church-parenthesis hypothesis. In the Darbyite, and now the dispensational, scheme of things, the seventieth week does not follow immediately after the sixty-ninth week. Dispensationalism, following Darby and the *Scofield Reference Bible*, teaches that the seventieth week is still future, and it's not Jesus who makes a "firm covenant with the many for one week" (Dan. 9:27)—*it's the antichrist!* It's not Jesus who "will put a stop to sacrifice and grain offering" through His shed blood (9:27)[9]—*it's the antichrist!* This interpretation is contrary to the New Testament's commentary on Daniel 9:24–27

> The sense of the passage, as given in the Septuagint version, which our Lord quoted in Matthew 24:15, is that the "one week" (the last of the 70, of which 69 had been previously accounted for) would witness the confirming of the new covenant with many (see Matt. 26:28, noting the words "covenant" and "many"), whereby the sacrifices and oblation of the old covenant were caused to cease (see Heb. 10:9), and the things predicted in verse 24 [of Daniel 9] were fulfilled.[10]

As Philip Mauro affirms, using Scripture to interpret Scripture, it is Jesus who "will make a firm covenant with the many," not the antichrist. This language is used by Jesus, not the antichrist, in Matthew 26:28 in addressing His *Jewish disciples* in the first century as a fulfillment of the seventieth week: "For this is My blood of the *covenant* which is poured out for *many* for forgiveness of sins." This covenant is "the new covenant in" His own blood (Luke 22:20). Nothing in the Book of Revelation, a book that supposedly describes a future seven-year great tribulation (Daniel's "postponed" seventieth week), mentions the antichrist making a covenant with the Jews and then breaking it. The New Testament fulfillment of the seventieth week of Daniel 9:27 is found in the redemptive work of the cross. Scripture could not be any more clear.

There is no reason to believe that there is a gap or that the antichrist is anywhere mentioned in Daniel 9:24–27. The period of seventy weeks of years—490 years—"is here predicted as one that will continue uninterruptedly from its *commencement* to its *close,* or completion, both with regard to the entire period of seventy [weeks of years], and also as to the several parts (7, 62, and 1) into which the seventy are divided. What can be more evident than this? *Exactly* seventy weeks in all are to elapse; and how can anyone imagine that there is an interval between the sixty-nine and the one, when these together make up the seventy?"[11] The seventy weeks are a unit: "The student of the Hebrew text will note that the masculine plural is here construed with a verb in the singular (*is decreed*). The seventy heptades are conceived as a unit, a round number, and are most naturally understood as so many sevens of years."[12]

Taking a Closer Look

For the dispensationalist, "Probably no single prophetic utterance is more crucial in the fields of Biblical Interpretation, Apologetics, and Eschatology" than the seventy-weeks prophecy of Daniel 9:24–27.[13] If the gap theory cannot be proved from a study of this messianic prophecy, then there is no validity to dispensationalism, and the entire end-time system called dispensationalism must be rejected. Because dispensationalists understand this, they must devise a way to create a gap between the sixty-ninth and seventieth weeks. Let's see if there is any justification for *any* gaps to be inserted when a specific number of years is given.

Forty Years and No Gap

There are thirteen instances of forty-year time periods with no gaps: (1) Moses is in Egypt for forty years (Acts 7:23); (2) Moses is in Midian for forty years (Acts 7:30); (3) Moses and Israel are in the wilderness for forty years (Deut. 8:2); (4) Othniel judges Israel for forty years (Judges 3:11); (5) Barak judges Israel for forty years (Judges 5:31); (6) the land of Israel "was undisturbed for forty years in the days of Gideon" (Judges 8:28); (7) Israel is enslaved by the Philistines for forty years (Judges 13:1); (8) Eli judges Israel for forty years (1 Sam. 4:18); (9) King Saul rules Israel for forty years (Acts 13:21); (10) King David rules Israel for forty years (2 Sam. 5:4); (11) King Solomon rules Israel for forty years (1 Kings 11:42); (12) King Joash rules Israel for forty years (2 Chron. 24:1); (13) God's judgment upon Egypt was to last forty years: "A man's foot will not pass through it, and the foot of a beast will not pass through it, and it will not be inhabited for forty years" (Ezek. 29:11).

In addition to the forty-year intervals of time, there are thirteen forty-day time periods found in Scripture. In each case, no gap is implied (Gen.

7:4, 12; 50:3; Ex. 24:18; 34:28; Num. 13:25; Deut. 9:18, 25; 1 Sam. 17:16; 1 Kings 19:8; Ezek. 4:5; Matt. 4:2; Acts 1:2).

Seventy Years and No Gap

Let's look at how the Bible presents the seventy-year time period. Because Israel refused to honor the Jubilee years—seventy in all—God sent the nation into captivity for seventy years so the land could enjoy its long overdue sabbath rest (Lev. 25:1–13, 18–22): "Then the land will enjoy its sabbaths all the days of the desolation, while you are in your enemies' land; then the land will rest and enjoy sabbaths. All the days of its desolation it will observe the rest which it did not observe on your sabbaths, while you were living in it" (Lev. 26:34–35, 43; 2 Chron. 36:21–23; Jer. 25:12; 29:10). Is there *any* indication of a gap in this seventy-year period? No! It is the near termination point of this seventy-year period that provokes Daniel to ask of the Lord when the "calamity"—seventy years of captivity—will come to an end (Dan. 9:2). What justification did Daniel have for asking God about the end of the judgment period? Was it presumption on his part? No. He took God at His word: seventy years meant seventy years.

The seventy-year period of captivity as described in Jeremiah 29:10 is a *pattern* for the "seventy weeks" in Daniel 9:24. "Therefore, as Jacques Doukhan has pointed out, 'The seventy weeks' prophecy must be interpreted with regard to *history* in as realistic a way as Daniel did for the prophecy of Jeremiah.'"[14] From this alone we can conclude that since the seventy years of captivity were consecutive *with no gap or parenthesis,* the "seventy weeks" must also be consecutive, seeing that there is nothing in the text to make us think otherwise. Daniel bases his prayer for restoration to the land on the certainty of the re-establishment promised by God when the seventy years were completed (Jer. 29:10). God made a covenant. What right do we have to conclude that God would somehow change the way time is ordinarily kept when we come to the use of seventy in the same chapter (Dan. 9:2, 24)?

Could God have placed a "gap" between the sixty-ninth and seventieth years of Israel's captivity, adding, say, a hundred years and still maintain that He had kept His word? There is no way He could have done it and remained a God of truth. But what if God came back and said, "I didn't actually *add* any years; I just *postponed* the final year by means of a 'gap' of 100 years. The 'gap' consisting of 100 years, which you assume to be additional years, should not be calculated in the overall accounting." This would mean that 170 years would have passed. Using "gap logic" the Bible could still maintain that Israel was in captivity for only seventy years. Let's call this what it is: nonsense.

What would we think of such a deal? Could God ever delay keeping His promise in such a way and still be called a covenant-keeping God? No! And yet this is exactly what dispensationalists do with the "seventy weeks of years" (490 years) of Daniel's prophecy. A "gap" of nearly two thousand years supposedly does nothing to change the integrity of a prophecy specifying the passage of only 490 years.

If we can find no gaps in the sequence of years in these examples, then how can a single exception be made with the "seventy weeks" in Daniel 9:24–27? Some maintain that the passage in Daniel lends itself to inserting a gap because of the division of weeks: seven weeks, sixty-two weeks, and one week. Since there is no gap between the seven and sixty-two weeks, what justification is there in inserting a gap between the sixty-ninth week (seven weeks + sixty-two weeks = sixty-nine weeks) and the seventieth week? Moses' life is divided up into three forty-year periods (Acts 7:23; 7:30; Deut. 8:2). Should we look for and expect gaps in the 120 years of Moses' life? No.

Randall Price claims there is justification for a gap based on "prophetic postponement" which he describes as "a distinct tenet of dispensational interpretation."[15] He offers what he believes are numerous examples of "Old Testament prophetic texts replete with examples of statements in which a partial fulfillment can be discerned in history but complete (or ultimate) fulfillment awaits a future, ideal time, usually the eschaton."[16] His examples are at best questionable. Even so, in none of the passages he cites is there a postponement or a gap when a specific amount of time is indicated, in this case, 490 years.

No Time In Between

One writer insists that the language of Daniel 9:26 is so clear that it is obvious that a gap exists *between* the two final weeks. Interpreters, he tells us,

> stumble and fall on the simple language of the text itself. There is but one natural interpretation—and that is the one which regards the events of

verse 26 as belonging to a period between the sixty-ninth and seventieth
weeks, when God has sovereignly set aside His people Israel, awaiting a
time of resumption of covenant relationship in the future, after Israel has
been restored to the land.[17]

As has already been noted, the text says nothing about "a period between
the sixty-ninth and seventieth-weeks." There can be no "period between"
any time period, whether seconds, minutes, hours, days, weeks, or years
unless a period of time is expressly given. It is impossible to insert time
between the end of one year and the beginning of another. January 1st
follows December 31st at the stroke of midnight. There is no "period between" the conclusion of one year and the beginning of the next year. Culver, therefore, begs the question. He first must prove that a period of time
should be placed between the sixty-ninth and seventieth weeks before he
can maintain that there is a "period between" the sixty-ninth and seventieth
weeks. The "simple language of the text" makes no mention of a gap. As
Hans LaRondelle points out, the text does not read, after the sixtytwo weeks
"but not in the seventieth."[18]

In addition, the text says nothing about the restoration of Israel to her
land as a fulfillment of some covenantal obligation. All the land promises
that God made to Israel were fulfilled (Joshua 21:43–45). Israel was in the
land at the end of the sixty-ninth week. She was still in the land when the
seventieth week commenced immediately after the end of the sixty-ninth
week. Israel was in the land when the temple was destroyed in A.D. 70.

Finally, if God destroys Israel again because of the breaking of a special
covenantal relationship, it would be an act of double jeopardy, punishing
Israel twice for the same transgression, a principle contrary to God's character. "Whatever you devise against the LORD, He will make a complete
end of it. Distress will not rise up twice" (Nahum 1:9). Israel was punished
by God for the rejection and crucifixion of His Son (Matt. 24, Mark 13,
and Luke 21). God ended Israel's judgment with the destruction of Jerusalem in A.D. 70.

"Silly-Putty" Exegesis

Placing a gap between the sixty-ninth and seventieth weeks of Daniel
9:24–27 "must be fixed" because of the system created by dispensationalists,

not because the Bible mentions anything about a gap. For an unintentionally humorous illustration of the absurdity of the "gap" interpretation, see "Daniel and Revelation Compared," a chart designed and drawn by Clarence Larkin and reproduced in George M. Marsden, *Fundamentalism and American Culture*.[19] We should be reminded that dispensationalists claim to interpret the Bible "literally." There is nothing literal about Larkin's interpretive illustration. In fact, it demonstrates that dispensationalism does not abide by its interpretive model. As with the time texts of Matthew 24:34 and Revelation 1:1, 3, dispensationalists force the Bible to comply to an already developed system that insists that these events cannot be describing first-century events. The system governs explicit texts.

Larkin's illustration of the "ten toes" of Daniel 2 shows the toes being stretched like "Silly-Putty" over more than two thousand years of history.[20] In similar fashion, Scripture must be "stretched" to make it fit the unbiblical "parenthesis" theory of dispensational premillennialism.

An objection that is often raised by those who insist that a gap is necessary to make sense of Daniel 9:24–27 is that the prophecy seems to predict that Jerusalem would be destroyed in the seventieth week. As history attests, Jerusalem was not destroyed until A.D. 70, nearly forty years after the end of the final week. This means, according to dispensationalists, that a forty-year gap is necessary to fulfill the content of the entire prophecy. This is a curious objection coming from those who see no problem in inserting a two-thousand-year gap between the sixty-ninth and seventieth weeks. Futurists skip over the A.D. 70 destruction of Jerusalem and conclude that Daniel is describing a future rebuilt temple.

If a gap is necessary to fulfill the content of the prophecy, could we not assume that a forty-year gap is much more logical than a gap of indeterminate length? Of course, a gap is not needed to make everything fit. More importantly, there is nothing in Daniel 9:24–27 that even intimates that a rebuilt temple is in view. All New Testament prophecies concerning the temple have reference to the temple that was standing in Jesus' day, the same temple that was destroyed in A.D. 70. John Lightfoot, in a sermon on Revelation 20:1–2, concludes that "where Daniel ends John begins, and goes no farther back, and where John begins Daniel ends, and goes no farther forward. For Daniel sheweth the state and persecutors of the Church of the Jews, from the building of Jerusalem by Cyrus, to the destruction of it by Titus, and he goes no farther."[21]

The Final Seven Years

A careful reading of 9:27 will show that the destruction of Jerusalem does not take place within the seventieth week. "Desolations are *determined*" within the seventieth week (9:26). Disowning "the Holy and Righteous One," asking "for a murderer to be granted" to them, and putting "to death the Prince of life" (Acts 3:14–15) were what "determined" that the "city and sanctuary" would become desolate (Dan. 9:26).

> Daniel is seeing this in the sixth century B.C., but it did not happen until A.D. 70, when Titus and his Roman legions fulfilled this prophecy exactly. The destruction of Jerusalem did not immediately follow Calvary, but it was an event which was determined by the fact that the Jews rejected Christ. It did not happen in the seventieth 'week', but was determined in the seventieth 'week'. Our Lord made it clear, both in His Olivet discourse and as He walked to the cross, that His rejection by the Jews would mean the destruction of their city and temple (Matt. 23:34–24:38; Luke 23:27–31).[22]

As the result of the Jews' rejection of Jesus, they would lose their inheritance. This would not occur for another forty years (Matt. 21:33–46; 22:1–14). Similarly, Jesus pronounced the temple "desolate" when He walked out of it even though its destruction did not come for another forty years (23:38). In principle, it was a "done deal" when He turned His back on the temple. It is no wonder that Jesus described the temple as "*your* house" (23:38). The temple's destruction was a *consequence*, a result, of the apostate Jews' rejection of Jesus (see 2 Sam. 13:32; Job 14:15; Isa. 10:22; Lam. 2:8; Luke 22:22).

> We might be helped at this point by thinking back to Adam. He was told that He would die on the very day that he ate the forbidden fruit. But he did not literally drop down dead. That day he died spiritually, and his physical death followed as a certain result. In the same way, Jerusalem's destruction was made certain by the Jewish rejection of their Messiah, but it was some little time before the certain event occurred. It did not take place in the seventieth 'week', but was most surely part and parcel of the events of that week.[23]

Another example will prove helpful. Nebuchadnezzar saw *one* statue depicting *four* kingdoms. The entire statue was seen "all at the same time," but we know that the kingdoms followed one another in time. Each kingdom was overthrown by the next kingdom. The kingdoms were not contemporaneous even though they were shown together and destroyed with a single strike from the stone (Dan. 2:34–35). Judgment was determined when Daniel interpreted the dream even though the destruction of each subsequent kingdom came hundreds of years later.

A judge will tell a convicted murderer: "It is the determination of this court that you will hang by the neck until you are dead." The sentence is determined on one day while the sentence may not be carried out until some time in the future. In similar fashion, we are told that the destruction of Jerusalem was "determined" within the seventy weeks while the sentence was not carried out until forty years later.

Notes

1. Anthony A. Hoekema, *The Bible and the Future* (Grand Rapids, MI: Eerdmans, 1979), 190.
2. Henry M. Morris, *The Genesis Record: A Scientific and Devotional Commentary on the Book of Beginnings* (Grand Rapids, MI: Baker Book House, 1976), 76.
3. Clarence Larkin, *Dispensational Truth or God's Plan and Purpose in the Ages* (Philadelphia, PA: Rev. Clarence Larkin Estate, 1920), 22–23.
4. Morris, *Genesis Record,* 76.
5. Leon J. Wood, *Daniel: A Study Guide Commentary* (Grand Rapids, MI: Zondervan, 1975), 39–40. Nebuchadnezzar saw *one* statue depicting *four* kingdoms. The entire statue was seen "all at the
6. The dispensationalist wants us to believe that the "kings" of Daniel 2:44 refer to the ten toes, not to the four kings of gold, silver, bronze, and iron. The toes are never referred to as kings or kingdoms.
7. J. Barton Payne, *The Imminent Appearing of Christ* (Grand Rapids, MI: Eerdmans, 1962), 148–49.
8. Philip Mauro, *Seventy Weeks and the Great Tribulation* (Swengel, PA: Reiner, n.d.), 74.
9. Those who separate the seventieth week from the sixty-ninth week maintain that sacrifices and grain offerings did not stop (Dan. 9:27). From God's covenantal and judicial perspective they did stop. Jesus put an end to them through His shed blood. This is why He could cry out, "It is finished" (John 19:30). This is the message of the Book of Hebrews.
10. Philip Mauro, *The Wonders of Bible Chronology* (Swengel, PA: Reiner, 1970), 97.
11. E.W. Hengstenberg, *Christology of the Old Testament and a Commentary on the Messianic Predictions,* 4 vols. (Grand Rapids, MI: Kregel, [1872–76] 1956), 3:143.
12. Milton S. Terry, *Biblical Apocalyptics: A Study of the Most Notable Revelations of God and of Christ* (Grand Rapids, MI: Baker Book House, [1898] 1988), 201.
13. A.J. McClain, *Daniel's Prophecy of the Seventy Weeks* (Grand Rapids, MI: Zondervan, 1940), 9. Quoted in Hans K. LaRondelle, *The Israel of God in Prophecy: Principles of Prophetic Interpretation* (Berrian Springs, MI: Andrews University Press, 1983), 170.
14. Jacques Doukhan, "The Seventy Weeks of Dan. 9: An Exegetical Study," *Andrews University Seminary Studies* 17 (Spring 1979), 8. Quoted in J. Randall Price, "Prophetic Postponement in Daniel 9 and Other Texts," *Issues in Dis-*

pensationalism, gen. eds. Wesley R. Willis and John R. Masters (Chicago, IL: Mood Press, 1994), 148. Price does not follow this methodology.

15. Price, "Prophetic Postponement in Daniel 9 and Other Texts," 160.

16. Price, "Prophetic Postponement in Daniel 9 and Other Texts," 159.

17. Robert Duncan Culver, *Daniel and the Latter Days* (Chicago, IL: Moody Press, 1954), 150.

18. LaRondelle, *The Israel of God in Prophecy,* 173.

19. George M. Marsden, *Fundamentalism and American Culture: The Shaping of Twentieth-Century Evangelicalism: 1870–1925* (New York: Oxford, 1980), 58–59.

20. Larkin, *Dispensational Truth,* 140–41. Larkin says that "what should happen between the 69 & 70 week[s] (the church dispensation) was not revealed to Daniel." Neither was it revealed to anyone else in the Bible. Dispensationalism is related, at least on this matter, to gnosticism—a special knowledge (*gnosis*) is needed to understand the system. That special *gnosis* comes in the form of notes found in the *Scofield Reference Bible.*

21. James Reid, *Memoirs of the Lives and Writings of those Eminent Divines, who Convened in the Famous Assembly at Westminster in the Seventeenth Century* (Paisley, England: n.p., 1811), 64.

22. Stuart Olyott, *Dare to Stand Alone* (Welwyn, Hertfordshire, England: Evangelical Press, 1982), 125.

23. Olyott, *Dare to Stand Alone,* 125.

Chapter Twenty-Six

TODAY'S WORLD IN PROPHECY

I thought it was the end of the world." Cesar Jamorawon believed the thunderous eruptions from Mount Pinatubo in the Philippines in July of 1991 were a punishment from God. "I thought that this must be a punishment from God because the world has forgotten Him. I have never experienced a graver crisis than this in my life."[1] From Jamorawon's perspective, the eruption of Mount Pinatubo was a unique eschatological experience, but was it a sign of coming prophetic events?

This was not the first eruption from the mouth of Mount Pinatubo. The volatile mount had erupted in 1380. There is little doubt that those who witnessed Pinatubo's fury more than six centuries ago expressed sentiments like those of Cesar Jamorawon. A similar reaction was heard in Kobe, Japan, in January 1995. Minoru Takasu "thought it was the end of the world"[2] when a devastating earthquake struck. It wasn't the end of the world then, and it's probably not a "sign" of the end of the world now.

Of course, we should see in events like earthquakes, volcanoes, famines, and floods a reminder that God does respond to a world that "has forgotten Him." John Wesley wrote of "The Cause and Cure of Earthquakes" in 1750:

Of all the judgments which the righteous God inflicts on sinners here, the most dreadful and destructive is an earthquake. This he has lately brought on our part of the earth, and thereby alarmed our fears, and bid us "prepare to meet our God!" The shocks which have been felt in divers places, since that which made this city tremble, may convince us that the danger is not over, and ought to keep us still in awe; seeing "his anger is not turned away, but his hand is stretched out still," Isa. x, 4.[3]

Wesley's assessment of earthquakes as an immediate judgment of God is quite different from saying that such events should be tied to texts that indicate the timing of a so-called rapture or the Second Coming. In 1756, Gilbert Tennent observed that earthquakes were "extraordinary in respect of number and dreadful Effects"[4] *in his day*. He saw them as indicators that "some extraordinary Revolutions [might] be near at Hand," not as signs of the soon coming of Jesus. James West Davidson writes:

> Ministers in 1755 as well as 1727, New Light as well as Old, accepted the prevailing assumptions that earthquakes were naturally caused, that they were inescapably meant as moral judgments, and that (most important) they were compatible with other moral judgments which God accomplished by using human instruments. They saw natural disasters as one proper part of the climax of history, not because of a preference for any specific millennial chronologies (once again a wide range of opinion appeared on that subject), but because catastrophes fell under the more general category of moral judgment, which was a necessary part of ultimate deliverance.[5]

"Perhaps because we are to such an extent 'strangers to the past,' we easily read into the events and circumstances of our own day a distinctiveness and uniqueness that may not actually be there."[6] Much of the speculative nature of today's Bible prophecy hysteria can be linked to "generational provincialism," that is, the belief that nothing has prophetic significance unless it happens to the present generation. Many who take this approach seem to be unaware that wars, earthquakes, famines, and plagues have been a part of the human condition since the Fall. At various crucial periods in human history, God has used these phenomena as warnings of impending judgment or as retribution for covenantal unfaithfulness (Num. 16:30, 32, 34; 26:10; Deut. 11:6). Of course, not every earthquake or famine has such a *special* meaning. Each occurrence, however, ought to serve as a reminder that we are sinners and our world has been ravaged by the effects of rebellion (John 9:1–3).

Political tyranny and religious apostasy are not necessarily signs of impending eschatological destruction. They, too, have been with us since the Fall. The light of the gospel was nearly extinguished as the church approached the sixteenth century. Few could ever have predicted what was about to happen, not only in terms of Christian revival but also in the explorer's spirit to open passages to unknown worlds. Explorers fought the heaviness of pessimism and charted dreams for parts unknown. How different is our day as we draw near not only to a new century but also to a new Millennium?

At the end of the year 1492 most men in Western Europe felt exceedingly gloomy about the future. Christian civilization appeared to be shrinking in area and dividing into hostile units as its sphere contracted. For over a century there had been no important advance in natural science, and registration in the universities dwindled as the instruction they offered became increasingly jejune and lifeless. Institutions were decaying, and many intelligent men, for want of something better to do, were endeavoring to escape the present through studying the pagan past.[7]

There is little in this chronicle of the times that could not serve as an accurate description of our own era. A general societal pessimism fills speculation about our future. Christian influence seems to be shrinking due to infighting among rival Christian groups. A general malaise hovers over the educational establishment. Educational reform is demanded from each end of the political spectrum and from everyone in between because of a deficient curriculum that cannot compete with our European and Japanese economic rivals. Escape is in the air as many turn to paganism through New Age humanism, the occult, and goddess worship. As in Columbus' day, Islam is "expanding at the expense of Christendom."[8]

If, as the writer of Ecclesiastes writes, "there is nothing new under the sun" (1:9), then how do we evaluate historical tumults prophetically? Five hundred years ago many in Christendom believed that the end was near. As we now know, their speculations were misguided. How can we now discern when such "signs" are prophetic indicators since "a generation goes and a generation comes" (1:4) but the end does not?

Four Prophetic Keys

Many reasons could be put forth to explain why our Christian counterparts of long ago were wrong about what they believed to be prophetic certainties. The signs seemed to fit the times. How can we avoid their mistakes? The following prophetic keys will help any interpreter unlock the door to the prophetic past and the prophetic future:

- The first prophetic key is to recognize that prophetic themes are most often set within established time frames. Failure to pay attention to a time frame can lead a person to assume that his generation is the generation experiencing the fulfillment when, in fact, the fulfillment is in the past.
- The second prophetic key is to recognize that as far as history records, little is unique about our era when it comes to calamities like plagues, earthquakes, and wars. This means that their contemporary manifestation does not necessarily carry any prophetic importance. In terms of a given time frame, the fulfillment of such prophecies is more than likely past.
- The third prophetic key is to determine historical context. Before an interpreter assumes a future fulfillment—if the time text is clear—he should search events within the given time frame for possible fulfillment.
- The fourth prophetic key is to distinguish fulfillment from application. There is much in Scripture that is fulfilled, but principles remain that can be applied to any era.

Of course, there are other rules of interpretation that apply to texts where prophecies are found as they would apply to Scripture in general. The four just listed, however, are the most misunderstood and misapplied when prophecy is the subject.

Prophetic Key Number One: Determining the Time Frame

One of the problems associated with interpreting prophecy is determining when a prophetic event is to take place. Many prophecies include time parameters. Abraham's descendants were strangers in the land of Egypt where they would be "enslaved and oppressed four hundred years" (Gen. 15:13). This prophecy was fulfilled "to the very day" (Ex. 12:40).

Joseph was told of seven years of plenty and seven years of famine (Gen. 45:6). Times of famine and plenty that follow these two seven-year intervals of time are irrelevant as a fulfillment of this prophecy.

Israel was to remain in the wilderness for forty years, a year for each day that the spies spied out the land (Num. 14:33–34). Subsequent forty-year periods of time are not a fulfillment of this prophecy.

Israel's captivity was seventy years in length, a year of captivity for each year of sabbath rest violated (2 Chron. 36:21; Lev. 26:33). Based on this certain timetable of God's binding word, Daniel prayed, petitioning God for the restoration of Israel to the land. To Daniel's method of calculation, the seventy years were nearing their completion (Dan. 9:2). Future seventy-year blocks of time are not a fulfillment of this prophecy.

Exactly 490 years were to pass for Daniel's people and the Holy City before the Messiah would appear (9:24). Those living in Jesus' day had made the calculations and were expecting "Messiah the Prince" to appear (9:25). The "magi from the east" were aware of the prophecy concerning the coming of a great king. This is why an unusual stellar phenomenon led them to Jerusalem to inquire about His birth (Matt. 2:1–2). It's possible that Daniel's prophecy of the "seventy weeks of years" (490 years) was known outside of Israel since Daniel was a ruler and wise man in Babylon (Dan. 2:46–49). Since Babylon was a center for trade and learning, Babylon's "wisdom," including Daniel's true wisdom, was in all likelihood exported with its commercial goods.

Simeon was "looking for the consolation of Israel" (Luke 2:25), as was Anna (2:36–38). Israel was beset with false messiahs. They, too, had calculated the time for His arrival and hoped to counterfeit His work (Acts 5:36–37). There was an anticipation of the "fullness of the time" (Gal. 4:4; cf. Mark 1:15).

Those who futurize prophecies, that is, those who see their fulfillment beyond A.D. 70, also realize the importance of time texts. Hal Lindsey sees Israel's becoming a nation again as a time indicator. He knows that a prophecy without a time text is almost impossible to interpret. With the establishment of the Jewish state in Israel in 1948, Lindsey believes "the whole prophetic scenario began to fall together with dizzying speed."[9] There is, however, little justification for Lindsey's timing scenario. He understands the "budding" of the fig tree in Matthew 24:32 to be a symbol of a restored national Israel. This is why he interprets "this generation" as the generation alive when Israel became a nation (1948–88). Nothing in Matthew 24:32 says anything about Israel becoming a nation again. This idea must be read into the passage. In addition, the New Testament is silent on the subject of Israel's restored nationhood. The Old Testament prophecies of Israel's restoration had been fulfilled in the return from the Babylonian captivity.[10]

We are back to determining what Jesus meant by the time text of "this generation." As has been demonstrated, "this generation" *always* means the generation to whom Jesus was speaking. *There are no exceptions!* This can only mean that the generation alive between A.D. 30 and 70 experienced the events described by Jesus in Matthew 24:1–34. Israel may yet have a role to play in prophecy, *but that role is not based on what Jesus said in Matthew 24 since He said nothing about Israel's becoming a nation again.* This means all of the events in Matthew 24:1–34 are fulfilled. Their meaning is associated with a past generation, not some future generation. When we read of wars, earthquakes, plagues, and famines in our generation, they are not prophetic signs for our day.

Prophetic Key Number Two: Evaluating the Historical Record

When the topic of the end times comes up in conversation, the usual first piece of evidence given that our generation is indeed the "Rapture Generation" is the state of the world, both its moral character and natural calamities. Nearly all prophetic writers point to the signs of wars, famines, plagues, lawlessness, and earthquakes as prime indicators that the whole prophetic scenario is beginning to fit together like some giant prophetic jigsaw puzzle. Here's one example among many: "I am not predicting Christ's imminent return in the year 2000. But we have sufficient evidence to substantiate that we are the 'Terminal Generation.' My personal conviction is that the deadly dangers now rising in the curve of probability will *require* the Second Coming of Christ before too long."[11] But what about similar disasters, wars, and seismic activity in the past? Is our generation unique? A look at plagues, earthquakes, and wars over the centuries will show that these "signs" are not unique to our age.

The Black Death

> Ring around a rosie,
> A pocket full of posies.
> Ashes, ashes,
> We all fall down.

A delightful nursery rhyme? Well, not quite. Its beginnings are rather ominous. "Ring around a rosie" is a description of the not-so-delightful Black Death, probably bubonic plague. The "ring" refers to the round, red rash that is the first symptom of the disease. The practice of carrying flowers and placing them around an infected person for protection is described in the phrase, "a pocket full of posies." "Ashes" is an imitation of the sneezing sounds made by the infected person. "We all fall down" describes the many deaths resulting from the disease.[12]

What is often forgotten by today's prophetic speculators is the horrendous death toll of the Black Death of 1347–50. Europe was nearly decimated. Millions died. The estimated death toll throughout Europe was about 30 percent of the population, or twenty-five million out of a population of about eighty million. "Worldwide, the scholarly estimates ... remain little more than medieval guesses: perhaps 75 million dead out of a total population of perhaps 500 million."[13] Today's pestilence catastrophes, including the AIDS epidemic, do not rival the Black Death, which has been described as the "most lethal disaster of recorded history."[14] The Black Death hit everyone.

Let's compare the Black Death with today's AIDS epidemic. At the time when the Bubonic Plague swept through Europe, the world's population was around 545 million. Estimates tell us that 70 million people died as a direct or indirect result of the plague (12.8% of the population). If 100 million people die from AIDS, out of today's population of 5 billion, this is only 2% of the population. In order to compete with the Bubonic Plague, AIDS would have to kill 640 million people (12.8% x 5,000,000,000 = 640,000,000). This calculation, however, is irrelevant in terms of the Olivet Discourse since the events described therein were fulfilled prior to A.D. 70.

Numerous records exist of epidemics that preceded the frightful pneumonic/bubonic plagues that visited Europe in 1347. As early as 1331 the epidemic broke out in Hopei Province in China, with reports that it killed nine out of every ten people. Numerous other plagues have been recorded, both before and after the Black Death. The bubonic plague, however, remains unrivaled.

This information is lost on the average Christian, who views only today's ills as important. When Hal Lindsey, for example, reads Jesus' words in Matthew 24, Mark 13, and Luke 21, he is sure that "WE ARE THE GENERATION HE WAS TALKING ABOUT!"[15] Those who suffered through the "great dying" of the fourteenth century thought *they* were the generation Jesus was talking about. All the facts seemed to fit. Death, dying, and starvation were everywhere as Jesus foretold. But did Jesus have the fourteenth century in mind? Many thought He did. Here is how one man described the era:

> "O happy posterity, who ... will look upon our testimony as a fable," wrote Petrarch. The poet nonetheless felt that the events of "that dreadful year 1348" must be recorded for the very posterity that would not believe the testimony. "Will posterity believe," he wrote from Parma in the late spring of 1349, "that there was a time when, with no deluge from heaven, no worldwide conflagration, no wars or other visible devastation, not merely this or that territory but almost the whole earth was depopulated? When was such a disaster ever seen, even heard of? In what records can we read that houses were emptied, cities abandoned, countrysides untilled, fields heaped with corpses, and a vast, dreadful solitude over all the world?"[16]

Their catastrophe was not a fulfillment of prophecy. Jesus had a different era in mind when He uttered words describing plagues, famines, earthquakes, and wars on the mount called Olivet. The disciples were to look for signs within *their* generation, and they found them.

The Lisbon Earthquake

What about the Lisbon earthquake of 1755? Surely, if the Black Plague was not a prelude to the end, Lisbon's encounter with the power of the earth and the "wrath of God" had to be a sign that the end was near. Had not Jesus told His hearers that "there will be great earthquakes" (Luke 21:11)? "The estimates of the death toll range from about 15,000 to more than 75,000. Modern historians incline to believe that the correct figure is probably about 30,000, which would be more than ten percent of the city's population, the equivalent of nearly a million in contemporary New York."[17]

Modern date setters do acknowledge past great earthquakes. But to make *our* generation unique in the annals of Bible prophecy, those engaged in predicting the time of the end assert that we should calculate the *frequency* of earthquakes. Again, the present must be seen as unusual to make the prophetic system work. Hal Lindsey wrote: "There have been many great earthquakes throughout history, but, according to surprisingly well-kept records, in the past they did not occur very frequently. The 20th century, however, has experienced an unprecedented increase in the frequency of these calamities. In fact, the number of earthquakes per decade has roughly doubled in each of the 10-year periods since 1950."[18] No statistical evidence is offered.

In fact, Lindsey is wrong. There is nothing unique about the number of earthquakes that the world is now experiencing. Certainly there are better detection devices. These alone would make their occurrences *seem* more numerous. In addition, because of a worldwide news network, communication satellites, and instant news analysis, we read about even the slightest seismic tremor in the morning paper.

The way some prophecy analysts talk, only a dozen or so major earthquakes have been recorded over the centuries. This is far from the truth. The Roman writer Seneca, before his death in A.D. 65, stated that frequent earthquakes had been a characteristic of the ancient world: "How often have cities in Asia, how often in Achaia, been laid low by a single shock of earthquake! How many towns in Syria, how many in Macedonia, have been swallowed up! How often has this kind of devastation laid Cyprus in ruins! How often has Paphos collapsed! Not infrequently are tidings brought to us of the utter destruction of entire cities."[19] Notice the date of Seneca's writing—A.D. 65—just five years before the destruction of Jerusalem and thirty-five years after Jesus' prophecy about earthquakes. After A.D. 70, earthquakes no longer have the same prophetic significance.

Today's reported earthquakes are not unique, as proven by a thorough study of history. The greatest student of earthquakes was a Frenchman, Count F. Montessus de Ballore. From 1885 to 1922 he devoted his time to studying and cataloging earthquakes and came to an astonishing conclusion. He cataloged 171,434 earthquakes from the earliest historic times! "The manuscript is stored in the library of the Geographical Society in Paris, where it occupies 26 meters (over 84 feet) of bookshelves."[20] As much as we might want to believe that we are the "Rapture Generation," there is no statistical or biblical evidence to support such a contention.

"Wars and Rumors of Wars"

No one doubts that in spite of the *Pax Romana,* wars were prevalent during the time leading up to the destruction of Jerusalem in A.D. 70. The Jews were instigators in a number of revolts that led Rome to increase its already iron grip on the nation. "The Jewish revolt against Rome was part of a more widespread rebellion that spread all over the Roman Empire and culminated in the year after Nero's death, A.D. 68–70, 'when Servius Galba, consul for the second time with Titus Vinius as his colleague, began the year that brought death to both and almost meant the downfall of Rome.'"[21] In fact, with the operation of the Roman Peace, any indication of war would have brought to mind Jesus' prediction of "wars and rumors of wars" since wars are not much of a sign during an era of wars. Based on the timing text of Matthew 24:34, the sign regarding wars is over.

But can't a case be made that the many wars of this century and the millions killed are a prelude to some end-time event? Not in terms of Matthew 24 since the time text refers to the generation to whom Jesus was speaking. Still, in comparing our century with previous centuries, there is little that is unique. "After the Goths annihilated the imperial army at Adrianople in 378, Saint Ambrose of Milan, who clearly identified the Goths with Ezekiel's Gog, proclaimed that 'the end of the world is coming upon us.'"[22] The Thirty Years' War (1618–48) involved ten nations. Experts estimate that thirty to forty percent of the total German population—seven to eight million civilians—died in the war. World War I was not as devastating for Germany.

The Manchu-Chinese war, which began with the invasion of the Manchus (from Manchuria) in 1644, resulted in twenty-five million deaths—about twice as many as were killed militarily in World War I. The War of the Spanish Succession (1701–14), a war involving ten European nations and their colonies in other parts of the world, resulted in the death of over a million. The famine which followed the war killed another million. The Napoleonic Wars (1792–1815) were equally destructive. France lost two million people in these wars. "The total death figure for the 23 years from 1792 to 1815 is set at 5 or 6 million!"[23]

The Taiping Rebellion (1850–64), described as "the most destructive war of the entire 19th century," resulted in the deaths of nearly thirty *million. "The Lopez War* (1864–1870), in which Paraguay fought against Argentina, Uruguay, and Brazil, cost more than 2 million lives. The war 'reduced the Paraguayan population from about 1,400,000 to some 221,000,' that is, by 84 percent! The other three countries 'lost an estimated 1,000,000 men.'"[24]

World War II certainly was devastating in terms of the number killed and the unleashing of two nuclear bombs. But considering all the wars that have been fought over the centuries—over fourteen thousand with estimates of over 3.6 billion killed—World War II just comes out as one war in a long history of wars.[25]

The *key* to understanding Jesus' prophecy of "wars and rumors of wars" in Matthew 24:6 is the time text that puts these words in perspective: The wars Jesus was speaking of were wars that would occur within a forty-year period after His crucifixion. With so many wars over the centuries, the text could not possibly have any meaning unless it was limited by time. That time is past.

Notes

1. Eileen Guerrero, "I thought this was the end of the world," *Marietta Daily Journal* (17 June 1991), 1A.

2. "'The end of the world,'" *Marietta Daily Journal* (18 January 1995), 1A.

3. John Wesley, "The Cause and Cure of Earthquakes" (1750), *Sermons on Several Occasions*, 2 vols. (New York: Carlton & Phillips, 1853), 1:506.

4. Gilbert Tennent (1703–64) quoted in James West Davidson, *The Logic of Millennial Thought: Eighteenth-Century New England* (New Haven, CT: Yale University Press, 1977), 102.

5. Davidson, *Logic of Millennial Thought*, 97.

6. Carl Olof Jonsson and Wolfgang Herbst, *The "Sign" of the Last Days—When?* (Atlanta, GA: Commentary Press, 1987), x. This book is filled with statistical and historical information that easily refutes the notion that our era is unique.

7. Samuel Eliot Morison, *Admiral of the Ocean Sea: A Life of Christopher Columbus* (Boston, MA: Little, Brown, 1942), 3.

8. Morison, *Admiral of the Ocean Sea*, 3.

9. Hal Lindsey, *The Promise* (New York: Bantam Books, [1982] 1984), 199.

10. William Hendriksen, *Israel and the Bible* (Grand Rapids, MI: Baker Book House, 1968), 16–31.

11. W.S. McBirnie, *2000 AD!: Nine Years to Doomsday?* (Glendale, CA: Voice of Americanism, 1991), 12.

12. J. Allen Varasdi, *Myth Information: An Extraordinary Collection of 590 Popular Misconceptions, Fallacies, and Misbeliefs* (New York: Ballantine, 1989), 205–206.

13. Otto Friedrich, *The End of the World: A History* (New York: Coward, McCann and Geoghegan, 1982), 115.

14. Barbara Tuchman, *A Distant Mirror: The Calamitous 14th Century* (London: 1979), xiii. Quoted in Jonsson and Herbst, *The "Sign" of the Last Days—When?*, 101.

15. Hal Lindsey, *The 1980s: Countdown to Armageddon* (King of Prussia, PA: Westgate Press, 1980), 181.

16. Friedrich, *End of the World*, 115–16.

17. Friedrich, *End of the World*, 188.

18. Lindsey, *The 1980s*, 30.

19. *Seneca Ad Lucilium Epistulae Morales*, trans. Richard M. Gummere, vol. 2 (London: 1920), 437. Quoted in Jonsson and Herbst, *The "Sign" of the Last Days—When?*, 75.

20. Jonsson and Herbst, *The "Sign" of the Last Days—When?*, 78.

21. Jonsson and Herbst, *The "Sign" of the Last Days—When?*, 127 note 9.

22. Friedrich, *End of the World,* 27.

23. Jonsson and Herbst, *The "Sign" of the Last Days—When?*, 147.

24. Jonsson and Herbst, *The "Sign" of the Last Days—When?*, 147.

25. Jonsson and Herbst, *The "Sign" of the Last Days—When?*, 152–56.

Chapter Twenty-Seven

MYSTERY BABYLON

"This report is written with much trepidation and with the realization that what I say may be mistaken as dogmatic assertions or prophetic utterances. Therefore, I must stress that those parts that constitute opinion are based on knowledge gleaned from years of study both in Scripture and historical records."[1] This author has done what dozens of writers had done before him, "gleaned from years of study both in Scripture and historical records" and come to the conclusion that the end must be near. Like others before him he assumed that the prophecies he was studying had *not* been fulfilled. He evaluated the conditions of modern nations and peoples by prophecies made long ago to empires that no longer exist.

Inevitably, the above writer's suppositions were wrong. Just one month after making some rather specific prophetic statements, he had to write another letter stating that he had jumped the prophetic gun. "Of course," he explains, "my prophetic scenario was predicated upon the *possibility* that this conflict could be the beginning of the end for the United States as the major economic and military might in the world. It wasn't an iron-clad prophecy or even a prediction. Even so, many people took it that way."

The problem is just that: Many people take such speculation as near certainty and structure their lives based on these prophetic "possibilities." Each news report is studied through the prophetic pronouncements of the latest biblical soothsayer. Gullible Christians are eager to believe the scenarios described by men and women who are "sure" about their predictions since they are thought to be "prophecy experts." Consider the following descriptions of Russia's role in prophecy over the years. Pay close attention to the dates.

- "The time cannot be far off when Russia's millions, augmented by the armies that she will gather from these and other nations, will be thrown by their rulers into Palestine in order to destroy the nation of the Jews [1916]."[2]
- "Russia is going to war with Palestine. That is coming.... There is where we are to-day. Therefore, we may expect very shortly that this conflict will take place [1928]."[3]
- "It is entirely possible that World War III will start in ninety days [1948]."[4]
- "Before Russia attacks Israel, however, it will first invade Iran, or Persia, as it is called in Ezekiel chapter 38, verse five. When we apply this prophecy to modern times, it becomes obvious that the Soviets will use their recent conquest of Afghanistan as a springboard to overthrow Iran and gain control of the Persian Gulf area [1980]."[5] Since Lindsey's prophetic conjecture, the former Soviet Union pulled out of Afghanistan, joined the United States in the defense of Kuwait and Israel in Desert Storm, and remains a third-rate world power.
- "Russia, who has been able to rebuild its economy and maintain its military strength through abstinence from the [Gulf] war, will eventually perceive that the only thing preventing its conquest of the world will be Israel and the European Community. It will attack Israel and the EC forces and be destroyed in its attempt at conquest [January 1991]."[6]

Europe, Russia, and Israel have played prominent roles in speculative prophetic declarations since World War I. Out of Europe, we are assured, Antichrist will arise to act as a unifier and peacemaker. Russia, the "Rosh" of Ezekiel 38 and 39, will gather its troops and attack Israel. Of course, Israel plays the prominent role as two-thirds of those living in their ancient homeland will be slaughtered by descending Gentile hordes.[7]

While this scenario is interesting and makes for fascinating reading, we must ask a fundamental question: Is it biblical? Bible experts have been involved in solving the prophetic puzzle for some time. Since World War I prophetic speculation has increased at a frenzied pace. Are today's prophetic declarations any more accurate? Can we find biblical and historical evidence that their timing is off?

Many so-called "predictions" are nothing more than the projection of already existing geopolitical trends that are then read back into Scripture to fabricate biblical support. When an ancient prophecy does not seem to fit our era—the depiction of bows and arrows instead of machine guns, for example—we are informed that "it was not possible for [a prophet] to describe modern weapons since he lived at a time when such inventions were beyond anyone's imagination."[8] They were not beyond God's imagination. Prophets, as "men moved by the Holy Spirit," speak "from God" (2 Peter 1:21). Modern weapons are not depicted because modern weapons are not intended.

Other futurists believe that Peter's prophecy in 2 Peter 3:10 refers to nuclear war—certainly a description of a "modern weapon." Ed Hindson tries to make the case that, "Peter's prophecy of a great end-times conflagration of the earth and its atmosphere uses precise terminology which accurately describes a nuclear explosion."[9] John Phillips also supports this view: "Peter described in accurate terms the untying of the atom and the resulting rushing, fiery destruction which follows it."[10]

The futurists cannot have it both ways. This supposed future war is going to be fought with either ancient weapons or highly modern weapons. These prophets are describing events that were to happen in their future, events that are history for us.

Prophetic Key Number Three: The Historical Context

Just as earthquakes, plagues, and wars are interpreted to justify an avalanche of prophetic sagas predicting an imminent Rapture or some other end-time event, today's geopolitical affairs are "analyzed" to sanction the belief that time is running out for the "late great planet earth" and that ours is the "terminal generation." Prophecies concerning ancient civilizations are applied to modern political territories. For example, modern Rome and Iraq are supposedly reincarnations of first-century Roman despotism (headed by the Pope) and pre-Christian dictatorial Babylon (headed by Saddam Hussein). In addition, events in Europe are supposedly the outworking of prophecies that were never entirely fulfilled (a revived Roman Empire). Saddam Hussein's Iraq, because it is located in the area once occupied by Nebuchadnezzar's

Babylon, must be a further fulfillment of prophetic pronouncements that are centuries old but are said to have remained dormant until the "fullness of time," that is, our time.

Babylon (Iraq) in Prophecy

When Saddam Hussein invaded Kuwait in 1990, a great deal of speculation arose concerning Iraq's role as a modern Babylon, supposedly a fulfillment of prophecies made centuries ago. Were the military actions of Saddam Hussein a long overdue culmination of prophecies set forth in the Book of Isaiah hundreds of years before Jesus was born? There were some who thought so. Charles Dyer, in *The Rise of Babylon: Sign of the End Times,* claimed that events depicted in Isaiah 13 were being fulfilled with the Iraqi invasion of Kuwait. He stated, "'The day of the Lord' described by Isaiah [in 13:6] refers to the tribulation period that is still to come. Babylon's destruction will come in the time of the tribulation—a short period of time just before the second coming of Christ."[11] Is this possible? No. Dyer's interpretation is based upon "gap theology," that is, an indeterminable period of time is placed between the sixty-ninth and seventieth weeks found in Daniel 9:24–27, a gap nearly two thousand years in length. Dyer's "time of the tribulation" (the sevenyear tribulation period following a supposed pre-tribulational "rapture") is Daniel's seventieth week. This *highly* questionable interpretation of Daniel 9:24–27 immediately makes his Babylonian scenario suspect.

There are additional reasons to reject Dyer's thesis. Isaiah 13:6 clearly states that "the day of the LORD is *near!*" Dispensationalists—who insist on a *literal* interpretation of Scripture—do not understand "near" to mean "near" as in "soon." The plain meaning of the text is thrown out the window to justify a *system* of theology that demands a futurist interpretation. Dyer, as a dispensationalist, alleges that the "day of the Lord" *always* has reference to the end times, specifically an interval called the Great Tribulation that is in the distant future. This is impossible since Isaiah states that Babylon's judgment is "near." If "near" means something other than "close at hand," then it does not mean anything.

The "day of the LORD" often refers to a time of judgment without referring to the final judgment. It is the "day of the LORD" any time God acts. In fact, Sunday, our day of worship, is called "the Lord's day" (Rev. 1:10) or "the day of the Lord." This is why it is important to pay attention to time indicators when determining when prophetic events take place. The Bible gives us a number of occasions when the "day of the LORD" was "near" for those hearing or reading the prophecy (Obad. 15; Isa. 34:5, 8; Ezek. 30:2–11; Zeph. 1:4, 7, 14).

The day of judgment was certainly near for Babylon in Isaiah's day: "Behold, the day of the LORD is coming.... And her days will not be prolonged" (Isa. 13:9, 22). The passage even tells us who God used to mete out His judgment: "Behold, I am going to stir up the Medes against them..." (13:17). We know that Babylon was conquered by the kingdom of silver—the Medes and Persians—during Israel's exile in Babylon (Dan. 2). The "day of the LORD" came during Belshazzar's feast: "That same night Belshazzar the Chaldean king was slain. So Darius the Mede received the kingdom at about the age of sixty-two" (Dan. 5:30–31).

In time the kingdom of bronze (Greece) conquered the Medes and Persians, and the kingdom of iron (Rome) conquered the Greeks. God's kingdom—the kingdom of stone cut without hands that became a mountain and filled the earth (2:44–45)—defeated all these kingdoms. This same Kingdom rolls over all earthly kingdoms that oppose the only legitimate Kingdom, God's kingdom (Psalm 2; Matt. 25:31–32).

But what of Saddam Hussein's reconstruction of the ancient city of Babylon? Hussein's building of ancient Babylon "was designed to attract tourists. Like the Shah's celebrations at Persepolis, this was a measure of understandable if chauvinistic nationalism rather than an aspiration to imperialism. If anything from the past inspired Hussein it was the glorious role of Baghdad in the Abbasid era (A.D. 749–1258)."[12] Mimicking the past does not fulfill prophecy.

John F. Walvoord believes "Saddam Hussein's ambition to destroy Israel motivated his move into Kuwait in August of 1990 as he attempted to set up a power base from which to attack Israel."[13] Walvoord's conclusions are colored by an interpretative system that forces him to see every contemporary event as some fulfillment of some yet to be fulfilled prophecy with Israel as the interpretative key. There are a number of problems with his position. First, the attacks on Israel were not made until *after* the allied forces threatened to force Saddam out of Kuwait. The Iraqis used Israel as a trump card. By attacking Israel, Saddam hoped to force Israel to go on the offensive. Saddam believed that once this happened the Arab part of the coalition would break away and join with him against the Western aggressors and Israel. Israel was not a consideration until Saddam realized he was backed into a military corner from which he had no chance of escaping.

Second, Saddam Hussein did not need Kuwait as a "power base from which to attack Israel." Iraq is much closer to Israel than Kuwait. The Scud missiles were launched from western Iraq, not from Kuwait.

Third, Hussein's invasion of Kuwait was motivated by ancient territorial disputes and economic factors. While some may want to read prophetic significance into his military venture, there is no justification for doing so.

Fourth, Saddam's "Babylonian" empire is now in shambles. This seems to support the secondary *application*—not fulfillment—of Bible prophecy: Saddam was judged like ancient Babylon and Rome. Any attempt to rebuild Babylon will be met with destruction (Isa. 13:20).

Should we expect a reconstituted Babylon in the future based upon events described in the Book of Revelation? Is Revelation's Babylon the same as the Babylon of the Old Testament? Are "Sodom and Egypt" (Rev. 11:8) and "Jezebel" (2:20) in the Book of Revelation further fulfillments of ancient prophecies? Not at all. This is a type of interpretive shorthand that has been used before: "They display their sin like Sodom" (Isa. 3:9; also 1:9–10). Babylon, as depicted in the Book of Revelation, has been interpreted in a number of ways: as a designation for first-century Rome, as a revived Roman empire comprising a ten-nation common market, as a literal revived Babylon, or as first-century Jerusalem.[14] Since the Book of Revelation was written around A.D. 66, we should be looking for a first-century application, either Rome or Jerusalem.[15] By going back to the first prophetic key—determining the time frame from the time texts—we can dismiss the distant futurist interpretations as untenable. Revelation tells us when the events prophesied will be fulfilled:

- The events "must *shortly take place*" (1:1).
- "For the time is *near*" (1:3).
- "I am coming to you *quickly*" (2:16).
- "I am coming *quickly*" (3:11).
- "The third woe is coming *quickly*" (11:14).
- "The things which must *shortly take place*" (22:6).
- "Behold, I am coming *quickly*" (22:7).
- "For the time is *near*" (22:10).
- "Behold, I am coming *quickly*" (22:12).
- "Yes, I am coming *quickly*" (22:20).

With the time frame established, our next step is to examine the historical context (the third key) using Scripture to interpret Scripture. Jerusalem and Babylon are both called "the great city" (Rev. 14:8; 11:8). The Harlot (Babylon) is "drunk with the blood of the saints" (17:6). Compare this with Matthew 23:34–36 where Jesus states that "all the righteous blood shed on earth, from the blood of righteous Abel to the blood of Zechariah, the son of Berechiah, whom you murdered between the temple and the altar" will be charged against the generation of Jews who rejected Him and spurned the Holy Spirit. The same theme is elsewhere used to describe Babylon: "And in her [Babylon] was found the blood of prophets and of saints and of all who have been slain on the earth" (Rev. 18:24). The Book of Acts confirms this testimony (Acts 7:51–52). Therefore, there is little doubt that the Babylon of Revelation is the first-century city of Jerusalem.

Jerusalem is also given pagan names designed to describe her treachery and apostasy. Jerusalem, the place where "their Lord was crucified" (Rev. 11:8), is "the great city which mystically is called Sodom and Egypt." Babylon is also described as "the great city" (14:8 and 17:5). Throughout the Bible when Israel is unfaithful, she is characterized as a "harlot" (Ezekiel 16). "Rome could not fornicate against God, for only Jerusalem was God's wife (Rev. 17:25, cp. Isa. 1:20; Jer. 31:31)."[16] In addition, "there is an obvious contrast between the Harlot and the chaste bride (cp. Rev. 17:25 with Rev. 21:1ff.) that suggests a contrast with the Jerusalem below and the Jerusalem above (Rev. 21:2; cp. Gal. 4:24ff.; Heb. 12:18ff.). The fact that the Harlot is seated on the seven-headed Beast (obviously representative of Rome) indicates not identity with Rome, but alliance with Rome against Christianity."[17] Israel's collaboration with Rome against Jesus in the first century is quite evident in John 18:28–32, 19:12–15, and Acts 17:7.

From this evidence we can conclude that the prophecies concerning Babylon of the Old Testament are fulfilled. The Babylon of Revelation is used "mystically" (Rev. 11:8) to refer to an apostate Israel of the *first century*. The traits of pagan Babylon are used to describe first-century Jerusalem, just as Old-Testament Jerusalem in rebellion shared the traits of Egypt (Ezek. 23:3, 8, 19, 28) and Sodom (Isa. 1:9–10; 3:9).

Notes

1. Albert James Dager, "The Gulf Crisis: The Beginning of the End for America?" *Media Spotlight: A Biblical Analysis of Religious and Secular Media* (January 1991), 1.

2. Arno C. Gaebelein, *Our Hope* XXIII (August 1916), 110. Quoted in Dwight Wilson, *Armageddon Now!: The Premillenarian Response to Russia and Israel Since 1917* (Tyler, TX: Institute for Christian Economics, [1977] 1991), 36.

3. F.E. Howitt, "Israel and Other Lands in Prophecy," *The Pentecostal Evangel* (10 March 1928), 2–3. Quoted in Wilson, *Armageddon Now!*, 79.

4. *The Pentecostal Evangel* (27 March 1948), 8. Quoted in Wilson, *Armageddon Now!*, 155.

5. Hal Lindsey, *The 1980s: Countdown to Armageddon* (King of Prussia, PA: Westgate Press, 1980), 73–74.

6. Dager, "The Gulf Crisis," 1. By 1998, Russia's economy was in shambles.

7. "The purge of Israel in their time of trouble is described by Zechariah in these words: 'And it shall come to pass, that in all the land, saith Jehovah, two parts therein shall be cut off and die; but the third shall be left therein. And I will bring the third part into the fire, and will refine them as silver is refined, and will try them as gold is tried' (Zech. 13:8, 9). According to Zechariah's prophecy, *two thirds of the children of Israel in the land will perish,* but the one third that is left will be refined and be awaiting the deliverance of God at the second coming of Christ which is described in the next chapter of Zechariah" (John F. Walvoord, *Israel in Prophecy* [Grand Rapids, MI: Zondervan/Academie, 1962], 108).

8. Erwin W. Lutzer, *Coming to Grips with the Role of Europe in Prophecy* (Chicago: Moody Press, 1990), 31.

9. Ed Hindson, *End Times, the Middle East, and the New World Order: How to Make Sense of World Events in Light of Bible Prophecy* (Wheaton, IL: Victor Books, 1991), 90.

10. John Phillips, *Only God Can Prophesy!* (Wheaten, IL: Harold Shaw, 1975), 111–12. Quoted in Hindson, *End Times, the Middle East, and the New World Order*, 90.

11. Charles H. Dyer, *The Rise of Babylon: Sign of the End Times* (Wheaton, IL: Tyndale, 1991), 19.

12. Edwin Yamauchi, "Updating the Armageddon Calendar," *Christianity Today* (29 April 1991), 51.

13. Quoted in Yamauchi, "Updating the Armageddon Calendar," *Christianity Today*, 51.

14. Joseph R. Balyeat, *Babylon: The Great City of Revelation* (Sevierville, TN: Onward, 1991).

15. Kenneth L. Gentry, Jr., *Before Jerusalem Fell: Dating the Book of Revelation*, 2nd ed. (Atlanta, GA: American Vision, 1999).

16. Gentry, *Before Jerusalem Fell*, 241 note 26.

17. Gentry, *Before Jerusalem Fell*, 241.

Chapter Twenty-Eight

ROSHING TO
JUDGMENT

In *The Edge of Time: The Final Countdown Has Begun*, Patti and Paul Lalonde write that "Bible scholars agree that 'Gog,' also described as the 'prince of Rosh,' is the leader of what is modern-day Russia."[1] Bible scholars do not agree, but this does not phase the Lalondes. They refuse to consider the overwhelming contrary opinions of noted Christian scholars and continue to mislead their readers. Here's how it works. In Ezekiel 38:2 and 39:1, the Hebrew word *rosh* is translated as if it were the name of a nation. That nation is thought to be modern Russia because *rosh* sounds like Russia. In addition, *Meshech* (38:2) is said to sound like Moscow, and *Tubal* (38:2) is similar to the name of one of the prominent Asiatic provinces of Russia, the province of Tobolsk. Edwin M. Yamauchi, noted Christian historian and archeologist, writes that *rosh* "can have nothing to do with modern 'Russia,'" and "all informed references and studies acknowledge that the association with Moscow and Tobolsk is untenable."[2]

Timothy J. Dailey writes in *The Gathering Storm* that the belief that Ezekiel 38 and 39 describe a "Russian-led invasion of the Middle East" is "so commonly held as to be almost taken for granted.... So ingrained is this theory that books on biblical prophecy have assumed routinely over the years that

Rosh equals Russian was beyond doubt. Without discussing the evidence, for example, John F. Walvoord concludes that the description in Ezekiel 38 and 39 'could only refer to what we know today as Russia.'[3] What is the evidence for this commonly held belief? In truth, the Russian invasion theory rests upon scanty foundations indeed."[4]

How should we understand the use of *rosh* in Ezekiel 38–39? Is it really a cryptic designation for modern Russia? Not if you know a little Hebrew. "*Rosh* in Hebrew means 'head' or 'chief'; *Russia* comes from *Rus*, a Scandinavian word that was introduced into Ukraine in the Middle Ages. Meshech and Tubal are attested in cuneiform texts as Mushku and Tabal, areas in central and eastern Turkey."[5]

North by Northeast

The belief that the Hebrew *rosh* is a prophetic reference to modern-day Russia has been popularized by the old *Scofield Reference Bible*. This view, however, did not begin with Scofield. "Dr. John Cumming, writing in 1864, said, 'This king of the North I conceive to be the autocrat of Russia. . . . That Russia occupies a place, and a very momentous place, in the prophetic world has been admitted by almost all expositors.'"[6] While it is true that Russia is north of Israel, it is also true that the Bible often uses north as a designation for a geographical area that includes the northeast. For example, Babylon was east of Israel, but Jeremiah 4:6 warns that the disaster comes "from the north" (Jer. 1:13–15; 3:18; 6:1, 22; 10:22; Zech. 2:6–7). The same is true for the Assyrians (Zeph. 2:13) and Persians (Isa. 41:25; Jer. 50:3). Is the Bible in error? Not at all. "From the perspective of the Holy Land, the invaders came down from the north, even if their place of origin was actually to the east. Ezekiel is giving the *direction* of the invasion, not the place of the invader's origin."[7]

Not So Fast

Scofield says, with the Lalondes supporting his errant conclusion, that "all agree" that Russia is designated here. Certainly *some* expositors hold this view, but many more do not. Ernst Wilhelm Hengstenberg writes that "the poor Russians have been here very unjustly arranged among the enemies of God's people. Rosh, as the name of a people, does not occur in all the Old Testament."[8] More recent commentators are beginning to reject the *Rosh* equals Russia hypothesis:

There is no evidence from the ancient Near East that a country named Rosh ever existed. Some would understand rosh as modern Russia. Proponents of this view usually appeal to etymology based on similar sounds (to the hearing) between two words. Such etymological procedures are not linguistically sound, nor is etymology alone a sound hermeneutical basis on which to interpret a word. The word "Russia" is a late eleventh-century A.D. term. Therefore, the data does [sic] not seem to support an interpretation of rosh as a proper name of a geographical region or country.[9]

The best translation of Ezekiel 38:2 is "the chief (head) prince of Meshech and Tubal," since Meshech and Tubal are normally connected (Gen. 10:2; 1 Chron. 1:5; Ezek. 27:13; 32:26). Even dispensational scholars are beginning to admit that *rosh* does not refer to Russia. Charles Ryrie even takes issue with the New American Standard translation of Ezekiel 38:2 when he writes: "*The prince of Rosh* (better, 'the chief prince of Meshech and Tubal'), the area of modern Turkey."[10]

Those dispensational scholars who admit that *rosh* does not refer to Russia, still maintain that Ezekiel 38–39 describes a battle that takes place during a future "Great Tribulation." Three reasons are given: "(1) Some of the countries named by Ezekiel were located in what is now Russia. (2) The armies are said to come 'from the far north' (Ezek. 38:6, 15; 39:2).... (3) Ezekiel spoke of a coalition of several nations, many of whom are today aligned with or under the influence of the Soviet Union. These include Iran ('Persia'), Sudan and northern Ethiopia ('Cush'), Libya ('Put'), and Turkey ('Meshech,' 'Tubal,' 'Gomer,' and 'Beth Togarmah'). All these nations (see 38:2–3, 5–6), possibly led by the Soviet Union, will unite to attack Israel."[11]

There is little in these three reasons to mandate that modern Russia is the leader of a confederation of nations to come against Israel.[12] The nations then located in the area that is *now* Turkey, Syria, northern Iran and Iraq, and western Russia were nations when Persia and Greece were in power in the second century B.C. In terms of Israel's location, these land masses constituted the "far north." An area between the Black and Caspian Seas was certainly far north in terms of Israel's location. "It may be surprising to learn that, in many cases, the geographical references to north in the Bible actually refer to the east. The Book of Jeremiah warns repeatedly of a coming invasion: 'Raise the signal to go to Zion! Flee for safety without delay! For

I am bringing disaster from the north, even terrible destruction' (Jeremiah 4:6)."[13] This passage is a reference to the Babylonian invasion that resulted in the downfall of the kingdom of Judah in 586 B.C. Babylon was more east than north. A study of similar passages will indicate similar geographical orientation (Jer. 1:14–15; 3:18; 6:1, 22; 10; 22; 46:24; Ezek. 26:7; Zeph. 2:13). Even Zion is called "the far north" (Psalm 48:2; cf. Isa. 14:13).

The third reason offered above proves that ancient peoples are indicated since their ancient names are given. If *rosh* is a prophetic name for Russia because it sounds like Russia, then why don't the other nations sound like their modern counterparts?

The most damaging piece of evidence to the theory that Ezekiel 38 and 39 refer to modern Russia's invasion of Israel during the Great Tribulation is that there is no mention of Gog and Magog or Meshech and Tubal in Revelation 4–19, yet this passage is where dispensationalists tell us the Great Tribulation is described. Revelation 20:8 describes the battle of Gog and Magog as coming *after* the thousand years. Moreover, its characteristics are quite different from the Ezekiel battle. This means, like "Jezebel" (Rev. 2:20), "Sodom and Egypt" (11:8), and "Babylon" (14:8), the Battle of Gog and Magog is *characteristic* of an Old Testament event, *but it is not the same event!* One is past (Ezek. 38–39); the other is future— *after* the "thousand years" (Rev. 20:8).

Is it true that this battle will take place after the people of Israel come back to their land in the "latter years" (Ezek. 38:8), in the "last days" (38:16)? First, as we saw above, there is no mention of a battle with "Gog and Magog" during the so-called Great Tribulation period. Second, the phrase "in the latter days" does not refer to events at the end of the world but simply to future events. In Hebrew there is no word for "in the future." Moses warned Israel that evil will befall the nation "in the latter days" (Deut. 31:29). When did this happen? Judges 2:20 tells us that "the anger of the LORD burned against Israel ...'Because this nation has transgressed My covenant which I commanded their fathers.'" Therefore, Deuteronomy 31:29 was fulfilled in Judges 2:20.

In Jeremiah 30 many judgments were pronounced upon Israel. They were to be realized in the "latter days" (30:24). We know that Israel suffered greatly under the Babylonian captivity, which took place in the "latter days" of which God spoke. But we also know that Israel was restored seventy years after the captivity began (Jer. 29:10; Dan. 9:2). "The fortunes of Moab" were to be restored "in the latter days," that is, "in the future" (Jer. 48:47). The fortunes of Elam were to be restored "in the last days" (49:39). The New International Version translates Jeremiah 48:47 and 49:39 as "in days to come." There is no reason to suppose that these passages are predicting events thousands of years in the future.

But doesn't Ezekiel 38:8 predict that Israel will be "gathered from many nations"? The futurists teach that Israel was scattered among many nations only after the destruction of Jerusalem in A.D. 70 and will be regathered from the nations in the years before the "Great Tribulation" which is still future. This is not what Scripture teaches. In Ezekiel 12:15 we are told that God scattered Israel "among the nations" (see 6:6–9). In Jeremiah 29:14 we are told that God will restore the fortunes of Israel and will gather them "from all the nations." When was this gathering "from all the nations" to be accomplished? "When seventy years have been completed" (Jer. 29:10), that is, after the Babylonian captivity.

Wooden Rifles?

The context of these two chapters makes it clear that the battle is an ancient one. *All* the soldiers are riding horses (Ezek. 38:15).[14] These horse soldiers are "wielding swords" (38:4) and carrying "bows and arrows, war clubs and spears" (39:9). The weapons are made of wood (39:10). Dispensationalists, who insist on literalism and a distant future battle, speculate that "this warfare will revert to use of old-fashioned weapons.... To maintain a forced literalism, some go beyond common sense and what the text actually requires: "The Russians have perfected an actual wooden rifle. They have compressed wood until it is harder than steel, but lighter to carry.[15] It is still combustible. The Germans used some wooden bullets during World War II; they were cheaper to make and had the desired effect."[16] The weapons of choice are swords, bows and arrows, and spears, indicators of an ancient battle in a pre-industrial age. It is amazing to read what some people will do to make this obvious ancient battle fit a modern context. In 1940, Harry Rimmer claimed that Russia would use wooden weapons because lasers would make metal weaponry inoperable in the future. Rimmer wrote: "The weirdest and most conclusive evidence that we are faced with in a foretelling of events yet to occur is the startling statement that this raiding army is armed only with wooden weapons!" Weird indeed.[17]

For Such a Time as This

If this battle is no longer a future event, then when and where in biblical history did this conflict take place? Instead of looking to the distant future, James B. Jordan believes that "it is in Esther that we see a conspiracy to plunder the Jews, which backfires with the result that the Jews plundered their enemies. This event is then ceremonially sealed with the institution of the annual Feast of Purim."[18] Jordan continues by establishing the context for Ezekiel 38–39:

> Ezekiel 34 states that God will act as Good Shepherd to Israel, and will bring them back into the land. He continues this theme in Ezekiel 36, saying that God will make a new covenant with Israel. The inauguration of this new covenant, which we can call the Restoration Covenant, is described in Zechariah 3, where God removes the filth from Joshua the High Priest and restores the Temple and Priesthood. . . . Ezekiel continues in Ezekiel 37 with the vision of the valley of dry bones. The Spirit of God would be given a greater measure than before (though of course not as great as at Pentecost in Acts 2), and the result would be restoration of the people. No longer would there be a cultural division between Judah and Ephraim, but all would be together as a new people. . . . At this point, Ezekiel describes the attack of Gog, Prince of Magog, and his confederates. Ezekiel states that people from all over the world attack God's people, who are pictured dwelling at peace in the land. God's people will completely defeat them, however, and the spoils will be immense. The result is that all nations will see the victory, and "the house of Israel will know that I am the Lord their God from that day onward" (Ezek. 39:21–23). . . . Chronologically this all fits very nicely. The events of Esther took place during the reign of Darius, after the initial rebuilding of the Temple under Joshua [the High Priest] and Zerubbabel and shortly before rebuilding of the walls by Nehemiah. . . . Thus, the interpretive hypothesis I am suggesting (until someone shoots it down) is this: Ezekiel 34–37 describes the first return of the exiles under Zerubbabel, and implies the initial rebuilding of the physical Temple. Ezekiel 38–39 describes the attack of Gog (Haman) and his confederates against the Jews. Finally, Ezekiel 40–48 describes in figurative language the situation as a result of the work of Nehemiah.[19]

The slaughter of Israel's enemies in Ezekiel 39 fits with the number of deaths listed in Esther 9:16 (75,000). In Esther 9:5 we read that "the Jews struck all their enemies with the *sword*, killing and destroying." Ezekiel 38:5–6 tells us that Israel's enemies come from "Persia, Ethiopia [*lit.*, Cush], and... from the remote parts of the north. . . ," all within the boundaries of the Persian Empire of Esther's day. From Esther we learn that the Persian Empire "extended from India to Ethiopia [*lit.*, Cush], 127 provinces. . ." in all (Esther 8:9). "In other words, the explicit idea that the Jews were attacked by people from all the provinces of Persia is in both passages."[20] The parallels are unmistakable.

Revising the Future

The breakup of the Soviet Empire has led some to discard the Rosh=Russia idea. Pat Robertson thought, like most futurists before him, "that the references in the prophetic writings to the nations of the North referred to the Soviet Union." He has since changed his views: "Now I have begun to believe it is more likely the Muslim republics—such as Kazakhistan, Tadzikhistan, Uzbekistan, and Azerbaijan."[21] This is a major revision. It is today's newspapers, however, not biblical exegesis, that bring about these revisions.

Europe in Prophecy

Next to seeing modern Russia attacking Israel in Ezekiel 38 and 39 during the "Great Tribulation," the second most talked-about prophetic scenario is that the establishment of a ten-nation European Common Market will be a fulfillment of Bible prophecy. This "United States of Europe," or European Economic Community (EEC), is to be ruled by a coming "antichrist" who is "alive somewhere in the world today."[22] According to Hal Lindsey, Dave Hunt, John F. Walvoord, and many others who write on prophecy, this "United States of Europe" constitutes a revived Roman Empire.

The idea of a newly confederated group of nations is based, for some, on the "ten toes" of Daniel 2:41–42 (the toes, however, are never referred to as kings), the "ten horns" and "ten kings" of Daniel 7:7, 20, 24, and the "ten horns" and "ten kings" of Revelation 13:1; 17:3, 7, 12, 16. These passages are futurized well beyond their historical time frame and catapulted into the distant future where they still await fulfillment. This is all done by inserting a gap of indeterminable time between the sixty-ninth and seventieth weeks of Daniel 9:24–27. As has been pointed out, *there is no biblical reason for inserting this mythical gap between these two sets of "years."* The sequence of years are a unit.

When we look at Scripture and peer into the facts of history, we learn that "ten kings" were allied "with the Beast" in the first century (Rev. 17:12). Rome actually had ten first-century imperial provinces. F.W. Farrar lists the following as the provinces that fulfilled the prediction of Revelation 17:12, and by way of application, Daniel 7:24–25 and Revelation 13:1: Italy, Achaia, Asia, Syria, Egypt, Africa, Spain, Gaul, Britain, and Germany.[23]

These provincial kings did what the Beast (Rome) commanded. Caesar ruled the Empire, but lesser rulers governed in the conquered territories and assisted Rome in the persecution of Jews and Christians. They, too, were called "kings." For example, Caesar was called "king" (John 19:15) while Agrippa, who was most assuredly under the rule and dominion of Caesar, was also called "king" (Acts 26:2). Dave Hunt obviously misunderstands history when he writes that "there never were ten kings that ruled the Roman Empire."[24] This improper reading of history and misapplied interpretation forces him to look for a future fulfillment when none is needed. As David A. Clark points out in his commentary on the Book of Revelation, a ten-nation confederacy made up of "kings" ruled Rome during the time of Nero:

> These verses [in Rev. 17:3, 12] tell us about the horns of the beast. He had not only seven heads; but ten horns. These ten horns were ten kings, not kings sitting on the throne of Rome, as I understand, but those kings and countries subjected by Rome, and which made the empire great. We know that Rome embraced at that time the countries of Europe that bordered on the Mediterranean Sea, and the northern part of Africa and considerable territory in Asia, and also in central Europe. Rome had conquered the world.[25]

There is no biblical or historical justification for believing that one day the Roman Empire will be revived as a fulfillment of prophecies made over two thousand years ago. Those with a short memory and little regard for history will not remember that the supposed revival of the Roman Empire has been identified in various ways, depending on who has been in power and how the status of nations and territories has been configured to make the scenario fit with "Bible prophecy." Mussolini's empire, the League of Nations, the United Nations, the European Defense Community, the Common Market, and NATO have all been certain candidates.[26]

Contemporary prophetic literature states that a "ten-nation confederation" will fulfill Bible prophecy. Hal Lindsey wrote in 1970: "When the Scripture says 'out of' it means the ten nations (ten kings) which will come out of Rome, since Rome was the fourth kingdom."[27] While many believe the EEC will fulfill this supposed prophecy of a revived Roman Empire, as of this writing, twelve nations have already joined the EEC with others surely to follow.

> The community is sure to expand by three to five states in the next few years, and by many more someday. Mr. [Jacques] Delors, who has to make proposals for dealing with enlargement, says he is thinking of an ultimate membership of 35, which will mean profound changes.[28]

For years we were told that *ten* was the magic number. Now we have twelve going on thirty-five, and we still have not gotten to the borders of the former Roman Empire which included parts of Asia, Syria, Israel, Egypt, and Africa! Today's prophecy pundits are simply following trends, "predicting a continuation of the thing that is already happening."[29] Biblical texts, more often than not ripped out of their historical and theological contexts, are made to fit the changes that one reads in the newspaper. Here is an example of prophetic speculation by way of social trends:

> One of the few advantages of the rapid acceleration of history is that we are increasingly able to decipher the mysteries of prophetic players and events that have lain shrouded in the mists of time. Some of these new insights are already vivid enough to shatter long-standing preconceptions; even those whose precise meanings remain elusive at least have us looking in the right direction.[30]

For decades we have been assured that current events line up with prophetic texts. We have been told that prophecy was being fulfilled before our eyes. Time and time again Christians were to look at the "signs of the times" as prophetic indicators that the end could not be far off. It seems, however, that every new geopolitical movement forces prophecy writers to revise their works.

They hope and pray that no one notices. Unfortunately, few people do take notice of the continual revisions that fail to include any apology that they were wrong in their assessments in their previous edition. Consider just *some* of the more popular examples of revisionist prophetic speculation:

- John F. Walvoord, *Armageddon, Oil and the Middle East Crisis* (1974, 1976). Updated and revised, 1990.
- Edgar C. James, *Armageddon and the New World Order* (1981). Updated and revised, 1991.
- Thomas S. McCall and Zola Levitt, *The Coming Russian Invasion of Israel* (1974). Updated and revised, 1987.
- Edgar C. James, *Arabs, Oil, and Armageddon* (1977). Updated and revised, 1991.
- Billy Graham, *Approaching Hoofbeats* (1983). Updated and revised as Storm Warning in 1992.

These authors do not constitute a comprehensive list of those who continue to write and revise books that simply apply a worn-out and discredited prophetic system to the latest newspaper headlines.[31]

Since there is no gap between the sixty-ninth and seventieth weeks of Daniel 9:24–27, there is no need to futurize the ten-king prophecies. Moreover, a study of history demonstrates that there were at least ten Roman provinces ruled by kings in the first century. Finally, the Book of Revelation makes it clear that the events described therein "must shortly take place" (1:1). Without this time text and others like it (1:3; 3:11; 22:7), the events of Revelation can be made to fit any era. Sure enough, this is exactly what we are experiencing today with the European Economic Community theory.

Prophetic Key Number Four: Distinguishing Fulfillment from Application

There remains, however, an applicational side to prophecy. While a certain prophecy may be fulfilled, a *principle* inherent in the prophetic event can have numerous contemporary applications. No one denies that there are plans for the development of a United States of Europe, although some nations are resisting union through independence movements in Eastern Europe, the former Soviet Union, Iraq, Yugoslavia, and South Africa. Political unions can be for good or evil. Under Napoleon and Hitler, a unified Europe was obviously evil. The former Soviet Union's effort to force such a union on conquered lands has fallen apart. Independence movements are in full bloom in the Baltic states. Now Europeans are questioning the wisdom of a United States of Europe.

> Despite the hot rhetoric and flaming spirit, not everyone is eagerly embracing an economically integrated Europe. Earlier this month [June 1991], for example, German Chancellor Helmut Kohl and [former] British Prime Minister John Major met in England and jointly expressed ambivalence about European monetary union. Several days later, a senior official at the Bundesbank, Germany's central bank, voiced reluctance about a single European currency. Other countries are similarly uneasy about a proposed value-added tax that would impose a uniform 15 percent levy across the continent. Great Britain, in particular, believes that a rigidly structured pan-European VAT would tie its hands on domestic fiscal policy and prevent it from making the proper government-spending choices. Economic reality, as much as nationalism or protectionism, threatens to sully Europe's fledgling confederacy.[32]

In the former Soviet Union we may find that another Napoleon or Hitler rises Phoenix-like out of the debris of failed communism. So far, no ideology, secular or spiritual, has taken the place of failed communism. This is dangerous. While communism may be dead, nationalism and socialism are not. The mixture of the two makes for a volatile compound: nationalism + socialism = nazism. We can find principles in the way God dealt with past tyrannies, both in specific prophetic events (Babylon and Rome) and later historical figures who acted like a Caesar (e.g., Mussolini) or a Nebuchadnezzar and his fiery furnace (e.g., Hitler and his gas ovens). While these prophetic events are past, they still retain a wealth of contemporary application.

Seeing the prophecies of the "ten kings" as fulfilled prophecy does not mean we should bury our heads in the political sand. Fulfilled prophecy gives us a reference point from which to make judgments regarding contemporary events. If Europe follows in the footsteps of Babylon, Greece, or Rome, we can expect the same type of judgment to befall her. The ruin of ungodly leaders such as Napoleon and Hitler gives credence to the biblical principle that rulers who rebel against God will meet certain doom.

Now therefore, O kings, show discernment;
Take warning, O judges of the earth.
Worship the LORD with reverence, and rejoice with trembling.
Do homage to the Son, lest He become angry, and you
perish in the way, For His wrath may soon be kindled.
How blessed are all who take refuge in Him!

(Psalm 2:10–12)

The Bible is a record of the reality of God acting in history. God destroyed all those nations that sought to build kingdoms that competed with His kingdom—from Babylon to Rome. God has set up His kingdom and it "will never be destroyed"; it will crush and put an end to all rival kingdoms, "but it will itself endure forever" (Dan. 2:45). Iraq, Russia, and Europe may raise their fists in rebellion against God, but God, as He has done in the past, will slap them down. One day they will all worship at His feet. "For He must reign until He has put all His enemies under His feet" (1 Cor. 15:25).

Notes

1. Peter and Patti Lalonde, *The Edge of Time: The Final Countdown Has Begun* (Eugene, OR: Harvest House, 1997), 216.
2. Edwin M. Yamauchi, *Foes from the Northern Frontier: Invading Hordes from the Russian Steppes* (Grand Rapids, MI: Baker Book House, 1982), 20, 24–25.
3. John F. Walvoord, *Armageddon, Oil, and the Middle East*, rev. ed. (Grand Rapids, MI: Zondervan, [1974, 1976] 1990), 141.
4. Timothy J. Daily, *The Gathering Storm* (Tarrytown, NY: Revell, 1992), 157–58.
5. Edwin M. Yamauchi, "Updating the Armageddon Calendar," *Christianity Today* (April 29, 1991), 51.
6. Hal Lindsey, *The Late Great Planet Earth* (Grand Rapids, MI: Zondervan, 1970), 63. Cumming's quotation comes from his *Destiny of Nations* (London: Hurst and Blackette, 1864), no page number cited.
7. Daily, *The Gathering Storm*, 166. Archeologist Barry Beitzel states that "the Bible's use of the expression 'north' denotes the direction from which a foe would normally approach and not the location of its homeland." (*The Moody Atlas of Bible Lands* [Chicago, IL: Moody Press, 1985], 5).
8. E. W. Hengstenberg, *The Prophecies of the Prophet Ezekiel*, trans. A.C. Murphy and J.G. Murphy (Edinburgh: T. and T. Clark, 1869), 333.
9. Ralph H. Alexander, "Ezekiel," *The Expositors Bible Commentary*, gen. ed. Frank E. Gaebelein, 12 vols. (Grand Rapids, MI: Zondervan, 1986), 6:930. For a discussion of five contemporary views of this battle, see Ralph H. Alexander, "A Fresh Look at Ezekiel 38 and 39," *Journal of the Evangelical Theological Society*, 17 (Summer 1974), 162–65.
10. Charles C. Ryrie, ed., *The Ryrie Study Bible* (Chicago, IL: Moody Press, 1978), 1285.
11. Charles H. Dyer, "Ezekiel," in *The Bible Knowledge Commentary: Old Testament*, eds. John F. Walvoord and Roy B. Zuck (Wheaton, IL: Victor Books, 1985), 1300.
12. The former Soviet Union offered to sell missiles to Israel. "It was the first time for someone from the Eastern bloc to come to us, and we were very happy," said Noah Schachar, spokesman for Rafael, an Israeli Defense Ministry agency (*Atlanta Journal/Constitution* [19 June 1991], A7). How does this fit in with Bible prophecy? Why would Israel's enemy be selling her arms?
13. Daily, *The Gathering Storm*, 165.
14. For some "literalists," horses can be made to mean "horse power." Rob Linsted, *The Next Move: Current Events in Bible Prophecy* (Wichita, KS: Bible Truth, n.d.), 41.

15. No reference is given for this claim. Compressed wood is very heavy. Just compare the weight of a tight-grained wood like oak with pine. Today's light military weapons are often made from composite materials and plastics, not wood.

16. Thomas S. McCall and Zola Levitt, *Coming: The End! Russia and Israel in Prophecy* (Chicago, IL: Moody Press, 1992), 56. This is a revised edition of *The Coming Russian Invasion of Israel*, first published by Moody in 1974 and revised in 1987.

17. Harry Rimmer, *The Coming War and the Rise of Russia* (Grand Rapids, MI: Eerdmans, 1940), 48–51.

18. James B. Jordan, *Esther: In the Midst of Covenant History* (Niceville, FL: Biblical Horizons, 1995), 5.

19. Jordan, *Esther*, 5–7.

20. Jordan, *Esther*, 7.

21. Pat Robertson, *The Secret Kingdom: Your Path to Peace, Love, and Financial Security* (Dallas, TX: Word, 1992), 255.

22. See John Ankerberg, *et al.*, *One World: Bible Prophecy and the New World Order* (Chicago: Moody Press, 1991), 25. This book is a rehash of decades of failed predictions.

23. F.W. Farrar, *The Early Days of Christianity* (New York: E.P. Dutton, 1882), 464 note 1.

24. Ankerberg, *One World*, 25.

25. David S. Clark, *The Message from Patmos: A Postmillennial Commentary* (Grand Rapids, MI: Baker Book House, 1989), 110.

26. Dwight Wilson, *Armageddon Now!: The Premillenarian Response to Russia and Israel Since 1917* (Tyler, TX: Institute for Christian Economics, [1977] 1991), 216.

27. Lindsey, *The Late Great Planet Earth*, 93.

28. Flora Lewis, "Europe's Last-Minute Jitters," *New York Times* (24 April 1992), A15.

29. George Orwell, "James Burnham and the Managerial Revolution," *Collected Essays, Journalism and Letters*, vol. 4 (New York: Harcourt Brace Jovanovich, 1968), 173. Quoted in Max Dublin, *Futurehype: The Tyranny of Prophecy* (New York: Dutton, 1991), 3.

30. George Otis, Jr., *The Last of the Giants: Lifting the Veil on Islam and the End Times* (Tarrytown, NY: Revell, 1991), 169.

31. Charles H. Dyer, *World News and Bible Prophecy* (Wheaton, IL: Tyndale, 1993). This is the same author who wrote *The Rise of Babylon*, a failed attempt to interpret Saddam Hussein's empire as a revived Babylonian kingdom.

32. Robert F. Black, "The Dark Side of Europe '92," *U.S. News and World Report* (24 June 1991), 48–49.

Appendix 1

GOD CAN TELL TIME

Prophetic commentator J. Dwight Pentecost writes that "It is to be observed that the time element holds a relatively small place in prophecy."[1] To the contrary, "the time element" plays a major role in prophecy. In fact, it plays the defining role. Without precision of meaning for the time texts prophetic pronouncements are meaningless. For example, what significance could be attached to Jonah's words of judgment in forty days if Nineveh did not repent? Could the Ninevites have stretched forty days into forty years or four-hundred years by claiming that the "time element holds a relatively small place in prophecy" by quoting a version of Psalm 90:4? "For a thousand years in Thy sight are like yesterday when it passes by, or as a watch in the night" (cf. 2 Peter 3:8). The nearness of the promised judgment led the Ninevites to repentance and an adverted judgment (Jonah 3:5).

Dispensationalists reject this literal approach to interpreting the time texts by fabricating a doctrine called *imminency* or the "any moment rapture of the church." The following definition by a dispensationalist is typical:

> The primary thought expressed by the word "imminency" is that something important is likely to happen, and could happen soon. While the event may not be immediate, or necessarily very soon, it is next on the program and may take place at any time.[2]

This is theological double talk. There is nothing in the time texts that would support this confusing definition. Words such as "likely," "could happen," and "may take place" are nowhere indicated. Taking a similar approach, Thomas Ice writes, "The fact that Christ could return at any moment *but not soon* is supported in the New Testament in the following passages: 1 Corinthians 1:7; 16:22; Philippians 3:20; 4:5; 1 Thessalonians 1:10; Titus 2:13; Hebrews 9:28; James 5:7–9; 1 Peter 1:13; Jude 21; Revelation 3:11; 22:7, 12, 17, 20. These verses state that Christ could return at any moment. . . ."[3] Not one of these verses supports his claim. Not one verse in the New Testament states that Jesus could return at any moment. Ice contradicts the Bible when he writes that Jesus could *not* return soon. Consider James 5:7–9:

> Be patient, therefore, brethren, until the coming of the Lord. Behold, the farmer waits for the precious produce of the soil, being patient about it, until it gets the early and late rains. You too be patient; strengthen your hearts, *for the coming of the Lord is at hand.* Do not complain, brethren, against one another, that you yourselves may not be judged; behold, *the Judge is standing right at the door* (James 5:7–9).

Contrary to what Ice contends, James tells his first readers that "the coming of the Lord is at hand" ("near"). And if you don't get his meaning, He defines "at hand" as "standing right at the door," the same words used by Jesus in Matthew 24:33: "Recognize that He is near, right at the door,"[4] not down the road or in the next county. Let's read James 5:8 following Ice's methodology: "You too be patient; strengthen your hearts, Christ could return at any moment *but not soon.*" Ice would have James writing the opposite of what the text actually states. James is clear: "For the coming of the Lord is at hand." It was near *for those who first read his letter.*

The biblical writers are straightforward in their claim that certain prophetic events were to happen "soon" for those who first read the prophecies. The eschatological events were *near* for *them.* No other interpretation is possible if the words are taken in their "plain, primary, ordinary, usual, or normal" sense; if they are interpreted literally.

If the biblical authors had wanted to be tentative, vague, or ambiguous in the way they described the timing of future events, they would have equivocated by using words expressing probability, similar to the way Paul expresses himself in 1 Corinthians 4:19: "But I will come to you soon [*taxu*], *if the Lord wills.* . ." (also see Acts 18:21: "I will return to you again, if God wills.") If the inspired New Testament writers wanted to tell their first readers that Jesus could come at "any moment," they would have written "any moment." They didn't. They said His coming was "at hand," that He was coming "quickly," that the time is "near." Ice completely negates the clear assertion of the Bible's time texts by turning them into the "manner" in which an event is to occur. For example, for Ice "quickly" simply means that an event happens fast when it happens. But how does this reinterpretation explain "near" and "shortly"? In what "manner" does one come "shortly"? After confusing his readers with his "manner" argument, Ice concludes that every time "quickly" is used "the actions all came about 'soon' after the prophecy was given. . . ."[5] Exactly!

Debate continues to rage over the use of words like "near," "soon," and "quickly," even though everyone knows what these words mean in normal conversation. Supposedly these time indicators are fluid. In fact, they are so fluid that they actually mean their opposite. For example, Revelation 1:1 tells us that the subsequent events outlined in the book "must shortly take place." In 1:3 we learn that "the time is near." Why are these definitive time indicators used if they hold a "small place in prophecy"? Why use time markers that in ordinary speech mean close at hand if their *real* meaning actually stretches time over centuries? There is no need to be ambiguous about the meaning of "near," "shortly," and "quickly." Translators chose these English words because they convey the proper meaning of their Greek counterparts. If these words really meant something else, then translators would have used the appropriate words.

How Literal are the Literalists?

These time markers indicate that the events depicted in the Book of Revelation were to happen without delay. Dispensational writers object. They realize that if these time indicators are taken literally they will have to concede that the events depicted in the Book of Revelation are history, fulfilled prophecy. We should be reminded at this point that dispensationalists insist on a literal hermeneutic. *Not* to interpret these texts literally fractures their system. Charles Ryrie has made this plain by stating that "dispensationalism claims to employ principles of literal, plain, normal, or historical-grammatical interpretation consistently."[6] Again on the topic of literalism, Ryrie writes: "Dispensationalists claim that their principle of hermeneutics is that of literal interpretation. This means interpretation that gives to every word the same meaning it would have in normal usage, whether employed in writing, speaking or thinking."[7] In another place Ryrie states: "Consistently literal, or plain, interpretation indicates a dispensational approach to the interpretation of Scripture. And it is this very consistency—the strength of dispensational interpretation—that seems to irk the nondispensationalist and becomes the object of his ridicule."[8] Actually, it is the *inconsistency* of the "literal or plain interpretation" that irks nondispensationalists. How consistent are dispensationalists in following the "literal, plain or normal" hermeneutical model when they deny the "literal, plain or normal" interpretation of "near," "shortly," and "quickly"?

Charles L. Feinberg

Charles Feinberg writes in his commentary on Revelation that the phrase "things which must shortly come to pass" in Revelation 1:1 "gives no basis for the historical interpretation of the book. Events are seen here from the perspective of the Lord and not from the human viewpoint (cf. II Pet 3:8). The same Greek words appear in Luke 18:7–8 (Gr *en tachei*), where the delay is clearly a prolonged one."[9] Feinberg follows the proper method—comparing Scripture with Scripture—but fails in his analysis of Luke 18:7–8. The unrighteous judge in Luke 18 gives justice to the widow *in her lifetime!* She receives justice before she dies. The point of the parable is to show how God brings about justice for His elect in a timely manner. "I tell you that He will bring about justice for them *speedily*" (18:8). If the woman received justice from the unrighteous judge in her lifetime, then how can we say that God acts "speedily" when nearly two thousand years have passed since John and the seven churches in Asia Minor were told that the "time is near" and that Jesus was "coming quickly"? Feinberg has made "speedily" and "shortly" to mean an extended period of time. The delay in Luke 18:8 is clearly *not* a prolonged one. Kurt Aland renders the true meaning of Revelation's time texts:

> To a certain extent, the words of Rev. 22:12 can be taken as the title of the Apocalypse: "Behold, I am coming soon, bringing my recompense." In the original text, the Greek word used is *tacu*, and this does not mean

"soon," in the sense of "sometime," but rather "now," "immediately." There-fore, we must understand Rev. 22:12 in this way: "I am coming now, bringing my recompense." The concluding word of Rev. 22:20 is: "He who testifies to these things says, 'Surely I am coming soon.'" Here we again find the word *tacu*, so this means: I am coming quickly, immedi-ately. This is followed by the prayer: "Amen. Come, Lord Jesus!" These words are a summary of the contents of Revelation, which uses continu-ally new images to paint the coming of the Lord. The Apocalypse ex-presses the fervent waiting for the end within the circles in which the writer lived—not an expectation that will happen at some unknown *X* in time (just to repeat this), but one in the immediate present.[10]

Feinberg ignores the obvious meaning of the time texts as described by Aland and develops a convoluted interpretation that is designed to force a futuristic interpretation.

Feinberg continues his argument with his comments on Revelation 1:3: "The time is at hand." "These words (Gr *ho kairos engus*)," he writes, "appear only twice in the Revelation. Neither reference indicates the possible length involved. Again, all is seen from the perspective of God."[11] There is no indica-tion in the Book of Revelation or the entire Bible that "at hand" and "near" are relative terms. There is no passage that points us to viewing time "from the perspective of God" as if when God says "near" He actually means an indefinite period of time. To make such a claim is practicing the fine art of *eisegesis*—reading an interpretation *into* a text so that it will say what you want it to say.

John F. Walvoord

John Walvoord takes a similar position in his interpretation of the time refer-ence "must shortly come to pass" (Revelation 1:1): "The idea is not that the event may occur soon, but when it does, it will be sudden (cf. Luke 18:8; Acts 12:7; 22:18; 25:4; Rom. 16:20)."[12] He interprets "the time is near [at hand]" (1:3) in the same way: "The expression 'at hand' indicates nearness from the standpoint of prophetic revelation, not necessarily that the event will immediately occur."[13] Apply the method of Feinberg and Walvoord to the following passages that contain time indicators. What do they tell you about the nearness of the events?

- "Now learn the parable from the fig tree: when its branch has already become tender, and puts forth its leaves, you know that summer *is near*"

(Matthew 24:32). How far away is summer after leaves appear? The analogy makes it apparent that "near" means chronological proximity: The appearance of leaves means that summer is near. A single growing season is in view.

- "Even so you too, when you see all these things, recognize that He is *near*, right at the door" (24:33). Here we find a brief commentary on what "near" means—"right at the door," not in the next county.
- Jesus said, "My time is *at hand* [*near*]" (Matt. 26:18). Jesus' trial and crucifixion were only hours away. Compare with John 7:6 where early in His ministry Jesus tells His disciples that His "time is not yet at hand."
- "Then He came to His disciples, and said to them, 'Are you still sleeping and taking your rest? Behold, the hour is *at hand* [*near*] and the Son of Man is being betrayed into the hands of sinners'" (Matt. 26:45).
- "Arise, let us be going; behold, the one who betrays Me is *at hand* [*near*]! And while He was *still speaking*, behold Judas, one of the twelve, came up, accompanied by a great multitude with swords and clubs, from the chief priests and elders of the people" (Matt. 26:46–47).
- "And the Passover of the Jews was *at hand*, and Jesus went up to Jerusalem" (John 2:13; cf. 6:4; 11:55). It was the nearness of the Passover that led Jesus to Jerusalem at this time.
- "Now the feast of the Jews, the Feast of Booths, was *at hand*" (John 7:2).

Every use of "near" or "at hand" in the New Testament means close in relation to time or distance. Because dispensationalists like Walvoord put "prophetic revelation" in a different interpretive category, literalism does not apply.

Walvoord's comment on Revelation 11:14, where he maintains that the word "quickly" is used to describe the timing of Jesus' coming after the rapture, demonstrates how exegetical gerrymandering takes place within the dispensational system: "The third woe contained in the seventh trumpet is announced as coming quickly. *The end of the age is rapidly approaching*."[14] How can "quickly" in Revelation 11:14 mean "rapidly approaching" but Jesus' coming cannot mean "rapidly approaching" in Revelation 2:16, 3:11, 22:7, 12, and 20? A similar question can be asked of Revelation 12:12 where the devil is said to know "that he has only a short time." Walvoord understands "short time" to mean not very long, no more than 3.5 years. The same is true of his interpretation of Revelation 6:11 where the martyrs are "told that they should rest for a little while longer." Why are the time texts in Revelation 6:11 and 12:12 taken literally by Walvoord but the many other time texts in Revelation are given a specialized meaning? The answer is quite simple: The interpretations in both cases are designed to fit an already developed system.

Robert L. Thomas

Similar to the way Pentecost, Feinberg, and Walvoord strip the time texts of Revelation of their natural and plain meaning, Robert Thomas dismisses the "plain and normal" interpretation because such an interpretation would mean "nearness of fulfillment for the events predicted."[15] The time texts are made to conform to an already-developed theological system. According to Thomas these events cannot mean "rapidly approaching" because such an interpretation

> would require the events to have taken place close to John's lifetime. As the matter stands, it has been almost nineteen hundred years since the prediction and much of what the book predicts still has not begun to happen. The response of this view to the seeming difficulty raised by the delay of more than nineteen hundred years is not that John was mistaken but that time in the Apocalypse is computed either relatively to the divine apprehension as here and in 22:10 (cf. also 1:3; 3:11; 22:7, 12, 20) or absolutely in itself as long or short (cf. 8:1; 20:2). *When measuring time, Scripture has a different standard from ours* (cf. 1 John 2:18) (Lee). The purpose of *en tachei* is to teach the imminence of the events foretold, not to set a time limit within which they must occur (Johnson). It must be kept in mind that God is not limited by considerations of time in the same way man is (cf. 2 Pet. 3:8).[16]

Thomas insists on a literal hermeneutic, as do all dispensationalists.[17] This principle avoided, however, when it comes to the plain meaning of certain time texts that do not support his position. Thomas writes that Scripture uses a "different standard from ours" when "measuring time." This just is not the case. The use of "quickly" in other contexts will show that "quickly" has but one meaning.

- John 11:29: "She arose quickly, and was coming to him."
- John 11:31: "Mary rose up quickly and went out."

- John 13:27: "'What you do, do quickly.'"
- Revelation 3:11: "I am coming quickly."
- Revelation 11:14: "The second woe is past; behold, the third woe is coming quickly."

What does "quickly" mean in these passages? Thomas begins with the premise that the events prophesied in Revelation have not taken place and then adjusts the meaning of the time texts to fit his futurist position. He assumes to be true what he must prove to be true, that the events have not taken place. If the time texts are understood in their "plain sense," then there are only two possible meanings: (1) John was mistaken and the Bible is filled with unreliable information,[18] an unacceptable position, or (2) the events described therein came to pass soon after the prophecy was given. Earlier in his commentary Thomas writes:

> The futurist approach to the book is the only one that grants sufficient recognition to the prophetic style of the book and a normal hermeneutical pattern of interpretation based on that style. It views the book as focusing on the last period(s) of world history and outlining the various events and their relationships to one another. *This is the view that best accords with the principle of literal interpretation.*[19]

Again and again Thomas abandons the literal method when he comes to the time texts. He uses 1 John 2:18 and 2 Peter 3:8 in an attempt to prove that "Scripture has a different standard from ours" when it comes to measuring time. This can only be true if one begins with the unproven premise that John was not describing some near eschatological event and that "near," "soon," and "quickly" have a specialized meaning in *some* sections of the Book of Revelation. John's readers had heard that Antichrist was coming. John assures them that "many antichrists have arisen" (1 John 2:18). For John and those who read his letter, this was evidence that it was the "last hour." For Thomas, "last hour" is nearly two thousand years long. Is this what dispensationalists mean by the "principle of literal interpretation"?

Thomas, however, reverses himself when he comes to Revelation 6:11 where the martyrs are told to rest for a "little while." He correctly reasons that "the identical expression comes from the lips of Jesus twice, once in John 7:33 and once in John 12:35. In the former case (John's gospel) the time is not more than about a year, and in the latter, just a matter of days."[20] We must ask Thomas why he does not follow the same procedure in his interpretation of "soon," "quickly," and "near" when he finds these words in the Book of Revelation. He chides those who do not interpret "little while" literally in Revelation 6:11.

> The proposal that it ["little while"] here points to the indefinite future, possibly hundreds of years from the persecution of Christianity under the Roman emperor Trajan to the time of the Waldensians (A.D. 98–1209) or later, is demeaning to the martyrs. Indefiniteness in such a situation is worse than no reply at all.[21]

The same can be said about Jesus' promises that "things must shortly take place" (Revelation 1:1) and the "time is near" (1:3). How would the martyrs have felt in the first century when they read that relief would be in a "little while"? Remember, the last book in the Bible is described as "the Revelation of Jesus Christ" (1:1). These are Jesus' words that the time stretchers are calling into question. Jesus made it clear that He would come in judgment upon Jerusalem within a short span of time. Thomas should follow his method consistently. Of course, if he did, he would no longer be a dispensationalist.

Ed Hindson

Ed Hindson, professor and dean of the Institute of Biblical Studies at Liberty University in Lynchburg, Virginia, writes in *Approaching Armageddon* that "there are no specific time indicators of when" the prophecies outlined in the Book of Revelation "will be fulfilled."[22] In what immediately follows this statement, Hindson contradicts himself and confuses any astute reader.

> The only indication of time is the phrase "the time is at hand" (Greek, *kairos engus*). This may be translated "near" or "soon." Taken with the phrase "come to pass shortly" (Greek, *en tachei*, "soon") in verse 1, the reader is left expecting the imminent return of Christ.

First he tells us that "there are *no* specific time indicators," and then he writes that there are two time indicators: "soon" in 1:1 and "near" or "at hand" in 1:3. After reading these specific time markers the reader is left with the expectation that Jesus' return is "imminent," that it is "near at hand."

Without explaining the obvious contradiction, Hindson moves on as if there is nothing to reconcile.

Earlier Hindson writes that Revelation "is the 'book of the unveiling,'" as the title indicates. It is meant to be understood! Thus, the *promise*: 'Blessed is he that readeth, and they that hear the words of this prophecy, and keep those things which are written therein' (Revelation 1:3)." If the Book of Revelation is "meant to be understood," and its first-century readers expected the "imminent return of Christ," then Jesus' return should have been "near" for *them*. By the way, Hindson does not quote *all* of Revelation 1:3. The verse concludes with, "the time is near."

In addition to words that express time, the Book of Revelation also describes *events* that are time sensitive. History records that the temple in Jerusalem was destroyed in A.D. 70 by Roman armies led by Titus. In Revelation 11:1–2 we read that the temple is standing and people "worship in it" (11:1). In his comments on this section of Scripture, Hindson writes that the temple mentioned in Revelation 11 "must be a third temple yet to be rebuilt by the Jews in Jerusalem in the future."[23] He claims that a "similar reference is made by Paul in 2 Thessalonians 2:3–4, where the 'man of sin' (Antichrist) 'sitteth in the temple of God' claiming to be God."[24] Why must the temple of Revelation 11:1 and 2 Thessalonians 2:4 be a "third temple yet to be rebuilt"? Hindson *assumes* that these temple references are describing a future rebuilt temple simply by stating what he must prove: "Both John (Revelation 11:1–2) and Paul (2 Thessalonians 2:3–4) indicate there will be a future temple in Jerusalem."[25] Where in all the New Testament does it say that there will be a rebuilt temple? Would Christians at Thessalonica have figured out that Paul was describing a rebuilt temple when the temple in Jerusalem was still standing when they received his letter? The description of the still operating temple in Revelation 11:1 is a key indicator as to when the Book was written, prior to the sacking of Jerusalem and the destruction of the temple in A.D. 70.

Fellow-dispensational writer Stanley D. Toussaint unwittingly destroys Hindson's logic. In determining when Matthew's gospel was written, Toussaint engages in a bit of logic of his own.

[Matthew's gospel] was written no doubt before 70 A.D. The city of Jerusalem was still standing at the time of writing. This is shown by the fact that Matthew refers to it as the "holy city" as though it was still in existence (4:5; 27:53). He does not mention its destruction as having been accomplished at any point.[26]

Toussaint's deduction can also apply to Revelation when the same principles are applied. Jerusalem is described as the "holy city" (11:2; 21:2, 10; 22:19), and John "does not mention its destruction," therefore the temple was still standing when John wrote. There is no need to conjure up a rebuilt temple. John's use of "shortly" and "near" in Revelation 1:1, 3 makes perfect sense.

A Modern Parable

You find that your son's room is a mess. Not an unusual occurrence. You give the following instructions: "Clean up your room, and do it *quickly*. I'll be back *soon* to check on your progress." An hour later you examine your son's work and find his room in the same state of disrepair as when you first saw it. You ask your son why his room is not clean, reminding him that you told him to do it *quickly* and that you would return *soon* to inspect it. He says, "Dad, you said you would be back 'soon.' As you know, the time element holds a relatively small place in room cleaning. Besides, when I start to clean it, I'll do it quickly! I could clean it today or next week, either way, I will follow your instructions to the letter."

There is no way around these texts. "Soon," "near," and "at hand" are explicit time indicators that are meant to describe a period of time in the near future. While days, weeks, months, and years are not specified, we can be certain that the events that are said to be "near," "soon," and coming "quickly" are not far off in time. Or as Walvoord describes it, the events that follow are "rapidly approaching."

Using 2 Peter 3:8 to Stretch Time

The favorite text of the time stretchers is 2 Peter 3:8. When all else fails the time extenders point to this passage as proof positive that time texts are not what they seem.

> But do not let this one fact escape your notice, beloved, that with the Lord one day is as a thousand years, and a thousand years as one day (2 Peter 3:8).

The argument goes something like this: "Yes, the Book of Revelation does use the words 'near,' 'quickly,' and 'shortly,' but words related to time must be interpreted in the light of 2 Peter 3:8. Remember, 'that with the Lord one day is as a thousand years, and a thousand years as one day.' While the Book of Revelation *seems* to teach that Jesus would come 'quickly' in judgment, and the time was 'near' for this event, we know that He was not discussing time from our perspective." Convenient but not very convincing.

Supposedly, while "near," "quickly," and "shortly" are used in a *literal* sense in *every other New Testament passage where they occur,* in the Book of Revelation we are told that they should be interpreted *figuratively,* except, of course, when they need to be interpreted literally. This line of argumentation is surprising when it is put forth by those who insist on a literal interpretation of Scripture. Why don't the literalists want to interpret "near," "quickly," and "shortly" literally in the Book of Revelation when they interpret these same words literally elsewhere in the Bible? Why doesn't 2 Peter 3:8 apply to all references to time? Why just in certain prophetic passages? The Book of Revelation on ten separate occasions, at the beginning (1:1, 3; 2:16; 3:11), in the middle (11:14), and at the end (22:6, 7, 10, 12, 20), speaks of the nearness of some great eschatological event.

Centuries before John wrote the Book of Revelation Daniel was told to conceal the words of the prophecy and "seal up the book until the end of time..." (Dan. 12:4). John, on the other hand, is told the opposite: "Do not seal up the words of the prophecy of this book, for the time is near" (Rev. 22:10). If we apply the 2 Peter 3:8 principle of measuring time to Daniel 12:4 and Revelation 22:10, we can conclude that Daniel's time was actually near and John's time is still in the distant future. One commentator writes: "It is true that history has shown that 'the things which must shortly come to pass' (1:1) have taken longer than John expected."[27] History has shown no such thing. God's Word is true. The Bible states without equivocation that the time was near for God to pour out His wrath on those who persecuted the saints. Since the Book of Revelation was written prior to the destruction of Jerusalem in A.D. 70, the time texts make perfect sense.[28]

At one point the martyred saints ask, "*How long,* O Lord, holy and true, wilt Thou refrain from judging and avenging our blood on those who dwell on the earth?" (Rev. 6:10). "They were told that they should rest for a *little while longer*" (6:11). What does "a little while longer" mean using 2 Peter

3:8? Those who suggest a non-literal interpretation of "near," "shortly," and "quickly" must also view "a little while longer" in the same way. But this calls into question the reliability of the Bible and makes nonsense of clear statements. Such an interpretation would be little comfort to those martyred saints who asked "How long, O Lord?"

In light of the time texts, how should 2 Peter 3:8 be applied? First, there is nothing in this passage or in any other passage that tells us that any time text should be filtered through 2 Peter 3:8. Second, if time texts are fluid in relation to 2 Peter 3:8, then we could never know what God means relative to time. In fact, we would have to conclude that time texts always mean their opposite. Third, 2 Peter 3:8 gives us a clue as to how *God* views time. Notice that 2 Peter 3:8 states that "*with the Lord* one day is *as* a thousand years." Fourth, we are not told that "with the Lord one day *is* a thousand years." Rather, "one day is *as* a thousand years." Are dispensationalists willing to admit that the thousand years of Revelation 20 can be reduced to a single day? Will the plagues described in Revelation 18:8 take a thousand years to come? Did Jesus really mean that He would take three thousand years to rebuild the temple (John 2:19)? Is Jesus still in Joseph of Arimathea's tomb since three days really means three thousand years (Matt. 27:63)?

> With all allowance for linguistic flexibility and comparative lengths of periods, it would be stretching language to the breaking point to make "shortly" mean several thousands of years. Such interpretations are only trifling with words, and the Word of God. The force of these words is decisive. The things that were to be shown in the visions were close at hand; they were to begin with the people to whom the book was written and not thousands of years in the future. God is His own interpreter and must be allowed to say what He means, and what God says in explanation of His own prophecies must be taken in its obvious meaning and regarded as authoritative.[29]

If the Bible can be interpreted so "soon" can mean "late," and "near" can mean "distant," and "shortly" can mean "delayed," and *vice versa*, then the Bible can mean anything and nothing. Does God have two methods of measurement? When God says "love," are we to read "hate?" Can we trust a God whose words can mean their opposite?

God's Own Commentary on Time

Ezekiel, as God's prophet, is called upon to take a message to the land of Israel: "An end! The end is coming on the four corners of the land" (Ezek. 7:2). How far off is this "end"? "The time has come, *the day is near*—tumult rather than joyful shouting on the mountains" (7:7). Ezekiel's message is that God "will *shortly* pour out" His wrath upon a covenant-breaking nation (7:8).[30]

The people did not listen to Ezekiel's prophetic word. Maybe they had Psalm 90:4 in mind when they heard that the judgment was "near": "For a thousand years in Thy sight are like yesterday when it passes by, or as a watch in the night." As an object lesson, so no one could misunderstand, God tells Ezekiel to prepare himself and his "baggage for exile" (12:3). He was to "go into exile by day in their sight" (12:3). Again and again Ezekiel acted out scenes depicting exile, an exile that was on the horizon (12:4–7). How did the people interpret the clear words of the prophet? They did just what the time stretchers do in our day: They concluded that "near" and "shortly" do not mean soon, impending, or approaching. God asks Ezekiel about a proverb that was going around: "Son of man, what is this proverb you people have concerning the land of Israel, saying, 'The days are long and every vision fails'?" (12:22). The people were disputing the nearness of the judgment by claiming that there was plenty of time. In fact, they asserted that Ezekiel's prediction about the nearness of judgment would fail to come to pass.

So as not to be misunderstood, God defines what He means by "near" and "shortly": "Therefore say to them, 'Thus says the Lord GOD, "I will make this proverb cease so that they will no longer use it as a proverb in Israel." But tell them, "The days draw near as well as the fulfillment of every vision"'" (12:23). Contrary to what the people thought, "The vision that [Ezekiel] sees" was not delayed "for many years from now." He is not prophesying "of times far off" (12:26). "They did not deny that a day of evil was coming, but indulged the hope that it might still be at a considerable distance."[31] God, through Ezekiel, set them straight.

Ezekiel's description of the imminent destruction of the temple and the city of Jerusalem parallels what happened to Israel after the ascension and enthronement of Jesus. A warning of impending doom had been given to the nation. Many ignored the warning and died in the conflagration that came upon the city in A.D. 70, one generation after Jesus pronounced His judgment (Matt. 24:14, 34; 1 Peter 4:7; Rev. 1:1, 3).

The Book of Genesis offers a commentary on the way God tells time. Pharaoh dreams of cows and ears of corn, some fat and some lean (Gen. 41:1–7). None of Pharaoh's magicians and wise men could interpret the dream (41:8). Joseph is finally called upon to try his hand at an interpretation. Through this dream God was telling Pharaoh that there would be seven years of plenty and seven years of famine in Egypt (41:17–31). Preparations were to be made during the seven years of abundance so the nation would survive during the seven years of famine. When would this happen? "Now as for the repeating of the dream to Pharaoh twice, it means that the matter is determined, and God *will quickly bring it about*" (41:32). How is "quickly" to be understood? The prophecy is fulfilled in Joseph's lifetime (41:46–49). Philip Mauro sets forth his reasons why he believes words that deal with time can only be interpreted literally:

> [T]he very first verse [in Revelation] states that God's purpose in giving the revelation to Jesus Christ was that he might "show unto His servants things which must *shortly come to pass*". These words are not at all ambiguous, and the simple-minded would never suspect that they could have been intended to convey any other than their ordinary and apparent meaning, namely, that the things foretold in "this prophecy" were to happen in the era that was just then beginning. The word here rendered "shortly" means *just that.* It is variously translated in other Scriptures by the words *quickly, speedily, soon.* Thus, in Acts 25:4, Festus, after commanding that Paul be kept at Caesarea, said that "he himself would depart *shortly* thither". In Philippians 2:19 Paul writes, "I trust to send Timotheus unto you *shortly*". And so also in 1 Timothy 3:14; Hebrews 13:23; and 2 Peter 1:14. In Galatians 1:6 we have, "so *soon* removed"; in Philippians 2:33, "so *soon* as I shall see how it will go with"; and in 2 Thessalonians 2:2, "That ye be not *soon* shaken in mind."[32]

Based on the way "quickly," "near," and "shortly" are used in Genesis through Revelation, any student of the Bible who does not interpret these time texts in the way the Bible uses them is in jeopardy of denying the integrity of the Bible.

Notes

1. J. Dwight Pentecost, *Things to Come: A Study in Biblical Eschatology* (Grand Rapids, MI: Zondervan/Academie, [1958] 1964), 46.

2. Gerald B. Stanton, "The Doctrine of Imminency: Is It Biblical?," in Thomas Ice and Timothy Demy, eds., *When the Trumpet Sounds* (Eugene, OR: Harvest House, 1995), 222.

3. Thomas Ice and Timothy Demy, *Fast Facts on Bible Prophecy* (Eugene, OR: Harvest House, 1997), 102–103. Emphasis added.

4. Does "right at the door" mean near for the dispensationalist during the tribulation period?

5. Thomas Ice, "The Great Tribulation is Future: The New Testament," in Thomas Ice and Kenneth L. Gentry, Jr., *The Great Tribulation: Past or Present?: Two Evangelicals Debate the Question* (Grand Rapids, MI: Kregel, 1999), 113.

6. Charles C. Ryrie, *Dispensationalism*, 2nd ed. (Chicago, IL: Moody Press, 1995), 20.

7. Ryrie, *Dispensationalism*, 80.

8. Ryrie, *Dispensationalism*, 40.

9. Charles L. Feinberg, "Revelation," *Liberty Bible Commentary*, eds. Edward E. Hindson and Woodrow M. Kroll (Lynchburg, VA: The Old-Time Gospel Hour, 1982), 2:790.

10. Kurt Aland, *A History of Christianity: From the Beginnings to the Threshold of the Reformation*, trans. James L. Schaff (Philadelphia, PA: Fortress Press, 1985), 88.

11. Feinberg, "Revelation," 2:790.

12. John F. Walvoord, *The Revelation of Jesus Christ* (Chicago, IL: Moody Press, [1966] 1987), 35.

13. Walvoord, *The Revelation of Jesus Christ*, 37.

14. Walvoord, *The Revelation of Jesus Christ*, 183.

15. Robert L. Thomas, *Revelation 1–7* (Chicago, IL: Moody Press, 1992), 55.

16. Thomas, *Revelation 1–7*, 55–56. Emphasis added.

17. Thomas, *Revelation 1–7*, 29–39.

18. "These events are 'soon to take place' (cf. 11:18; 22:10). These words have troubled commentators. The simplest solution is to take the preterist view and to say that John, like the entire Christian community, thought that the coming of the Lord was near, when in fact they were wrong. Our Lord himself seems to share this error in perspective in the saying: 'This generation will not pass away before all these things take place' (Mark 13:30).... How-

ever, the simple meaning cannot be avoided. The problem is raised by the fact that the prophets were little interested in chronology, and the future was always viewed as imminent." (George Eldon Ladd, *A Commentary on the Revelation of John* [Grand Rapids, MI: Eerdmans, 1972], 22).

19. Thomas, *Revelation 1–7*, 32. Emphasis added.

20. Thomas, *Revelation 1–7*, 447.

21. Thomas, *Revelation 1–7*, 448–49.

22. Ed Hindson, *Approaching Armageddon: The World Prepares for War With God* (Eugene, OR: Harvest House, 1997), 36.

23. Hindson, *Approaching Armageddon*, 172.

24. Hindson, *Approaching Armageddon*, 172.

25. Hindson, *Approaching Armageddon*, 174.

26. Stanley D. Toussaint, *Behold the King: A Study of Matthew* (Portland, OR: Multnomah, 1981), 333.

27. Robert H. Mounce, *The Book of Revelation* (Grand Rapids, MI: Eerdmans, 1977), 243.

28. J. Barton Payne, a premillennialist, wrote that "internal evidence, which is drawn from the predictions contained within the book itself, is more suited to the days of Nero [A.D. 64–68]. Unless John's reference in 11:1 to the (Jerusalem) temple be taken figuratively, this structure's mere existence would require a date before 70; the writer's silence in respect to the course of the Jewish War, and his *predictions* of its devastation and 3 1/2-year duration in 11:2, suggest a date prior to the winter of 66; and his symbolical specification in 17:10 of the currently reigning Roman emperor as the sixth of this line of rulers accords most easily with the historical position of Nero." (*Encyclopedia of Biblical Prophecy: The Complete Guide to Scriptural Predictions and Their Fulfillment* [Grand Rapids, MI: Baker Book House (1973) 1980], 592).

29. David S. Clark, *The Message from Patmos: A Postmillennial Commentary on the Book of Revelation* (Grand Rapids, MI: Baker Book House, 1989), 22–23.

30. I am indebted to Don K. Preston's *Can God Tell Time?* (Ardmore, OK: Don K. Preston, 1992) for the material in this section.

31. Patrick Fairbairn, *An Exposition of Ezekiel* (Evansville, IN: Sovereign Grace Publishers, 1960), 123.

32. Philip Mauro, *The Patmos Visions: A Study of the Apocalypse* (Boston, MA: Scripture Truth Depot, 1925), 24–25.

Appendix 2

FRUITLESS TREES AND NATIONAL ISRAEL

Israel becoming a nation again in 1948 is the key to much of today's prophetic speculation regarding the last days. For support of this view, futurists appeal to Matthew 24:32: "Now learn the parable of the fig tree: when its branch has already become tender, and puts forth its leaves, you know that summer is near." This text has been made to read: "Now learn about restored nationhood for Israel. When Israel becomes a nation again, similar to the way a fig tree puts forth leaves to herald the coming of summer, then you will know that I am near to rapture the church." Of course, this is not what the text says. These questionable ideas are imported into the text from an already developed eschatological system.

Hal Lindsey has made the most popular case for the view. He writes that "the figure of speech 'fig tree' has been a historic symbol of national Israel."[1] This claim, of course, is irrelevant since we are looking for *biblical* symbols. For the moment, however, let us assume that Lindsey is correct, and the "fig tree" is a *biblical* symbol of national Israel. Let us go further and assert that Jesus is using the "fig tree" illustration in Matthew 24:32 to say something about the fate of national Israel. In what way does the Bible apply the fig tree to Israel's national destiny? For blessing or cursing?

Jerusalem's Judgment

There is not a single verse in the New Testament that supports the claim that there is prophetic significance in Israel's restoration as a nation. Beyond A.D. 70, Israel as a nation plays no prophetic role. The New Testament only addresses Israel's near destruction never its distant restoration. There is no mention of a temple being rebuilt or Jews returning to their land as was predicted in the Old Testament. The Jews did return to their land as prophesied (Jer. 29:14), "when seventy years have been completed for Babylon" (29:10; cf. Dan. 9:2). The temple was eventually rebuilt as predicted (Ezra 5:16; John 2:20). These prophecies have been fulfilled. Isaiah 11:11 does mention Israel returning to their land "the second time." A remnant of Israelites returned to their land after the Babylonian captivity. The first time was "the day that they came up out of the land of Egypt" (11:16).[2] There is no mention of a third time. If the Old Testament is the pattern, then we should expect to see specific New Testament prophecies regarding the future reestablishment of Israel as a nation and the rebuilding of the temple.

Some futurists maintain that the land promises were never completely fulfilled. Walter Kaiser offers his opinion contrary to what the Bible actually says.

> Oftentimes students of the Bible point to three passages that appear to suggest that the promise of land to Israel has indeed been fulfilled: Joshua 21:43–45; 23:14–15; Nehemiah 9:8. These texts assert that "not one of all the LORD's good promises to the house of Israel failed; every one was fulfilled" (Josh. 21:45; cf. 23:14).

> However, the boundaries mentioned in Numbers 34:2–12 are not the ones reached in the accounts of Joshua and Judges. For example, Joshua 13:1–7 and Judges 3:1–4 agree in maintaining that there was much land that remained to be taken.[3]

The Bible tells a different story: "So the LORD gave Israel all the land which He had sworn to their fathers, and they possessed it and lived in it" (Josh. 21:43). To establish this point, we read, "Not one of the good promises which the LORD had made to the house of Israel failed; all came to pass" (21:45). Could the Bible be any more clear? God kept all of His promises to the letter. God is not obligated to do more than He pledged.

Futurists acknowledge the absence of any direct reference to a rebuilt temple, restored nationhood, or reestablishment to the land in the New Testament, so they insist that the fig tree illustration in Matthew 24:32 compensates for this silence. Contrary to what futurists assert, a study of *all* the New Testament texts that compare Israel to a fig tree points to Jerusalem's destruction not its restoration.

Trees Without Fruit

Matthew 21 and the parallel passages in Mark and Luke shed a great deal of light on the fig tree illustration in Matthew 24:32. Matthew 21 begins with the triumphal entry of Jesus into Jerusalem and the people "cutting branches from the trees, and spreading them in the road," honoring Him as the "Son of David" (Matt. 21:8–9). Mark writes that they had spread "*leafy* branches" (Mark 11:8). As Jesus approached Jerusalem, He "wept over it" because of its persistent unbelief and its soon-to-be revealed fate (Luke 19:39–40).

Mark tells us that Jesus "entered Jerusalem and came into the temple; and after looking all around, He departed for Bethany with the twelve, since it was already late" (Mark 11:11). Was He looking for "fruit" (*i.e.,* good works) from those who frequented the temple? On His return from Bethany to Jerusalem, from a distance, Jesus saw "a fig tree in *leaf*" and upon closer inspection "found nothing but *leaves*" (11:13). He cursed the fruitless, leaves-only tree: "May no one ever eat fruit from you again!" (11:14). Matthew tells it this way: "'No longer shall there *ever* be any fruit from you.' And at once the fig tree withered" (Matt. 21:19). "The cursing of the figtree signifies that the entry to Jerusalem and the temple story should not be understood as a Messianic purification, but as a visitation in judgment upon the temple."[4] The nineteenth-century dispensationalist author John Cumming understands what Jesus had in mind when He cursed the fig tree:

> All who have compared the context and the circumstances in which that miracle was wrought, have one unanimous conclusion, that in blasting the fig-tree it could not possibly be a momentary ebullition of anger, or an expression of disappointment, in the Son of God; nor was the fig-tree regarded as a responsible and therefore guilty thing; it was a lesson to the Jews, adorned with the leaves of a magnificent profession; watered,

tended, sunned, and showered on for many generations past, but with no fruit corresponding to their privileges, or at all to justify their loud and boasting profession; our Lord blasted the fig-tree, and pronounced a lasting anathema upon it, not because the fig-tree was guilty, but to teach the nation of whom it was a symbol, that their hypocrisy at last had filled up their cup, and that the day of their destruction, dispersion, and judgment was now at hand.[5]

Cumming is correct. But we must go one step further. If the nation of Israel is to be identified with the fig tree, then Jesus makes it clear that as a nation she will never produce fruit.[6] Those who insist that Matthew 24:32 is describing renewed *covenantal* status for Israel as a significant eschatological sign conveniently overlook what Jesus said about fruit *never* coming from the fig tree: "No longer shall there *ever* be any fruit from you." Jesus forces the Jews to view the temple in a new light.

Mark's Gospel reveals a significant re-evaluation of Jerusalem's Temple. Although Jesus affirms the significance of the Temple within God's purposes (hence his quoting Isaiah's reference to it as '*my* house'), he declares in word and deed that it now stands under judgement. Jesus enters the Temple as the Lord himself inspecting his own property and judging it for its lack of fruit. In due course, it will be destroyed. Its destruction, however, is also integrally linked to the person of Jesus, whom Mark portrays as God's appointed replacement of the Temple. Now that the new has come, the old must pass away.[7]

After His encounter with the fig tree, Jesus returned to Jerusalem and, entering the temple, "began to cast out those who were buying and selling in the temple" (Mark 11:15). It was at this point that the "chief priests and the scribes ... began seeking how to destroy Him" (11:18). Once again Jesus leaves the city and comes upon "the fig tree withered from the roots up" (11:20).

The encounter with the fig tree is not a minor literary diversion. The cursing of the fig tree and the cleansing of the temple are related. Jerusalem, the temple, the people, and the religious leaders were fruitless. They had the outward appearance of religion (leaves) but produced no works (fruit) (Matt. 3:8, 10; 7:17–19; 12:33; 13:23; 21:43; 23:27). Jesus was looking for the fruit of repentance from Israel. Finding no fruit, Jesus promised to cut down the fig tree (Israel).

> And He began telling this parable: "A certain man had a fig tree which had been planted in his vineyard; and he came looking for fruit on it, and did not find any. And he said to the vineyard keeper, 'Behold, for three years I have come looking for fruit on this fig tree without finding any. Cut it down! Why does it even use up the ground?' And he answered and said to him, 'Let it alone, sir, for this year too, until I dig around it and put in fertilizer; and if it bears fruit next year, fine; but if not, cut it down'" (Luke 13:6–9).

This parable is an obvious reference to Jerusalem's impending judgment (cf. Isa. 5:1–7). Jesus was in the third year of His ministry when He concluded that the nation was not worth preserving. He would give it one more growing season before passing judgment. The response of the Jewish leadership to Jesus' disciples meant that God would cut Israel down (Luke 13:9). When would this come to pass? "For the days shall come upon you when your enemies will throw up a bank before you, and surround you, and hem you in on every side, and will level you to the ground and your children within you, and they will not leave one stone upon another, because you did not recognize the time of your visitation" (Luke 19:43–44). What was the "visitation" that they "did not recognize"? "He came to His own, and those who were His own did not receive Him" (John 1:11). Only when Jesus came to destroy Jerusalem in A.D. 70 did the apostate Jews of that generation recognize His visitation (Matt. 24:30; John 19:37; Rev. 1:7).

> The incident about the unproductive fig tree (Mk. 11:12–14, 20–21) involves a prophetic warning of the terrible fate that would come upon the nation. Jesus saw an ownerless fig tree full of leaves but without fruit growing on it. The grand display of foliage was nothing but empty pretense, just as the glorious temple of gold and marble and its ceremony lacked the presence of God-fearing people. Jesus cursed the tree and it soon withered, indicating that judgment awaited Jerusalem.[8]

Israel had not displayed the fruit of righteousness required by God (cf. Hosea 2:12). Notice that Jesus does not say, "Now learn the parable from the fig tree: when it puts forth its *fruit*, you know that summer is near." The tree only showed *leaves*. Every instance of a leaves–only tree in the gospels is a sign of Israel's judgment, a judgment that came in A.D. 70. Matthew 24:32 has to be embellished in order to make it contradict Matthew 21:19 where Jesus emphatically states that no fruit will ever come forth from the fig tree. David Reagan writes: "Now, the next day, Jesus calls the fig tree to mind and says, 'Watch it. When it *reblossoms*, all these things will happen.'"[9] Cumming, who believes that there is prophetic significance to Israel's renewed national status, mentions a future tree that puts "forth its *buds*."[10] Jesus told His disciples the day before that the fig tree would never produce fruit. Reagan and Cumming have Jesus contradicting Himself. The fig tree of Matthew 24:32 only puts forth "leaves." There is no mention of "blossoms" or "buds."

From the Roots

Unfortunately, the clear testimony of the Bible does not convince those who are intent on making the Bible fit their preconceived view of prophecy. Philip N. Moore, a self-proclaimed "researcher for Hal Lindsey," demonstrates the absurd measures one must go through in order to get a text to fit unproven assumptions about the Bible.

Moore believes that the cursing of the fig tree is temporary. When the Bible says "from the roots," Moore claims that "the trunk and the branches and the leaves all withered away, but not the roots."[11] Moore calls on M. R. DeHaan to support his conclusion:

> Mark tells us a very interesting detail, which is well worth repeating: "And in the morning, as they passed by, they saw the fig tree dried up from the roots" (Mark 11:20). The last three words of this verse tell the story. *From the roots*. Remember *from* the roots. In other words, the trunk and the branches and the leaves all withered away, but *not the roots*. The root remained alive while the rest of the tree withered away. Now the trunk and the branches and leaves are the visible part of the tree, the roots are beneath the ground and are the invisible part of the tree.[12]

Moore concludes, "Surely language could be no plainer than that."[13] I don't know what horticulture school DeHaan and Moore attended, but when the trunk, leaves, and branches wither *it's because the roots are dead*. A counter example might help to illustrate the absurdity of their line of argument. Nebuchadnezzar had a dream of a large tree that was chopped down, its branches removed, and its foliage and fruit scattered (Dan. 4:14). The stump remained "with its roots in the ground, but with a band of iron and bronze around it" (4:15). Notice that the tree was fruit-producing (4:14). The roots remained alive with the band squeezed around its trunk to inhibit growth for a season. The lesson? Nebuchadnezzar was judged for a time but was later restored (4:24–27). When the band was later removed, the tree once again produced fruit. No such promise is made in reference to the fig tree. The fig tree is withered "from the roots."

Moore maintains that "from the roots" does not include the roots. Such an interpretation shows how desperate he is to gain support for his dispensational view. I don't know of anyone who would exclude the roots with the phrase "from the roots." Let's put Moore's outrageous theory to the test by turning to the Bible. Every time you read "from" keep in mind that Moore would see it as an exclusion.

- "Therefore all the generations from Abraham to David" (Matt. 1:17). Following Moore's interpretation, Abraham would not be included.
- "From two years and under" (Matt. 2:16). According to Moore, no baby two-years-old would have been included in Herod's slaughter.
- "Then Jesus arrived from Galilee at the Jordan" (Matt. 3:13). According to Moore, Jesus really arrived from somewhere else other than Galilee.
- "Shake off the dust from the soles of your feet" (Mark 6:11). According to Moore, the soles of the disciples' feet were to remain dusty.
- "From childhood" (Mark 9:21). According to Moore, childhood was not included.

As you can see, Moore's interpretation is absurd. "From the roots" includes the roots just as it includes whatever the word "from" precedes in a phrase. The fig tree withered because the roots were dead. To quote Moore, "Surely language could be no plainer than that."

A Double Negation

To further compound his error, Moore once again abandons his call for the literal interpretation of the Bible. After Jesus curses the fig tree, He says,

"'No longer shall there ever be any fruit from you,' And at once the fig tree withered." Mark tells it this way: "May no one ever eat fruit from you again!" (Mark 11:14). Once again, drawing on DeHaan for support, Moore concludes that "The word translated *forever* is *aion* in the Greek original, and means an *age*, a period of time, or a dispensation. So what Jesus really said was 'Let no fruit grow on thee for an age, or a dispensation, for a period of time.'"[13] Moore and DeHaan are mistaken. In addition to the Greek word *aion*, two other Greek words are used which are translated "no longer" and "no one." When coupled with *aion*, they create an idiom. In this case, "*May no one ever eat* is a special form of utterance which has parallels in some languages in a simple future 'no one will ever' or with a somewhat more emphatic introductory expression, 'it will be very so that no one will ever'. The form is that of a curse upon the fig tree."[14] C. F. D. Moule in his *Idiom-Book of New Testament Greek* calls the phrase "most vehemently prohibitive."[15] In *A Greek-English Lexicon to the New Testament*, citing Matthew 21:19 and Mark 11:14, the authors state that the wording is designed as a "piling up of negatives . . . a double negation."[16]

Using the fig tree illustration in Matthew 24:32 to support the claim that all Bible prophecy hinges on Israel's national restoration is a weak reed. Why would God choose a metaphor as the key sign? It doesn't make any sense. If dispensationalists still want to maintain that Israel is the fig tree in Matthew 24:32, then they must live with the implications of the cursed fig tree in Matthew 21:19.

Notes

1. Hal Lindsey, *The Late Great Planet Earth* (Grand Rapids, MI: Zondervan, 1970), 53–54.

2. William Hendriksen, *Israel In Prophecy* (Grand Rapids, MI: Baker Books, 1968).

3. Walter C. Kaiser, Jr., *Back Toward the Future: Hints for Interpreting Biblical Prophecy* (Grand Rapids, MI: Baker Books, 1989), 111.

4. Kent E. Brower, "'Let the reader Understand': Temple and Eschatology in Mark," *Eschatology in Bible and Theology: Evangelical Essays at the Dawn of a New Millennium*, Kent E. Brower and Mark W. Elliott, eds. (Downers Grove, IL: InterVarsity Press, [1997] 1999), 135. Brower's observations are based on the seminal work of W. R. Telford, *The Barren Temple and the Withered Tree* (JSNTSS 1. Sheffield: JSOT, 1980).

5. John Cumming, *The End: or, The Proximate Signs of the Close of this Dispensation* (Boston, MA: John P. Jewett and Co., 1855), 139–40.

6. We can expect individual *Israelites* to produce both good and bad fruit (Jer. 24; Matt. 3:7–10; John 1:47). Of course, the same is true of Gentiles (Matt. 7:17–19).

7. P.W.L. Walker, *Jesus and the Holy City: New Testament Perspectives on Jerusalem* (Grand Rapids, MI: Eerdmans, 1996), 12–13.

8. Stanley W. Paher, *If Thou Hadst Known* (Las Vegas, NV: Nevada Publications, 1978), 54.

9. David Reagan, *The Master Plan: Making Sense of the Controversies Surrounding Bible Prophecy Today* (Eugene, OR: Harvest House, 1993), 183. Emphasis added.

10. Cumming, *The End*, 140. Emphasis added.

11. Philip N. Moore, *A Liberal Interpretation on the Prophecy of Israel—Disproved* (Atlanta, GA: The Conspiracy, Incorporated, 1997), 9.

12. M. R. DeHaan, *The Jew and Palestine in Prophecy*, 2nd ed. (Grand Rapids, MI: Zondervan, 1950), 149.

13. Moore, *A Liberal Interpretation on the Prophecy of Israel—Disproved*, 9.

14. DeHaan, *The Jew and Palestine in Prophecy*, 148.

15. C. F. D. Moule, *An Idiom-Book of the Greek New Testament*, 2nd ed. (London, England: Cambridge Univesity Press, [1959] 1977), 136.

16. William F. Arndt and F. Wilbur Gingrich, *A Greek-English Lexicon to the New Testament and Other Early Christian Literature*, 4th ed. (Chicago, IL: University of Chicago Press, 1952), 520.

Appendix 3

"ANTI-SEMITISM" AND ESCHATOLOGY

I n *The Living End,* Charles Ryrie sets forth his belief that the Bible predicts "the time of Israel's greatest bloodbath."[1] This is true, Ryrie contends, because the Bible is "history prewritten."[2] Indeed, the Bible does predict a judgment on the Jews, but this event is now history. Instead of encouraging Jews to emigrate to the doomed city, Jesus warned the inhabitants of Jerusalem to flee from a judgment that was near at hand for them (Matt. 24:16).[3] Ryrie and other dispensationalists have futurized prophecies related to the destruction of Jerusalem beyond their intended first-century time frame and audience. As we will see, this method has had dire consequences for the Jews.

Name Calling

Why have some dispensationalists shifted their attack against non-dispensationalists from exegetical arguments to *ad hominem* attacks? There is one simple answer: They can no longer defend their system by an appeal to the Bible or to history. Rank and file dispensationalists are jumping ship, and those who remain are redefining the system out of existence. Here is an example:

For years, dispensational theology, with its differentiation of God's program for the church and for Israel, shaped conservative evangelical views. Its literal interpretation of prophecy, promoted by the Scofield Bible and scholars from Dallas Theological Seminary, marked the restoration of Israel as the starting point for many other end-times prophecies, culminating in Christ's return.

But some say the influence of traditional dispensationalism has declined in the past decade. Others, like Darrell Bock, professor of New Testament at Dallas, say it's entering a new phase. He sees it going through a period of self-assessment. A new, "progressive dispensationalism" is emerging, one that is less "land-centered" and "future-centered" than past versions.[4]

Others are questioning dispensational "orthodoxy." For example, Robert L. Saucy, tells us, "Over the past several decades the system of theological interpretation commonly known as dispensationalism has undergone considerable development and refinement." [5] The change has been radical enough to warrant the giving of a new label—progressive dispensationalism—"to distinguish the new interpretations from the older version of dispensationalism.[6]

In *Dispensationalism, Israel and the Church: The Search for Definition*, the contributors describe how dispensationalism has changed and will continue to change. One writer states that "dispensationalism has been in the process of change since its earliest origins within the Plymouth Bretheren [*sic*] movement of the nineteenth century."[7] In the same series, Craig Blaising admits and welcomes "modifications currently taking place in dispensational thought."[8]

A few old-school dispensationalists remain, but they can no longer turn to their more scholarly counterparts for exegetical backup support, so they resort to a highly effective form of name calling: "If a person does not believe that the Bible teaches that Old Testament prophecies predict a future re-establishment of national Israel he or she is *anti-semitic*."[9] Those who study the Old Testament prophecies related to Israel note that these prophecies have been fulfilled in (1) the return of the Jews after their exile into Assyria and Babylon and (2) the first-century establishment of the Jewish church.[10]

A careful study of dispensational rhetoric, reasoning, history, and theology will demonstrate that dispensationalism has within its system the seeds of "theological anti-semitism."

Messianic Vision?

Sid Roth, host of "Messianic Vision," on the September 18, 1991, edition of the "700 Club," stated that "two-thirds of the Jewish people [living in Israel] will be exterminated." He, along with other futurists, bases this belief on a futurized interpretation of Zechariah 13:8–9. He sees incidents like that of Blacks against Jews in New York as a prelude to a coming great persecution. Pat Robertson asked Roth: "You don't foresee some kind of persecution against Jews in America, do you?" Roth responded: "Unfortunately, I believe God foresees this." Roth believes that the end (pre-tribulational rapture) is near. Since he believes that Jews are destined to suffer, based on a futurized interpretation of Zechariah 13:8–9,[11] he postulates that today's anti-semitism is a prelude to a greater, future tribulation. The reality of violent acts against Jews today is all part of the inevitabilities that come with dispensational premillennialism. What is the origin of this position?

The Rupture of Theology

The pre-tribulational rapture is the key to dispensational eschatology. The pre-tribulational rapture separates dispensationalism from other forms of premillennialism as well as amillennialism and postmillennialism. This is what makes it a "fourth view" of eschatology.[12] According to dispensationalism, prior to the rapture, *Israel has no prophetic significance*. This is carried to a consistent extreme by some dispensationalists who claim that Jews once again must be ejected from their homeland and brought back as *believing* Israelites. Dr. Paige Patterson stated this position on a Dallas, Texas, radio program (KCBI) on May 15, 1991. He said:

> The present state of Israel is not the final form. The present state of Israel will be lost, eventually, and Israel will be run out of the land again, only to return when they accept the Messiah as Savior.

It is only in this way, so the theory goes, that the prophecies concerning Israel's restoration can literally be fulfilled in prophetic time, that is, after the rapture of the church. Israel's expulsion occurs prior to the rapture with the church looking on. Would Christians be fighting against God if they helped the Jews hold on to their land? Would they be anti-semitic if they allowed prophecy to unfold and saw millions of Jews persecuted by their enemies?

The Parenthesis

Standard dispensationalism has always taught that the prophetic time clock stopped ticking when Israel rejected Jesus as the Messiah. This rejection put the conclusion of Daniel's seventy weeks (490 years) on hold. Israel experienced 483 years of the prophecy outlined by God in Daniel 9:24-27. The final week—the seven years that will complete the prophecy—is still to take place. This is the period of "Jacob's trouble" when Israel will go through never before experienced persecution. Of course, as with much of dispensationalism, there are no verses that support this view. One must be an expert in reading between the verses.

The result of such a system means that *Israel has no prophetic significance in God's program until the church is raptured prior to the seven-year tribulation period* (Daniel's 70th week). This is the dispensational view as ably articulated by E. Schuyler English:

> An intercalary period of history, after Christ's death and resurrection and the destruction of Jerusalem in A.D. 70, has intervened. This is the present age, the Church age. . . . *During this time God has not been dealing with Israel nationally, for they have been blinded concerning God's mercy in Christ.* . . . However, God will again deal with Israel as a nation. This will be in Daniel's seventieth week, a seven-year period yet to come.[13]

According to dispensationalism, God is now dealing with His Church, His "heavenly people." God is *not*, according to dispensationalism, dealing with Israel, His "earthly people." The promises made to Israel are "postponed." Technically speaking, with this unusual dispensational view in mind, there can be no such thing as "anti-semitism" as Lindsey and other dispensationalists describe it! The Jews are like everybody else: They are lost in their sins until they embrace Christ as their Lord and Savior. "Anti-Semitism," according to the dispensational view, is no different from anti-Japanese, anti-Italian, anti-Arab, anti-Irish, or anti-German attitudes. Jews are not God's chosen people this side of the rapture. *This is the dispensational view!*

Consider this as well. If the promises to Israel as a people and nation are postponed, as dispensationalism teaches, then the land promise, and the promise of "those who bless you, I will bless," also have been set aside until the prophetic clock ticks once again when the Church is raptured. Treating Jews with care or persecuting them will affect God in no special way *prior to the rapture*. God is not obligated to keep a promise that has been postponed. Again, these are the implications of the dispensational view of prophecy.

A number of dispensationalists understand the problem of how to view Israel before the rapture. Stan Rittenhouse has written the following about present-day Israel:[14]

- "A curse has been put on Israel."
- "Israel will again be made desolate."
- "Today's Israel is not of God."
- "Today's Israel is not of Christ but rather that of the Devil."
- "The Israel of today is a Satanic counterfeit."
- "Israel must first be destroyed."

Why does Rittenhouse write such inflammatory things about the *present* state of Israel? Like a good dispensationalist, he believes that "Today is an in-between age which is commonly called the Age of Grace, the Age of the Holy Spirit, or the Church Age (the Church being the body of believers in Christ, the total and complete group, whosoever that may be, Gentile or Jew). During this period in between the First and Second Coming[s] of Jesus Christ, a Satanic counterfeit—political Zionism—masquerading as the State of 'Israel' will be established."[15]

According to dispensationalism, God has a special place for Israel, *but only until after the rapture when the church will no longer be earthbound*. This means that Israel has no special significance between the first and second comings of Christ. Dispensational premillennialism, which had its start sometime in the nineteenth century, does not have a place for Israel until *after* the rapture. And even then, two-thirds of the Jews living in Israel will be destroyed.

The establishment of the State [of Israel] is seen as a sign that the Second Coming is near, to be preceded by a Soviet attack on Israel. These groups profess simple biblical values and clear cut support for Israel, but their political activity raises complex, troubling questions for Jews.[16]

It is this part of dispensationalism that rarely gets public and scholarly scrutiny. If any group within evangelicalism, other than dispensationalists, claimed that Israel has no special redemptive significance until after the rapture, they would be condemned and labeled anti-Semitic.

Armageddon Now!

Modern-day Jews are bothered by the potential for harm that resides in dispensationalism. Their fear is justified in light of history. Dwight Wilson, author of *Armageddon Now!*, convincingly demonstrates that dispensational premillennialism advocated a "hands off" policy regarding Nazi persecutions of the Jews during World War II. Since, according to dispensational views regarding Bible prophecy, "the Gentile nations are permitted to afflict Israel in chastisement for her national sins," there is little that should be done to oppose it.[17] Wilson writes that "It is regrettable that this view allowed premillennialists to expect the phenomenon of 'anti-Semitism' and tolerate it matter-of-factly."[18] Wilson describes himself as "a third-generation premillenarian who has spent his whole life in premillennialist churches, has attended a premillennialist Bible college, and has taught in such a college for fourteen years."[19]

Wilson describes "premillenarian views" opposing "anti-Semitism" in the midthirties and thereafter as "ambivalent."[20] There was little moral outcry "among the premillenarians . . . against the persecution, since they had been expecting it."[21] He continues:

> Another comment regarding the general European anti-Semitism depicted these developments as part of the on-going plan of God for the nation; they were "Foregleams of Israel's Tribulation." Premillennialists were anticipating the Great Tribulation, "the time of Jacob's trouble." Therefore, they predicted, "The next scene in Israel's history may be summed up in three words: purification through tribulation." It was clear that although this purification was part of the curse, God did not intend that Christians should participate in it. Clear, also, was the implication that He did intend for the Germans to participate in it (in spite of the fact that it would bring them punishment)—*and that any moral outcry against Germany would have been in opposition to God's will. In such a fatalistic system, to oppose Hitler was to oppose God.*[22]

Other premillennial writers placed "part of the blame for anti-Semitism on the Jews: 'The Jew is the world's archtroubler. Most of the Revolutions of Continental Europe were fostered by Jews.' The Jews—especially the German Jews—were responsible for the great depression."[23]

Wilson maintains that it was the premillennial view of a predicted Jewish persecution prior to the Second Coming that led to a "hands off" policy when it came to speaking out against virulent "anti-Semitism." "For the premillenarian, the massacre of Jewry expedited his blessed hope. Certainly he did not rejoice over the Nazi holocaust, he just fatalistically observed it as a 'sign of the times.'"[24] Wilson offers this summary:

> Pleas from Europe for assistance for Jewish refugees fell on deaf ears, and "Hands Off" meant no helping hand. So in spite of being theologically more pro-Jewish than any other Christian group, the premillenarians also were apathetic—because of a residual anti-Semitism, because persecution was prophetically expected, because it would encourage immigration to Palestine, because it seemed the beginning of the Great Tribulation, and because it was a wonderful sign of the imminent blessed hope.[25]

Dispensationalism sees a great persecution yet to come where "two thirds of the children of Israel in the land will perish" during the "Great Tribulation."[26]

Dispensational "Anti-Semitism"

Let me recount another bit of history related to this issue. Dispensational premillennialist James M. Gray of the Moody Bible Institute believed in the authenticity of the *Protocols of the Elders of Zion*. He defended Henry Ford when Ford published installments of the *Protocols* in his self-funded *Dearborn Independent* newspaper.

In a 1927 editorial in the *Moody Bible Institute Monthly*, Gray claimed that Ford "had good grounds for publishing some of the things about the Jews. . . . Mr. Ford might have found corroborative evidence [of the Jewish conspiracy] had he looked for it."[27] As time went on, Gray was coming under increasing pressure to repudiate the *Protocols* as a forgery. Not only Gray, but *Moody Bible Institute Monthly* was being criticized by the evangelical *Hebrew Christian Alliance* for not condemning the manufactured *Protocols*. Gray grew indignant and once again voiced his belief that the *Protocols* were authentic. He did this in the *Moody Bible Institute Monthly*, a dispensational magazine still in publication today as *Moody Monthly*! Gray, of course, pointed out that "Moody Bible Institute had always worked for the highest interests of Jews by training people to evangelize them."[28]

Even so, Gray went on to assert that "Jews were at least partly to blame for their ill treatment." He supported this contention by referring his readers to an article written by Max Reich, a faculty member at the Moody Bible Institute. Reich wrote: "Without religion, the Jew goes down and becomes worse than others, as a corruption of the best is always the worst corruption."[29]

Charges of "anti-Semitism" were not abated by Gray's attempts at clarification. His views concerning the Jews remained. "By the beginning of 1935, Gray was fending off charges from the *American Hebrew and Jewish Tribune*, the *Bulletin of the Baltimore Branch of the American Jewish Congress*, and even *Time* magazine that persons connected with Moody had been actively distributing the *Protocols*."[30]

Of course, Gray was not the only dispensational premillennialist who vouched for the genuineness of the *Protocols* and had rather negative ("anti-semitic"?) things to say about the Jews. Arno C. Gaebelein, an editor of the *Scofield Reference Bible*, believed that the *Protocols* were authentic, that they accurately revealed a "Jewish conspiracy." His *Conflict of the Ages*[31] would be viewed today as an "anti-semitic" work because it fostered the belief that communism had Jewish roots and that the Bolshevik revolution of 1917 had been masterminded by a group of well-trained Jewish agitators. At the same time that Gaebelein was using anti-semitic rhetoric, he had a thriving evangelistic ministry to Jews in New York City. Why the double mindedness? Dispensationalism requires both the persecution and salvation of Jews.[32]

Dispensationalism's Future Holocaust?

Over against the clear statements of Scripture and the corroboration of unbiased secular historians who were living at the time of the destruction of Jerusalem in A.D. 70, dispensationalists maintain that the events of Matthew 24:1–34 refer to a future seven-year tribulation period where the entire world will suffer untold persecution and slaughter at the hands of the antichrist and his armies. John Walvoord, a leading dispensationalist spokesman, writes that these supposed future judgments will be "without parallel in the history of the world. According to Revelation 6:7 the judgments attending the opening of the fourth seal involve the death with sword, famine, and wild beasts of one fourth of the world's population. If this were applied to the present world population now approaching three billion, it would mean that 750,000,000 people would perish, more than the total population of North America, Central America, and South America combined."[33]

Hal Lindsey supports Walvoord's position, affirming that during the "Great Tribulation" there will be "*death on a massive scale*. It staggers the imagination to realize that one-fourth of the world's population will be destroyed within a matter of days. According to projected census figures this will amount to nearly one billion people!"[34] Of course, with the latest census figures, with the dispensational view in mind, nearly 1.25 *billion* people will die. Not only does the world come in for a beating under the dispensational hermeneutic, but Israel is specifically hit hard. Walvoord, with his view of a future seven-year "Great Tribulation," must claim that a large number of Jews living in Israel will be slaughtered. He writes:

> The purge of Israel in their time of trouble is described by Zechariah in these words: "And it shall come to pass, that in all the land, saith Jehovah, two parts therein shall be cut off and die; but the third shall be left therein. And I will bring the third part into the fire, and will refine them as silver is refined, and will try them as gold is tried" (Zechariah 13:8, 9). According to Zechariah's prophecy, *two thirds of the children of Israel in the land will perish*, but the one third that are left will be refined and be awaiting the deliverance of God at the second coming of Christ which is described in the next chapter of Zechariah.[35]

Israel's present population is around 4,500,000. If two-thirds of the Jews living in Israel at the time of the "Great Tribulation" are to die, this will mean the death of nearly 3,000,000! In addition, there is continued immigration from the former Soviet Union supported by Christian organizations like "On Wings of Eagles." Financial support is raised by Christians to fund Jewish settlements in the occupied territories. "'This is a biblical issue,' says Theodore T. Beckett, a Colorado developer who founded the Christian-sponsored, adopt-a-settlement program. 'The Bible says in the last days the Jews will be restored to the nation of Israel.'"[36] For every three people who enter, two of them will be killed during the "Great Tribulation." Why aren't today's dispensationalists warning Jews about this coming holocaust by encouraging them to leave Israel until the conflagration is over? Instead, we find dispensationalists supporting and encouraging the relocation of Jews to the land of Israel. For what? A future holocaust?

Eugene Merrill, while not discussing Zechariah 13:8 in his commentary on that biblical book, does describe how a future holocaust of the Jews is in view in Zechariah 14:2. Merrill writes:

> The restoration and dominion cannot come until all the forces of evil that seek to subvert it are put down once and for all. Specifically, the redemption of Israel will be accomplished on the ruins of her own suffering and those of the malevolent powers of this world that, in the last day, will consolidate themselves against her and seek to interdict forever any possibility of her success. The nations of the whole earth will come against Jerusalem, and, having defeated her, will divide up their spoils of war in her very midst.[37]

If this is to be the future of Jews living in Israel, then why aren't dispensationalists warning Jews to flee the city? Israel was warned by Jesus to "flee to the mountains" (Matthew 24:16). The New Testament is filled with warnings about the coming A.D. 70 holocaust with no encouragement to take up residence in Jerusalem. In fact, there was a mass exodus from the city by those who understood the world-wide implications of the gospel message and the approaching destruction of what was the center of Jewish worship (John 4:21-24).

A Past and Confined Holocaust

Preterists believe that the events described in Matthew 24:1-34 were fulfilled in the events leading up to and including the destruction of Jerusalem in A.D. 70. "The guilt of all the righteous blood shed on earth, from the blood of righteous Abel to the blood of Zechariah, the son of Berechiah, whom [they] murdered between the temple and the altar" (Matthew 23:35) fell upon the generation of Jews who "did not recognize the time of [their] visitation" (Luke 19:44) and crucified "the Lord of glory" (1 Corinthians 2:8). How do we know this? Because Jesus told us: "Truly I say to you, all these things shall come upon *this generation*" (Matthew 23:36 and 24:34). No future generation of Jews is meant here.

Unfortunately, by futurizing this prophecy, Jews through the centuries have been reliving this past (preterist) judgment at the hands of misguided men who have been driven by bad theology. For example, in the Bavarian Alpine village of Oberammergau, controversy has arisen over the re-enact-ment of Christ's Passion. "The classic folk drama originated in 1634, after villagers vowed to re-enact Christ's Passion regularly if they were spared from the Black Death."[38] The most severe criticism has arisen because of a single verse from Matthew's gospel: "His blood be on us and on our chil-dren!" (27:25). While a number of alterations have been made in the play, the verse from Matthew has not be cut.

> The commission voted narrowly to retain the controversial line, prompt-ing criticism from Rabbi A. James Rudin of the American Jewish Com-mittee, who is calling for a completely new play that "should reflect the reality of the 'cursed' Jewish people living in a reborn and independent state of Israel."[39]

The play does not need to be rewritten; it just needs a more biblical inter-pretation. The curse had its end in A.D. 70 upon the generation that uttered the oath. To continue to futurize the events that are of a certainty fulfilled prophecy can only do more harm. Much of modern-day evangelicalism and fundamentalism unwittingly contributes to wide-spread "anti-semitism" be-cause of their continued futurization of texts that have been fulfilled. Secular writers have picked up on this element in dispensationalism:

> Convinced that a nuclear Armageddon is an inevitable event within the divine scheme of things, many evangelical dispensationalists have committed themselves to a course for Israel that, by their own admission, will lead directly to a holocaust indescribably more savage and wide-spread than any vision of carnage that could have generated in Adolf Hitler's criminal mind.[40]

Jews are always in jeopardy of being persecuted as long as dispensation-alists push a false interpretation of prophecy that makes Jews the scapegoat for a distorted theological system.

Jewish "Anti-Semitism"?

Even Jews can sound like theological anti-Semites. Orthodox Rabbi Eliezer Schach suggested that millions of Jews were murdered during World War II because of their sinfulness.

> The Almighty keeps a balance sheet of the world, and when the sins become too many, he brings destruction. We don't know how long his patience holds out, sometimes 20 years, sometimes 10, and sometimes only a year. . . . The last time he brought destruction, it was the Holocaust. . . . Because of the sins, the Almighty may bring another Holocaust upon us, and it may already be tomorrow.[41]

Auschwitz survivor Menachem Russak said Schach "exonerated the Nazi murderers, but turned them into messengers of God who were sent to punish the people of Israel for not observing the Torah."[42]

Dispensational premillennialist Hal Lindsey could be doing the same when he writes: "Until Messiah comes again and Israel turns to him, the nation is still officially under God's divine discipline."[43] Lindsey concludes that the destruction of the temple in A.D. 70 "*began* the long period called by Jesus the 'times of the Gentiles.' As Moses predicted, during this long period the Jewish people would be wanderers from place to place with no assurance of safety or acceptance."[44] A preterist, someone who believes that the prophecies relating to Jerusalem's destruction were fulfilled in A.D. 70, maintains that the destruction of the temple in A.D. 70 *ended* the forty year period Jesus outlined in Matthew 24. While Lindsey awaits a future Jewish holocaust, preterists assert it is over. Sure enough, Lindsey's futurist interpretation is a reality. "For nearly two thousand years now," Lindsey writes, "this prophecy has been a horrible reality in the life of God's chosen people. No nation in the history of the world has undergone such persecution and distress."[45] Lindsey is still awaiting a time when God will "purge" Israel of sin.[46] These comments from Lindsey come from a chapter titled "The Holocaust."

We should bear in mind at this point that anti-semitism is an overused and often misunderstood term that is applied indiscriminately. Consider the charge of anti-semitism leveled against the Willowband Declaration, produced at a meeting convened by the World Evangelical Fellowship in April of 1989. An international consultation on Jewish evangelism challenged Christians "to stop looking for excuses for not sharing the gospel of Jewish Christ with Jews."[47] What was the response of A. James Rudin, a rabbi and national interreligious affairs director of the American Jewish Committee? "He called it a 'blueprint for spiritual genocide' and expressed the hope that it will be 'repudiated by Christians everywhere.'"[48] For Rabbi Rudin, *evangelizing Jews is anti-semitic!* The belief that Jews are in need of redemption teaches "contempt for Jews and Judaism," says Rabbi Rudin.

Conclusion

What is the answer to anti-semitism? First, we must reject the simplistic treatments of dispensational writers who consider anyone who does not agree with their future holocaust view as being an anti-semite. "Being opposed to the policies of the modern state of Israel for its West Bank atrocities or for its socialism or for its anti-Christian laws will not suffice as anti-Semitism." Being "opposed to the policies of Israel's government…is not he same as being opposed to Jews as such."[49] For decades Christians have opposed the Soviet Union. This did not mean that Christians were prejudiced against the Russian people or their heritage.

Second, we must understand that minority groups of all kinds suffer persecution. There was a period in our nation when blacks were enslaved. For a time, the Irish were often treated worse than blacks. "In the pre-Civil War South, Irish laborers were often used in work considered too dangerous for slaves, who represented a sizable capital investment. . . . The native public's reaction to the Irish included moving out of neighborhoods *en masse* as the immigrants moved in; stereotyping them all as drunkards, brawlers, and incompetents; and raising employment barriers exemplified in the stock phrase, 'No Irish need apply.'"[50] Even today we find continued persecution of blacks, Asians, and Jews. Little is said by our dispensational brethren, however, when Israel discriminates against Christians or when Arab nations are just as hostile toward Christians as they are against Jews.

> Many conflicts around the globe can be traced to religious intolerance, [Carl] Henry noted, such as: the Nazi extermination of Jews, the Chinese Communist massacre of Christians, Israel's official hard-line policy toward Jews who consider themselves Reformed, Conservative and Messi-

anic Jews (Christians), the fighting among Irish Protestants and Catholics, and Islam's persecution of Muslim converts to other religions.[51]

To what in eschatology can we attribute these acts of persecution? Are we to assume that only dispensationalism can save us from these centuries-old rivalries?

Third, the Jews will be safe when Christians can teach others that it is wrong to do harm to a neighbor, no matter what their race or religion. The issue, therefore, is ethics, not eschatology.

Notes

1. Charles Caldwell Ryrie, *The Living End* (Old Tappan, NJ: Revell, 1976), 81. "A Bloodbath for Israel" is the title of chapter 8.

2. Ryrie, *The Living End*, 80.

3. A number of Christian ministries raise funds to help Russian Jews to immigrate to Israel. Why do they do this when they know that two-thirds of the Jews living in Israel during the Great Tribulation will be slaughtered?

4. Ken Sidey, "For the Love of Zion," *Christianity Today* (March 9, 1992), 50.

5. Robert L. Saucy, *The Case for Progressive Dispensationalism: The Interface Between Dispensationalism and Non-Dispensational Theology* (Grand Rapids, MI: Zondervan, 1993), 8.

6. Saucy, *The Case for Progressive Dispensationalism*, 8.

7. Stanley N. Gundry, "Foreword," *Dispensationalism, Israel and the Church: The Search for Definition* (Grand Rapids, MI: Zondervan, 1992), 11.

8. Craig A. Blaising, "Dispensationalism: A Search for Definition," *Dispensationalism, Israel and the Church*, 15. See Craig A. Blaising and Darrell L. Bock, *Progressive Dispensationalism: An Up-to-Date Handbook of Contemporary Dispensational Thought* (Wheaton, IL: Victor/Bridgepoint Books, 1993).

9. Those who accuse non-dispensationalists of being "anti-semitic" rarely define the term. Instead, they manufacture a new term called "theological anti-semitism" to suit their defamatory tactics. True anti-semitism is defined as prejudice against semitic people because they are semites.

10. See William Hendriksen, *Israel and Prophecy* (Grand Rapids, MI: Baker Book House, 1968), 16–31. The first church was made up almost exclusively of Jews. Later, Gentile believers were grafted into an already existing Jewish Church (Rom. 11:19). These believers, consisting of Jews and Gentiles, are the true "Jews" (Rom. 2:28–29), the true "circumcision" (Phil. 3:3), the true "seed of Abraham" (Gal. 3:7, 29), the "children of promise" (4:28), the "commonwealth of Israel" (Eph. 2:12, 19).

11. Zechariah was describing a future holocaust. It was fulfilled in A.D. 70 with the destruction of Jerusalem and the slaughter of 1,100,000 Jews at the hands of the Romans.

12. Robert G. Clouse, ed., *The Meaning of the Millennium: Four Views* (Downers Grove, IL: InterVarsity Press, 1977).

13. E. Schuyler English, *A Companion to the New Scofield Reference Bible* (New York: Oxford University Press, 1972), 135. Emphasis added.

14. Stan Rittenhouse, °*"For Fear of the Jews"* (Vienna, VA: The Exhorters, 1982), 7, 8, 9, 45, 169, 179.

15. *"For Fear of the Jews,"* 7.

16. *The B'Nai B'Rith International Jewish Monthly* (Sept. 1981), 17.

17. Dwight Wilson, *Armageddon Now!: The Premillenarian Response to Russia and Israel Since 1917* (Grand Rapids, MI: Baker Book House, 1977), Reprinted by the Institute for Christian Economics in 1991 with an updated foreword by the author.

18. Wilson, *Armageddon Now!*, 16.

19. Wilson, *Armageddon Now!*, 13.

20. Wilson, *Armageddon Now!*, 94.

21. Wilson, *Armageddon Now!*, 94.

22. Wilson, *Armageddon Now!*, 94. Emphasis added.

23. Wilson, *Armageddon Now!*, 95.

24. Wilson, *Armageddon Now!*, 95.

25. Wilson, *Armageddon Now!*, 96–97. See comments on page 217.

26. John F. Walvoord, *Israel in Prophecy* (Grand Rapids, MI: Zondervan/Academie, [1962] 1988), 108.

27. Timothy P. Weber, *Living in the Shadow of the Second Coming: American Premillennialism, 1875-1982* (Grand Rapids, MI: Zondervan/Academie, 1983), 189.

28. Weber, *Living in the Shadow of the Second Coming,* 189.

29. Quoted in Weber, *Living in the Shadow of the Second Coming,* 190.

30. Weber, *Living in the Shadow of the Second Coming,* 189.

31. Arno Clemens Gaebelein, *The Conflict of the Ages: The Mystery of Lawlessness: Its Origin, Historic Development and Coming Defeat* (New York: Publication Office "Our Hope," 1933).

32. Timothy P. Weber, "A Reply to David Rausch's 'Fundamentalism and the Jew,'" *Journal of the Evangelical Theological Society* (March 1981), 70.

33. Walvoord, *Israel in Prophecy,* 108.

34. Hal Lindsey, *There's a New World Coming* (New York: Bantam Books, [1973] 1984), 90. Emphasis in original.

35. Walvoord, *Israel in Prophecy,* 108. Emphasis added.

36. Ann LoLordo, "Evangelical Christians Come to Jews' Aid," *Atlanta Constitution* (August 8, 1997), A8.

37. Eugene H. Merrill, *An Exegetical Commentary: Haggai, Zechariah, Malachi* (Chicago, IL: Moody Press, 1994), 342.

38. Michael Walsh, "Oberammergau's Blood Curse," *Time* (June 4, 1990), 89.

39. Walsh, "Oberammergau's Blood Curse," 89.

40. Grace Halsell, *Prophecy and Politics: Militant Evangelists on the Road to Nuclear War* (Westport, CT: Lawrence Hill & Co., 1986), 195.

41. "Rabbi sees Holocaust as God's punishment; Israelis are outraged," *The Atlanta Journal* (December 28, 1990), B5. A shorter version of this Associated Press news story appeared in *USA Today* (December 28, 1990), 4A.

42. "Rabbi sees Holocaust as God's punishment; Israelis are outraged," B5.

43. Hal Lindsey, *The Promise* (New York: Bantam Books, 1994), 190.

44. Lindsey, *Promise*, 190.

45. Lindsey, *Promise*, 190.

46. Lindsey, *Promise*, 191.

47. Arthur H. Matthews, "Evangelism To Jews Supported by Gathering, But Blasted by Rabbi," *World* (May 20, 1989), 12.

48. Matthews, "Evangelism To Jews Supported by Gathering," 12.

49. Kenneth L. Gentry, Jr., "Anti-Semitism, Reconstruction, and Dispensationalism," *Chalcedon Report* (August 1997), 11.

50. Thomas Sowell, *Ethnic America: A History* (New York: Basic Books, 1981), 27 and 17.

51. Carey Kinsolving, "Southern Baptist warned of Saudi Arabia's Religious Persecution," *The Washington Post* (March 7, 1992).

Appendix 4

SOLA SCRIPTURA
AND PROPHECY

Assembling historical support for a particular theological position is a common practice among evangelicals, especially in the area of eschatology. Standard dispensational works include historical studies to support their position.[1] Of course, there is nothing wrong with historical analysis as long as the evidence is not used to bolster weak exegetical arguments.

To bolster the claim that much of New Testament prophecy has not been fulfilled, futurists rummage through the writings of the early Church Fathers. Since these men are only a generation or two removed from the apostolic era, so the reasoning goes, their insights are considered invaluable for a right understanding of biblical prophecy. Unfortunately, these writers are read selectively and with a predisposition to an already accepted prophetic perspective. For example, premillennial pastor Steve Hogan asks, "What do the early Church Fathers say about the Antichrist?"[2] After surveying eight Church Fathers from Justin Martyr (*c.* 100–164) to Augustine (354–430) on their views of the antichrist and the great tribulation, Hogan asks a follow-up question:

> Doesn't it seem strange to you that if Nero was the antichrist, and if the great tribulation had already occurred, then these church fathers would have said so?[3]

In fact, they did. "All the earliest Christian writers on the Apocalypse, from Irenaeus down to Victorinus of Pettau and Commodian in the fourth, and Andreas in the fifth, and St. Beatus in the eighth century, connect Nero, or some Roman Emperor, with the Apocalyptic Beast."[4] In Christian writings, "Nero is the Anti-Christ whose persecution of the Christians heralds the destruction of Rome. This view of Nero as Anti-Christ continued to be celebrated by the Church Fathers and by later Christian writers. The picture of him as the incarnation of evil triumphed as Christianity triumphed."[5] Tertullian (145–200), in chronicling the sufferings of the apostles, wrote, "At Rome Nero was the first who stained with blood the rising faith" [6]

The Bible is the Standard

In terms of *sola Scriptura*, however, it does not matter what these men believed. The Bible is the standard. If the Bible says the Beast (antichrist) appeared in the first century, then it happened, no matter what certain early Church Fathers assert.[7] From the first century to the present, godly men have been wrong in their interpretation and application of prophetic texts.[8] Moreover, there is little if any consensus among the supporters of the historicist and futurist schools of biblical prophecy down through the centuries as to the identity of the antichrist/beast.[9]

Second-Hand Sources

Why do we assume that men like Justin Martyr, Cyprian, Irenaeus, and others are exempt from misapplication and error? Is it because of their proximity to the events?

> Their physical and spiritual fathers and grandfathers would have told them about this incredibly wicked person, the antichrist, and would have included this important information in their writings.[10]

So now we are dependent on second and third-hand testimony to support a futuristic view of prophecy even though the Bible states unequivocally that the events of Matthew 24 took place before "this generation" passed away (v. 34). The *biblical* time references "near," "shortly," and "quickly" are dismissed in favor of opinions by uninspired writers written decades after the fact. When John tells his first-century readers that the presence of antichrist in *their day* is evidence that "it is the last hour" (1 John 2:18), we are told that historical evidence nullifies such a conclusion. Proximity to an event does not assure future generations that past events will be reported or remembered acurately.[11] People still believe that religious leaders in the fifteenth century taught that the earth was flat and Columbus wanted to prove it was round even though there is no evidence to substantiate this commonly held fable.[12]

Immediacy or Imminency?

Once historical sources are used as authoritative, futurists then move to the next level of analysis by reformulating the debate just enough to obscure the issue. For example, Hogan, like other futurists, states, "the early church fathers were expecting the antichrist and the great tribulation to come *sometime in the future*."[13] A close reading of their writings gives an altogether different perspective. Ignatius writes around the year A.D. 100 that "the last times are come upon us,"[14] words that echo those of the Apostle Paul when he writes that "the ends of the ages" had come upon him and the Corinthian Church (1 Cor. 10:11). They both can't be right. Given a choice, I'll stick with Paul. Cyprian (c. 200–258) writes "that the day of affliction *has begun* to hang over our heads, and the end of the world and the time of the Antichrist . . . draw near, so that we must all stand prepared for the battle."[15] This was a constant theme in Cyprian's writings. These men, along with most of their contemporaries, believed that they were living in the last days, that the time of the end was near for *them*. They were wrong because they misapplied the time texts. Today's "prophecy experts" repeat their errors.

What happens when futurists encounter time texts which speak of the near return of Christ? A new doctrine is manufactured called "imminency" or the "any moment" return of Christ. The following definition is typical:

> The primary thought expressed by the word "imminency" is that something important is likely to happen, and could happen soon. While the event may not be immediate, or necessarily very soon, it is next on the program and may take place at any time.[16]

There is nothing in the time texts that would support this definition.[17] Words such as "likely," "could happen," and "may take place" are nowhere indicated. The biblical writers are straightforward in their claim that the events described were to happen "soon" for those who first read the prophecies. No other interpretation is possible if the words are taken in their "plain, primary, ordinary, usual, or normal" sense, something dispensationalists insist upon.[18]

If the biblical authors wanted to communicate uncertainty about the timing of future events, they would have equivocated by using words expressing probability. So then, any time a dispensationalist sees a passage that states without reservation that Jesus' coming is "near," he substitutes "any moment," a clear violation of sound biblical exegesis. Thomas Ice and Timothy Demy try but fail to find biblical support for a similar view by modifying the meaning of words dealing with time.

> The fact that Christ could return at any moment but may not soon is supported in the New Testament in the following passages: 1 Corinthians 1:7; 16:22; Philippians 3:20; 4:5; 1 Thessalonians 1:10; Titus 2:13; Hebrews 9:28; James 5:7–9; 1 Peter 1:13; Jude 21; Revelation 3:11; 22:7, 12, 17, 20.[19]

These passages offer no support for an "any moment" return of Christ. For example, James 5:7–9 states clearly that "the coming of the Lord is *at hand*," that "the Judge is standing *right at the door*." The Christians of Corinth[20] were "awaiting eagerly" the coming of the Lord (1 Corinthians 1:7), a coming that all first-century Christians were told was near.

Renald Showers makes a surprising admission that contradicts the notion of imminency as advocated by Ice, Demy, and himself. He asserts that a "person cannot legitimately say that an imminent event will happen soon. The term 'soon' implies that an event *must* take place 'within a short time (after a particular point of time specified or implied).'"[21] This means that time words such as "soon," "near," and "at hand" mean just what they seem to mean. The conclusion? Jesus' coming had to be near for the first-century church since "'soon' implies that an event *must* take place 'within a short time.'" This is confirmed to us when we read in Revelation that "the time is near" (1:3).

A Closer Look at History

Dispensationalists are fond of quoting the early Church Fathers to support their contention that the Church taught the "imminent" or "any moment" return of Christ. As the following survey will illustrate, they believed no such thing. They believed that end time events were contemporary with their generation, as these examples demonstrate:

- "Even in Justin Martyr's time there was still the expectation of an immediate Parousia (*Dial. c. Tryph.* 80)."[22] Justin believed that "the Antichrist would be a person who was *close at hand*, and who would reign three and a half years."[23]
- Justin applied the fulfillment of Matthew 24:11 to his own day: "For what things He predicted would take place in His name, *these we do see being actually accomplished in our sight.* For He said, 'For many shall come in My name, clothed outwardly in sheep's clothing, but inwardly they are ravening wolves' [Matt. 7:15]. And, 'There shall be schisms and heresies' [1 Cor. 11:19]. . . . And, 'Many false Christs and false prophets shall arise, and shall deceive many of the faithful' [Matt. 24:11]."[24]
- "Irenaeus also thought that Antichrist, as foreshadowed by the Wild Beast, would be a man; and that 'the number of the Beast' represented *Lateinos*, 'a Latin.'"[25]
- "Hippolytus compares the action of the False Prophet giving life to the Beast's image, to Augustus inspiring fresh force into the Roman Empire."[26]
- St. Victorinus (about A.D. 303) identifies Nero as the Beast.[27]

There is ample evidence to prove that these writers understood that aspects of the Olivet Discourse applied to the destruction of Jerusalem in A.D. 70. At the same time, they believed that they were living in the last days, that the Beast was among them, and Jesus' return was near *for them*. This only shows that they were as confused about Bible prophecy as today's prophetic speculators.

First-Century Testimony

There is earlier extra-biblical evidence to support the claim that first-century Christians clearly understood that Jesus would return in judgment before their generation passed away. A story is told about James, the brother of Jesus, stating that Jesus' coming was "about to take place."[28] Second-century ecclesiastical writer Hegesippus, quoting what James said to a group of Scribes and Pharisees, "reflects the tradition of the early church on [the subject of the immediacy of the second advent] by stating that Jesus 'is about to come on the clouds of heaven.'"[29] When asked about the "Son of Man," James responded: "He is now sitting in the heavens, on the right hand of great Power, *and is about to come on the clouds of heaven.*"[30] The Greek word *mello*, "about to," "communicates a sense of immediacy."[31] "If the author had not wished to stress the immediate aspect of Christ's coming, he could still have stressed the certainty of Christ's coming with *erketai*, thereby omitting the immediate factor."[32]

After hearing James' statement—an obvious allusion to Matthew 26:64—the officials of the temple cast him down from the "wing of the temple," as Hegesippus tells it, and later stoned him and beat out his brains with a club. This was in A.D. 63. "Immediately after this," Hegesippus writes, "Vespasian invaded and took Judea."[33] James identifies the coming of Jesus "on the clouds of heaven" with the destruction of Jerusalem in A.D. 70. Here is an eyewitness to the life and words of Jesus confirming the biblical testimony that Matthew 24:30 would be fulfilled in the very near futuare.

Even with history favoring the preterist position, F. W. Farrar concludes that the Bible clearly states that Jesus would return in judgment within the lifetime of the apostolic writers. While history is instructive, in the final analysis the Bible is the only infallible standard to which we can appeal:

> But to me it seems that the founder of the Preterist School is none other that St. John himself. For he records the Christ as saying to him when he was in the Spirit, 'Write the things which thou sawest, and THE THINGS WHICH ARE, and the things which are about to happen (*a mellei ginesthai*) after these things.' No language surely could more clearly define the bearing of the Apocalypse. It is meant to describe the contemporary state of things in the Church and the world, and the events which were to follow in immediate sequence. If the Historical School can strain the latter words into an indication that we are (contrary to all analogy) to have a symbolic and unintelligible sketch of many centuries, the Preterist School may at any rate apply these words, *ha eisen*, 'THE THINGS WHICH ARE,' to vindicate the application of a large part of the Apocalypse to events nearly contemporary, while they also give the natural meaning to the subsequent clause by understanding it of events which were then on the horizon. The Seer emphatically says that the future events which he has to foreshadow will occur *speedily* (*en taxei*) and the recurrent burden of his

whole book is the nearness of the Advent (*ho kairos engus* ["the time is near"]). Language is simply meaningless if it is to be so manipulated by every successive commentator as to make the words "speedily" and "near" imply any number of centuries of delay.[34]

Further evidence will show that second-century writers did not believe in imminency. Like today's prophetic speculators, they misapplied the time texts to their day.

Second-Century Testimonies

Second-century writers believed that the return of Christ was near for them. Henry Clarence Thiessen writes that "the church looked for [Jesus] to come in their day. . . . We may assume that the early church lived in the constant expectation of their Lord, and hence was not concerned with the possibility of a tribulation period in the future."[35] If the early church (post A.D. 70) believed that Jesus was to come in their day, then they were wrong. Trying to make their words say something different is not honest.

Alan Patrick Boyd, a dispensationalist who deals honestly with their writings, shows that the ante-Nicene[36] fathers believed in the "immediacy of the Second Advent."[37] He states "that Clement perceived the *apostolic* message to be the proclamation of the immediacy of the kingdom of God"[38] and "the immediacy of the Second Advent."[39] The author of "2 Clement also believed in the immediacy of Christ's return."[40] The writer of the "Epistle of Barnabas purports a credence in immediacy."[41] "The Didache also maintains immediacy. . . . [I]n direct dependence on Luke 12.35, 37, 40 and Matthew 24:42, 44, he warns the readers to be ready because of the immediacy of Christ's return."[42] "Ignatius held to immediacy as well. . . . Furthermore, he employs the term *prosdoka* (Polyc. 3.2) of waiting for Christ—a clear indication of Ignatius' belief in immediacy."[43]

Conclusion

J. L. Neve states that ". . . the time of the Apostolic Fathers, like that of primitive Christianity, was thoroughly eschatological in tendency. Men had the consciousness that they were living in the last times. The *immediate return of Jesus was anticipated*. It was this expectation which held the congregation together."[44] George Eldon Ladd notes: "The early church lived in expectation of Christ's return." Ladd quotes 1 Clement 23 in support: "Ye perceive how in a little time the fruit of a tree comes to maturity. Of a truth, soon and suddenly shall His will be accomplished, as the Scripture also bears witness, saying, 'Speedily will He come and will not tarry,' and 'The Lord shall suddenly come to His temple, even the Holy One, for whom ye look.'" Ladd continues:

> To deduce from this attitude of expectancy a belief in a pretribulation rapture and an any-moment coming of Christ, as has often been done, is not sound. The expectation of the coming of Christ *included the events which would attend and precede His coming.* The early fathers who emphasized an attitude of expectancy believed that this entire complex of events—Antichrist, tribulation, return of Christ—would soon occur. This is not the same as an any-moment coming of Christ.[45]

Many ante-Nicene writers "thought that the Roman persecution which they were undergoing at the time was the foretold tribulation period and that the current emperor was the Anti-Christ. Therefore they were expecting the return of Christ momentarily to deliver them from the tribulation and the Anti-Christ."[46]

The time texts—"near," "shortly," "quickly"—could, if stretched, still be interpreted somewhat literally in the second and third centuries. As time passed, however, a reassessment of these time texts in relation to world conditions had taken place. A strong futurism replaced preterism. "From the 4th century on, the belief in the millennium declined. . . . The persecutions against the church drew to an end with the conversion of Constantine, and the church saw a new day of peace dawning."[47] Biblical scholars began to reassess prophetic texts. Most adopted a futurist view, reinterpreting and relativizing the time texts and, thus, obscuring the plain teaching of the Bible.

Notes

1. John F. Walvoord, *The Millennial Kingdom* (Grand Rapids, MI: Dunham Publishing Co., 1959), 37–58, George N. H. Peters, *The Theocratic Kingdom of Our Lord Jesus Christ, as Covenanted in the Old Testament and Presented in the New Testament*, 3 vols. (Grand Rapids, MI: Kregel Publications, [1884] 1972), and Grant R. Jeffrey, *Apocalypse: The Coming Judgment of the Nations* (Toronto, Ontario: Frontier Research Publications, 1992), 313–22 are representative examples. For a critique of these works and a different historical perspective, see Kenneth L. Gentry, Jr., *He Shall Have Dominion: A Postmillennial Eschatology* (Tyler, TX: Institute for Christian Economics, 1992), 73–93.

2. Steve Hogan, "Matthew 24—The Future is Coming," (unpublished manuscript, 1997), 21.

3. Hogan, "Matthew 24—The Future is Coming," 21.

4. Frederic W. Farrar, *Early Days of Christianity* (New York: E. P. Dutton, 1882), 472.

5. Miriam T. Griffin, *Nero: The End of a Dynasty* (New Haven, CT: Yale University Press, [1984] 1985), 15.

6. Tertullian, "Scorpiace: Antidote for the Scorpion's Sting," in "The Writings of Tertullian," 2:8, *The Ante-Nicene Fathers* (Grand Rapids, MI: Eerdmans, 1956), 3:648.

7. Much of what the Church Fathers wrote remains untranslated in Latin (*Patrologia Latina*: 218 volumes) and Greek (*Patrologia Graeca*: 166 volumes), therefore, we cannot be dogmatic in asserting what the early Church Fathers believed. "The patrologies combined weigh in at over a million pages." R. Howard Bloch, *God's Plagiarist: Being An Account of the Fabulous Industry and Irregular Commerce of the Abbe Migne* (Chicago: The University of Chicago Press, 1994), 1.

8. See Leroy Edwin Froom, *The Prophetic Faith of Our Fathers: The Historical Development of Prophetic Interpretation* (Washington, D.C.: Review and Herald, 1950), 4 vols.

9. Farrar, *Early Days of Christianity*, 434–35.

10. Hogan, "Matthew 24—The Future is Coming," 21.

11. Paul F. Boller, Jr., *Not So!: Popular Myths About America from Columbus to Clinton* (New York: Oxford University Press, 1995) and Paul F. Boller, Jr. and John George, *They Never Said It: A Book of Fake Quotes, Misquotes, and Misleading Attributions* (New York: Oxford University Press, 1989).

12. Jeffrey Burton Russell, *Inventing the Flat Earth: Columbus and Modern Historians* (New York: Praeger, 1991).

13. Hogan, "Matthew 24—The Future is Coming," 21. Emphasis added.

14. *The Epistle of Ignatius to the Ephesians*, chapter 11, in *Ante-Nicene Fathers*, 1:54. Quoted in Froom, *Prophetic Faith*, 1:209.

15. *The Epistles of Cyprian*, Epistle 55.

16. Gerald B. Stanton, "The Doctrine of Imminency: Is It Biblical?," in Thomas Ice and Timothy Demy, eds., *When the Trumpet Sounds* (Eugene, OR: Harvest House, 1995), 222.

17. Matthew 10:22–23; 16:27–28; 24:34; 26:64; John 21:21–22; Romans 13:11–12; 16:20; 1 Corinthians 7:29; 7:31; 10:11; 2 Thessalonians. 2:6–7; Philippians 4:5; Hebrews 9:26; 10:25, 37; James 5:3, 7–9; 1 Peter 4:7; 5:4; 1 John 2:18; Revelation 1:1, 3; 3:10–11; 11:14; 17:8; 22:6, 7, 10, 12, 20.

18. Elmer L. Towns, "Literal Interpretation of Prophecy," in Mal Couch, gen. ed., *Dictionary of Premillennial Theology* (Grand Rapids, MI: Kregel Publications, 1996), 317–19.

19. Thomas Ice and Timothy Demy, *Fast Facts on Bible Prophecy* (Eugene, OR: Harvest House, 1997), 102.

20. Notice the second person plural ("you") throughout the passage (1:1–9).

21. Renald Showers, *Maranatha: Our Lord Come!* (Bellmawr, NJ: The Friends of Israel Ministry, 1995), 128. Quoted in Ice and Demy, *Fast Facts on Bible Prophecy*, 102.

22. Farrar, *Early Days of Christianity*, 108, note 1.

23. *Dialog with Trypho*. Farrar, *Early Days of Christianity*, 433.

24. Justin Martyr, "Dialogue with Trypho," *The Ante-Nicene Fathers: Translations of the Writings of the Fathers down to A.D. 325*, eds. Alexander Roberts and James Donaldson (Grand Rapids, MI: Eerdmans, 1956), chap. xxxv, 1:212.

25. Farrar, *Early Days of Christianity*, 433.

26. *De Antichristo*, 6. Farrar, *Early Days of Christianity*, 433.

27. Farrar, *Early Days of Christianity*, 433.

28. W. Montgomery, "James, the Lord's Brother," *Dictionary of the Apostolic Church*, ed. James Hastings, 2 vols. (New York: Charles Scribner's Sons, 1916), 1:628.

29. Alan Patrick Boyd, "A Dispensational Premillennial Analysis of the Eschatology of the Post-Apostolic Fathers (Until the Death of Justin Martyr)" (unpublished master's thesis, Dallas Theological Seminary, 1977), 28. Boyd cites Eusebius, *Ecclesiastical History*, 2.33. The correct reference is 2:23.

30. *Eusebius' Ecclesiastical History*, "The martyrdom of James, who was called the

brother of the Lord," 2.23 (Grand Rapids, MI: Baker, 1958), 77-78. The same account can be found in volume 8 of the *Ante-Nicene Fathers*, 763.

31. Boyd, "A Dispensational Premillennial Analysis of the Eschatology of the Post-Apostolic Fathers," 28.

32. Boyd, "A Dispensational Premillennial Analysis of the Eschatology of the Post-Apostolic Fathers," 28. Also see William F. Arndt and F. Wilbur Gingrich, *A Greek-English Lexicon of the New Testament and Other Early Christian Literature*, 4th ed. (Chicago, IL: University of Chicago Press, 1954), s.v. *mellow*, I.c.a., 502.

33. *Eusebius' Ecclesiastical History*, 77-78.

34. Farrar, *Early Days of Christianity*, 432–33. In a note on page 432, Farrar expresses surprise at how commentators explain away the time expressions of words like "speedily" and "immediately": "It is curious to see with what extraordinary ease commentators explain the perfectly simple and [un]ambiguous expression 'speedily' (*en taxei*), to mean any length of time which they may choose to demand. The word 'immediately,' in Matt. xxiv. 29, has been subject to similar handling, in which indeed all Scripture exegesis abounds. The failure to see that the Fall of Jerusalem and the end of the Mosaic Dispensation was a 'Second Advent'—and *the* Second Advent contemplated in many of the New Testament prophecies—has led to a multitude of errors."

35. Henry C. Thiessen, *Lectures in Systematic Theology*, revised by Vernon D. Doerksen (Grand Rapids, MI: Eerdmans [1949] 1986), 372.

36. Those who wrote *before* (*ante*) the Council of Nicea called by Emperor Constantine in 325.

37. Boyd, "A Dispensational Premillennial Analysis of the Eschatology of the Post-Apostolic Fathers, 28.

38. Boyd, "A Dispensational Premillennial Analysis of the Eschatology of the Post-Apostolic Fathers, 32.

39. Boyd, "A Dispensational Premillennial Analysis of the Eschatology of the Post-Apostolic Fathers, 32.

40. Boyd, "A Dispensational Premillennial Analysis of the Eschatology of the Post-Apostolic Fathers, 32.

41. Boyd, "A Dispensational Premillennial Analysis of the Eschatology of the Post-Apostolic Fathers, 33.

42. Boyd, "A Dispensational Premillennial Analysis of the Eschatology of the Post-Apostolic Fathers, 33, 35.

43. Boyd, "A Dispensational Premillennial Analysis of the Eschatology of the Post-Apostolic Fathers, 35.

44. J.L. Neve, *A History of Christian Thought,* 1:43. Quoted in William Everett Bell, *A Critical Evaluation of the Pretribulation Rapture Doctrine in Christian Eschatology,* 1, note 1 and 49. Emphasis added. Also quoted in Boyd, 28, note 1.

45. George Eldon Ladd, *The Blessed Hope* (Grand Rapids, MI: Eerdmans, 1956), 20.

46. William Everett Bell, Jr., "A Critical Evaluation of the Pretribulation Rapture Doctrine in Christian Eschatology" (unpublished doctoral dissertation, New York University, 1967), 54. Conclusion based on P. Allan Carlsson, "A Historical Approach to the Doctrine of the Rapture" (unpublished Master's thesis, Wheaton College, Wheaton, Illinois, 1956), 119–24.

47. Thiessen, *Lectures in Systematic Theology,* 366.

Appendix 5

ZECHARIAH 14 AND THE COMING OF CHRIST

In the premillennial view of Bible prophecy, the events depicted in Zechariah 14 are most often interpreted as depicting the second coming of Christ when Jesus will descend from heaven and stand on the Mount of Olives and from there set up His millennial kingdom. The chronology outlined in Zechariah, however, does not fit this scenario. Events actually begin in chapter thirteen where it is prophesied that the Shepherd, Jesus, will be struck and the sheep will be scattered (Zech. 13:7). This was fulfilled when Jesus says, "You will all fall away, because it is written, 'I WILL STRIKE DOWN THE SHEPHERD, AND THE SHEEP SHALL BE SCATTERED'" (Mark 14:27).

What follows describes events leading up to and including the destruction of Jerusalem in A.D. 70. God will act as Judge of Jerusalem and its inhabitants. As the king, He will send "his armies" and destroy "those murderers, and set their city on fire" (Matt. 22:7).

> For I will gather all the nations [the Roman armies] against Jerusalem to battle, and the city will be captured, the houses plundered [Matt. 24:17], the women ravished [Luke 17:35], and half the city exiled [Matt.

24:16], but the rest of the people will not be cut off from the city [Matt. 24:16]" (Zech. 14:2).

This happened when the Roman armies, made up of soldiers from the nations it conquered, went to war against Jerusalem. Rome was an empire consisting of all the known nations of the world (see Luke 2:1). The Roman Empire "extended roughly two thousand miles from Scotland south to the headwaters of the Nile and about three thousand miles from the Pillars of Hercules eastward to the sands of Persia. Its citizens and subject peoples numbered perhaps eighty million."[1] Rome was raised up, like Assyria, to be the "rod of [God's] anger" (Isa. 10:5). "So completely shall the city be taken that the enemy shall sit down in the midst of her to divide the spoil. *All nations* (2), generally speaking were represented in the invading army, for Rome was the mistress of many lands."[2] Thomas Scott, using supporting references from older commentators and cross references to other biblical books, writes that Zechariah is describing the events surrounding Jerusalem's destruction in A.D. 70.

> The time when the Romans marched their armies, composed of many nations, to besiege Jerusalem, was "the day of the Lord" Jesus, on which he came to "destroy those that would not that he should reign over them" [Matt. 22:1–10; 24:3, 23–35; Luke 19:11–27, 41–44]. When the Romans had taken the city, all the outrages were committed, and the miseries endured, which are here predicted [Luke 21:20–24]. A very large proportion of the inhabitants were destroyed, or taken captives, and sold for slaves; and multitudes were driven away to be pursued by various perils and miseries: numbers also, having been converted to Christianity, became citizens of "the heavenly Jerusalem" and thus were "not cut off from the city" of God [Gal 4:21–31; Heb. 12:22–25].[3]

Forcing these series of descriptive judgments to leap over the historical realities of Jerusalem's destruction in A.D. 70 so as to fit a future judgment scenario is contrived and unnecessary. A proximate fulfillment is more logical and consistent with basic hermeneutical principles.

> Then the LORD will go forth and fight against those nations, as when He fights on a day of battle (14:3).

After using Rome as His rod to smite Jerusalem, God turns on Rome in judgment. Once again, Assyria is the model: "I send it against a godless nation and commission it against the people of My fury to capture booty and to seize plunder, and to trample them down like mud in the streets . . . . So it will be that when the Lord has completed all His work on Mount Zion and on Jerusalem, He will say, 'I will punish the fruit of the arrogant heart of the king of Assyria and the pomp of his haughtiness'" (Isa. 10:5–6, 12–13). "It is significant that the decline of the Roman Empire dates from the fall of Jerusalem."[4] Thomas Scott concurs: "It is also observable, that the Romans after having been thus made the executioners of divine vengeance on the Jewish nation, never prospered as they had done before; but the Lord evidently fought against them, and all the nations which composed their overgrown empire; till at last it was subverted, and their fairest cities and provinces were ravaged by barbarous invaders."[5]

> And in that day His feet will stand on the Mount of Olives, which is in front of Jerusalem on the east; and the Mount of Olives will be split in its middle from east to west by a very large valley, so that half of the mountain will move toward the north and the other half toward the south (Zech. 14:4).

It is this passage that dispensationalists use to support the view that Jesus will touch down on planet earth and set up His millennial kingdom. Of course, one of the problems in making Zechariah 14:4 refer to Christ's second coming is the absence of any reference to Him coming down. But let's assume that Jesus' coming is *implied*. How else would Jehovah be able to "stand on the Mount of Olives"? Numerous times in the Bible we read of Jehovah "coming down" to meet with His people. In most instances His coming is one of judgment. In no case was He physically present.

Mountains, like sun, moon, and stars, are often used to represent tribes, nations, and kingdoms. For example, Israel is depicted as a mountain (Amos 4:1; Zech. 4:7; John 4:21; Rev. 8:8; 21:10).

> The symbolic nature of mountains comes from the Apostle John's Jewish heritage. John was a Jew, and the book of Revelation must be interpreted with one eye on the Old Testament: "The Book of Revelation is the most thoroughly Jewish in its language and imagery of any New

Testament book. This book speaks not the language of Paul, but of the Old Testament Prophets Isaiah, Ezekiel, and Daniel."[6]

In the Old Testament, a mountain was often a symbolic reference to a kingdom or national power. The prophet Isaiah wrote of a time when "the mountain of the LORD's temple will be established as chief among the mountains; it will be raised above the hills, and all nations will stream to it" (Isaiah 2:2). In Jeremiah 51:25, God issued a stern warning to the nation of Babylon: "'I am against you, O destroying mountain, you who destroy the whole earth,' declares the LORD, 'I will stretch out my hand against you, roll you off the cliffs, and make you a burned-out mountain.'"

The prophet Daniel saw a vision in which "the rock that struck the statue became a huge mountain and filled the whole earth" (Daniel 2:35). What did the mountain symbolize? "In the time of those kings, the God of heaven will set up a kingdom that will never be destroyed, nor will it be left to another people. It will crush all those kingdoms and bring them to an end, but it will itself endure forever" (2:44).

The Old Testament uses the figure of a mountain to refer to a kingdom.[7]

Jesus describes Israel's judgment in terms of a mountain being "taken up and cast into the sea" (Matt. 21:21; Mark 11:23). Jesus delivered His judgment discourse concerning the destruction of the temple from the Mount of Olives (Matt. 24–25). Notice how many times God's coming is associated with mountains.

- "So I have *come down* to deliver them from the power of the Egyptians, and to bring them up from that land to a good and spacious land, to a land flowing with milk and honey. . . (Ex. 3:8).
- "Then Thou didst *come down* on Mount Sinai, and didst speak with them from heaven. . . (Neh. 9:13a).
- "Bow Thy heavens, O LORD, and *come down*; touch the mountains, that they may smoke" (Psalm 144:5).
- "For thus says the LORD to me, 'As the lion or the young lion growls over his prey, against which a band of shepherds is called out, will not be terrified at their voice, nor disturbed at their noise, so will the LORD of hosts *come down* to wage war on Mount Zion and on its hill'" (Isa. 31:4).
- "Oh, that Thou wouldst rend the heavens and *come down*, that the mountains might quake at Thy presence— (Isa. 64:1).

- "When Thou didst awesome things which we did not expect, Thou didst *come down*, the mountains quaked at Thy presence" (Isa. 64:3).

In Micah 1:3 we are told that God "is coming forth from His place" to "*come down* and tread on the high places of the earth." How is this descriptive language different from the Lord standing on the Mount of Olives with the result that it will split? Micah says "the mountains will melt under Him, and *the valleys will be split*, like wax before the fire, like water poured down a steep place" (1:4). "It was not uncommon for prophets to use figurative expressions about the Lord 'coming' down, mountains trembling, being scattered, and hills bowing (Hab. 3:6, 10); mountains flowing down at his presence (Isaiah 64:1, 3); or mountains and hills singing and the trees clapping their hands (Isaiah 55:12)."[8]

Isaiah 40:4 is descriptive of earth-moving events that did not literally take place.

> Clear the way for the LORD in the wilderness; make smooth in the desert a highway for our God. Let every valley be lifted up, and every mountain and hill be made low; and let the rough ground become a plain, and the rugged terrain a broad valley.

The New Testament specifies how we should interpret these verses by applying them to the coming of Christ. Christ's coming is preceded by "every mountain and hill" being brought "low" (Luke 3:5). Was there a major realignment of the topography of Judea when Jesus came on the scene after the announcement of John the Baptist? Was *any* mountain or hill "made low"? And yet, the prophecy was fulfilled in the first century.

What is the Bible trying to teach us with this descriptive language of the Mount of Olives "split in its middle"? The earliest Christian writers applied Zechariah 14:4 to the work of Christ *in His day*. Tertullian (A.D. 145—220) wrote: "'But at night He went out to the Mount of Olives.' For thus had Zechariah pointed out: 'And His feet shall stand in that day on the Mount of Olives' [Zech. xiv. 4]."[9] Tertullian was alluding to the fact that the Olivet prophecy set the stage for the judgment coming of Christ that would once for all break down the Jewish/Gentile division. Matthew Henry explains the theology behind the prophecy in this way:

The partition-wall between Jew and Gentiles shall be taken away. The *mountains about Jerusalem*, and particularly this, signified it to be an enclosure, and that it stood in the way of those who would approach to it. Between the Gentiles and Jerusalem this *mountain of Bether*, of *division*, stood, Cant. ii. 17. But by the destruction of Jerusalem this mountain shall be made to *cleave in the midst*, and so the Jewish pale shall be taken down, and the church laid in common with the Gentiles, who were made one with the Jews by the breaking down of this *middle wall of partition*, Eph. ii. 14.[10]

You will notice that there is no mention of a thousand year reign following the presence of Jehovah on the Mount of Olives. While we are told that "the LORD will be king over all the earth" (14:9), this does not mandate an earthly millennial reign of Christ. This language is neither new or foward looking. "For the LORD Most High is to be feared, *a great King over all the earth*. He subdues peoples under us, and nations under our feet" (Psalm 47:2, 3). This is exactly what happened with the destruction of Jerusalem in A.D. 70.

Notes

1. Otto Friedrich, *The End of the World: A History* (New York: Coward, McCann and Geoghegan, 1982), 28.

2. G. N. M. Collins, "Zechariah," *The New Bible Commentary*, F. Davidson, ed., 2nd ed. (Grand Rapids, MI: Eerdmans, 1954), 761.

3. Thomas Scott, *The Holy Bible, Containing the Old and New Testaments, According to the Authorised Version; with Explanatory notes, Practical Observations, and Copious Marginal References*, 3 vols. (New York: Collins and Hannay, 1832), 2:955

4. Collins, "Zechariah," 761.

5. Scott, *The Holy Bible, etc.*, 956.

6. Ferrel Jenkins, *The Old Testament in the Book of Revelation*, 22.

7. Charles H. Dyer, *World News and Bible Prophecy* (Wheaton, IL: Tyndale, 1993), 150–51.

8. Ralph Woodrow, *His Truth is Marching On: Advanced Studies on Prophecy in the Light of History* (Riverside, CA: Ralph Woodrow Evangelistic Association, 1977), 110.

9. "Tertullian Against Marcion," Book 4, chapter XL, in *The Ante-Nicene Fathers*, 3:417.

10. Matthew Henry, *Matthew Henry's Commentary on the Whole Bible*, 6 vols. (New York: Fleming H. Revell, n.d.), 4:1468.

Index

Prophecy Books & Tapes
Available from American Vision

P.O. Box 220, Powder Springs, Georgia 30127
1-800-628-9460 (Orders Only) • **770–222–7266**
americanvision.org • prophecybooks.com

Before Jerusalem Fell

By Kenneth L. Gentry, Jr. The Book of Revelation is one of the most misunderstood books of the Bible. Much of this misunderstanding is due to confusion regarding when Revelation was written. The dating of the book is central to understanding its purpose and audience. Kenneth Gentry uses indisputable evidence, internal and external within Revelation itself and gathers facts from historical records to prove that the book was written before A.D. 70 and the destruction of Jerusalem. It is now up to those who date Revelation after the destruction of Jerusalem to answer *Before Jerusalem Fell*. Over 450 pages. Hardbound. _____ $29.95

End-Time Visions

By Richard Abanes. The author is the director of the Religious Information Center. He has appeared on the television shows *Extra*, *Hard Copy*, and the Fox Television Network special *Prophecies of the Millennium*. Abanes shows the dark side of prophetic speculation. In addition, he is not afraid to take on the more popular evangelical prophetic writers: Jack Van Impe, Tex Marrs, Chuck Missler, Chuck Smith, Tim LaHaye, Don McAlvany, Pat Robertson, and Hal Lindsey. It's a mystery that these men are taken seriously by the majority of Christians today. Their own words indict them. You must order this book! This brief review cannot do it justice. 428 pages. Hardbound. _____ $25.95

Days of Vengeance

By David Chilton. The book of Revelation is not about our future as most believe. Chilton hammers home this point over and over again in this extraordinary verse-by-verse expedition through prophecy. To the dismay of some, Chilton literally demystifies Revelation. The vials, trumpets, beasts, and even the glassy sea are decloaked for all to see and understand. *Days of Vengeance* is a modern marvel of eschatological understanding. 721 pages. Hardbound. _____ $24.95

The Beast of Revelation

By Kenneth L. Gentry, Jr. One of the greatest mysteries of all time is the identity of the dread Beast of Revelation. The Bible describes him as the ultimate villain in human history. He is the archetype of evil. Ken Gentry claims that previous prophecy detectives overlooked one of the major keys to the puzzle. The author makes an ironclad case for identifying the Beast. 209 pages. Softcover. _____ $9.95

The Parousia

By James Stuart Russell. This is one of the classic books on the topic of the parousia. It is a careful look at the New Testament doctrine of the Lord's second coming. Originally published in 1878. 561 pages. Softcover. _____ $16.95

Armageddon NOW!

By Dwight Wilson. Most Christians who read books on Bible prophecy seem to have short memories. How many recall Hal Lindsey's prediction in *The Late Great Planet Earth* that Jesus would return before 1988? Dwight Wilson goes back to 1917 to show that Lindsey is not alone in making predictions that did not come to pass. Since 1917, premillennial authors have repeatedly identified so-called antichrists, beasts, and numerous other "literal fulfillments" of Bible prophecy. In each and every case, as Wilson demonstrates, these authors have been wrong. This 1991 edition of *Armageddon NOW!* has a new foreword by the author bringing the work up to date. A masterful work of scholarship. 261 pages. Softcover. _____ $9.95

Three Views on the Millennium and Beyond

Edited by Darrell L. Bock. Eschatology is a hot topic. Dispensational premillennialism has dominated the field for decades. But no more. The best thing about this book is Ken Gentry's exposition of postmillennialism and his responses to amillennialism and premillennialism. As always, Ken is clear and to the point. He covers it all, a difficult task with the confines of space limitations. Also included are indexes and select bibliographies. A great book on the millennial issue. 330 pages. Softcover. _____ $16.99

Revelation: Four Views

Edited by Steve Gregg. We have to buy this book by the case to keep it in stock! It is one of those books that belongs on everyone's bookshelf regardless of one's prophetic view. Verse by verse, Steve Gregg presents the book of Revelation from four popular views: Historicist, Preterist, Futurist, and Spiritual. 528 pages. Hardbound. _____ $29.99

Four Views on the Book of Revelation

Edited by C. Marvin Pate. The authors compare and contrast four popular views on the book of Revelation: Preterist, Idealist, Progressive Dispensationalist, and Classical Dispensationalist. Contributions from C. Marvin Pate, Kennneth L. Gentry, Sam Hamstra, Jr., and Robert L. Thomas. 248 pages. Softcover. _____ $16.99

The Great Tribulation

By Thomas Ice and Kenneth L. Gentry Jr. This engaging book brings together two opposing viewpoints regarding an issue at the heart of prophetic study: Are the events of the book of Revelation yet to be fulfilled or were they fulfilled in the first century? Presented in a friendly debate format, this work will inform and challenge readers regardless of their own position. 224 pages. Softcover. _____ $13.99

The Three R's

By Dave MacPherson. The three R's are Rapture, Revisionism, and Robbery. The author traces the character of Pretribulation Rapturism from 1830 to Hal Lindsey. This book is the latest installment of the author's 30-year research odyssey in dispensational history. 141 pages. Softcover. _____ $9.95

Paradise Restored

By David Chilton. A genuine prophecy primer. *Paradise Restored* is focused and extremely fun to read. Chilton's wit and well-honed penetration of Biblical truth is served up to the reader in terms anyone can understand. Chilton teaches us how to interpret prophecy and gives us the keys to understanding modern eschatology. 311 pages. Softcover. _____ $17.95

An Evening In Ephesus

By Bob Emery. If you were a Christian in the first century and had received John's letter from Patmos, how would you have understood the references to: The Beast? 666? Babylon, Mother of Harlots? The 1000-year reign? The new Jerusalem? In this dramatic commentary, you join a meeting in the home of a prominent Christian from Ephesus. The apostle John, released from his exile, unveils the mysteries of the prophetic word. 125 pages. Softcover. _____ $9.95

The Puritan Hope

By Iain H. Murray. Does the Church of Jesus Christ have a future? Prior to the nineteenth century and the rise of dispensational premillennialism, mission enterprises were energized by the belief that the gospel would go into all the world and be successful. Murray traces the "Puritan Hope" from John Calvin to Charles H. Spurgeon, showing that the modern missionary movement is linked to postmillennialism and that premillennialism is "one of the oddities of Church history." The appendix on "C.H. Spurgeon's Views on Prophecy" is alone worth the price of the book. Great historical reading. 288 pages. Softcover. _____ $9.95

Postmillennialism

By Keith A. Mathison. Premillennialism dominates the eschatological scene today. It seems that everyone has their bags packed, waiting to be taken to heaven in the "rapture." The belief is that the world is only going to get worse. Keith Mathison dismisses the pessimistic rhetoric and outlines an optimistic eschatology based on a thorough study of the Bible. He also includes an historical perspective on the various millennial positions. He then undertakes a systematic study of the subject, beginning with Genesis and concluding with Revelation. Included are several appendixes on Daniel's 70 weeks prophecy and 1 and 2 Thessalonians. A great book for anyone wanting a good introduction to postmillennialism. 286 pages. Softcover. _____ $14.99

The Last Days are Here Again

By Richard Kyle. Kyle shows that prophetic speculation is not new or confined to Christian groups. Beginning with early Christianity, the book takes the reader on a fascinating trip through the writings and movements of numerous prophetic speculators. *The Last Days are Here Again* is more than an historical account; it analyzes numerous contemporary eschatological trends, from dispensational premillennialism and the Jesus People to UFOlogists and a racist Armageddon that is the heart of the Nation of Islam. Kyle ends his fascinating study by taking us into the future of prophetic thinking. What's in store as we approach the year 2000? Anyone interested in Bible prophecy should have a copy. 255 pages. Softcover. _____ $14.99

The Last Days According to Jesus

By R.C. Sproul. Dispensationalism is dead. Unfortunately, the majority of Christians don't know it. Dispensationalists continue to vote for popular prophecy writers by purchasing their books and videos even though their prophetic pronouncements fail to come to pass. Uninformed Christians keep the position alive. R.C. Sproul has gone out on a limb by taking on the dispensational establishment and presenting a biblical case for preterism. While Sproul rehearses the arguments of others—DeMar and Gentry included—he breaks new ground by dealing with issues generally not covered by preterist and futurist authors. 253 pages. Hardbound. _____ $16.99

When Will These Things Be?

By Douglas J. Enick. Many authors, it seems, attempt to outdo each other in creating a flurry of excitement about current events and their possible relation to the Second Coming of Christ. Their speculation knows no bounds as they envision cobra helicopters, nuclear bombs, computer chips embedded in the skin, the hole in the ozone, war between Russia and Israel and a one-world government. This book is different. It seeks to let Scripture interpret Scripture and provides a calm and sober approach to Bible prophecy. 152 pages. Softcover. _____ $8.99

The Rapture Plot

By Dave MacPherson. Early in the 1800s, a complicated and disruptive view spread a pall of pessimism which has since then weakened Christian unity and effectiveness—the now pervasive view of the any-moment, pretribulation rapture. After 25 years of intensive research, Dave MacPherson has become the world's leading scholar on the origin, development, and history of this view. In this book, he reveals the surprising tale of doctrinal plagiarism, revisionism, and intrigue—and frees the reader from its sinister clutch. 290 pages. Softcover. _____ $14.95

He Shall Have Dominion

By Kenneth L. Gentry, Jr. Today, millions of Christian believe that the Church will be "raptured" soon, removing them from the turmoils and responsibilities of this life. But this has not always been the case. A mere two centuries ago, Protestant Christians believed that they would die before Jesus came back to earth. This affected the way they thought, prayed, worked, and planned for the future. Simply stated, they built for the future. This book is a positive book. It teaches that Christians will exercise dominion in history. It therefore teaches responsibility. This is why its message is hated by those seeking an "easy out" theology. 620 pages. Hardbound. _____ $19.95

Last Days Madness: A Debate

This audio tape is a radio debate between Gary DeMar and Dr. Robert Thomas of the Masters Seminary. A spirited but cordial exchange that pinpoints the issue over the timing of prophetic fulfillment. Thomas, who claims to interpret the Bible "literally," spiritualizes the time texts which emphatically state that Jesus' coming was "near." Audio tape._____ $5.95

A Short Course on Bible Prophecy

This is one of our most popular tapes. It consists of two, forty-five minute lectures given by Gary DeMar at a Dallas, Texas, conference. Gary covers Matthew 24, including interpretation skills, the crucial time texts, and methodology. 2-part audio tape. _____ $9.95

Timing Is Everything

In this easy-to-digest video, Ralph Barker interviews Gary DeMar about Bible prophecy and what it means for those living in the final days of the twentieth century. Gary DeMar covers key areas of interest such as Bible interpretation skills, methodology, and the essential, crucial test of "timing" when studying prophecy. 2-hour video cassette. _____ $19.95

Demystifying Revelation

Gary DeMar and Ken Gentry tackle the questions all prophecy students ask, "What is mystery Babylon?" "Who is the Beast?" "What is the secret of 666?" "Are these the last days?" The viewer quickly discovers that the most mysterious book of the ages isn't really mysterious at all. Get out your Bible, pop in this fascinating video, and uncover the secrets of Revelation. 2-hour video cassette. _____ $22.95

Millennial Madness

Produced by Plain Truth Ministries. Gary DeMar, Hank Hanegraaff (Bible Answer Man), Gordon Fee, and other prophecy experts focus on the various approaches to end-times teaching. Regardless of where you land on the prophetic landscape, you will learn fascinating facts about the history of prophecy and of the various millennial views. 2 1/4-hours on two video cassettes. _____ $24.95

Identifying the Man of Lawlessness

Many would agree that the most difficult Scripture in the Bible concerning the end-times is 2 Thessalonians Chapter 2. It has been the subject of debate since the Church was established. Many commentators won't even address this troublesome passage. Through this study with Gary DeMar you will gain an understanding about the "man of sin," " the great apostasy," and the "restrainer." Comes complete with syllabus and protective storage case. Three audio tapes. _____ $19.95

Are We Living in the Last Days?

This is the question of the day, "Are we living in the last days?" Gary DeMar focuses on two difficult and misunderstood texts: Matthew 24 and Daniel 9 (The 70 weeks of years). Comes complete with syllabus and protective storage case. Eight audio tapes. _____ $39.95

Gary DeMar Under Fire

If you like "talk radio" you will love this four-tape audio series. Gary DeMar teaches, defends, and answers questions about *Last Days Madness* for over five hours. Aired live on radio and now preserved for you in this unique set. Four audio tapes. _____ $24.95

---

*PRICES SUBJECT TO CHANGE WITHOUT NOTICE. Check for availability before ordering.